Spurgeon'

SPURGEON'S TEACHING ON THE HOLY SPIRIT

By Charles H. Spurgeon

ISBN: 9781521412381

May 2017

MAIN CONTENTS

PART I

WHO IS THE HOLY SPIRIT?

THE HOLY SPIRIT IN THE COVENANT

"And I will put My Spirit within you."
Ezekiel 36:27

A Sermon Delivered On Sunday Morning: 1856

THE Holy Spirit is the third Person in the Covenant. We have considered "God in the Covenant" and "Christ in the Covenant" [See Sermons #93 and 103, Volume 2–GOD IN THE COVENANT and CHRIST IN THE COVENANT– Read/download the entire sermon, free of charge, at http://www.spurgeongems.org.] and now, this morning, we have to consider the Holy Spirit in the Covenant. For, remember, it is necessary that the Triune God should work out the salvation of the Lord's people if they are to be saved at all. And it was absolutely requisite that when the Covenant was made, all that was necessary should be put into it and, among the rest, the Holy Spirit, without whom all things done even by the Father and by Jesus Christ would be ineffectual, for He is needed as much as the Savior of men, or the Father of spirits. In this age, when the Holy Spirit is too much forgotten, and but little honor is accorded to His sacred Person, I feel that there is a deep responsibility upon me to endeavor to magnify His great and holy name. I almost tremble, this morning, in entering on so profound a subject, for which I feel myself so insufficient. But, nevertheless, relying on the aid, the guidance and the witness of the Holy Spirit, Himself, I venture upon an exposition of this text, "I will put My Spirit within you."

The Holy Spirit is given, in the Covenant, to all the children of God and received by each in due course. And yet upon our Lord Jesus Christ did the Spirit first descend and alighted upon Him as our Covenant Head, "like the precious ointment upon the head that ran down upon the beard, even Aaron's beard; that went down to the skirts of his garments." The Father has given the Holy Spirit without measure unto His Son–and from Him, in measure, though still in abundance, do all "the brethren who dwell together in unity" (or union with Christ) partake of the Spirit. This holy anointing flows down from Jesus, the Anointed One, to every part of His mystical body, to every individual member of His Church. The Lord's declaration concerning Christ was, "I have put My Spirit upon HIM." And He said, "The Spirit of the Lord is upon ME, because He has anointed Me to preach the Gospel to the poor; He has sent

4

Me to heal the broken-hearted." The Spirit was first poured upon Christ and from Him descends to all those who are in union with His adorable Person. Let us bless the name of Christ if we are united to Him—and let us look up to our Covenant Head, expecting that from Him will flow down the heavenly unction which shall anoint our souls!

My text is one of the unconditional promises of Scripture. There are many conditional promises in the Word of God given to certain characters, although even these promises are in some sense unconditional, since the very condition of the promise is by some other promise secured as a gift—but this one has no condition whatever. It does not say, "I will put My Spirit within them if they ask for Him." It says plainly, without any reservation or stipulation, "I will put My Spirit within them." The reason is obvious. Until the Spirit is put within us we cannot feel our need of the Savior, neither can we ask for or seek Him and, therefore, it is necessary that there should be an absolutely unconditional promise made to all the elect children of God—that they should have given to them the waiting Grace, the desiring Grace, the seeking Grace, the believing Grace which shall make them pant and hunger and thirst after Jesus! To everyone who is like Christ—"chosen of God and precious"—to every redeemed soul, however sunken in sin, however lost and ruined by the Fall, however much he may hate God and despise his Redeemer, this promise still holds good, "I will put My Spirit within you" and, in due course, every one of them shall have that Spirit who shall quicken them from the dead, lead them to seek pardon, induce them to trust in Christ and adopt them into the living family of God!

The promise is also concerning an internal blessing to be bestowed—"I will put My Spirit within you." Remember, we have the Spirit of God in His written Word and with every faithful minister of the Gospel the Spirit is likewise vouchsafed to us in the ordinances of Christ's Church. God is perpetually giving the Spirit to us by these means. But it is in vain for us to hear of the Spirit, to talk of Him, or to believe in Him unless we have a realization of His power within us! Here, therefore, is the promise of such an internal blessing—"I will put My Spirit within you."

We come now to consider this promise in all its comprehensiveness. May the Holy Spirit Himself assist us in so doing! We shall take the various works of the Holy Spirit, one by one, and shall remember that in all the works which He performs, the Spirit is put in the Covenant to be possessed by every Believer.

In the first place we are told by Christ, "IT IS THE SPIRIT THAT QUICKENS." Until He is pleased to breathe upon the soul, it is dead to any spiritual life. It is not until the Spirit, like some heavenly wind, breathes upon the dry bones and puts life into them, that they can ever live. You may take a corpse and dress it in all the garments of external decency. You may wash it with the water of morality—yes, you may bedeck it with the crown of profession and put upon its brow a tiara of beauty. You may paint its cheeks until you make it like life itself. But remember, unless the Spirit is there, corruption will, before long, seize on the body. So, Beloved, it is the Spirit who is the Quickener—you would have been as "dead in trespasses and sins" now as ever you were if it had not been for the Holy Spirit who made you alive! You were lying, not simply "cast out in the open field," but worse than that—you were the very prey of mortality! Corruption was your father, the worm was your mother and your sister—you were noxious in the nostrils of the Almighty. It was thus that the Savior beheld you in all your loathsomeness and said to you, "Live." In that moment you were "begotten again unto a lively hope by the resurrection of Jesus Christ from the dead." Life entered into you at His bidding—then it was that the Spirit quickened you! The words of Jesus, so He told His disciples, "They are Spirit, and they are life." You were made alive entirely through the might of the quickening Spirit—

"The Spirit, like some heavenly wind
Blows on the sons of flesh—
Creates a new—a heavenly mind
And forms the man afresh."

If, then, you feel at any time death working in you, as doubtless you will, withering the bloom of your piety, chilling the fervor of your devotions and quenching the ardor of your faith, remember that He who first quickened you must keep you alive. The Spirit of God is the sap that flowed into your poor, dry branch because you were grafted into Christ. And as by that sap you were first made green with life, so it is by that sap, alone, you can ever bring forth fruit unto God. By the Spirit you drew your first breath when you cried out for mercy—and from the same Spirit you must draw the breath to praise that mercy in hymns and anthems of joy! Having begun in the Spirit, you must be made perfect in the Spirit. "The flesh profits nothing." The works of the Law will not help you. The thoughts and devices of your own hearts are of no avail. You would be cut off from Christ, you would be more depraved than you were before your conversion, you would be more corrupt than you were previous to your being regenerated–"twice dead, plucked up by the roots"–if God the Holy Spirit were to withdraw from you! You must live in His life, trust in His power to sustain you and seek of Him fresh supplies when the tide of your spiritual life is running low.

II. WE NEED THE HOLY SPIRIT AS AN ASSISTANT SPIRIT IN ALL THE DUTIES WE HAVE TO PERFORM.

The most common Christian duty is that of prayer, for the meanest child of God must be a praying child. Remember,then, that it is written, "The Spirit also helps our infirmities, for we know not what to pray for as we ought." The Spirit of God is in the Covenant as the Great Aid to us in all our petitions to the Throne of Grace. Child of God, you know not what to pray–rely, then, on the Spirit as the Inspirer of prayer who will tell you how to pray! Sometimes you know not how to express what you desire–rely upon the Spirit, then, as the One who can touch your lips with the "live coal from off the altar," whereby you shall be able to pour out your fervent wishes before the Throne of God. Sometimes even when you have life and power within you, you cannot express your inward emotions–then rely upon that Spirit to interpret your feelings, for He "makes intercession for us with groans which cannot be uttered." When, like Jacob, you are wrestling with the Angel and are nearly thrown down, ask the Holy Spirit to nerve your arms. The Holy Spirit is the chariot wheel of prayer. Prayer may be the chariot, the desire may draw it forth, but the Spirit is the very wheel whereby it moves. He propels the desire and causes the chariot to roll swiftly on and to bear to Heaven the supplication of the saints when the desire of the heart is "according to the will of God."

Another duty to which some of the children of God are called is that of preaching. And here, too, we must have the"Lo, I am with you always, even unto the end of the world." It is a solemn thing to enter upon the work of the ministry. I will just make an observation here for in this place there are young men who are striving to enter into the ministry before they scarcely know the alphabet of the Gospel. They set themselves up as preachers of God's Word when the first thing they ought to do is to join the infant class in a school and learn to read properly. I know there are some to whom God has given the desire to seek the glory of His name and the welfare of souls and who humbly wait till He has opened the way. God bless them and speed them! But–would you believe it?–a young man was baptized and received into the Church one

Sunday–and he positively went off to a College on the Monday or Tuesday to ask if they would receive him! I asked him whether he had ever preached before, or addressed half-a-dozen Sunday scholars. He said, "No." But what surprised me most was that he said he was called to the work before he was converted! It was a call from the devil, I verily believe–not a call from God in the least degree! Take heed that you touch not God's Ark with unholy fingers! You may all preach if you can, but take care that you do not set yourselves up in the ministry without having a solemn conviction that the Spirit from on high has set you apart–for if you do, the blood of souls will be found on your skirts! Too many have rushed into the Holy Place uncalled of God who, if they could have rushed out of it on their dying beds would have had eternal cause for gratitude! But they ran presumptuously, then preached unsent and, therefore, unblessed! And when dying, they felt a greater condemnation from the fact that they had taken on themselves an office to which God had never appointed them! Beware of doing that! But if God has called you, however little talent you may have, fear not anyone's frown or rebuke. If you have a solemn conviction in your souls that God has really ordained you to the work of the ministry and if you have obtained a seal to your commission in the conversion of even one soul, let not death or Hell stop you–go straight on and never think you must have certain endowments to make a successful preacher! The only endowment necessary for success in the ministry is the endowment of the Holy Spirit.

When preaching in the presence of a number of ministers last Friday, I told the Brothers, when one of them asked how it was God had been pleased to bless me so much in this place, "There is not one of you whom God could not bless ten times as much if you had ten times as much of the Spirit." For it is not any ability of the man–it is not any human qualification–it is simply the influence of God's Spirit that is necessary! And I have been delighted to find myself abused as ignorant, unlearned and void of eloquence–all which I knew long before, but so much the better–for then all the glory belongs to God! Let men say what they please, I will always confess to the truth of it. I am a fool! "I have become a fool in glorying," if you please. I will take any opprobrious title that worldlings like to put upon me, but they cannot deny the fact that God blesses my ministry, that harlots have been saved, that drunks have been reclaimed, that some of the most abandoned characters have been changed and that God has worked such a work in their midst as they never saw before in their lives! Therefore, give all the Glory to His holy name! Cast as much reproach as you like on me, you worldlings–the more honor shall there be to

God who works as He pleases, and with what instrument He chooses, irrespective of man!

Again, dearly-Beloved, whatever is your work, whatever God has ordained you to do in this world, you are equally certain to have the assistance of the Holy Spirit in it. If it is the teaching of an infant class in the Sunday school, do not think you cannot have the Holy Spirit! His succor shall be granted as freely to you as to the man who addresses a large assembly. Are you sitting down by the side of some poor dying woman? Believe that the Holy Spirit will come to you there as much as if you were administering the sacred elements of the Lord's Supper. Let your strength for the lowliest work as much as for the loftiest be sought from God! Spiritual plowman, sharpen your plowshare with the Spirit! Spiritual sower, dip your seed in the Spirit so it shall germinate—and ask the Spirit to give you Grace to scatter it that it may fall into the right furrows! Spiritual warrior, whet your sword with the Spirit and ask the Spirit, whose Word is a two-edged sword, to strengthen your arm to wield it!

III. The next point we refer to shall be that THE HOLY SPIRIT IS GIVEN TO THE CHILDREN OF GOD AS A SPIRIT OF REVELATION AND OF INSTRUCTION.

He brings us "out of darkness into marvelous light." By nature we are ignorant, extremely so, but the Holy Spirit teaches the family of God and makes them wise. "You have an unction from the Holy One," said the Apostle John, "and you know all things." Student in the School of Christ, would you be wise? Ask not the theologian to expound to you his system of divinity, but, sitting down meekly at the feet of Jesus, ask that His Spirit may instruct you. For I tell you, student, though you should read the Bible many a year and continually turn over its pages, you would not learn anything of its hidden mysteries without the Spirit. But perhaps, in a solitary moment of your study, when suddenly enlightened by the Spirit, you may learn a Truth of God as swiftly as you see the lightning flash. Young people, are you laboring to understand the Doctrine of Election? It is the Holy Spirit alone who can reveal it to your heart and make you comprehend it. Are you tugging and toiling at the Doctrine of Human Depravity? The Holy Spirit must reveal to you the depth of wickedness of the human heart. Are you wanting to know the secret of the life of the Believer as he lives by the faith of the Son of God and the mysterious fellowship with the Lord he enjoys? It will always be a mystery to you unless the Holy Spirit shall unfold it to your heart. Whenever you read the Bible, cry to the Spirit, "Open my eyes that I may behold wondrous things out of Your Law." The Spirit gives eye-salve to the blind and if your eyes are not now open, seek the eye-salve and so you shall see–yes, and see so clearly that he who has only learned in man's school, shall ask, "How knows this man letters, having never learned?"

Those who are taught of the Spirit often surpass those who are taught of man. I have met with an entirely uninstructed clod-hopper in the country who never went to school for one hour in his life–who yet knew more about the Holy Scriptures than many a clergyman trained at the University! I have been told that it is a common practice for men in Wales, while they are at work breaking stones on the road, to discuss difficult points in theology which many a Divine cannot master! How? Because they humbly read the Scriptures, trusting only to the guidance of the Holy Spirit, believing that He will lead them into all Truth–and He is pleased so to do. All other instruction is very well. Solomon says "that the soul be without knowledge, it is not good." We should all seek to know as much as can be known, but let us remember that in the work of salvation real knowledge must be obtained by the teaching of the Holy Spirit. And if we would learn in the heart and not merely in the head, we must be taught entirely by the Holy Spirit. What you learn from man, you can unlearn–but what you learn of the Spirit is fixed indelibly in your heart and conscience–and not even Satan himself can steal it from you. Go, you ignorant ones, who often stagger at the Truths of Revelation–go and ask the Spirit, for He is the Guide of benighted souls! Yes, and the Guide of His own enlightened people, too, for without His aid, even when they have been "once enlightened, and have tasted of the heavenly gift," they would not understand all Truths of God unless He led them into it.

IV. I desire further to mention that GOD WILL GIVE THE SPIRIT TO US AS A SPIRIT OF APPLICATION.

Thus it was that Jesus said to His disciples, "He shall glorify Me, for He shall receive of Mine, and shall show it unto you." To make the matter still more plain, our Lord added, "All things that theFather has are Mine: therefore said I, that He shall take of Mine, and shall show it unto you." Let me remind you how frequently Jesus impressed on His disciples the fact that He spoke to them the words of His Father–"My Doctrine," said He, "is not Mine, but His that sent Me." And again, "The words that I speak unto you, I speak not of Myself: but the Father that dwells in Me, He does the works." As Christ thus made known the will of God the Father to His people, so the Holy Spirit makes known to us the words of Christ. I could almost affirm that Christ's words would be of no use to us unless they were applied to us by the Holy Spirit! Beloved, we need the application to assure our hearts that they are our own, that they are intended for us and that we have an interest in their blessedness! And we need the unction of the Spirit to make them bedew our hearts and refresh our souls.

Did you ever have a promise applied to your heart? Do you understand what is meant by application as the exclusive work of the Spirit? It is as Paul says the Gospel came to the Thessalonians, "not in word only, but also in power, and in the Holy Spirit, and in much assurance." Sometimes it comes all of a sudden—your heart may have been the scene of a thousand distracting thoughts, billow dashing against billow till the tempest rose beyond your control. But soon some text of Scripture, like a mighty fiat from the lips of Jesus, has stilled your troubled breast and immediately there has been a great calm—and you have wondered from where it came. The sweet sentence has rung like music in your ears. Like a wafer made of honey it has moistened your tongue. Like a charm it has quelled your anxieties while it has dwelt uppermost in your thoughts all day—reining in all your lawless passions and restless strivings. Perhaps it has continued in your mind for weeks! Wherever you went, whatever you did, you could not dislodge it nor did you wish to do so, so sweet, so savory was it to your soul. Have you not thought of such a text as that as the best in the Bible, the most precious in all the Scriptures? That was because it was so graciously applied to you!

Oh, how I love applied promises! I may read a thousand promises as they stand recorded on the pages of this Sacred Volume and yet get nothing from them. My heart would not burn within me for all the richness of the store—but one enough for forty days for many of the Lord's Elijahs! How sweet it is, in the times of deep affliction, to have this promise applied to the heart—"When you pass through the waters, I will be with you; and through the rivers, they shall not overflow you: when you walk through the fire, you shall not be burned, neither shall the flame kindle upon you"! Perhaps you say, "That is all enthusiasm." Of course it appears so to you, if, as natural men you discern not the things of the Spirit! But we are talking about spiritual things to spiritual men and to them it is no mere enthusiasm—it is often a matter of life or death. I have known numerous cases where almost the only plank on which the poor troubled saint was able to float was just one text of which, somehow or other, he had got so tight a grasp that nothing could take it away from him! Nor is it only His Word which needs to be applied to us. "He shall receive of Mine, and shall show it unto you," may be referred, likewise, to our Savior's precious blood. We sometimes sing–

"There is a Fountain filled with blood"–
and we talk of bathing in it. Now faith does not apply the blood to the soul–that is the work of the Spirit. True, I seek it by faith, but it is the Spirit who washes me in "the fountain opened...for sin and for uncleanness." It is the Spirit who receives of the things of Christ and shows them to me. You would never have a drop of blood sprinkled on your heart unless it was sprinkled by the hand of the Spirit. So, too, the robe of Christ's righteousness is entirely fitted on us by Him. We are not invited to appropriate the obedience of Christ to ourselves– but the Spirit brings all to us which Christ has made for us. Ask, then, of the Spirit, that you may have the Word applied, the blood applied, pardon applied andGrace applied–and you shall not ask in vain–for Jehovah has said, "I will put My Spirit within you."

But now we have to mark another very important point. WE MUST RECEIVE THE SPIRIT AS A SANCTIFYING SPIRIT.

Perhaps this is one of the greatest works of the Holy Spirit–sanctifying the soul. It is a great work to purge the soul from sin. It is greater than if one should wash a leopard till all his spots were obliterated, or an Ethiopian till his sable skin became white, for our sins are more than skin-deep–they have entered into our very nature! Should we be outwardly washed white this morning, we would be black and polluted before tomorrow! And if all the spots were taken away today, they would grow again tomorrow, for we are black all through! You may scrub the flesh, but it is black to the last–our sinfulness is a leprosy that lies deep within. But the Holy Spirit sanctifies the soul. He enters the heart, beginning the work of sanctification by conversion. He keeps possession of the heart and preserves sanctification by perpetually pouring in fresh oil of Grace till at last He will perfect sanctification by making us pure and spotless, fit to dwell with the blest inhabitants of Glory!

The way the Spirit sanctifies is this–first He reveals to the soul the evil of sin and makes the soul hate it. He shows it to be a deadly evil, full of poison–and when the soul begins to hate it, the next thing the Spirit does is to show it that the blood of Christ takes all the guilt away and, from that very fact, to lead it to hate sin even more than it did when it first knew its blackness. The Spirit takes it to "the blood of sprinkling, that speaks better things than that of Abel." And there He tolls the death-knell of sin as He points to the blood of Christ and says, "He shed this for you, that He might purchase you unto Himself to be one of His peculiar people, zealous of good works." Afterwards, the Holy Spirit may, at times, allow sin to break out in the heart of the child of God that it may be more strongly repressed by greater watchfulness in the future. And when the heir of Heaven indulges in sin, the Holy Spirit sends a sanctifying chastisement upon the soul until the heart, being broken with grief by the blueness of the wound, evil is cleansed away and Conscience, feeling uneasy, sends the heart to Christ who removes the chastisement and takes away the guilt!

Again, remember Believer, all your holiness is the work of the Holy Spirit. You have not a Grace which the Spirit did not give you! You have not a solitary virtue which He did not work in you. You have no goodness which has not been given to you by the Spirit. Therefore, never boast of your virtues or of your Graces. Have you now a sweet temper, whereas you once were passionate? Boast not of it—you will be angry if the Spirit leaves you. Are you now pure, whereas you were once unclean? Boast not of your purity, the seed of which was brought from Heaven—it never grew within your heart by nature—it is God's gift. Is unbelief prevailing against you? Do your lusts, your evil passions and your corrupt desires seem likely to master you? Then I will not say, "Up, and at 'em!" but I will say—Cry mightily unto God that you may be filled with the Holy Spirit—so shall you conquer at last and become more than conqueror over all your sins—seeing that the Lord has engaged to put His Spirit "within you."

VI. When I have spoken of two more points, I shall conclude. THE SPIRIT OF GOD IS PROMISED TO THE HEIRS OF HEAVEN AS A DIRECTING SPIRIT to guide them in the path of Providence.

If you are ever in a position in which you know not what road to take, remember that your "strength is to sit still," and your wisdom is to wait for the directing voice of the Spirit saying to you, "This is the way, walk you in it." I trust I have proved this myself and I am sure every child of God who has been placed in difficulties must have felt, at times, the reality and blessedness of this guidance. And have you never prayed to Him to direct you? If you have, did you ever find that you went wrong afterwards? I do not mean the sort of prayers that they present who ask counsel, but not of the Lord—"who walk to go down into Egypt...to strengthen themselves in the strength of Pharaoh," and then ask God to bless them in a way that He never sanctioned. No, you must start fairly by renouncing every other trust. It is only thus that you can make proof of His promise, "Commit your way unto the Lord; trust also in Him, and He shall bring it to pass." Take with you, then, child of God, an open confession. Say, "Lord, I desire, like a sheet of water, to be moved by the breath of the Spirit. Here I lie, 'passive in Your hands.' Gladly would I know no will but Yours. Show me Your will, O Lord! Teach me what to do and what to refrain from doing."

To some of you this may seem all fanaticism. You believe not that God the Holy Spirit ever guides men in the way they should take. So you may suppose if you have never experienced His guidance. We have heard that when one of our English travelers in Africa told the inhabitants of the intense cold that sometimes prevailed in his country, by which water became so hard that people could skate and walk upon it, the king threatened to put him to death if he told anymore lies, for he had never felt or seen such things. And what one has never seen or felt is certainly fit subject for doubt and contradiction. But with regard to the Lord's people who tell you that they are led by the Spirit, I advise you to give heed to their sayings and seek to make the trial for yourselves! It would be a good thing if you were just to go to God, as a child, in all your distresses. Remember that as a Solicitor whom you may safely consult, as a Guide whose directions you may safely follow, as a Friend on whose protection you may safely rely, the Holy Spirit is personally present in the Church of Christ and with each of the disciples of Jesus! And there is no fee to pay but the fee of gratitude and praise, because He has directed you so well!

VII. Just once more–THE HOLY SPIRIT WILL BE GIVEN TO GOD'S CHILDREN AS A COMFORTING SPIRIT.

This is peculiarly His office. Have you ever felt, immediately before a great and grievous trouble, you have had a most unaccountable season of joy? You scarcely knew why you were so happy or so tranquil. You seemed to be floating upon a very Sea of Elysium–there was not a breath of wind to ruffle your peaceful spirit, all was serene and calm. You were not agitated by the ordinary cares and anxieties of the world. Your whole mind was absorbed in sacred meditation. By-and-by, the trouble comes and you say, "Now I understand it all. I could not, before, comprehend the meaning of that grateful lull, that quiet happiness, but I see now that it was designed to prepare me for these trying circumstances. If I had been low and dispirited when this trouble burst upon me, it would have broken my heart. But now, thanks be to God, I can perceive through Jesus Christ how this 'light affliction, which is but for a moment,' works for me, 'a far more exceeding and eternal weight of glory.'" But, mark you, I believe that it is worthwhile to have the troubles in order to get the comfort of the Holy Spirit—it is worthwhile to endure the storm in order to realize the joys!

Sometimes my heart has been shaken by disgrace, shame and contempt, for many a brother minister, of whom I thought better things, has reviled me—and many a Christian has turned on his heels away from me because I had been misrepresented to him and he has hated me without a cause. But it has so happened that at that very time, if the whole Church had turned its back on me and the whole world had hissed me, it would not have greatly moved me, for some bright ray of spiritual sunshine lit up my heart and Jesus whispered to me those sweet words, "I am My Beloved's, and My Beloved is Mine." At such times the consolations of the Spirit have been neither few nor small with me! O Christian, if I were able, I would bring you yet further into the depths of this glorious passage but, as I cannot, I must leave it with you. It is full of honey—only put it to your lips and get the honey from it. "I will put My Spirit within you."

In winding up, let me add a remark or two. Do you not see here the absolute certainty of the salvation of everyBeliever? Or rather, is it not absolutely certain that every member of the family of God's Israel must be saved? For it is written, "I will put My Spirit within you." Do you think that when God puts His Spirit within men, they can possibly be damned? Can you think God puts His Spirit into them and yet they perish and are lost? You may think so if you please, Sir, but I will tell you what God thinks—"I will put My Spirit within you, and cause you to walk in My statutes; and you shall keep My judgments, and do them." Sinners are far from God by wicked works and they will not come unto Him that they may have life. But when God says, "I will put My Spirit within you," He compels them to come to Him!

What a vain pretense it is to profess to honor God by a Doctrine that makes salvation depend on the will of man! If it were true, you might say to God, "We thank You, O Lord, for what You have done—You have given us a great many things and we offer You Your wages of praise, which are justly due to Your name, but we think we deserve more, for the deciding point was in our free will." Beloved, do not any of you swerve from the free Grace of God, for the babblings about man's free agency are neither more nor less than lies, right contrary to the Truth of Christ and the teachings of the Spirit.

How certain, then, is the salvation of every elect soul! It does not depend on the will of man—he is "made willing" in the day of God's power. given by God to Mr. Spurgeon in his sleep, during the night of Saturday, April 12, 1856, and preached by him the next morning!] He shall be called at the set time and his heart shall be effactually changed, that he may become a trophy of the Redeemer's power. That he was unwilling before is no hindrance, for God gives him the will, so that he is then of a willing mind. Thus, every heir of Heaven must be saved because the Spirit is put within him and thereby his disposition and affections are molded according to the will of God!

Once more, how useless is it for any persons to suppose that they can be saved without the Holy Spirit! Ah, dearFriends, men sometimes go very near to salvation without being saved—like the poor man who lay by the side of the pool of Bethesda, always close to the water, but never getting in. How many changes in outward character there are which very much resemble conversion but, not having the Spirit in them, they fail after all! Deathbed repentances are often looked upon as very sincere, although too frequently, we fear, they are but the first gnawing of the worm that never dies. I have read, this week, an extraordinary anecdote, told by Dr. Campbell, of a woman who, many years ago, was condemned to death for murdering her child and was hung in the Grass Market at Edinburgh. She very diligently improved the six weeks allowed her by the Scottish law, previous to her execution, and the ministers who were with her continually gave it as their opinion that she died in the sure and certain hope of salvation. The appointed day came. She was hung, but it being very rainy, and no awning having been prepared, those who had the charge of her execution were in a great hurry to complete it and get under shelter—so she was cut down before the legal time and, as the custom is, the body was given up to her friends to be buried. A coffin was provided and she was moved in it to East Lothian where her husband was going to bury her. They stopped at a public-house on the road, to refresh themselves, when, to their great surprise and alarm, in rushed a boy and said he heard a noise in the coffin! They went out and found that the woman was alive! The vital powers had been suspended, but the life was not extinct and the jolting of the cart had restored her circulation. After a few hours she became quite well.

They moved their residence and went to another part of the country. But the sad part of the tale is that the woman was as bad a character afterwards as she ever was before and, if anything, worse. She lived as openly in sin and despised and hated religion even more than she had previously done.

This is a most remarkable case. I believe that you would see that the great majority of those who profess to repent on their deathbeds, if they could rise again from their graves, would live a life as profane and godless as ever. Rely on this—it is nothing but the Grace of the Spirit of God that makes sure work of your souls. Unless He shall change you, you may be changed, but it will not be a change that will endure! Unless He shall put His hand to the work, the work will be marred, the pitcher spoiled on the wheel. Cry unto Him, therefore, that He may give you the Holy Spirit, that you may have the evidence of a real conversion and not a base counterfeit! Take heed, Sirs, take heed! Natural fear, natural love, natural feelings are not conversion! Conversion, in the first instance, and by all subsequent edification, must be the work of the Holy Spirit and of Him alone! Never rest comfortable, then, until you have the Holy Spirit's operations most surely effected in your hearts!

THE PERSONALITY OF THE HOLY SPIRIT

"And I will pray the Father and He shall give you another Comforter, that He may abide with you forever: even the Spirit of Truth, whom the world cannot receive, because it sees Him not, neither knows Him: but you know Him for He dwells with you and shall be in you."
John 14:16, 17

A Sermon Delivered On Sunday Morning: 21 January 1855

You will be surprised to hear me announce that I do not intend this morning to say anything about the Holy Spirit as the Comforter. I propose to reserve that for a special Sermon this evening. In this discourse I shall endeavor to explain and enforce certain other doctrines which I believe are plainly taught in this text and which I hope God the Holy Spirit may make profitable to our souls.

Old John Newton once said that there were some books which he could not read, they were good and sound enough, but, he said, "they are books of halfpence—you have to take so much in quantity before you have any value. There are other books of silver and others of gold, but I have one book that is a book of bank notes. And every leaf is a bank note of immense value."

So I found with this text—that I had a bank note of so large a sum, that I could not preach on it all this morning. I should have to keep you several hours before I could unfold to you the whole value of this precious promise—one of the last which Christ gave to His people.

I invite your attention to this passage, because we shall find in it some instruction on four points, first, concerning the true and proper personality of the Holy Spirit. Secondly, concerning the united agency of the glorious Three Persons in the work of our salvation. Thirdly, we shall find something to establish the doctrine of the indwelling of the Holy Spirit in the souls of all Believers. And fourthly, we shall find out the reason why the carnal mind rejects the Holy Spirit.

First of all, we shall have some little instruction concerning the proper PERSONALITY OF THE HOLY SPIRIT. We are so much accustomed to talk about the influence of the Holy Spirit and His sacred operations and graces that we are apt to forget that the Holy Spirit is truly and actually a Person–that He is a subsistence–an existence. Or as we Trinitarians usually say, one Person in the essence of the Godhead. I am afraid that though we do not know it, we have acquired the habit of regarding the Holy Spirit as an emanation flowing from the Father and the Son, but not as being actually a Person Himself. I know it is not easy to carry about in our mind the idea of the Holy Spirit as a Person.

I can think of the Father as a Person, because His acts are such as I can understand. I see Him hang the world in ether. I behold Him swaddling a newborn sea in bands of darkness. I know it is He who formed the drops of hail, who leads forth the stars by their hosts and calls them by their name, I can conceive of Him as a Person because I behold His operations. I can realize Jesus, the Son of Man, as a real Person because He is bone of my bone and flesh of my flesh. It takes no great stretch of my imagination to picture the Babe in Bethlehem, or to behold the, "Man of Sorrows and acquainted with grief." I can easily realize the King of martyrs, as He was persecuted in Pilate's hall, or nailed to the accursed tree for our sins.

Nor do I find it difficult at times to realize the Person of my Jesus sitting on His Throne in Heaven. Or girt with clouds and wearing the diadem of all creation, calling the earth to judgment and summoning us to hear our final sentence. But when I come to deal with the Holy Spirit–His operations are so mysterious, His doings are so secret, His acts are so removed from everything that is of sense and of the body–that I cannot so easily get the idea of His being a Person.

But a Person He is. God the Holy Spirit is not an influence, an emanation, a stream of something flowing from the Father. He is as much an actual Person as either God the Son, or God the Father. I shall attempt this morning a little to establish the doctrine and to show you the truth of it–that God the Holy Spirit is actually a Person.

The first proof we shall gather from the pool of holy Baptism. Let me take you down, as I have taken others, into the pool. It is now concealed, but I wish it were always open to your view. Let me take you to the baptismal font, where Believers put on the name of the Lord Jesus and you shall hear me pronounce the solemn words, "I baptize you in the name,"–mark–"in the name," not names–"of the Father, and of the Son, and of the Holy Spirit." Everyone who is baptized according to the true form laid down in Scripture must be a

Trinitarian–otherwise his Baptism is a farce and a lie and he himself is found a deceiver and a hypocrite before God.

As the Father is mentioned and as the Son is mentioned, so is the Holy Spirit and the whole is summed up as being a Trinity in unity, by its being said, not the names, but the "name"–the glorious name–the Jehovah name, "of the Father, and of the Son, and of the Holy Spirit." Let me remind you that the same thing occurs each time you are dismissed from this house of prayer. In pronouncing the solemn closing benediction, we invoke on your behalf the love of Jesus Christ, the grace of the Father and the fellowship of the Holy Spirit. And thus, according to the Apostolic manner, we make a manifest distinction between the Persons showing that we believe the Father to be a Person, the Son to be a Person and the Holy Spirit to be a Person. Were there no other proofs in Scripture, I think these would be sufficient for every sensible man. He would see that if the Holy Spirit were a mere influence, He would not be mentioned in conjunction with two whom we all confess to be actual and proper Persons.

A second argument arises from the fact that the Holy Spirit has actually made different appearances on earth. The Great Spirit has manifested Himself to man. He has put on a form so that while He has not been beheld by mortal men, He has been so veiled in appearance that He was seen, so far as that appearance was concerned, by the eyes of all beholders. Do you see Jesus Christ our Savior? There is the river Jordan, with its shelving banks and its willows weeping at its side. Jesus Christ, the Son of God, descends into the stream and the holy Baptist, John, plunges Him into the waves.

The doors of Heaven are opened. A miraculous appearance presents itself–a bright light shinning from the sky, brighter than the sun in all its grandeur–and down in a flood of glory descends something which you recognize to be a dove. It rests on Jesus–it sits upon His sacred head and as the old painters put a halo round the brow of Jesus, so did the Holy Spirit shed a resplendence around the face of Him who came to fulfill all Righteousness and therefore commenced with the ordinances of Baptism. The Holy Spirit was seen as a dove–to mark His purity and His gentleness–and He came down like a dove from Heaven to show that it is from Heaven alone that He descends.

Nor is this the only time when the Holy Spirit has been manifest in a visible shape. You notice that company of disciples gathered together in an upper room—they are waiting for some promised blessing—by-and-by it shall come. Hark, there is a sound as of a rushing mighty wind! It fills all the house where they are sitting. Astonished, they look around them, wondering what will come next. Soon a bright light appears, shining upon the heads of each—cloven tongues of fire sat upon them. What were these marvellous appearances of wind and flame but a display of the Holy Spirit in His proper Person? I say the fact of an appearance manifests that He must be a Person. An influence could not appear—an attribute could not appear—we cannot see attributes—we cannot behold influences. The Holy Spirit must, then, be a Person—since He was beheld by mortal eyes and came under the cognizance of mortal sense.

Another proof is from the fact that personal qualities are, in Scripture, ascribed to the Holy Spirit. First, let me read to you a text in which the Holy Spirit is spoken of as having understanding. In the 1st Epistle to the Corinthians, Chapter2, you will read, "But as it is written, eye has not seen, nor ear heard, neither has it entered into the heart of man, the things which God has prepared for them that love Him. But God has revealed them unto us by His Spirit—for the Spirit searches all things, yes, the deep things of God. For what man knows the things of a man, save the spirit of man which is in him? Even so the things of God knows no man, but the Spirit of God."

Here you see an understanding—a power of knowledge is ascribed to the Holy Spirit. Now, if there are any persons here whose minds are of so preposterous a complexion that they would ascribe one attribute to another and would speak of a mere influence having understanding—then I give up! But I believe every rational man will admit that when anything is spoken of as having an understanding it must be an existence—it must, in fact, be a Person. In the 12th Chapter,11th verse of the same Epistle, you will find a will ascribed to the Holy Spirit. "But all these work that one and the selfsame Spirit, dividing to every man severally as He will."

So it is plain the Spirit has a will. He does not come from God simply at God's will, but He has a will of His own, which is always in keeping with the will of the infinite Jehovah, but is, nevertheless, distinct and separate. Therefore I say He is a Person. In another text power is ascribed to the Holy Spirit and power is a thing which can only be ascribed to an existence. In Romans 15:13, it is written, "Now the God of hope fill you with all joy and peace in believing, that you may abound in hope through the power of the Holy Spirit." I need not insist upon it, because it is self-evident, that wherever you find understanding, will and power—you must also find an existence. It cannot be a mere attribute. It cannot be a metaphor. It cannot be a personified influence. It must be a Person.

But I have a proof which, perhaps, will be more telling upon you than any other. Acts and deeds are ascribed to the Holy Spirit—therefore He must be a Person. you read in the first chapter of the Book of Genesis, that the Spirit brooded over the surface of the earth, when it was as yet all disorder and confusion. This world was once a mass of chaotic matter. There was no order. It was like the valley of darkness and of the shadow of death. God the Holy Spirit spread His wings over it. He sowed the seeds of life in it—the germs from which all beings sprang were implanted by Him. He impregnated the earth so that it became capable of life.

Now it must have been a Person who brought order out of confusion. It must have been an existence who hovered over this world and made it what it now is. But do we not read in Scripture something more of the Holy Spirit? Yes, we are told that "holy men of old spoke as they were moved by the Holy Spirit." When Moses penned the Pentateuch, the Holy Spirit moved his hand. When David wrote the Psalms and discoursed sweet music on his harp, it was the Holy Spirit that gave his fingers their Seraphic motion. When Solomon dropped from his lips the words of the Proverbs of wisdom, or when he hymned the Canticles of love it was the HOLY SPIRIT who gave him words of knowledge and hymns of rapture.

Ah, and what fire was that which touched the lips of the eloquent Isaiah? What hand was that which came upon Daniel? What might was that which made Jeremiah so plaintive in his grief? Or what was that which winged Ezekiel and made him, like an eagle, soar into mysteries aloft and see the mighty unknown beyond our reach? Who was it that made Amos, the herdsman, a Prophet? Who taught the rough Haggai to pronounce his thundering sentences? Who showed Habakkuk the horses of Jehovah marching through the waters? Or who kindled the burning eloquence of Nahum? Who caused Malachi to close up the book with the muttering of the word "curse"? Who was in each of these, save the Holy Spirit? And must it not have been a Person who spoke in and through these ancient witnesses? We must believe it. We cannot avoid believing it, when we recall that, "holy men of old spoke as they were moved by the Holy Spirit."

And when has the Holy Spirit ceased to have an influence upon men? We find that still He deals with His ministers and with all His saints. Turn to the Acts and you will find that the Holy Spirit said, "Separate me Paul and Barnabas for the work." I never heard of an attribute saying such a thing! The Holy Spirit said to Peter, "Go to the centurion and what I have cleansed, that call not you common." The Holy Spirit caught away Philip after he had baptized yon eunuch and carried him to another place. And the Holy Spirit said to Paul, "you shall not go into that city, but shall turn into another." And we know that the Holy Spirit was lied unto by Ananias and Sapphira, when it was said, "you have not lied unto man, but unto God."

Again, that power which we feel every day who are called to preach–that wondrous spell which makes our lips so potent–that power which gives us thoughts which are like birds from a far-off region, not the natives of our soul. That influence which I sometimes strangely feel, which, if it does not give me poetry and eloquence, gives me a might I never felt before and lifts me above my fellow man. That majesty with which He clothes His ministers, till in the midst of the battle they cry, aha! like the war-horse of Job and move themselves like leviathans in the water. That power which gives us might over men and causes them to sit and listen as if their ears were chained, as if they were entranced by the power of some magician's wand–that power must come from a Person–it must come from the Holy Spirit.

But is it not said in Scripture and do we not feel it, dear Brethren, that it is the Holy Spirit who regenerates the soul? It is the Holy Spirit who quickens us. "You has He quickened who were dead in trespasses and sins." It is the Holy Spirit who imparts the first germ of life, convicting us of sin, of righteousness and of judgment to come. And is it not the Holy Spirit who after that flame is kindled, still fans it with the breath of His mouth and keeps it alive? Its Author is its Preserver. Oh, can it be said that it is the Holy Spirit who strives in men's souls, that it is the Holy Spirit who brings them to the foot of Sinai and then guides them into the sweet place that is called Calvary–can it be said that He does all these things and yet is not a Person? It may be said, but it must be said by fools. For he never can be a wise man who can consider that these things can be done by any other than a glorious Person–a Divine Person.

Allow me to give you one more proof and I shall have done. Certain feelings are ascribed to the Holy Spirit, which can only be understood upon the supposition that He is actually a Person. In the 4th Chapter of Ephesians, verse 30, it is said that the Holy Spirit can be grieved–"Grieve not the Holy Spirit of God, whereby you are sealed unto the day of redemption." In Isaiah 63:10 it is said that the Holy Spirit can be vexed–"But they rebelled and vexed His Holy Spirit, therefore He was turned to be their enemy and He fought against them." In Acts 7:51 you read that the Holy Spirit can be resisted–"you stiff-necked and uncircumcised in heart and ears, you do always resist the Holy Spirit; as your fathers did, so do you."

And in the 5th verse of the same book, you will find that the Holy Spirit may be tempted. We are there informed that Peter said to Ananias and Sapphira, "How is it that you have agreed together to tempt the Spirit of the Lord?" Now, these things could not be emotions which might be ascribed to a quality or an emanation–they must be understood to relate to a Person. An influence could not be grieved. It must be a Person who can be grieved, vexed, or resisted. And now, dear Brethren, I think I have fully established the point of the personality of the Holy Spirit.

Allow me now, most earnestly, to impress upon you the absolute necessity of being sound unto the doctrine of the Trinity. I knew a man, a good minister of Jesus Christ he was–I believe he was before he turned aside unto heresy–he began to doubt the glorious divinity of our blessed Lord and for years did he preach the heterodox doctrine. Then one day he happened to hear a very eccentric old minister preaching from the text, "But there the glorious Lord shall be unto us a place of broad rivers and streams, wherein shall go no galley with oars, neither shall gallant ship pass thereby. Your tackle is loosed– they could not well strengthen their mast, they could not spread the sail."

"Now," said the old minister, "you give up the Trinity and your tackle is loosed, you cannot strengthen your masts. Once give up the doctrine of three Persons and your tackle is all gone. Your mast, which ought to be a support to your vessel, is a rickety one and shakes." A Gospel without a Trinity? It is a pyramid built upon its apex! A Gospel without the Trinity? It is a rope of sand that cannot hold together! A Gospel without the Trinity? Then, indeed, Satan can overturn it. But, give me a Gospel with the Trinity and the might of Hell cannot prevail against it. No man can any more overthrow it than a bubble could split a rock, or a feather break in halves a mountain.

"Get the thought of the three Persons and you have the marrow of all divinity. Only know the Father and know the Son and know the Holy Spirit to be One and all things will appear clear. This is the golden key to the secrets of nature. This is the silken clue of the labyrinths of mystery and he who understands this, will soon understand as much as mortals ever can know."

II. Now for the second point–the UNITED AGENCY of the Three Persons in the work of our salvation. Look at the text and you will find all the three Persons mentioned. "I,"–that is the Son–"will pray the Father and He shall give you another Comforter." There are the three Persons mentioned–all of them doing something for our salvation. "I will pray," says the Son. "I will send," says the Father. "I will comfort," says the Holy Spirit. Now, let us for a few moments discourse upon this wondrous theme–the unity of the Three Persons with regard to the great purpose of the salvation of the elect.

When God first made man, He said, "Let Us make man," not let Me, but "Let Us make man in Our own image." The covenant Elohim said to each other, "Let Us unitedly become the Creator of man." So, when in ages far gone by in eternity, they said, "Let Us save man," it was not the Father who said, "Let Me save man," but the Three Persons conjointly said with One consent, "Let Us save man." It is to me a source of sweet comfort to think that it is not one Person of the Trinity that is engaged for my salvation. It is not simply one Person of the Godhead who vows that He will redeem me, but it is a glorious Trio of Godlike ones and the Three declare, unitedly, "We will save man."

Now, observe here that each Person is spoken of as performing a separate office. "I will pray," says the Son–that is intercession. "I will send," says the Father–that is donation. "I will comfort," says the Holy Spirit–that is supernatural influence. Oh, if it were possible for us to see the three Persons of the Godhead, we should behold one of them standing before the Throne with outstretched hands crying day and night, "O Lord, how long?" We should see one girt with Urim and Thummim, precious stones, on which are written the twelve names of the tribes of Israel. We should behold Him crying unto His Father, "Forget not Your promises, forget not Your covenant." We should hear Him make mention of our sorrows and tell forth our griefs on our behalf, for He is our intercessor.

And could we behold the Father, we should not see Him a listless and idle spectator of the intercession of the Son. We should see Him with attentive ears listening to every word of Jesus and granting every petition. Where is the Holy Spirit all the while? Is He lying idle? Oh no, He is floating over the earth and when He sees a weary soul, He says, "Come to Jesus, He will give you rest." When He beholds an eye filled with tears, He wipes away the tears and bids the mourner look for comfort on the Cross. When He sees the tempest-tossed Believer, He takes the helm of his soul and speaks the word of consolation. He helps the broken in heart and binds up their wounds.

And ever on His mission of mercy, He flies around the world, being everywhere present. Behold how the Three Persons work together. Do not then say, "I am grateful to the Son"–you ought to be, but God the Son no more saves you than God the Father. Do not imagine that God the Father is a great tyrant and that God the Son had to die to make Him merciful. It was not to make the Father's love flow towards His people. Oh, no. One loves as much as the other. The Three are conjoined in the great purpose of rescuing the elect from damnation.

But you must notice another thing in my text which will show the blessed unity of the Three–the one Person promises to the Other. The Son says, "I will pray the Father." "Very well," the disciples may have said, "We can trust You for that." "And He will send you." You see here is the Son signing a bond on behalf of the Father. "He will send you another Comforter." There is a bond on behalf of the Holy Spirit, too. "And He will abide with you forever." One person speaks for the other and how could they if there were any disagreement between them? If one wished to save and the other not, they could not promise on one another's behalf. But whatever the Son says, the Father listens to. Whatever the Father promises, the Holy Spirit works. And whatever the Holy Spirit injects into the soul–God the Father fulfils.

So the Three together mutually promise on one another's behalf. There is a bond with three names appended–Father, Son and Holy Spirit. By three immutable things, as well as by two, the Christian is secured beyond the reach of death and Hell. A Trinity of Securities, because there is a Trinity of God.

III. Our third point is the INDWELLING of the Holy Spirit in Believers. Now Beloved, these first two things have been matters of pure doctrine–this is the subject of experience. The indwelling of the Holy Spirit is a subject so profound and so having to do with the inner man, that no soul will be able truly and really to comprehend what I say, unless it has been taught of God. I have heard of an old minister, who told a Fellow of one of the Cambridge Colleges that he understood a language that he never learnt in all his life. "I have not," he said, "even a smattering of Greek and I know no Latin, but thank God I can talk the language of Canaan and that is more than you can."

So, Beloved, I shall now have to talk a little of the language of Canaan. If you cannot comprehend me, I am much afraid it is because you are not of Israelite extraction–you are not a child of God nor an inheritor of the kingdom of Heaven.

We are told in the text, that Jesus would send the Comforter, who would abide in the saints forever–who would dwell with them and be in them. Old Ignatius, the martyr, used to call himself Theophorus, or the God-bearer, "because," said he, "I bear about with me the Holy Spirit." And truly every Christian is a God-bearer. Know you not that you are temples of the Holy Spirit? For He dwells in you. That man is no Christian who is not the subject of the indwelling of the Holy Spirit.

He may talk well, he may understand theology and be a sound Calvinist. He will be the child of nature finely dressed, but not the living child. He may be a man of so profound an intellect, so gigantic a soul, so comprehensive a mind and so lofty an imagination that he may dive into all the secrets of nature. He may know the path which the eagle's eye has not seen and go into depths where mortals reach not. But he shall not be a Christian with all his knowledge. He shall not be a son of God with all his researches, unless he understands what it is to have the Holy Spirit dwelling in him and abiding in him– yes and that forever.

Some people call this fanaticism and they say, "you are a Quaker, why not follow George Fox?" Well we would not mind that much–we would follow anyone who followed the Holy Spirit. Even he, with all his eccentricities, I doubt not, was, in many cases, actually inspired by the Holy Spirit. And whenever I find a man in whom there rests the Spirit of God, the Spirit within me leaps to hear the Spirit within him and he feels that we are one. The Spirit of God in one Christian soul recognizes the Spirit in another. I recollect talking with a good man, as I believe he was, who was insisting that it was impossible for us to know whether we had the Holy Spirit within us or not.

I should like him to be here this morning, because I would read this verse to him–"But you know Him, for He dwells with you and shall be in you." Ah, you think you cannot tell whether you have the Holy Spirit or not? Can I tell whether I am alive or not? If I were touched by electricity, could I tell whether I was or not? I suppose I should. The shock would be strong enough to make me know where I stood. So, if I have God within me—if I have Deity tabernacling in my breast—if I have God the Holy Spirit resting in my heart and making a temple of my body—do you think I shall not know it? Call it fanaticism if you will. But I trust that there are some of us who know what it is to be always, or generally, under the influence of the Holy Spirit—always in one sense—generally in another.

When we have difficulties we ask the direction of the Holy Spirit. When we do not understand a portion of Holy Scripture, we ask God the Holy Spirit to shine upon us. When we are depressed, the Holy Spirit comforts us. You cannot tell what the wondrous power of the indwelling of the Holy Spirit is—how it pulls back the hand of the saint when he would touch the forbidden thing. How it prompts him to make a covenant with his eyes. How it binds his feet, lest they should fall in a slippery way, how it restrains his heart and keeps him from temptation.

O you who know nothing of the indwelling of the Holy Spirit, despise it not. O despise not the Holy Spirit, for it is the unpardonable sin. "He that speaks a word against the Son of Man, it shall be forgiven him, but he that speaks against the Holy Spirit, it shall never be forgiven him, either in this life, or that which is to come." So says the Word of God. Therefore, tremble, lest in anything you despise the influences of the Holy Spirit.

But before closing this point, there is one little word which pleases me very much. That is, "forever." You knew I should not miss that. You were certain I could not let it go without observation. "Abide with you forever." I wish I could get an Arminian here to finish my sermon. I fancy I see him taking that word, "forever." He would say, "for—forever." He would have to stammer and stutter. For he never could get it out all at once. He might stand and pull it about and at last he would have to say, "the translation is wrong." And then I suppose the poor man would have to prove that the original was wrong, too. Ah, but blessed be God, we can read it—"He shall abide with you forever." Once give me the Holy Spirit and I shall never lose Him till "forever" has run out—till eternity has spun its everlasting rounds!

IV. Now we have to close up with a brief remark on the reason why the world rejects the Holy Spirit. It is said, "Whom the world cannot receive, because it sees Him not, neither knows Him." You know what is sometimes meant by "the world"–those whom God, in His wondrous sovereignty, passed over when He chose His people–the preterite ones. Those passed over in God's wondrous preterition–not the reprobates who were condemned to damnation by some awful decree, but those passed over by God, when He chose out His elect. These cannot receive the Spirit. Again, it means all in a carnal state are not able to procure themselves this Divine influence. And thus it is true, "Whom the world cannot receive."

The unregenerate world of sinners despises the Holy Spirit, "because it sees Him not." Yes, I believe this is the great secret why many laugh at the idea of the existence of the Holy Spirit–because they see Him not. You tell the worldling, "I have the Holy Spirit within me." He says, "I cannot see it." He wants it to be something tangible–a thing he can recognize with his senses. Have you ever heard the argument used by a good old Christian against an infidel doctor? The doctor said there was no soul and he asked, "Did you ever see a soul?" "No," said the Christian. "Did you ever hear a soul?" "No." "Did you ever smell a soul?" No." "Did you ever taste a soul?" "No." "Did you ever feel a soul?"

"Yes," said the man–"I feel I have one within me." "Well," said the doctor, "there are four senses against one–you have only one on your side." "Very well," said the Christian, "Did you ever see a pain?" "No." "Did you ever hear a pain?" "No." "Did you ever smell a pain?" "No." "Did you ever taste a pain?" "No." "Did you ever feel a pain?" "Yes," "And that is quite enough, I suppose, to prove there is a pain?" "Yes." So the worldling says there is no Holy Spirit, because he cannot see it. Well, but we feel it. You say that is fanaticism and that we never felt it. Suppose you tell me that honey is bitter, I reply "No, I am sure you cannot have tasted it. Taste it and try."

So with the Holy Spirit. If you did but feel His influence, you would no longer say there is no Holy Spirit because you cannot see it. Are there not many things, even in nature, which we cannot see? Did you ever see the wind? No. But you know there is wind when you behold the hurricane tossing the waves about and rending down the habitations of men. Or when in the soft evening zephyr it kisses the flowers and makes dewdrops hang in pearly coronets around the rose. Did you ever see electricity? No, but you know there is such a thing, for it travels along the wires for thousands of miles and carries our messages. Though you cannot see the thing itself, you know there is such a thing. So you must believe there is a Holy Spirit working in us, both to will and to do, even though it is beyond our senses.

But the last reason why worldly men laugh at the doctrine of the Holy Spirit is because they do not know it. If they knew it by heart-felt experience and if they recognized its agency in the soul–if they had ever been touched by it. If they had been made to tremble under a sense of sin–if they had had their hearts melted–they would never have doubted the existence of the Holy Spirit.

And now, Beloved, it says, "He dwells with you and shall be in you." We will close up with that sweet recollection–the Holy Spirit dwells in all Believers and shall be with them.

One word of comment and advice to the saints of God and to sinners and I have done. Saints of the Lord! You have this morning heard that God the Holy Spirit is a Person. You have had it proved to your souls. What follows from this? Why, it follows how earnest you should be–in prayer to the Holy Spirit, as well as for the Holy Spirit. Let me say that this is an inference that you should lift up your prayers to the Holy Spirit, that you should cry earnestly unto Him, for He is able to do exceeding abundantly above all you can ask or think.

See this mass of people? What is to convert it? See this crowd–who is to make my influence permeate through the mass? You know this place has now a mighty influence–and God blessing us, it will continue to have an influence–not only upon this city but upon England at large. We now enjoy the press as well as the pulpit and certainly, I should say before the close of the year, more than two hundred thousand of my productions will be scattered through the land–words uttered by my lips, or written by my pen. But how can this influence be rendered for good? How shall God's glory be promoted by it? Only by incessant prayer for the Holy Spirit–by constantly calling down the influence of the Holy Spirit upon us.

We want Him to rest upon every page that is printed and upon every word that is uttered. Let us then be doubly earnest in pleading with the Holy Spirit, that He would come and own our labors, that the whole Church at large may be revived thereby and not ourselves only, but the whole world share in the benefit.

Then to the ungodly I have this one closing word to say. Ever be careful how you speak of the Holy Spirit. I do not know what the unpardonable sin is and I do not think any man understands it. But it is something like this—"He that speaks a word against the Holy Spirit, it shall never be forgiven him." I do not know what that means—but tread carefully! There is danger. There is a pit which our ignorance has covered by sand—tread carefully—you may be in it before the next hour. If there is any strife in your heart today, perhaps you will go to the ale-house and forget it. Perhaps there is some voice speaking in your soul and you will put it away.

I do not tell you you will be resisting the Holy Spirit and committing the unpardonable sin. But it is somewhere there. Be very careful. Oh, there is no crime on earth so black as the crime against the Holy Spirit. You may blaspheme the Father and you shall be damned for it unless you repent. You may blaspheme the Son—and Hell shall be your portion, unless you are forgiven. But blaspheme the Holy Spirit and thus says the Lord, "There is no forgiveness, neither in this world, nor in the world which is to come." I cannot tell you what it is. I do not profess to understand it. But there it is.

It is the danger signal. Stop, Man, stop! If you have despised the Holy Spirit, if you have laughed at His revelations and scorned what Christians call His influence, I beseech you, stop! This morning seriously deliberate—perhaps some of you have actually committed the unpardonable sin. Stop! Let fear stop you. Sit down. Do not drive on so rashly as you have done. You who are such a profligate in sin, you who have uttered such hard words against the Trinity, stop!

Ah, it makes us all stop. It makes us all draw up and say, "Have I not perhaps so done?" Let us think of this and let us not at any time trifle either with the words, or the acts of God the Holy Spirit.

THE HOLY SPIRIT COMPARED TO THE WIND

"The wind blows where it wishes and you hear the sound of it, but cannot tell from where it comes and where it goes. So is everyone that is born of the Spirit."
John 3:8

A Sermon Delivered In: 1865

AT the present moment I am not able to enter fully into the subject of the new birth. I am very weary, both in body and mind and cannot attempt that great and mysterious theme. To everything there is a season and a time for every purpose under Heaven and it is not the time to preach upon regeneration when the head is aching, nor to discourse upon the new nature when the mind is distracted. I selected my text with the intention of fixing upon one great illustration which strikes me just now as being so suggestive, and with Divine assistance I may be able to work it out with profit to you and ease to myself.

I shall endeavor to bring before you the parallel which our Savior here draws between the wind and the Holy Spirit. It is a remarkable fact, known, I dare say to most of you, that both in the Hebrew and Greek languages the same word is used for spirit and for wind–so that our Savior, as it were, rode upon the wings of the wind, while he was instructing the seeking Rabbi in the deep things of God. He caught at the very name of the wind as a means of fastening a spiritual truth upon the memory of the enquirer, hinting to us that language should be watched by the teacher that he may find out suitable words and employ those which will best assist the disciple to comprehend and to retain his teaching. "The wind," said He, "blows," and the very same word would have been employed if He had meant to say, "The Spirit blows where He wishes."

There was intended, doubtless, to be a very close and intimate parallel between the Spirit of God and the wind, or otherwise the great Ruler of Providence who invisibly controlled the confusion of Babel would not have fashioned human language so that the same word should stand for both. Language, as well as nature, illustrates the wisdom of God! It is only in His light that we see light–may the Holy Spirit be graciously pleased to reveal Himself in His Divine operations to all our waiting minds.

We are taught in God's Word that the Holy Spirit comes upon the sons of men and makes them new creatures. Until He enters them they are "dead in trespasses and sins." They cannot discern the things of God because Divine Truths of God are spiritual and spiritually discerned–and unrenewed men are carnal and possess not the power to search out the deep things of God. The Spirit of God creates new in the children of God and then in their new-born spirituality they discover and come to understand spiritual things, but not before. And, therefore, my beloved Hearers, unless you possess the Spirit, no metaphors, however simple, can reveal Him to you.

Let us not mention the name of the Holy Spirit without due honor. Forever blessed are You, most glorious Spirit, co-equal and co-eternal with the Father and with the Son! Let all the angels of God worship You! Be You had in honor world without end!

We will consider IN WHAT SENSE THE HOLY SPIRIT MAY BE COMPARED TO THE WIND. The Spirit of God, to help the spiritually-minded in their study of His Character and Nature condescends to compare Himself to dew, fire, oil, water and other suggestive types. And among the rest our Savior uses the metaphor of wind. What is the first thought here but that of mystery? It was the objection on the score of mystery which our Lord was trying to remove from the mind of Nicodemus. Nicodemus in effect, said, "I cannot understand it. How can it be? A man born again when he is old, created over again and that from an invisible agency from above? How can these things be?"
Jesus at once directed his attention to the wind, which is none the less real and operative because of its mysterious origin and operation. You cannot tell from where the wind comes–you know it blows from the north or from the that it is blowing to the east or to the west, but where is it going? From where did these particles of air originate which rush so rapidly past? Where are they going? By what law are they guided in their course and where will their journey end?

The gale may be blowing due east here, but it may be driving west a hundred miles away In one district tho wind may be rushing from the north and yet not far from it there may be a strong current from the south. Those who ascend in balloons tell us that they meet with crosscurrents–one wind blowing in this direction and another layer of air moving towards an opposite quarter–how is this? If you have watched the skies you must occasionally have noticed a stream of clouds hurrying to the right, while higher up, another company is sailing to the left! It is a question whether thunder and lightning may not be produced by the friction of two currents of air traveling in different directions. But why is it that this current takes it into its head to go this way, while another steers for quite another port? Will they meet across each other's path in regions far away?

Are there whirlpools in the air as in the water? Are there eddies, currents, rivers of air, lakes of air? Is the whole atmosphere like the sea, only composed of less dense matter? If so, what is it that stirs up that great deep of air and bids it howl in the hurricane and then constrains it to subside into the calm? The philosopher may scheme some conjecture to prove that the "trade winds" blow at certain intervals because of the sun crossing the equator at those periods and that there must necessarily be a current of air going towards the equator because of the rarefaction. But he cannot tell you why the weathercock on yonder church steeple turned this morning from south-west to due east.

He cannot tell me why it is that the sailor finds that his sails are at one time filled with wind and in a few minutes they fall loosely about so that he must steer upon another tack if he would make headway. The various motions of the air remain a mystery to all but the infinite Jehovah. My Brethren, the like mystery is observed in the work of the Spirit of God. His Person and work are not to be comprehended by the mind of man. He may be here tonight, but you cannot see Him—He speaks to one heart, but others cannot hear His voice. He is not recognizable by the unrefined senses of the unregenerate.

The spiritual man discerns Him, feels Him, hears Him and delights in Him, but neither wit nor learning can lead a man into the secret. The Believer is often bowed down with the weight of the Spirit's Glory, or lifted up upon the wings of His majesty. But even he knows not how these feelings are worked in him. The fire of holy life is at seasons gently fanned with the soft breath of Divine comfort, or the deep sea of spiritual existence stirred with the mighty blast of the Spirit's rebuke. But still it is forevermore a mystery how the eternal God comes into contact with the finite mind of His creature, man. God is filling all Heaven, meanwhile, and yet dwelling in a human body as in a temple—occupying all space and yet operating upon the will, the judgment, the mind of the poor insignificant creature called man.

We may enquire, but who can answer us? We may search, but who shall lead us into the hidden things of the Most High? He brooded over chaos and produced order, but who shall tell us after what fashion He worked? He overshadowed the Virgin and prepared a body for the Son of God, but into this secret who shall dare pry? His is the anointing, sealing, comforting and sanctifying of the saints—but how does He work all these things? He makes intercession for us according to the will of God. He dwells in us and leads us into all the Truths of God—but who among us can explain to his fellow man the order of the Divine working?

Though veiled from human eye like the Glory which shone between the cherubim, we believe in the Holy Spirit and therefore see Him. But if our faith needed to sustain it, we should never believe at all. Mystery is far from being all which the Savior would teach by this simile. Surely He meant to show us that the operations of the Spirit are like the wind for Divinity. Who can create a wind? The most ambitious of human princes would scarcely attempt to turn, much less to send forth, the wind! These steeds of the storm know no bit nor bridle, neither will they come at any man's bidding. Let our senators do what they will, they will scarcely have the madness to legislate the winds!

Old Boreas, as the heathens called him, is not to be bound with chains and welded on an earthly anvil, or in a vulcanian forge. "The wind blows where it wishes." And it does so because God directs it and suffers it not to stay for man nor to tarry for the sons of men. So with the Spirit of God. All the true operations of the Spirit are due in no sense whatever to man, but always to God and to His Sovereign will. Revivalists may get up excitement with the best intentions and may warm peoples' hearts till they begin to cry out, but all this ends in nothing unless it is Divine work. Have I not said scores of times from this pulpit, "All that is of Nature's spinning must be unraveled"?

Every particle which Nature puts upon the foundation will turn out to be but "wood, hay and stubble," and will be consumed. It is only "the gold, the silver and the precious stones" of God's building that will stand the fiery test. "You must be born again from above," for human regenerations are lies. You may blow with your mouth and produce some trifling effects upon trifles as light as air. Man in his zeal may set the windmills of silly minds in motion. But, truly, to stir men's hearts with substantial and eternal Truths of God needs a celestial breeze such as the Lord alone can send!

Did not our Lord also intend to hint at the Sovereignty of the Spirit's work? For what other reason did He say, "The wind blows where it wishes?" There is an arbitrariness about the wind. It does just as it pleases and the laws which regulate its changes are unknown to man. "Free as the wind," we say–"the wild winds." So is the mighty working of God! It is a very solemn thought and one which should tend to make us humble before the Lord–that we are, as to the matter of salvation–entirely in His hands! If I have a moth in my hand tonight I can bruise its wings, or I can crush it at my will and by no attempts of its own can it escape from me. And every sinner is absolutely in the hands of God and–let him remember he is in the hand of an angry God, too.

The only comfort is that he is in the hand of a God who, for Jesus' sake, delights to have mercy upon even the vilest of the vile. Sinner, God can give you the Holy Spirit if He wills. But if He should say concerning you, "Let him alone," your fate is sealed, your damnation is sure! It is a thought which some would say is "enough to freeze all energy." Beloved, I would to God it would freeze the energy of the flesh and make the flesh dead in the sense of powerlessness–for God never truly begins to show His might till we have seen an end of all human power. I tell you, Sinner, you are as dead concerning spiritual things as the corpse that is laid in its coffin! No, as the corpse that is rotting in its grave and has become, like Lazarus in the tomb, stinking and offensive.

There is a voice that can call you forth out of your sepulcher, but if that voice comes not remember where you are–justly damned, justly ruined, justly cut off forever from all hope. What do you say? Do you tremble at this? Do you cry, "O God! Have pity upon me"? He will hear your cry, Sinner, for there never yet was a sincere cry that went up to Heaven, though it were ever so feeble, but what it had an answer of peace. When one of the old saints lay dying, he could only say, "O Lord, I trust You languida fide," with a languid faith. It is poor work that, but, oh, it is safe work. You can only trust Christ with a feeble faith. If it is such a poor trembling faith that it does not grip Him, but only touches the hem of His garment, it nevertheless saves you!

If you can look at Him, though it is only a great way off, yet it saves you. And oh, what a comfort this is, that you are still on pleading terms with Him and in a place of hope! "Whoever believes is not condemned." But, oh, do not trifle with the day of Divine Grace, lest having frequently heard the warning, and hardened your neck just as often, you should "suddenly be destroyed and that without remedy!" If He shuts you out, none can bid you come in! If He does but close the iron bar, you are shut out in the darkness of obstinacy, obduracy and despair forever—the victim of your own delusions!

Sinner, if God saves you, He shall have all the glory—for He has a right to do as He wills—for He says, "I will have mercy on whom I will have mercy and I will have compassion on whom I will have compassion." But still, I think I have not yet brought out what is in the text. Do you not think that the text was intended to show the varied methods in which the Spirit of God works in the conversion and regeneration of men? "The wind blows where it wishes." Now observe the different force of the wind. This afternoon the wind seemed as if it would tear up every tree and doubtless, had they been in leaf, many of those noble princes of the forest must have stretched themselves prone upon the earth. But God takes care that in these times of boisterous gales there should be no leaf and therefore the wind gets but little purchase with which to drag up a tree.

But the wind does not always blow as it did this afternoon. On a summer's evening there is such a gentle zephyr that even the gnats who have been arranging a dance among themselves are not disturbed, but keep to their proper places. Yes, the aspen seems as if it could be quiet, though you know it keeps forever quivering, according to the old legend that it was the tree on which the Savior hung and therefore trembles still as though through fear of the sin which came upon it. It is but a legend. There are times when all is still and calm, when everything is quiet and you can scarcely detect the wind at all.

Now just so it is with the Spirit of God. To some of us He came like a "rushing mighty wind." Oh, what tearing of soul there were then! My spirit was like a sea tossed up into tremendous waves, made, as Job says, "To boil like a pot," till one would think the deep were hoary. Oh, how that wind came crashing through my soul and every hope I had was bowed as the trees of the wood in the tempest! Read the story of John Bunyan's conversion—it was just the same. Turn to Martin Luther—you find his conversion of the same sort. So might I mention hundreds of biographies in which the Spirit of God came like a tornado sweeping everything before it and the men could not but feel that God was in the whirlwind.

To others He comes so gently they cannot tell when first the Spirit of God came. They recollect that night when mother prayed so with brothers and sisters and when they could not sleep for hours because the big tears stood in their eyes on account of sin. They recollect the Sunday school and the teacher there. They remember that earnest minister. They cannot say exactly when they gave their hearts to God and they cannot tell about any violent convictions. They are often comforted by that text, "One thing I know, whereas I was blind, now I see." But they cannot get any farther—they sometimes wish they could.

Well, they need not wish it, for the Spirit of God, as a Sovereign, will always choose His own way of operation. And if it is but the wind of the Holy Spirit, remember it is as saving in its gentleness as in its terror and is as efficient to make us new creatures when it comes with the zephyr's breath as when it comes with the hurricane's force. Do not quarrel with God's way of saving you! If you are brought to the Cross be thankful for it—Christ will not mind how you got there. If you can say, "He is all my salvation and all my desire," you never came to that without the Spirit of God bringing you to it. Do not, therefore, think you came the wrong way, for that is impossible!

Again, the wind not only differs in force, but it differs in direction. We have been saying several times the wind is always shifting. Perhaps there never were two winds that did blow exactly in the same direction. I mean that if we had power to detect the minute points of the compass, there would be found some deviation in every current, although, of course, for all practical purposes it blows from certain distinct points which the mariner marks out. Now, the Spirit of God comes from different directions.

You know very well, dear Friends, that sometimes the Spirit of God will blow with mighty force from one denomination of Christians. Then suddenly they seem to be left and God will raise up another body of Christians, fill them with Himself and qualify them for usefulness. In the days of Wesley and Whitefield there was very little of the Divine Spirit anywhere except among the Methodists. I am sure they have not a monopoly of Him now. The Divine Spirit blows also from other quarters. Sometimes He uses one man, sometimes another. We hear of a revival in the North of Ireland. By-and-by it is in the South of Scotland. It comes just as God wills, for direction.

And you know, too, dear Friends, it comes through different instrumentalities in the same Church. Sometimes the wind blows from this pulpit—God blesses me to your conversion. Another time it is from my good sister, Mrs. Bartlett's class. On a third occasion it is the Sunday school. Again, it may be another class, or the preaching of the young men, or from the individual exertion of private Believers. God causes that wind to blow just which way He wills. He works, also, through different texts of Scripture. You were converted and blessed under one text—it was quite another that was made useful to me.

Some of you were brought to Christ by terrors, others of you by love, by sweet wooing words. The wind blows as God directs. Now, dear Friends, whenever you take up a religions biography, do not sit down and say, "Now I will see whether I am just like this person." Nonsense! God never repeats Himself. Men make steel pens—thousands of grosses of them—all alike, but I will be bound to say that in quills from the common, there are no two of them precisely the same. If you look, you will soon discover that they differ in a variety of ways. Certain gardeners cut their trees into the shape of cheeses and a number of unnatural forms, but God's trees do not grow that way, they grow just anyway—gnarl their roots and twist their branches.

Great painters do not continually paint the same picture again and again and again, and my Divine Master never puts His pencil on the canvas to produce the same picture twice. Every Christian is a distinct work of Divine Grace on God's part which has in it some originality, some portion distinct from all others. I do not believe in trying to make all history uniform. It is said that Richard III had a humpback. Whether he really was deformed, or whether history gave him the humpback, I cannot tell. But it is said that all his courtiers thought it was the most beautiful humpback that ever was seen and they all began to grow humpbacks, too!

And I have known ministers who had some peculiar idiosyncrasy of experience which was nothing better than a spiritual humpback—but their people all began to have humpbacks, too—to think and talk all in the same way and to have the same doubts and fears. Now that will not do! It is not the way in which the Most High acts with regard to the wind and if He chooses to take all the points of the compass and make use of them all, let us bless and glorify His name! Are not the different winds various in their qualities? Few of us like an east wind. Most of us arc very glad when the wind blows from the south. Vegetation seems to love much the south-west.

A stiff northeaster is enough to make us perish. And long continuance of the north may well freeze the whole earth! While from the west the wind seems to come laden with health from the deep blue sea. And though sometimes too strong for the sick, yet it is never a bad time when the west wind blows. The ancients all had their different opinions about wind. Some were dry, some were rainy. Some affected this disease, some touched this part of men, some the other. Certain it is that God's Holy Spirit has different qualities. In the Canticles He blows softly with the sweet breath of love. Look farther and you get that same Spirit blowing fiercely with threats and denunciation.

Sometimes you find Him convicting the world "of sin, of righteousness, of judgment." That is the north wind. At other times opening up Christ to the sinner and giving him joy and comfort. That is the south wind that blows softly and gives a balminess in which poor troubled hearts rejoice. And yet "all these works the same Spirit." Indeed, my subject is all but endless, and therefore I must stop. But even in the matter of duration you know how the wind will sometimes blow six weeks in this direction and, again, continue in another direction. And the Spirit of God does not always work with us–He does as He pleases–He comes and He goes. We may be in a happy hallowed frame at one time, and at another we may have to cry, "Come from the four winds, O Breath!"

II. We will consider. in the second place, THE PARALLEL BETWEEN THE HOLY SPIRIT AND THE EFFECTS OF THE WIND. "You hear the sound of it." Ah, that we do! The wind sometimes wails as if you could hear the cry of mariners far out at sea, or the moans of the widows that must weep for them. And, oh, the Spirit of God sets men wailing with an exceedingly bitter cry for sin, as one that is in sorrow for his first-born.

"You hear the sound of it." Oh, it is a blessed sound, that wailing! Angels rejoice over "one sinner that repents." Then comes the wind at another time with a triumphant sound, and if there is an Aeolian harp in the window, how it swells, sweeps, descends–then rises again! It gives all the tones of music and makes the air glad with its jubilant notes. So with the Holy Spirit–sometimes He gives us faith, makes us bold–other times full of assurance, confidence, joy and peace in believing. "You hear the sound" of a full diapason of the Holy Spirit's mighty melody within the soul of man filling him with peace and joy and rest and love.

Sometimes the wind comes, too, with another sound as though it were contending. You heard it, perhaps, this afternoon. We who are a little in the country hear it more than you do–it is as though giants were struggling in the sky together. It seems as if two seas of air, both lashed to fury, met and dashed against some unseen cliffs with terrible uproar. The Spirit of God comes into the soul sometimes and makes great contention with the flesh. Oh, what a stern striving there is against unbelief, against lust, against pride, against every evil thing.

"You hear the sound of it." You that know what Divine experience means–you know when to go forth to fight your sins. When you can hear "the sound of a going in the tops of the mulberry trees," then you bestir yourself to destroy your sins. Sometimes the wind comes with a sweep as though it were going on forever. It comes past and dashes through the trees, sweeping away the rotten branches. Then away it goes across the Alps, dashing down an avalanche in its course, still onward. And as it flies, it blows away everything that is frail and weak. And on, on, on it speeds its way to some unknown goal.

And thus it is sometimes the Spirit of God will come right through us, as if He were bearing us away to that spiritual heritage which is our sure future destiny–bearing away coldness, barrenness, everything before it. We do not lament then that we do not pray. We do not believe that we cannot pray–"I can do everything," is our joyful shout as we are carried on the wings of the wind. "You hear the sound of it." I hope you have heard it sometimes in all its powerful, overwhelming, mighty influence till your soul has been blown away.

"You hear the sound of it." But then the wind does something more than make a sound. And so does the Holy Spirit. It WORKS and produces manifest results. Just think what the wind is doing tonight. I cannot tell at what pitch it may be now. It is just possible that in some part of the ocean a vessel scuds along almost under bare poles. The mariners do their best to reef the sails– away she goes–now the mast is gone–they do their best to bear up but they find that in the teeth of the gale they cannot stand.

The ship dashes on the rocks and she is wrecked. And, oh, the Spirit of God is a great wrecker of false hopes and carnal confidences! I have seen the Spirit of God come to a sinner like a storm to a ship at sea. He had to take down the top gallants of the sinner's pride. Then every thread of carnal confidence had to be reefed and then his hope, itself, had to be cut away. And on, on the vessel went, until she struck a rock and down she went. The man from that time never dared trust in his merits for he had seen his merits wrecked and broken in pieces by the wind.

The wind, too, remember, is a great leveller. It always aims at everything that is high. If you are down low in the street you escape its fury. But climb to the top of the Monument, or St. Paul's and see whether you do not feel it! Get into the valley, it is all right. The lower branches of the trees are scarcely moved, but the top branches are rocked to and fro by it. It is a great leveller! So is the Holy Spirit. He never sees a man high but He brings him down. He makes every high thought bow before the majesty of His might.

And if you have any high thoughts tonight, rest assured that when the Spirit of God comes He will lay them low, even with the ground. Now do not let this make you fear the Holy Spirit. It is a blessed thing to be rocked so as to have our hopes tested and it is a precious thing to have our carnal confidences shaken. And how blessedly the wind purifies the atmosphere! In the Swiss valleys there is a heaviness in the air which makes the inhabitants unhealthy. They take quinine and you see them going about with big swellings in their necks.

From Martigny to Bretagne, there is a great valley in which you will see hundreds of persons diseased. The reason is that the air does not circulate. They are breathing the same air, or some of it, that their fathers breathed before them. There seems to be no ventilation between the two parts of the giant Alps and the air never circulates. But if they have a great storm which sweeps through the valleys it is a great blessing to the people. And so the Spirit of God comes and cleanses out our evil thoughts and vain imaginations—and though we do not like the hurricane, yet it brings spiritual health to our soul.

Again the wind is a great trier of the nature of things. Here comes a great rushing up the street. It sweeps over the heaps of rubbish lying in the road. Away goes all the light chaff, paper and other things which have no weight in them! They cannot stand the brunt of its whirling power. But see, the pieces of iron, the stones and all weighty things are left unmoved. In the country you will often see the farmer severing the chaff from the wheat by throwing it up into a current of air and the light husks all blow away, while the heavy wheat sinks on the heap, cleansed and purified. So is the Holy Spirit the great testing power and the result of His operations will be to show men what they are.

Here is a hypocrite, he has passed muster up to now and reckons himself to be a true and genuine man. But there comes a blast from Heaven's mighty Spirit and he finds himself to be lighter than vanity–he has no weight in him, he is driven on and has no rest. He can find no peace. He hurries from one refuge of lies to another. "There is no peace, says my God, to the wicked." Thus also we try the doctrines of men, we bring the breath of Inspiration to bear upon them–do they abide the test? Or are they driven away? Can you hold that truth in the presence of God? Can you cling to it and find it stable in the hour of trial?

Is it a nice pleasant speculation for a sunny day when all is calm and bright, or will it bear the rough rude blast of adversity when God's Holy Spirit is purifying you with His healthful influence? True Christians and sound doctrines have ballast and weight in them–they are not moved nor driven away. But empty professors and hollow dogmas are scattered like chaff before the wind when the Lord shall blow upon them with the breath of His Spirit. Therefore examine yourselves–try the doctrines and see if they are of God. "What is the chaff to the wheat?" says the Lord.

Have root in yourselves–then you will not wither in the hot blast, nor be driven away in the tempestuous day. Is not the Spirit moreover like unto the wind in its developing of character? See the dust is lying all over the picture, you cannot see the fair features of the beauteous sketch beneath. Blow off the dust and the fine colors will be seen and once more the skill of the painter will be admired. Have you ever noticed some piece of fine mosaic, or perhaps some well-cut engraving on metal all hidden and the fine lines filled up with dust?

You have blown off the accumulation and then you could admire the work. So does the Spirit of God. Men get all covered with dust in the hot dusty roadside of life till they are nearly the color of the earth itself. But they come to the hilltop of Calvary and here they stand till the wind of Heaven has cleansed them from all the dust that has gathered around their garments. Oh there is nothing like communion with the Spirit of God to counteract the earthly tendencies of a business life! There are some men that get covered with a yellow dust till they are almost hidden by it. They can talk of nothing else but money. Gold, gold, gold is getting to occupy nearly every thought.

Now I have no quarrel with money in its right place, but I do not like to see men live in it. I always try to drive away that mean and grovelling spirit which lives for nothing else but to accumulate money, but I cannot always succeed. Now the Spirit of God will make a man see his folly and put his money into its right position and place the Graces of the Christian character where men can see them and glorify God in them. Never let your business character or professional skill dim and hide your Christianity. If you do, God's Spirit will come to brighten you up and He will have no mercy on these, but will, in love to your soul, cleanse and give luster to God's work which is worked in you.

I have also noticed how helpful the wind is to all who choose to avail themselves of it. In Lincolnshire, where the country is flat and below the level of the sea, they are obliged to drain the land by means of windmills and hundreds of them may be seen pumping up the water so as to relieve the land of the excess moisture. In many parts of the country nearly all the wheat and corn is ground by means of the wind. If it were not for the wind the inhabitants would be put to great inconvenience.

The Spirit of God is thus also a mighty helper to all who will avail themselves of His influences. You are inundated with sin, a flood of iniquity comes in—you can never bale out the torrent. But with the help of God's Spirit it can be done! He will so assist that you shall see the flood gradually descending and your heart once more purified. You need always to ask His help—fresh sin, like falling showers, will be poured into you by every passing day and you will need a continuous power to cast it out—you may have it in God's Spirit! He will, with ceaseless energy, help you to combat sin and make you more than a conqueror!

Or, on the other hand, if you need some power to break up and prepare your spiritual food for you, you will find no better help than what God's Spirit can give. In Eastern countries they grind corn by hand, two sitting at a small stone mill. But it is a poor affair at best—so are our own vain attempts to prepare the bread of Heaven for ourselves. We shall only get a little and that little badly ground. Commentators are good in their way, but give me the teaching of the Holy Spirit. He makes the passage clear and gives me to eat of the finest wheat. How often we have found our utter inability to understand some part of Divine Truth—we asked some of God's people and they helped us a little—but after all, we were not satisfied till we took it to the Throne of heavenly Grace and implored the teachings of the blessed Spirit!

Then how sweetly it was opened to us! We could eat of it spiritually. It was no longer husk and shell, hard to be understood. It was as bread to us and we could eat to the full. Brethren, we must make more use of the wisdom which comes from above, for the Spirit, like the wind, is open to us all to employ for our own personal benefit. I see also here a thought as to the co-operation of man and the Spirit in all Christian work. It has pleased God to make us co-workers with Him–fellow laborers–both in the matter of our own salvation and also in the effort to benefit others. Look for a moment at yon stately boat–she moves not because of her sails but she would not reach the desired haven without them.

It is the wind which propels her forward–but the wind would not act upon her as it does unless she had the rigging all fixed–her masts standing and her sails all bent so as to catch the passing breeze. But now that human seamanship has done its best, see how she flies! She will soon reach her haven with such a favoring gale as that. You have only to stand still and see how the wind bears her on like a thing of life. And so it is with the human heart. When the Spirit comes to the soul that is ready to receive such influences, then He helps you on to Christian Grace and Christian work and makes you bear up through all opposition till you come to the port of peace and can anchor safely there. Without Him we can do nothing–without us He will not work.

We are to preach the Gospel to every creature and while one plants and another waters, God adds the increase. We are to work out our own salvation–He works in us to will and to do of His own good pleasure. We must go up to possess the goodly land with our own spear and sword–but the hornet goes before us to drive out the foe. Jericho shall be captured by a Divine and miraculous interference, but even there rams' horns shall find a work to do and must be employed. The host of Midian shall be slain, but our cry is, "The sword of the Lord and of Gideon." We give God all the glory, nevertheless we use the means.

The water of Jordan must be sought out and used by all who desire a cleansing like Naaman the Syrian. A lump of figs must be used if other Hezekiahs are to be healed–but the Spirit is, after all, the great Cleanser and Healer of His people Israel. The lesson is clear to all–the wind turns mills that men make. It fills sails that human hands have spread. And the Spirit blesses human effort, crowns with success our labors, establishes the work of our hands upon us and teaches all through that, "the hand of the diligent makes rich." And, "if a man will not work, neither shall he eat."

Another thought suggests itself to my mind in connection with the wind and human effort. It is this—How completely dependent men are upon the wind as to what it shall do for them. They are entirely at its mercy as to its time of blowing, its strength and the direction it will take. I have already dwelt upon this thought of the sovereignty of the wind, but it comes up here in a more practical form. The steamer now can steer almost anywhere they please and at all times it will proceed on its voyage.

But the sailing ship must tack according to the wind and when becalmed must wait for the breeze to spring up. The watermill and steam mill can be worked night and day, but the mill that depends upon the wind must abide by the wind's times of blowing and must turn round its sails so as to suit the direction of the current of air. In like manner we are compelled to wait on the pleasure of the Spirit. There is no reservoir of water which we can turn on when we will and work as we please. We would forget God far more than we do now if that were the case. The sailor who is depending on the wind anxiously looks up to the masthead to see how the breeze is shifting and turning round the vane. And he scans the heavens to see what weather he is likely to have.

He would not need to care nearly so much as he does now that he is absolutely dependent on the wind, if he had steam power so as to sail in the very teeth of the storm if he so willed. God, then, keeps us looking up to Heaven by making us to be completely at His mercy as to the times and ways of giving us His helping power. It is a blessed thing to wait on God, watching for His hand and in quiet contentment leaving all to Him. Brethren, let us do our part faithfully, spread every sail, make all as perfect as human skill and wisdom can direct and then in patient continuance in well-doing, wait the Spirit's propitious gales, neither murmuring because He tarries, nor be taken unawares when He comes upon us in His Sovereign pleasure to do that which seems good in His sight.

Now tonight I have only given you some hints on this subject—you can work it out for yourselves. As you hear the wind you may get more sermons out of it than I can give you just now. The thing is perfectly inexhaustible. And I think the business of the minister is not to say all that can be said about the subject.

Somebody remarked concerning a certain minister that he was a most unfair preacher because he always exhausted the subject and left nothing for anybody else to say.

That will never be said of me and I would rather that it should not. A minister should suggest germs of thought, open up new ways and present, if possible, the Truth of God in such a method as to lead men to understand that the half is not told them. And now, my dear Hearer, whether you listen often to my voice or have now stepped in for the first time I would like to ring this in your ear. Do you know the Spirit of God? If you have not the Spirit, you are none of His. "You must be born again." "What, Lord, 'MUST?' Do You not mean 'may?' " No, you must. "Does it not mean, 'You can be?' " No, you must. When a man says, "must," it all depends upon who he is. When God says, "must," there it stands and it cannot be questioned.

There are the flames of Hell—would you escape from them? You must be born again. There are Heaven's glories sparkling in their own light—would you enjoy them? You must be born again! There is the peace and joy of a Believer, would you have it? You must be born again. What, not a crumb from off the table without this? No, not one. Not a drop of water to cool your burning tongues except you are born again. This is the one condition that never changes. God never alters it and never will.

You must, must, MUST. Which shall it be? Shall your will stand, or God's will? O, let God's "must" ride right over you and bow yourselves down and say, "Lord, I must! Then I will! Ah, and it has come to this—I must tonight. Give me Christ, or else I die. I have hold of the knocker of the door of Your mercy and I must, I WILL get that door open. I will never let You go except You bless me! You say, must, Lord, and I say, must, too." "You must, you must be born again." God fulfill the "must" in each of your cases, for Jesus Christ's sake. Amen.

THE SUPERLATIVE EXCELLENCE OF THE HOLY SPIRIT

"Nevertheless I tell you the truth. It is expedient for you that I go away: for if I go not away, the Comforter will not come unto you; but if I depart, I will send Him unto you."
John 16:7

A Sermon Delivered On Sunday Morning: 12 June 1864

THE saints of God may very justly reckon their losses among their greatest gains. The adversities of Believers minister much to their prosperity. Although we know this, through the infirmity of the flesh we tremble at soul-enriching afflictions and dread to see those black ships which bring us such freights of golden treasure. When the Holy Spirit sanctifies the furnace, the flame refines our gold and consumes our dross, yet the dull ore of our nature likes not the glowing coals and had rather lie quiet in the dark mines of earth. As silly children cry because they are called to drink the medicine which will heal their sicknesses, even so do we.

Our gracious Savior, however, loves us too wisely to spare us the trouble because of our childish fears. He foresees the advantage which will spring from our griefs and therefore thrusts us into them out of wisdom and true affection. It was a very great trouble to these first Apostles to lose their Teacher and Friend. Sorrow had filled their hearts at the thought that He should depart, but yet His departure was to give them the greater blessing of the Holy Spirit. And therefore their entreaties and tears cannot avert the dreaded separation. Christ will not gratify their wishes at so vast an expense as the withholding of the Spirit. Mourn as they may under the severe trial, Jesus will not remain with them because His departure is in the highest degree expedient.

Beloved, let us expect to be subject to the same loving discipline. Let us reckon upon losing happy frames and choice enjoyments when Jesus knows that the loss will be better for us than the enjoyment. God has given two great gifts to His people—the first is His Son for us. The second is His Spirit to us. After He had given His Son for us, to become Incarnate, to work righteousness, and to offer an Atonement—after that gift had been fully bestowed there remained no more to be conferred in that respect. "It is finished!" proclaimed the completion of Atonement and His Resurrection showed the perfection of Justification. It was not, therefore, necessary that Christ should remain any longer upon earth since His work below is forever finished.

Now is the season for the second gift, the descent of the Holy Spirit. This could not be bestowed until Christ had ascended, because this choice favor was reserved to grace, with highest honor, the triumphant ascension of the great Redeemer. "When He ascended up on high, He led captivity captive and gave gifts unto men." This was, as Peter tells us, the great promise which Jesus received of His Father. "Therefore being by the right hand of God exalted and having received of the Father the promise of the Holy Spirit, He has shed forth this, which you now see and hear." That His triumphal entrance into Heaven might be stamped with signal Glory, the gifts of the Spirit of God could not be scattered among the sons of men until the Lord had gone up with a shout, even the Lord with the sound of trumpet.

The first gift being completed, it became necessary that He, whose Person and work make up that priceless gift, should withdraw Himself that He might have power to distribute the second benefit by which alone the first gift becomes of any service to us. Christ Crucified is of no practical value to us without the work of the Holy Spirit. And the Atonement which Jesus worked can never save a single soul unless the blessed Spirit of God shall apply it to the heart and conscience. Jesus is never seen until the Holy Spirit opens the eyes–the water from the Well of Life is never received until the Holy Spirit has drawn it from the depths.

As medicine unused for want of the physician's word. As sweets untasted because out of reach. As treasure unvalued because hidden in the earth–such is Jesus the Savior–until the Holy Spirit teaches us to know Him and applies His blood to our souls. It is to the honor of the Holy Spirit that I desire to speak this morning and O, may the same hallowed flame which of old sat upon the Apostles now rest upon the preacher and may the Word come with power to our hearts!

We shall commence our discourse by the remark that THE BODILY PRESENCE OF CHRIST MUST HAVE BEEN EXCEEDINGLY PRECIOUS. How precious those alone can tell who much love Christ. Love always desires to be in the company of the thing beloved and absence causes grief. What is fully meant by the expression, "Sorrow has filled your heart," those only can know who anticipate a like painful bereavement. Jesus had become the Joy of their eyes, the Sun of their days, the Star of their nights—like the spouse, as she came up from the wilderness—they leaned upon their Beloved. They were as little children and now that their Lord and Master was going, they felt they should be left orphans.

Well might they have great sorrow of heart! So much love, so much sorrow, when the object of love is withdrawn. Judge, my Brethren, the joy which the bodily Presence of Christ would give to us this morning, and then you can tell how precious it must be. Have we not, some of us, been looking for years for the personal advent of Christ? We have lifted up our eyes in the morning and we have said, "Perhaps He will come this day." And when the day has closed we have continued our watching in our sleepless hours and renewed our hopes with the rising of the sun. We longingly expect Him according to His promise. And like men who watch for their Lord, we stand with loins girt about waiting for His appearing.

We are looking for and hastening unto the Day of the Lord. This is the bright hope which cheers the Christian, the hope that the Savior shall descend to reign among His people gloriously. Suppose Him to appear suddenly on this platform now—how would you clap your hands! Why, the lame among you would, at the joy of His appearance, leap like a hart and even the dumb might sing for joy! The Presence of the Master! What rapture! Come quickly! Come quickly, Lord Jesus!

It must be, indeed, a precious thing to enjoy the corporeal Presence of Christ. Think of the advantage it would be in the instruction of His people. No mystery need puzzle us if we could refer all to Him. The disputes of the Christian Church would soon be ended for He would tell us what His Word meant beyond dispute. There would be no discouragement to the Church in her work of faith and labor of love, for the Presence of Christ would be the end of all difficulties and insure conquest over all enemies. We should not have to mourn as we now do over our forgetfulness of Jesus, for we should sometimes catch a look at Him. And a sight of Him would give us a store of joy so that like the Prophet of Horeb we could go forty days in the strength of that meat!

It were a delightful thing to know that Christ was somewhere upon earth, for then He would take the personal supervision of His universal Church. He could warn us of apostates. He could reject the hypocrites. He would comfort the feeble-minded and rebuke the erring. How delightful would it be to see Him walking among the golden candlesticks, holding the stars in His right hand! Churches need not, then, be subdivided and rent with evil passions. Christ would create unity. Schism would cease to be and heresy would be rooted out. The Presence of Jesus, whose countenance is as the sun shining in his strength, would ripen all the fruits of our garden, consume all the weeds, and quicken every plant!

The two-edged sword of His mouth would slay His foes and His eyes of fire would kindle the holy passions of His friends. But I shall not enlarge upon that point because it is one in which fancy exercises itself at the expense of judgment. I question whether the pleasure, which the thought of Christ's being here in the flesh has given us just now, may not have had a leaven of carnality in it. I question whether the Church is yet prepared to enjoy the corporeal Presence of her Savior without falling into the error of knowing Him after the flesh. It may be it shall need centuries of education before the Church is fit to see her Savior in the flesh on earth again, because I see in my own self—and I suppose it is so in you—that much of the delight which I expect from the company of Christ is according to the sight of the eyes and the judgment of the mind. And sight is ever the mark and symbol of the flesh.

II. However, leaving that point, we come to the second, which is THAT THE PRESENCE OF THE COMFORTER, AS WE HAVE IT UPON EARTH, IS VERY MUCH BETTER THAN THE BODILY PRESENCE OF CHRIST. We have fancied that the bodily Presence of Christ would make us blessed and confer innumerable benefits. But according to our text the Presence of the Holy Spirit working in the Church is more expedient for the Church. I think this will be clear to you, if you think for a moment, that the bodily Presence of Christ on earth, however good it might be for the Church, would in our present condition involve many inconveniences which are avoided by His Presence through the Holy Spirit.

Christ, being most truly Man, must as to His Manhood inhabit a certain place and in order to get to Christ, it would be necessary for us to travel to His place of residence. Conceive all men compelled to travel from the ends of the earth to visit the Lord Jesus Christ, dwelling upon Mount Zion, or in the city of Jerusalem. What a lengthened voyage would that be for those who live in the far-off ends of the world!

Doubtless they would joyfully undertake it and as pence would be universal and poverty be banished, men might not be restrained from taking such a journey, but might all be able to accomplish it? As they could not all live where they could every morning see Christ, they must be content with every now and then getting a glimpse of Him. But see, my Brethren, the Holy Spirit, the vicar of Christ, dwells everywhere! And if we wish to apply to the Holy Spirit, we have no need to move an inch. In the closet we can find Him, or in the streets we can talk with Him. Jesus Christ could not be present in this congregation after the flesh and yet present in a neighboring Church, much less present in America and in Australia and in Europe and in Africa, at the same time.

But the Holy Spirit is everywhere! And through that Holy Spirit Christ keeps His promise, "Where two or three are met together in My name, there am I in the midst of them." He could not keep that promise according to the flesh—at least we are quite unable to conceive of His so doing. But through the Holy Spirit we sweetly enjoy His Presence and hope to do so to the world's end. Think again—access to Christ—if He were here in His corporeal Personality, would not be very easy to all Believers. There are only twenty-four hours in the day and if our Lord never slept, if, as a Man, He could still live and, like the saints above, rest not day nor night, yet there are only the twenty-four hours. And what were twenty-four hours for the supervision of a Church which we trust will cover the whole earth?

How could a thousand millions of Believers all receive immediate personal comfort either from His lips or the smiles of His face? Even at the present moment there are some millions of true saints upon earth—what could one man do by his personal presence—even though that one man were Incarnate Deity? What could He do in one day for the comfort of all of these? Why, we could not possibly expect each one of us to see Him every day—no, we could scarcely expect to have our turn once in the year!

But, Beloved, we can now see Jesus every hour and every moment of every hour! So often as you bow the knee, His Spirit, who represents Him, can commune with you and bless you. No matter whether it is in the dead of night that your cry goes up, or under the blaze of burning noon—there is the Spirit waiting to be gracious and your sighs and cries climb up to Christ in Heaven and return with answers of peace. These difficulties did not occur to you, perhaps, in your first thoughts. But if you meditate awhile you will see that the

Presence of the Spirit, avoiding that difficulty, makes Christ accessible to every saint at all times. Not to a few choice favorites, but to every believing man and woman the Holy Spirit is accessible and thus the whole body of the faithful can enjoy present and perpetual communion with Christ.

We ought to consider yet once more that Christ's Presence in the flesh upon earth, for any other purpose than that of ending the present dispensation, would involve another difficulty. Of course every Word which Christ had spoken from the time of the Apostles until now would have been Inspired. Being Inspired it would have been a thousand pities that it should fall to the ground. Busy scribes would therefore be always taking down Christ's Words. And, my Brethren, if in the short course of three years our Savior managed to do and to say so much that one of the Evangelists informs us that if all had been written the world itself could not have contained the books which would have been written—I ask you to imagine what a mass of literature the Christian Church would have acquired if she had preserved the Words of Christ throughout these one thousand eight hundred and sixty-four years!

Certainly we should not have had the Word of God in the simple compact form of a pocket Bible—it would have consisted of innumerable volumes of the sayings and deeds of the Lord Jesus Christ! Only the studious, no, not even the studious could have read all the Lord's teachings! And the poor and the illiterate must ever have been at a great disadvantage. But now we have a Book which is finished within a narrow compass with not another line to be added to it. The canon of Revelation is sealed up forever and the poorest man in England, believing in Christ, going with a humble soul to that Book and looking up to Jesus Christ who is present through His Spirit, though not after the flesh, may, in a short time comprehend the Doctrines of Grace and understand with all saints what are the heights and depths and know the love of Christ which passes knowledge.

So then, on the score of inconvenience, precious as the corporeal Presence of Christ might be, it is infinitely better for the Church's good that, until the day of her Millennial Glory, Christ should be present by His Spirit and not in the flesh. Yet more, my Brethren! If Jesus Christ were still present with His Church in the flesh, the life of faith would not have such room for its display as it now has. The more there is visible to the eyes, the less room for faith—the least faith, the most show. The Romish Church, which has little enough of true faith, provides everything to work upon the senses—your nostrils are regaled with incense and your ears are delighted with sweet sounds. The more faith grows, the less it needs outward helps. And when faith shows her true character and is clean divorced from sense and sight, then she wants absolutely nothing to rest upon but the invisible power of God!

She then has learned to hang as the world hangs—upon no seen support! Just as the eternal arch of yon blue sky springs right up without props, so faith rests upon the invisible pillars of God's Truth and faithfulness, needing nothing to shore or buttress her. The Presence of Christ Jesus here in bodily flesh and the knowing of Him according to the flesh, would be the bringing back of the saints to a life of sight and in a measure spoil the simplicity of naked trust. You remember the Apostle Paul says, "We now know no man after the flesh. Yes," says he, "though we have known Christ after the flesh, yet now after the flesh know we Him no more." To the skeptic, who should ask us, "Why do you believe in Christ?" if Jesus had remained upon the earth, we could always give an easy answer—"There He is—there is the Man. Behold Him as He continues still to work miracles."

There would be very little room for faith's holy adherence to the bare Word of God and no opportunity for her to glorify God, trusting where she cannot trace. But now, Beloved, the fact that we have nothing visible to point to which carnal minds can understand—this very fact makes the path of faith more truly congenial with its noble character—

"Faith, mighty faith, the promise sees,
And looks to that alone,"

which she could hardly do, if she could look upon the visible Person of a present Savior. Happy day will it be for us when faith enjoys the full fruition of her hopes in the triumphant advent of her Lord! But His absence, alone, can train and educate her to the needed point of spiritual refinement.

Furthermore, the Presence of Jesus Christ on earth would materially affect the character of God's great battle against error and sin. Suppose that Christ were to destroy the preachers of error by miracle. Suppose that persecuting monarchs had their arms dried up, or that all men who would oppose Christ were suddenly devoured by fire. Why then it would be more a battle between physical greatness and moral evil, than a warfare in which only spiritual force is employed on the side of right. But now that Christ has gone, the fight is all between Spirit and spirit–between God the Holy Spirit and Satan–between Truth and error. It is between the earnestness of believing men and the infatuation of unbelieving men. Now the fight is fair.

We have no miracles on our side–we do not want them–the Holy Spirit is enough! We call no fire from Heaven–no earthquake shakes the ground beneath our foemen's feet. Korah is not swallowed up. Dathan does not go down alive into the pit. Physical force is left to our enemies–we do not ask for it. Why? Because by the Divine working we can vanquish error without it. In the name of the Holy One of Israel, in whose cause we have been enlisted–by His might we are enough–no need for miracles and signs and wonders. If Christ were here still working miracles, the battle were not so spiritual as it now is. But the absence of the corporeal Savior makes it a spiritual conflict of Spirit of the noblest and most sublime order.

Again, dear Friends, the Holy Spirit is more valuable to the Church in her present militant state than the Presence of Christ could be conceived to be, because Christ must be here in one of two ways–either He must be here suffering, or not suffering. If Christ were here suffering, then how could we conclude that His Atonement was finished? Is it not much better for our faith that our blessed Lord, having once and for all made expiation for sin, should sit at the right hand of the Father? Is it not much better, I ask, than to see Him still struggling and suffering here below? "Oh, but," you say, "perhaps He would not suffer!" Then I pray you, do not wish to have Him here till our warfare is accomplished, for to see an unsuffering Christ in the midst of His suffering people–to see His face calm and clear when yours and mine are wrinkled with grief–to see Him smiling when we are weeping, this were intolerable! No, it could not be! Brethren, if He is a suffering Christ in our sight, then we should suspect that He had not finished His work.

And, on the other hand, if He is an unsuffering Christ, then it would look as if He were not a faithful High Priest made like unto His Brethren. These two difficulties throw us back into a state of thankfulness to God that we have not the dilemma to answer, but that the Spirit of God, who is Christ present on earth, relieves us from these difficulties and gives us all the advantage we could expect from Christ's Presence in a tenfold degree. Only this one further remark, that the personal Presence of Christ, much as we think of it, did not produce very great results in His disciples until the Spirit was poured forth from on high.

Christ was their Teacher—how much did they learn? Why, there is Philip—Christ has to say to him, "Have I been so long time with you and yet have you not known Me, Philip?" They were puzzled by questions which little children can now answer! You can see that at the end of their three years course of training with Christ, they had made but slender progress. Christ is not only their Teacher, but their Comforter—yet how frequently Christ failed to console them because of their unbelief. After He had uttered that delightful discourse which we have been reading, He found them sleeping for sorrow. In this very chapter, when He is trying to comfort them, He adds, "But because I have said these things unto you, sorrow has filled your heart."

Christ's object was to foster the Graces of His disciples—but where were their Graces? Here is Peter—he has not even the Grace of courage and consistency, but denies his Master while the rest of them forsake Him and flee. There was not even the Spirit of Christ infused into them! Their zeal was not tempered with love, for they wanted fire from Heaven to consume His adversaries and Peter drew a sword to cut off the High Priest's servant's ear. They scarcely knew the Truths which their Master taught and they were far enough from imbibing His heavenly Spirit. Even their endowments were slender. It is true they once worked miracles and preached, but with what success?

Do you ever hear of Peter winning three thousand sinners under a sermon till the Holy Spirit came? Do you find any of them able to edify others and build up the Church of Christ? No, the ministry of our Lord Jesus Christ, considered only as to its immediate fruits, was not to be compared with ministries after the descent of the Spirit. "He came unto His own and His own received Him not." His great work as a Redeemer was a complete triumph from beginning to end. But as a Teacher, since the Spirit of God was only upon Him and not upon the people, His words were rejected, His entreaties were despised and His warnings unheeded by the great multitude of the people.

The mighty blessing came when the words of Joel were fulfilled, "And it shall come to pass afterward, that I will pour out My Spirit upon all flesh. And your sons and your daughters shall prophesy, your old men shall dream dreams, your young men shall see visions: and also upon the servants and upon the handmaids in those days will I pour out My Spirit." That was the blessing and a blessing which, we venture to say again, was so rich and so rare that it was, indeed, expedient that Jesus Christ should go, that the Holy Spirit might descend.

III. I now pass on to the third point of the subject with brevity. We have come thus far–the Presence of Christ admitted to be precious, but the Presence of the Holy Spirit most clearly shown to be of more practical value to the Church of God than the corporeal Presence of the Lord Jesus Christ. Advance, then, to the third point, THE PRESENCE OF THE COMFORTER IS SUPERLATIVELY VALUABLE. We may gather this, first, from the effects which were seen upon the day of Pentecost. On the day of Pentecost the heavenly Wind sounded the alarm of war. The soldiers were ill prepared for it. They were a slender band, having only this virtue–they were content to wait until power was given to them.

They sat still in the upper room. That mighty sound was heard across Jerusalem. The forceful Whirlwind travels on until it reaches the chosen spot. It fills the place where they are sitting. Here was an omen of what the Spirit of God is to be to the Church! It is to come mysteriously upon the Church according to the Sovereign will of God. But when He comes like the Wind, it is to purge the moral atmosphere and to quicken the pulse of all who spiritually breathe. This is a blessing, indeed! A gift which the Church greatly wants–I would that this rushing mighty Wind would come upon this Church with an irresistible force which should carry everything before it–the force of Truth, but of more than Truth–the force of God driving His Truth home upon the heart and conscience of men!

I would that you and I could breathe this Wind and receive its invigorating influence that we might be made champions of God and of His Truth. O that it would drive away our mists of doubt and clouds of error! Come, Sacred Wind, England needs You–the whole earth requires You! The foul gases which brood in this deadly calm would fly if Your Divine lightning enlightened the world and set the moral atmosphere in commotion. Come, Holy Spirit, come. We can do nothing without You! If we have Your Wind, we spread our sails and speed onward towards Glory!

Then the Spirit came as fire. A fire-shower accompanied the rushing mighty Wind. What a blessing is this to the Church! The Church wants fire to quicken her ministers, to give zeal and energy to all her members. Having this fire, she burns her way to success! The world meets her with the fire of firewood, but she confronts the world with the fire of kindling spirits and of souls aglow with the love of Jesus Christ. She trusts not to the wit and eloquence and wisdom of her preachers, but to the Divine Fire which clothes them with energy. She knows that men are irresistible when they are filled with hallowed enthusiasm sent from God. She trusts, therefore, in this and her cry is, "Come, Holy Fire, abide upon our pastors and teachers! Rest upon every one of us!" This Fire is a blessing Christ did not bring us in Person, but which He now gives through His Spirit to the Church.

Then there came from the fire-shower a descent of tongues. This, too, is the privilege of the Church. When the Lord gave the Apostles different tongues, He did, as it were, give them the keys of the various kingdoms. "Go," says He, "Judea is not My only dominion. Go and unlock the gates of every empire. Here are the keys, you can speak every language." Dear Friends, though we can no longer speak with every man in his own tongue, yet we have the keys of the whole world swinging at our girdle if we have the Spirit of God with us. You have the keys of human hearts if the Spirit of God speaks through you. I have this day the keys of the hearts of the multitudes here if the Holy Spirit wills to use them!

There is an efficacy about the Gospel, when the Spirit is with us, little dreamed of by those who call it the foolishness of men. I am persuaded that the results which have followed ministry in our lifetime are trivial and insignificant compared with what they would be if the Spirit of God were more mightily at work in our midst. There is no reason in the nature of the Gospel or the power of the Spirit why a whole congregation should not be converted under one sermon! There is no reason in God's Nature why a nation should not be born in a day and why, within a single twelve months, a dozen ministers preaching throughout the world might not be the means of converting every elect son and daughter of Adam to a knowledge of the Truth of God. The Spirit of God is perfectly Irresistible when He puts forth His full power!

His power is so Divinely Omnipotent that the moment He goes forth the work is achieved, The great prophetic event, we see, occurred on the day of Pentecost. The success given was only the first fruits—Pentecost is not the harvest. We have been accustomed to look on Pentecost as a great and wonderful display of Divine power not at all to be equaled in modern times. Brethren, it is to be exceeded! I stand not upon Pentecost as upon a towering mountain, wondering at my height, but I look at Pentecost as a little rising knoll from which I am to look up to mountains far loftier! I look not to Pentecost as the shouting of our harvest home and the bringing in of the sheaves into the garner. No! But as an offering of the first wave sheaf before the altar of God!

You must expect greater things, pray for greater things, long for greater things! Here is this England of ours, sunk in stolid ignorance of the Gospel. Weighing like a nightmare upon her bosom we have baptismal regeneration supported by a horde of priests who either believe that dogma, or hold their benefices by subscribing to a lie. How is this incubus to be shaken off from the living bosom of England? "Not by might, nor by power, but by My Spirit, says the Lord." There is France cursed with infidelity, fickle, gay, given up to pleasure—how is she to be made sober and sanctified unto God? "Not by might, but by My Spirit, says the Lord." Yonder is Germany, with her metaphysical skepticism, her half Romanism, that is to say, Lutheranism—and her abounding Popery! How is she to arise? "Not by might, nor by power, but by My Spirit, says the Lord." Away there in Italy sits old Rome, the harlot of the seven hills, still reigning queen triumphant over the great part of the earth! How is she to die? Where is the sword which shall find out her heart? "Not by might, nor by power, but by My Spirit, says the Lord."

The one thing, then, which we need, is the Spirit of God! Do not say that we need money—we shall have it soon enough when the Spirit touches men's hearts. Do not say that we need buildings, Churches, edifices—all these may be very well in subservience—but the main need of the Church is the Spirit and men into whom the Spirit may be poured! If there were only one prayer which I might pray before I died, it should be this: "Lord, send to Your Church men filled with the Holy Spirit and with fire." Give to any denomination such men and its progress must be mighty—keep back such men, send them college gentlemen of great refinement and profound learning, but of little fire and Grace—dumb dogs which cannot bark—and straightway that denomination must decline. Let the Spirit come and the preacher may be rustic, simple, rough, unmannered—but the Holy Spirit being upon him—none of his adversaries shall stand against him! His word shall be with power to the shaking of the gates of Hell!

Beloved, did I not say well when I said that the Spirit of God is of superlative importance to the Church and that the day of Pentecost seems to tell us this? Remember, Brethren, and here is another thought which should make the

Spirit very dear to you—without the Holy Spirit no good thing ever did or ever can come into any of your hearts—no sigh of penitence! No cry of faith! No glance of love! No tear of hallowed sorrow! Your heart can never palpitate with Divine life except through the Spirit! You are not capable of the smallest degree of spiritual emotion, much less spiritual action, apart from the Holy Spirit! Dead you lie, living only for evil, and absolutely dead for God until the Holy Spirit comes and raises you from the grave!

There is nothing good in you today, my Brothers and Sisters, which was not put there. The flowers of Christ are all exotics—"In me, that is, in my flesh, dwells no good thing." Who can bring a clean thing out of an unclean? No one! Everything must come from Christ and Christ gives nothing to men except through the Spirit of all Grace. Prize, then, the Spirit as the channel of all good which comes into you. And further, no good thing can come out of you apart from the Spirit. Let it be in you, yet it lies dormant except God works in you to will and to do of His own good pleasure. Do you desire to preach? How can you unless the Holy Spirit touches your tongue? Do you desire to pray? Alas, what dull work it is unless the Spirit makes intercession for you! Do you desire to subdue sin? Would you be holy? Would you imitate your Master? Do you desire to rise to superlative heights of spirituality? Are you wanting to be made like the angels of God, full of zeal and ardor for the Master's cause? You cannot without the Spirit—"Without Me you can do nothing."

O branch of the vine, you can have no fruit without the sap! O child of God, you have no life within you apart from the life which God gives you through His Spirit! Said I not well, then, that the Holy Spirit is superlatively precious, so that even the Presence of Christ after the flesh is not to be compared to His Presence for glory and for power?

IV. This brings us to the conclusion, which is a practical point. Brethren, if these things are so, let us, who are believers in Christ, view the mysterious Spirit with deep awe and reverence. Let us so reverence Him as not to grieve Him or provoke Him to anger by our sins. Let us not quench Him in one of His faintest motions in our soul. Let us foster every suggestion and be ready to obey every prompting. If the Holy Spirit is, indeed, so mighty, let us do nothing without Him. Let us begin no project and carry on no enterprise and conclude no transaction without imploring His blessing. Let us pay Him the due homage of feeling our entire weakness apart from Him, and then depending alone upon Him, having this for our prayer, "Open my heart and my whole being to

Your incoming and uphold me with Your free Spirit when I shall have received that Spirit in my inward parts."

You who are unconverted, let me beseech you, whatever you do, never despise the Spirit of God. Remember, there is a special honor put upon Him in Scripture–"All manner of sin and of blasphemy shall be forgiven unto men, but the sin against the Holy Spirit shall never be forgiven, neither in this world nor in that which is to come." Remember, "If a man speaks a word against the Son of Man, it shall be forgiven him. But if he speaks a word against the Holy Spirit, it shall never be forgiven him." This is the sin which is unto death, of which even the loving John says–"I do not say that you shall pray for it." Tremble, therefore, in His Presence! Take your shoes off, for when His name is mentioned, the place where you stand is holy ground. Let the Spirit be treated with reverence.

In the next place, as a practical remark, let us, viewing the might of the Spirit, take courage today. We know, Brethren, that we, as a body of people seeking to adhere closely to Scripture and to practice the ordinances and hold the doctrines as we have received them from the Lord Himself, are but poor and despised. And when we look at the great ones of the earth, we see them on the side of the false and not of the true. Where are the kings and the nobles? Where are the princes, and where are the mighty men?

Are they not against the Lord of Hosts. Where is the gold? Where is the silver? Where is the architecture? Where is the wisdom? Where is the eloquence? Is it not banded against the Lord of Hosts? What? Shall we, then, be discouraged? Our fathers were not! They bore their testimony in the stocks and in the prison, but they feared not for the good old cause! As John Bunyan, they learned to rot in dungeons, but they learned not to play the coward. They suffered and they testified that they were not discouraged. Why? Because they knew (not that Truth is mighty and will prevail, for Truth is not mighty and will not prevail in this world until men are different from what they are), but they knew that the Spirit of God is mighty and will prevail!

Better to have a small Church of poor men and the Spirit of God with them, than to have a hierarchy of nobles, to have an army of titled princes and prelates without the Holy Spirit! For this is not merely the sinew of strength, but it is strength itself! Where the Spirit of God is–there is liberty and power! Courage then, Brethren! We have only to seek for that which God has promised to give and we can do wonders. He will give the Holy Spirit to them that ask Him. Wake up, members of this Church, to earnest prayer. And all Believers throughout the world, cry aloud unto God to let His bare arm be seen. Wake, children of God, for you know the power of prayer!

Give the Covenant angel no rest till he speaks the word and the Spirit works mightily among the sons of men. Prayer is work adapted to each of you who are in Christ. You cannot preach, you cannot teach, but you can pray! And your private prayer, unknown by men, shall be registered in Heaven, Those silent but earnest cries of yours shall bring down a blessing. The other morning, when we were holding special prayer, there were some Brethren present who kept saying during the prayer to themselves, scarcely loud enough to be heard, "Do Lord! Do! Grant it! Hear it!" That is a kind of praying which I love in Prayer Meetings!

I would not care for the loud shouts of some of our Methodist Brethren, though if they like they are welcome to it. But I do like to hear friends praying with the groaning which cannot be uttered, "Lord, send the Spirit! Send the Spirit, Lord! Work! Work! Work!" During sermon time it is what numbers of Churches should be doing, crying out to God in their hearts. As you walk the streets when you see sin you should pray, "Lord, put it down by Your Spirit!" And when you mark a struggling Brother striving to do good, you should cry, "Lord, help him! Help him by Your Spirit." I am persuaded we only need more prayer and there is no limit to the blessing! You may evangelize England, you may evangelize Europe, you may Christianize the world–if you do but know how to pray.

Prayer can get anything of God, prayer can get everything–God denies nothing to the man who knows how to ask. The Lord never shuts His storehouse till you shut your mouth! God will never stop His arm till you stop your tongue. Cry aloud and spare not! Give Him no rest till He sends forth His Spirit once again to stir the waters and to brood over this dark world till light and life shall come! Cry day and night, O you elect of God, for He will avenge you speedily. The time of battle draws near! Rome sharpens her sword for the fight! The men of error gnash their teeth in rage! Now for the sword of the Lord and of Gideon! Now for the old might and majesty of the ancient days! Now for the shaking of the walls of Jericho, even though we have no better weapons than rams' horns! Now for the driving out of the heathen, and for the establishment of God's Israel in the land! Now for the coming of the Holy Spirit with such might and power that as Noah's flood covered the mountaintops, Jehovah's flood of Glory shall cover the highest summits of sin and iniquity and the whole world over, the Lord God Omnipotent shall reign!

You who have not the Spirit pray for it. May He prompt you to pray this morning! Unconverted Sinners, may the Spirit give you faith! Remember that the Holy Spirit tells you to trust Christ. If you honor the Holy Spirit, trust Christ. I know you must be regenerate, for the man who trusts Christ is regenerate. You must repent, you must be holy, but the man who trusts Christ shall repent and shall be made holy. The germs of repentance and holiness are in him already. Trust Christ, Sinner! It is the Holy Spirit's mandate to you this morning. May He constrain you to trust Him and He shall have the Glory, world without end. Amen.

THE OUTPOURING OF THE HOLY SPIRIT

"While Peter yet spoke these words, the Holy Spirit fell on all them which heard the Word."
Acts 10:44

A Sermon Delivered On Sunday Morning: 20 June 1858

The Bible is a book of the Revelation of God. The God after whom the heathen blindly searched and for whom reason gropes in darkness is here plainly revealed to us in the pages of Divine authorship. He who is willing to understand as much of Godhead as man can know, may here learn it if he is not willingly ignorant and willfully obstinate. The doctrine of the Trinity is specially taught in Holy Scripture. The word certainly does not occur, but the three Divine Persons of the One God are frequently and constantly mentioned. Holy Scripture is exceedingly careful that we should all receive and believe that great truth of the Christian religion–that the Father is God, that the Son is God, that the Spirit is God–and yet there are not three Gods but one God. Though They are each of them very God of very God, yet three in One and One in three is the Jehovah whom we worship.

You will notice in the works of Creation how carefully the Scriptures assure us that all the three Divine Persons took their share. "In the beginning Jehovah created the heavens and the earth." And in another place we are told that God said, "Let Us make man"–not one Person, but all three taking counsel with each other with regard to the making of mankind. We know that the Father has laid the foundations and fixed those solid beams of light on which the blue arches of the sky are sustained. But we know with equal certainty that Jesus Christ, the eternal Logos, was with the Father in the beginning and "without Him was not anything made that was made."

Moreover we have equal certainty that the Holy Spirit had a hand in Creation, for we are told that "the earth was without form and void and darkness was upon the face of the earth. And the Spirit of the Lord moved upon the face of the waters." And brooding with His dove-like wings, He brought out of the egg of chaos this mighty thing, the fair round world. We have the like proof of the three Persons in the Godhead in the matter of Salvation. We have abundant proof that God the Father chose His people from before the foundations of the world. That He did invent the plan of salvation and has always given His free, willing and joyous consent to the salvation of His people.

With regard to the share that the Son had in salvation, that is apparent enough to all. For us men and for our salvation He came down from Heaven. He was incarnate in a mortal body. He was crucified, dead and buried. He descended into Hades. The third day He rose again from the dead. He ascended into Heaven. He sits at the right hand of God, where also He makes intercession for us. As to the Holy Spirit, we have equally sure proof that the Spirit of God works in conversion. For everywhere we are said to be begotten of the Holy Spirit. Continually it is declared that unless a man be born again from above, he cannot see the kingdom of God.

All the virtues and the graces of Christianity are described as being the fruits of the Spirit, because the Holy Spirit does from first to last work in us and carry out that which Jesus Christ has beforehand worked for us in His great redemption, which also God the Father has designed for us in His great predestinating scheme of salvation.

Now, it is to the work of the Holy Spirit that I shall this morning specially direct your attention. And I may as well mention the reason why I do so. It is this. We have received continually fresh confirmations of the good news from a far country which has already made glad the hearts of many of God's people. In the United States of America there is certainly a great awakening. No sane man living there could think of denying it. There may be something of spurious excitement mixed up with it, but that good—lasting good has been accomplished—no rational man can deny.

Two hundred and fifty thousand persons—that is a quarter of a million—profess to have been regenerated since December last—have made a profession of their faith—and have united themselves with different sections of God's Church. The work still progresses, if anything, at a more rapid rate than before and that which makes me believe the work to be genuine is just this—that the enemies of Christ's holy Gospel are exceedingly wroth at it. When the devil roars at anything, you may rest assured there is some good in it. The devil is not like some dogs we know of. He never barks unless there is something to bark at. When Satan howls we may rest assured he is afraid his kingdom is in danger.

Now this great work in America has been manifestly caused by the outpouring of the Spirit, for no one minister has been a leader in it. All the ministers of the Gospel have co-operated in it, but none of them have stood in the van. God himself has been the leader of His own hosts. It began with a desire for prayer. God's people began to pray. The Prayer Meetings were better attended than before. It was then proposed to hold meetings at times that had never been set apart for prayer—these also were well attended. And now, in the city of Philadelphia, at the hour of noon every day in the week, three thousand persons can always be seen assembled together for prayer in one place.

Men of business, in the midst of their toil and labor, find an opportunity of running in there and offering a word of prayer and then return to their occupations. And so, throughout all the States, Prayer Meetings, larger or smaller in number, have been convened. And there has been real prayer. Sinners beyond all count, have risen up in the Prayer Meeting and have requested the people of God to pray for them—thus making public to the world that they had a desire after Christ. They have been prayed for and the Church has seen that God verily does hear and answer prayer.

I find that the Unitarian ministers for a little while took no notice of it. Theodore Parker snarls and raves tremendously at it, but he is evidently in a maze. He does not understand the mystery and acts with regard to it as swine are said to do with pearls. While the Church was found asleep and doing very little, the Socinian could afford to stand in his pulpit and sneer at anything like evangelical religion. But now that there has been an awakening, he looks like a man that has just awakened out of sleep. He sees something. He does not know what it is. The power of religion is just that which will always puzzle the Unitarian, for he knows but little about that.

At the form of religion he is not much amazed, for he can to an extent endorse that himself. But the supernaturalism of the Gospel—the mystery—the miracle—the power—the demonstration of the Spirit that comes with the preaching is what such men cannot comprehend. They gaze and wonder and then become filled with wrath—but still they have to confess there is something there they cannot understand, a mental phenomenon that is far beyond their philosophy—a thing which they cannot reach by all their science nor understand by all their reason.

Now, if we have the like effect produced in this land, the one thing we must seek is the outpouring of the Holy Spirit. I thought, perhaps, this morning in preaching upon the work of the Holy Spirit, that text might be fulfilled–"Him that honors Me I will honor." My sincere desire is to honor the Holy Spirit this morning and if He will be pleased to honor His Church in return, unto Him shall be the glory forever.

"While Peter yet spoke these words, the Holy Spirit fell on all them which heard the word." In the first place, I shall endeavor to describe the method of the Spirit's operation. Secondly, the absolute necessity of the Holy Spirit's influence if we would see men converted. In the third place I shall suggest the ways and means by which under Divine grace we may obtain a like falling down of the Spirit upon our Churches.

In the first place, then, I will endeavor to explain THE METHOD OF THE HOLY SPIRIT'S OPERATIONS. But let me guard myself against being misunderstood. We can explain what the Spirit does but how He does it–no man must pretend to know. The work of the Holy Spirit is the peculiar mystery of the Christian religion. Almost any other thing is plain, but this must remain an inscrutable secret into which it were wrong for us to attempt to pry. Who knows where the winds are begotten? Who knows, therefore, how the Spirit works, for He is like the wind. "The wind blows where it likes and you hear the sound thereof but cannot tell from where it comes and where it goes. So is everyone that is born of the Spirit."
In Holy Scripture certain great secrets of nature are mentioned as being parallel with the secret working of the Spirit. The procreation of children is instanced as a parallel wonder, for we know not the mystery thereof. How much less, therefore, shall we expect to know that more secret and hidden mystery of the new birth and new creation of man in Christ Jesus. But let no man be staggered at this, for they are mysteries in nature–the wisest man will tell you there are depths in nature into which he cannot dive and heights into which he cannot soar.

He who pretends to have unraveled the knot of creation has made a mistake. He may have cut the knot by his rough ignorance and by his foolish conjectures–but the knot itself must remain beyond the power of man's unraveling, until God Himself shall explain the secret. There are marvelous things, that, as yet, men have sought to know in vain. They may, perhaps, discover many of them–but how the Spirit works–no man can know.

But now I wish to explain what the Holy Spirit does, although we cannot tell how He does it. I take it that the Holy Spirit's work in conversion is two-fold. First it is an awakening of the powers that man already has. Secondly, it is an implantation of powers which he never had at all.

In the great work of the new birth, the Holy Spirit first of all awakens the mental powers. The Holy Spirit never gives any man new mental powers. Take for instance reason—the Holy Spirit does not give men reason—for they have reason prior to their conversion. What the Holy Spirit does is to teach our reason, right reason—to set our reason in the right track, so that we can use it for the high purpose of discerning between good and evil—between the precious and vile.

The Holy Spirit does not give man a will—for man has a will before. But He makes the will that was in bondage to Satan free to the service of God. The Holy Spirit gives no man the power to think, or the organ of belief—for man has power to believe or think as far as the mental act is concerned. But He gives that belief which is already there a tendency to believe the right thing. He gives to the power of thought the propensity to think in the right way so that instead of thinking irregularly, we begin to think as God would have us think and our mind desires to walk in the steps of God's revealed Truth.

There may be here, this morning, a man of enlarged understanding in things political—but his understanding is darkened with regard to spiritual things. He sees no beauty in the Person of Christ—he sees nothing desirable in the way of holiness. He chooses the evil and forsakes the good. Now the Holy Spirit will not give him a new understanding, but He will cleanse his old understanding so that it will discern between things that differ and shall discover that it is but a poor thing to enjoy "the pleasures of sin for a season," and let go an "eternal weight of glory."

There shall be a man here, too, who is desperately set against religion and wills not to come to God. And do what we will, we are not able to persuade him to change his mind and turn to God. The Holy Spirit will not make a new will in that man, but He will turn his old will. Instead of willing to do evil He will make him will to do right—He will make him will to be saved by Christ—He will make him "willing in the day of His power." Remember, there is no power in man so fallen but that the Holy Spirit can raise it up. However debased a man may be, in one instant, by the miraculous power of the Spirit, all his faculties may be cleansed and purged. Ill-judging reason may be made to judge rightly. Stout, obstinate wills may be made to run willingly in the ways of God's Commandments. Evil and depraved affections may in an instant be turned to Christ. And old desires that are tainted with vice may be replaced by heavenly aspirations.

The work of the Spirit on the mind is the remodeling of it. The new forming of it. He does not bring new material to the mind—it is in another part of the man that He puts up a new structure—but He puts the mind that had fallen out of order into its proper shape. He builds up pillars that had fallen down and erects the palaces that had crumbled to the earth. This is the first work of the Holy Spirit upon the mind of man.

Besides this, the Holy Spirit gives to men powers which they never had before. According to Scripture, I believe man is constituted in a three-fold manner. He has a body—by the Holy Spirit that body is made the temple of the Lord. He has a mind—by the Holy Spirit that mind is made like an altar in the temple. But man by nature is nothing higher than that. He is mere body and soul. When the Spirit comes, he breathes into him a third higher principle which we call the spirit. The Apostle describes man as man, "body, soul and spirit." Now if you search all the mental writers through, you will find they all declare there are only two parts—body and mind. And they are quite right, for they deal with unregenerate man. But in regenerate man there is a third principle as much superior to mere mind as mind is superior to dead animal matter—that third principle is that with which a man prays. It is that with which he lovingly believes—or rather it is that which compels the mind to perform their acts. It is that which, operating upon the mind, makes the same use of the mind as the mind does of the body.

When, after desiring to walk I make my legs move, it is my mind that compels them. And so my spirit, when I desire to pray, compels my mind to think the thought of prayer and compels my soul also. As the body without the soul is dead, so the soul without the spirit is dead and one work of the Holy Spirit is to quicken the dead soul by breathing into it the firing spirit. As it is written, "The first man, Adam, was made a living soul, but the second Adam was made a quickening Spirit"—and, "as we have borne the image of the earthy, so must we bear the image of the heavenly." That is, we must have in us, if we would be converted, the quickening spirit, which is put into us by God the Holy Spirit.

I say again, the spirit has powers which the mind never has. It has the power of communion with Christ—which to a degree is a mental act—but it can no more be performed by man without the spirit, than the act of walking could be performed by man, if he were destitute of a mind to suggest the idea of walking. The spirit suggests the thoughts of communion which the mind obeys and carries out. No, there are times, I think, when the spirit leaves the mind altogether, times when we forget everything of earth and one almost ceases to think, to reason, to judge, to weigh, or to will. Our souls are like the chariots of Amminadab, drawn swiftly onwards without any powers of volition. We lean upon the breast of Jesus—and in rhapsody Divine and in ecstasy celestial—we enjoy the fruits of the land of the blessed and pluck the clusters of Eschol before entering into the land of promise.

I think I have clearly put these two points before you. The work of the Spirit consists, first, in awakening powers already possessed by man—but which were asleep and out of order. And in the next place in putting into man powers which he had not before. And to make this simple to the humblest mind, let me suppose man to be something like a machine—all the wheels are out of order, the cogs do not strike upon each other, the wheels do not turn regularly, the rods will not act, the order is gone.

Now the first work of the Holy Spirit is to put these wheels in the right place, to fit the wheels upon the axles, to put the right axle to the right wheel, then to put wheel to wheel, so that they may act upon each other. But that is not all His work. The next thing is to put fire and steam so that these things shall go to work. He does not put fresh wheels—He puts old wheels into order—and then He puts the motive power which is to move the whole. First He puts our mental powers into their proper order and condition. Then He puts a living quickening spirit, so that all these shall move according to the holy will and Law of God.

But, mark you, this is not all the Holy Spirit does. For if He were to do this and then leave us, none of us would get to Heaven. If any of you should be so near to Heaven that you could hear the angels singing over the walls—if you could almost see within the pearly gates—still, if the Holy Spirit did not help you the last step you would never enter there. All the work is through His Divine operation. Hence it is the Holy Spirit who keeps the wheels in motion and who takes away that defilement which, naturally engendered by our original sin, falls upon the machine and puts it out of order. He takes this away and keeps the machine constantly going without injury, until at last He removes man from the place of defilement to the land of the blessed–a perfect creature–as perfect as he was when he came from the mold of his Maker.

And I must say, before I leave this point, that all the former part of what I have mentioned is done instantaneously. When a man is converted to God, it is done in a moment. Regeneration is an instantaneous work. Conversion to God, the fruit of regeneration, occupies all our life, but regeneration itself is effected in an instant. A man hates God. The Holy Spirit makes him love God. A man is opposed to Christ, he hates His Gospel, does not understand it and will not receive it. The Holy Spirit comes, puts light into his darkened understanding, takes the chain from his bandaged will, gives liberty to his conscience, gives life to his dead soul, so that the voice of conscience is heard–and the man becomes a new creature in Christ Jesus. And all this is done, mark you, by the instantaneous supernatural influence of God the Holy Spirit working as He wills among the sons of men.

II. Having thus dwelt upon the method of the Holy Spirit's work, I shall now turn to the second point, THE ABSOLUTE NECESSITY OF THE SPIRIT'S WORK IN ORDER TO CONVERSION. In our text we are told that, "while Peter spoke these words, the Holy Spirit fell on all them which heard the word." Beloved, the Holy Spirit fell on Peter first, or else it would not have fallen on his hearers. There is a necessity that the preacher himself, if we are to have souls saved, should be under the influence of the Spirit.

I have constantly made it my prayer that I might be guided by the Spirit even in the smallest and least important parts of the service. For you cannot tell but that the salvation of a soul may depend upon the reading of a hymn, or upon the selection of a chapter. Two persons have joined our Church and made a profession of being converted simply through my reading a hymn–"Jesus, lover of my soul."

They did not remember anything else in the hymn, but those words made such a deep impression upon their mind that they could not help repeating them for days afterwards. And then the thought arose, "Do I love Jesus?" Then they considered what strange ingratitude it was that He should be the lover of their souls and yet they should not love Him.

Now I believe the Holy Spirit led me to read that hymn. And many persons have been converted by some striking saying of the preacher. But why was it the preacher uttered that saying? Simply because he was led thereunto by the Holy Spirit. Rest assured, Beloved, that when any part of the sermon is blessed to your heart, the minister said it because he was ordered to say it by his Master. I might preach today a sermon which I preached on Friday and which was useful then—but there might be no good whatever come from it now—because it might not be the sermon which the Holy Spirit would have delivered today.

But if with sincerity of heart I have sought God's guidance in selecting the topic and He rests upon me in the preaching of the Word, there is no fear but that it shall be found adapted to your immediate wants. The Holy Spirit must rest upon your preachers. Let them have all the learning of the wisest men and all the eloquence of such men as Demosthenes and Cicero—still the Word cannot be blessed to you, unless first of all the Spirit of God has guided the minister's mind in the selection of his subject and in the discussion of it.

But if Peter himself were under the hand of the Spirit, that would fail unless the Spirit of God, then, did fall upon his hearers. And I shall endeavor now to show the absolute necessity of the Spirit's work in the conversion of men.

Let us remember what kind of thing the work is and we shall see that other means are altogether out of the question. It is quite certain that men cannot be converted by physical means. The Church of Rome thought that she could convert men by means of armies. So she invaded countries and threatened them with war and bloodshed unless they would repent and embrace her religion. However, it availed but little and men were prepared to die rather than leave their faith. She therefore tried those beautiful things—stakes, racks, dungeons, axes, swords, fire—by these things she hoped to convert men.

You have heard of the man who tried to wind up his watch with a pickax. That man was extremely wise compared with the man who thought to touch mind through matter. All the machines you like to invent cannot touch mind. Talk about tying angel's wings with green withes, or manacling the cherubim with iron chains—and then talk about meddling with the minds of men through physical means. Why, the things don't set. They cannot act. All the king's armies that ever were and all the warriors clothed with mail, with all their ammunition, could never touch the mind of man. That is an impregnable castle which is not to be reached by physical agency.

Nor, again, can man be converted by moral argument. "Well," says one, "I think he may. Let a minister preach earnestly and he may persuade men to be converted." Ah, Beloved, it is for want of knowing better that you say so. Melancthon thought so, but you know what he said after he tried it–"Old Adam is too strong for young Melancthon." So will every preacher find it, if he thinks his arguments can ever convert man. Let me give you a parallel case. Where is the logic that can persuade an Ethiopian to change his skin? By what argument can you induce a leopard to renounce his spots? Even so may he that is accustomed to do evil learn to do well.

But if the Ethiopian's skin is changed it must be by a supernatural process. And if the leopard's spots be removed, He that made the leopard must do it. Even so is it with the heart of man. If sin were a thing ab extra and external, we could induce man to change it. For instance, you may induce a man to leave off drunkenness or swearing, because those things are not a part of his nature–he has added that vice to his original depravity. But the hidden evil in the heart is beyond all moral persuasion. I dare say a man might have enough argument to induce him to hang himself, but I am certain no argument will ever induce him to hang his sins–to hang his self-righteousness–and to come and humble himself at the foot of the Cross.

For the religion of Christ is so contrary to all the propensities of man that it is like swimming against the stream to approach it. The stream of man's will and man's desire is exactly the opposite of the religion of Jesus Christ. If you wanted proof of that, at the lifting of my finger there are thousands in this hall who would rise to prove it, for they would say, "I have found it so Sir, in my experience. I hated religion as much as any men. I despised Christ and His people. I know not to this day how it is that I am what I am, unless it is the work of God."

I have seen the tears run down a man's cheeks when he has come to me in order to be united to the Church of Christ. He has said, "Sir, I wonder how it is I am here today–if anyone had told me a year ago that I should think as I now think and feel as I now feel–I would have called him a born fool for his pains. I used to say I never would be one of those canting Methodists. I liked to spend my Sunday in pleasure and I did not see why I was to be cooping myself up in the house of God listening to a man talk. I said the best Providence in all the world was a good strong pair of hands–and to take care of what you got. If any man talked to me about religion, why I would slam the door in his face and pretty soon put him out.

"But the things that I loved then, I now hate. And the things that then I hated, now I love. I cannot do or say enough to show how total is the change that has been worked in me. It must have been the work of God. It could not have been worked by me, I feel assured. It must be Someone greater than myself who could thus turn my heart." I think these two things are proofs that we want something more than nature and since physical agency will not do–and mere moral persuasion will never accomplish it. There is an absolute necessity for the Holy Spirit.

But again, if you will just think a minute what the work is, you will soon see that none but God can accomplish it. In the Holy Scripture conversion is often spoken of as being a new creation. If you talk about creating yourselves, I should feel obliged if you would create a fly first. Create a gnat. Create a grain of sand–and when you have created that–you may talk about creating a new heart. Both are alike impossible, for creation is the work of God. But still, if you could create a grain of dust, or create even a world, it would not be half the miracle–for you must first find a thing which has created itself. Could that be? Suppose you had no existence, how could you create yourself? Nothing cannot produce anything. Now, how can man re-create himself? A man cannot create himself into a new condition, when he has no being in that condition, but is, as yet, a thing that is not.

Then, again, the work of creation is said to be like the resurrection. "We are alive from the dead." Now, can the dead in the grave raise themselves? Let any minister who thinks he can convert souls, go and raise a corpse. Let him go and stand in one of the cemeteries and bid the tombs open wide their mouths and make room for those once buried there to awaken. He will have to preach in vain. But if he could do it, that is not the miracle–it is for the dead to raise themselves–for an inanimate corpse to kindle in its own breast the spark of life anew. If the work is a resurrection, a creation–does it not strike you that it must be beyond the power of man? It must be worked in him by no one less than God Himself.

And there is yet one more consideration and I shall have concluded this point. Beloved, even if man could save himself, I would have you remember how averse he is to it! If we could make our hearers all willing, the battle would be accomplished. "Well," says one, "If I am willing to be saved, can I not be saved?" Assuredly you can, but the difficulty is we cannot bring men to be willing. That shows, therefore, that there must be a constraint put upon their will. There must be an influence exerted upon them which they have not in themselves, in order to make them willing in the day of God's power.

And this is the glory of the Christian religion. The Christian religion has within its own heart power to spread itself. We do not ask you to be willing first. We come and tell you the news and we believe that the Spirit of God working with us will make you willing. If the progress of the Christian religion depended upon the voluntary assent of mankind it would never go an inch further–but because the Christian religion has within an omnipotent influence, constraining men to believe it, it is therefore what it is and must be triumphant, "till like a sea of glory it spreads from shore to shore."

III. Now I shall conclude by bringing one or two thoughts forward with regard to WHAT MUST BE DONE AT THIS TIME IN ORDER TO BRING DOWN THE HOLY SPIRIT. It is quite certain, Beloved, if the Holy Spirit willed to do it, that every man, woman and child in this place might be converted now. If God, the Sovereign Judge of all, would be pleased now to send out His Spirit, every inhabitant of this million-peopled city might be brought at once to turn unto the living God. Without instrumentality, without the preacher, without books, without anything–God has it in His power to convert men.

We have known persons about their business, not thinking about religion at all, who have had a thought injected into their heart and that thought has been the prolific mother of a thousand meditations. And through these meditations they have been brought to Christ. Without the aid of the minister, the Holy Spirit has thus worked and today He is not restrained. There may be some men, great in infidelity, staunch in opposition to the Cross of Christ–but, without asking their consent–the Holy Spirit can pull down the strong man and make the mighty man bow himself. When we talk of the Omnipotent God, there is nothing too great for Him to do. But, Beloved, God has been pleased to put great honor upon instrumentality.

He could work without it if He pleased but He does not do so. However, this is the first thought I want to give you. If you would have the Holy Spirit exert Himself in our midst, you must first of all look to Him and not to instrumentality. When Jesus Christ preached, there were very few converted under Him and the reason was because the Holy Spirit was not abundantly poured forth. He had the Holy Spirit without measure Himself—but on others the Holy Spirit was not as yet poured out. Jesus Christ said, "Greater works than these shall you do because I go to my Father, in order to send the Holy Spirit."

And remember that those few who were converted under Christ's ministry were not converted by Him, but by the Holy Spirit that rested upon Him at that time. Jesus of Nazareth was anointed of the Holy Spirit. Now then, if Jesus Christ, the great Founder of our religion, needed to be anointed of the Holy Spirit, how much more our ministers? And if God would always make the distinction even between His own Son as an instrument and the Holy Spirit as the agent—how much more ought we to be careful to do that between poor puny men and the Holy Spirit?

Never let us hear you say again, "So many persons were converted by So-and-So." They were not. If converted they were not converted by man. Instrumentality is to be used, but the Spirit is to have the honor of it. Pay no more a superstitious reverence to man. Think no more that God is tied to your plans and to your agencies. Do not imagine that so many city missionaries, so much good will be done. Do not say, "So many preachers. So many sermons—so many souls saved." Do not say, "So many Bibles, so many tracts—so much good done." Not so, use these, but remember it is not in that proportion the blessing comes. It is so much Holy Spirit, so many souls in-gathered.

And now another thought. If we would have the Spirit, Beloved, we must each of us try to honor Him. There are some Chapels into which if you were to enter, you would never know there was a Holy Spirit. Mary Magdalene said of old, "They have taken away my Lord and I know not where they have laid Him." And the Christian might often say so, for there is nothing said about the Lord until they come to the end—and then there is just the benediction—or else you would not know that there were three Persons in one God at all. Until our Churches honor the Holy Spirit, we shall never see Him abundantly manifested in our midst. Let the preacher always confess before he preaches that he relies upon the Holy Spirit. Let him burn his manuscripts and depend upon the Holy Spirit. If the Spirit does not come to help him, let him be still and let the people go home and pray that the Spirit will help him next Sunday.

And do you also, in the use of all your agencies, always honor the Spirit? We often begin our religious meetings without prayer. It is all wrong. We must honor the Spirit—unless we put Him first, He will never make crowns for us to wear. He will get victories, but He will have the honor of them and if we do not give to Him the honor, He will never give to us the privilege and success. And best of all, if you would have the Holy Spirit, let us meet together earnestly to pray for Him.

Remember, the Holy Spirit will not come to us as a Church unless we seek Him. "For this thing will I be enquired of by the house of Israel to do it for them." We purpose during the coming week to hold meetings of special prayer, to supplicate for a revival of religion. On the Friday morning I opened the first Prayer Meeting at Trinity Chapel, Brixton. And, I think, at seven o'clock, we had as many as two hundred and fifty persons gathered together. It was a pleasant sight. During the hour, nine brethren prayed, one after the other. And I am sure there was the spirit of prayer there.

Some persons present sent up their names, asking that we would offer special petitions for them. And I doubt not the prayers will be answered. At Park Street, on Monday morning, we shall have a Prayer Meeting from eight to nine. Then during the rest of the week there will be a Prayer Meeting in the morning from seven to eight. On Monday evening we shall have the usual Prayer Meeting at seven, when I hope there will be a large number attending. I find that my brother, Baptist Noel, has commenced morning and evening Prayer Meetings and they have done the same thing in Norwich and many provincial towns, where, without any pressure, the people are found willing to come.

I certainly did not expect to see so many as two hundred and fifty persons at an early hour in the morning meet together for prayer. I believe it was a good sign. The Lord has put prayer into their hearts and therefore they were willing to come. "Prove Me now here, says the Lord of Host, and see if I do not pour you out a blessing so that there shall not be room enough to receive it." Let us meet and pray and if God does not hear us, it will be the first time He has broken His promise.

Come, let us go up to the sanctuary. Let us meet together in the house of the Lord and offer solemn supplication. And I say again, if the Lord does not make bare His arm in the sight of all the people, it will be the reverse of all His previous actions–it will be the contrary of all His Promises and contradictory to Himself. We have only to try Him and the result is certain in dependence on His Spirit. If we only meet for prayer, the Lord shall bless us–and all the ends of the earth shall fear Him. O Lord, lift up Yourself because of Your enemies. Pluck Your right hand out of Your bosom, O Lord our God, for Christ's sake. Amen.

PART II

THE WORK OF THE HOLY SPIRIT

THE WORK OF THE HOLY SPIRIT

"Are you so foolish? Having begun in the Spirit, are you now made perfect by the flesh?"
Galatians 3:3

A Sermon Delivered On Thursday Evening: 5 November 1857

YES, we are just so foolish. Folly is bound up not only in the heart of a child but in the heart of even a child of God. And though the rod may be said to bring folly out of a child, it will take many a repetition of the rod of affliction upon the shoulders of a Christian before that folly is taken out of him. I suppose we are all of us very sound as a matter of theory upon this point. If any should ask us how we hope to have our salvation worked in us we should without the slightest hesitation declare our belief that salvation is of the Lord alone. And we should declare that as the Holy Spirit first of all commenced our piety in us, we look alone to His might to continue and to preserve and at last to perfect the sacred work.

I say we are sound enough on that point as a matter of theory, but we are all of us very heretical and unsound as a matter of practice. For alas, you will not find a Christian who does not have to mourn over his self-righteous tendencies. You will not discover a Believer who has not at certain periods in his life to groan because the spirit of self-confidence has risen in his heart– and prevented him from feeling the absolute necessity of the Holy Spirit. He has then put his confidence in the mere strength of nature, the strength of good intentions, the strength of strong resolutions, instead of relying upon the might of God the Holy Spirit alone.

This one thing I know, Brethren, that while as a preacher I can tell you all that the Holy Spirit must work all our works in us and that without Him we can do nothing, yet as a man I find myself tempted to deny my own preaching, not in my words, but to deny them in fact by endeavoring to do deeds without looking first to the Holy Spirit. While I should never be unsound in the didactic part of it, yet in that part which concerns the working of it out in common with all that love the Lord Jesus but who are still subject to the infirmities of flesh and blood, I have to groan that I repeatedly find myself, having begun in the Spirit, seeking to be made perfect in the flesh. Yes, we are just as foolish as that. And, my Brethren, it is well for us if we have a consciousness that we are foolish–for when a man is foolish and knows it–there is the hope that he will one day be wise, by God's grace.

To know one's self to be foolish is to stand upon the doorstep of the temple of wisdom. To understand the wrongness of any position is half way towards amending it. To be quite sure that our self-confidence is a heinous sin and folly and an offense towards God and to have that thought burned into us by God's Holy Spirit is going a great length towards the throwing of our self-confidence away. This helps bring our souls in practice, as well as in theory, to rely wholly upon the power of God's Holy Spirit.

This evening, however, I shall run away from my text somewhat. Having just in a few words endeavored to explain the meaning of the whole sentence, I intend only this evening to dwell upon the doctrine which incidentally the Apostle teaches us. He teaches us that we begin in the Spirit–"Having begun in the Spirit" I have already illustrated the whole text sufficiently for our understanding if God the Holy Spirit shall enlighten us. And I shall now, I say, confine myself to the thought that Christians begin in the Spirit–that the early part of Christianity is of God's Spirit and of God's Spirit only, while it is equally true that all the way through we must lean upon the same power and depend upon the same strength.

And I have selected this text for this reason. We have a very large influx of young Believers, month after month–week after week I may say. Every week we receive a considerable number of additions to the Church. Month after month these hands baptize into a profession of faith of the Lord Jesus many of those who are yet young in the faith of the Gospel. Now I am astonished to find those persons that thus come before me so well instructed in the doctrines of grace. And they are so sound in all the Truths of the Covenant, insomuch that I may think it my boast and glory, in the name of Jesus, that I know not that we have any members whom we have received into the Church who do not give their full assent and consent unto all the doctrines of the Christian religion, commonly called Calvinistic doctrines.

Those which men are likely to laugh at as being high doctrinal points are those which they most readily receive, believe and rejoice in. I find, however, that the greatest deficiency lies in this point–forgetfulness of the work of the Holy Spirit. I find them very easily remembering the work of God the Father.

They do not deny the great doctrine of election. They can see clearly the great sentence of justification passed by the Father upon the elect through the vicarious sacrifice and perfect righteousness of Jesus. And they are not backward in understanding the work of Jesus, either. They can see how Christ was the Substitute for His people and stood in their place. Nor do they for one moment impugn any doctrine concerning God's Spirit. But they are not clear upon the point. They can talk upon the other points better than they can upon those which more particularly concern the blessed work of that all adorable Person of the Godhead, God the Holy Spirit.

I thought, therefore, that I would just preach as simply as ever I could upon the work of the Holy Spirit and begin at the beginning. Hoping on succeeding evenings at different times, as God the Holy Spirit shall guide me, to enter more fully into the subject of the work of the Spirit from the beginning even to the end. But let me say, it is no use your expecting me to preach a course of sermons. I know a great deal better than that. I don't believe God the Holy Spirit ever intended men to publish three months before hand, lists of sermons that they were going to preach.

There always will arise changes in Providence and different states of mind both in the preacher and the hearer and he will be a very wise man who has got an Old Moore's Almanac correct enough to let him know what would be the best sort of sermon to preach three months ahead. He had better leave it to his God to give him in the same hour what he shall speak and look for his sermons, as the Israelites looked for the manna, day by day. However, we now commence by endeavoring to narrate the different points of the Spirit's work in the beginning of salvation.

And first, let me start by asserting that THE COMMENCEMENT OF SALVATION IS THE HOLY SPIRIT'S WORK. Salvation is not begun in the soul by the means of grace apart from the Holy Spirit. No man in the world is at liberty to neglect the means that God has appointed. If a house is built for prayer, that man must expect no blessing who neglects to tread its floor. If a pulpit is erected for the ministration of the Word, no man must expect (although we do sometimes get more than we expect) to be saved except by the hearing of the Word. If the Bible is printed in our own native language and we can read it, He who neglects Holy Scripture and ceases from its study, has lost one great and grand opportunity of being blessed.

There are many means of grace and let us speak as highly of them as ever we can. We would be far from depreciating them. They are of the highest value. Blessed are the people who have them. Happy is the nation which is blessed with the means of grace. But my Brethren, no man was ever saved by the means of grace apart from the Holy Spirit. You may hear the sermons of the man whom God delights to honor. You may select from all your Puritanical divines the writings of the man whom God did bless with a double portion of His Holy Spirit. You may attend every meeting for prayer. You may turn over the leaves of this blessed Book. But in all this, there is no life for the soul apart from the breath of the Divine Spirit.

Use these means. We exhort you to use them and use them diligently. But recollect that in none of these means is there anything that can benefit you unless God the Holy Spirit shall own and crown them. These are like the conduit pipes of the market place—when the fountain head flows with water then they are full and we derive a blessing from them. But if the stream are stopped, if the fountain head does cease to give forth its current, then these are wells without water, clouds without rain. And you may go to ordinances as an Arab turns to his skin bottle when it is dry and with your parched lips you may suck the wind and drink the whirlwind but receive neither comfort, nor blessing nor instruction, from the means of grace.

Nor is the salvation of any sinner commenced in him by a minister or by a priest. God forgive the man that ever called himself a priest, or suffered anyone else to call him so since the days of our Lord Jesus. The other morning at family prayer I read the case of King Uzziah, who, having the kingly office, thrust himself into the tabernacle of the Lord and took the place of the priests. You remember how the priests withstood him and said, "This is not your portion, O Uzziah." And you remember how he seized the censer and would burn incense as a priest before the Lord God. And while they yet spoke, lo, the leprosy did rise in his face and he went out a leper, as white as snow, from the house of God.

Ah, my Brethren, it is no mean offense against God for any man to call himself a priest. Remember that all the saints have a priestly office through Christ Jesus. But when any man puts to the idea a specialty as applicable to himself above his fellows and claims to be a priest among men, he commits a sin before God. A sin which, even though it is a sin of ignorance, is indeed great and grievous and leads unto many great and deadly errors—the guilt of which must lie partly upon the head of the man who gave foothold for those errors by allowing the title to be applied to himself.

Well, there is no man–call him priest if you like, by way of ill courtesy–that can begin the work with us–no, not in the use of the ceremony. The Papist may tell us and the Papist masked–the devil in white, the Puseyite–may tell us that grace begins in the heart at the dropping of the water upon the child's brow. But he tells a lie, a lie before God, that has not even so much as the shadow of truth to justify the liar. There is no power in man, though he were ordained by one who could most assuredly claim succession from the Apostles–though he were endowed with miraculous gifts, though he were the Apostle Paul himself–if he did assert that he had in himself power to convert, power to regenerate, let him be accursed! He has denied the truth and Paul himself would have declared him anathema, for having departed from the everlasting Gospel, one cardinal point of which is regeneration, the work of God the Holy Spirit–the new birth–a thing that is from above.

And, my Brethren, it is quite certain that no man ever begins the new birth himself. The work of salvation never was commenced by any man. God the Holy Spirit must commence it. Now, the reasons why no man ever commenced the work of grace in his own heart is very plain and palpable. First, because he cannot. Secondly, because he won't. The best reason of all is because he cannot–he is dead. Well, the dead may be made alive, but the dead cannot make themselves alive, for the dead can do nothing. Besides, the new thing to be created as yet has no being. The uncreated cannot create.

"No," but you say, "that man can create." Yes, can Hell create Heaven? Then sin may create grace. What? Will you tell me that fallen human nature that has come almost to a level with the brutes is competent to rival God? That it can emulate the Divinity in working as great marvels and in imparting as Divine a life as even God Himself can give? It cannot. Besides, it is a creation. We are created anew in Christ Jesus. Let any man create a fly and afterwards let him create a new heart in himself. Until he has done the less he cannot do the greater. Besides, no man will.

If any man could convert himself, there is no man that would. If any man says he would, if that is true, he is already converted. For the will to be converted is in great part conversion. The will to love God, the desire to be in unison with Christ is not to be found in any man who has not already been brought to be reconciled with God through the death of His Son. There may be a false desire, a desire grounded upon a misrepresentation of the truth. But a true desire after true salvation by the true Spirit is a certain index that the salvation already is there in the germ and in the bud and only needs time and grace to develop itself. But certain it is that man neither can nor will–being on the one hand utterly impotent and dead and on the other hand utterly depraved and unwilling–hating the change when he sees it in others and most of all despising it in himself. Be certain, therefore, that God the Holy Spirit must begin, since none else can.

And now, my Brethren, I must just enter into the subject very briefly, by showing what the Holy Spirit does in the beginning. Permit me to heard of an assembly of Divines who once debated whether men did repent first or believe first. And after a long discussion, someone wiser than the rest suggested another question, whether in the new-born child the lungs did first heave, or the blood did first circulate. "Now," said he, "when you shall ascertain the one, you may be able to ascertain the other." You shall not know which comes first. They are, very likely, begotten in us at the same moment. We are not able, when we mention these things in order, exactly to declare and testify that these do all happen according to the order in which we mention them. But we only, according to the judgment of men, according to our own experience, seek now to set forth what is the usual way of acting with God the Holy Spirit in the work of salvation.

The first thing, then, that God the Holy Spirit does in the soul is to regenerate it. We must always learn to distinguish between regeneration and conversion. A man may be converted a great many times in his life, but regenerated only once. Conversion is a thing which is caused by regeneration, but regeneration is the very first act of God the Spirit in the soul. "What?" you say, "Does regeneration come before conviction of sin?" Most certainly. There could be no conviction in the dead sinner. Now, regeneration quickens the sinner and makes him live. He is not competent to have true spiritual conviction worked in him until, first of all, he has received life.

It is true that one of the earliest developments of life is conviction of sin. But before any man can see his need of a Savior he must be a living man. Before he can really, I mean, in a spiritual position, in a saving, effectual manner understand his own deep depravity, he must have eyes with which to see the depravity. He must have ears with which to hear the sentence of the Law. He must have been quickened and made alive–otherwise he could not be capable of feeling, or seeing, or discerning at all. I believe, then, the first thing the Spirit does is this–He finds the sinner dead in sin, just where Adam left him. He breathes into him a Divine influence. The sinner knows nothing about how it is done, nor do any of us understand it. "You understand not the wind–it blows where it lists." But we see its effects.

Now, none of us can tell how the Holy Spirit works in men. I doubt not there have been some who have sat in these pews and in the middle of a sermon or in prayer, or singing–they knew not how it was–the Spirit of God was in their hearts. He had entered into their souls. They were no longer dead in sin, no longer without thought, without hope, without spiritual capacity–they had begun to live. And I believe this work of regeneration, when it is done effectually–and God the Spirit would not do it without doing it effectually–is done mysteriously, often suddenly and it is done in many manners. But still it has always this mark about it–that the man, although he may not understand how it is done, feels that something is done. The what, the how, he does not know. But he knows that something is done. And he now begins to think thoughts he never thought before. He begins to feel as he never felt before. He is brought into a new state, there is a change wrought in him–as if a dead post standing in the street were on a sudden to find itself possessed of a soul and did hear the sound of the passing carriages and listen to the words of the passengers. There is something quite new about it.

The fact is, the man has got a Spirit. He never had one before. He was nothing but a body and a soul. But now, God has breathed into him the third great principle, the new life, the Spirit and he has become a spiritual man. Now he is not only capable of mental exercise, but of spiritual exercise. Having a soul before, he could repent–he could believe as a mere mental exercise. He could think thoughts of God and have some desires after Him. But he could not have one spiritual thought, nor one spiritual wish or desire, for he had no powers that could educe these things. But now, in regeneration, he has got something given to him and being given, you soon see its effects.

The man begins to feel that he is a sinner. Why did he not feel that before? Ah, my Brethren, he could not, he was not in a state to feel. He was a dead sinner. And though he used to tell you and tell God, by way of compliment, that he was a sinner, he did not know anything about it. He said he was a sinner. Yes, but he talked about being a sinner just as the blind man talks about the stars that he has never seen, as he talks about the light, the existence of which he would not know unless he were told of it. But now it is a deep reality. You may laugh at him, you who have not been regenerated. But now he has got something that really puts him beyond your laughter. He begins to feel the exceeding weight and evil of transgression. His heart trembles, his very flesh quivers–in some cases the whole frame is affected.

The man is sick by day and night. His flesh creeps on his bones for fear. He cannot eat, his appetite fails him. He cannot bear the sound of melody and mirth. All his animal spirits are dried up. He cannot rejoice, he is unhappy, he is miserably downcast, distressed. In some cases he is almost ready to go mad–though in the majority of cases it takes a lighter phase and there are the gentle whispers of the Spirit. But even then the pangs and pains caused by regeneration, while the new life discovers the sin and evil of the past condition of the man are things that are not to be well described or mentioned without tears. This is all the work of the Spirit.

And having brought the soul thus far, the next thing the Holy Spirit does is, to teach the soul that it is utterly incapable of saving itself. It knew that before, maybe, if the man sat under a Gospel ministry. But he only knew it with the ear and understood it with the mind. Now, it has become part of his very life. He feels it–it has entered into his soul and he knows it to be true. Once he thought he would be good and thought that would save him. The Holy Spirit just knocks the brains out of that thought. "Then," he says, "I will try ceremonies and see whether I cannot gain merit so." God the Holy Spirit shoots the arrow right through the heart of that thought and it falls dead before him and he cannot bear the sight of the carcass, so that, like Abraham said of Sarah, he exclaims, "Bury the dead out of my sight." Though once he loved it dearly, now he hates the sight of it.

He thought once that he could believe. He had an Arminian notion in his head that he could believe when he liked and repent when he liked. Now, God the Spirit has brought him in such a condition that he says, "I can do nothing." He begins to discover his own death, now that he is made alive. He did not know anything about it before. He now finds that he has no hand of faith to lift, though the minister tells him to do it. He now discovers, when he is bid to pray, that he would, but cannot pray. He now finds that he is powerless and he dies in the hand of God like clay in the hand of the potter and is made to cry out, "O Lord, my God, unless You save me, I am damned to all eternity. For I cannot lift a finger in this matter until You first of all give me strength."

And if you urge him to do anything he longs to be doing he is so afraid that it should only be fleshly doings and not the doings of the Spirit that he meditates and stops until he groans and cries. And feeling that these groans and cries are the real work of the Spirit and prove that he has spiritual life, he then begins in right earnest to look to Jesus Christ the Savior. But mark, all these things are by the Spirit and none of them can ever be produced in the soul of any man or woman, apart from the Divine influence of God the Holy Spirit.

This being done—the soul being now weaned from all confidence and despairing and brought to its last standing place, yes, laid prostrate on the ground, the rope being about its neck and the ashes and sackcloth on its head—God the Holy Spirit next applies the blood of Jesus to the soul. He gives the soul the grace of faith whereby it lays hold of Jesus and gives it an anointing of holy consolation and unction of assurance, whereby, casting itself wholly on the blood and righteousness of Jesus, it receives joy, knows itself to be saved and rejoices in pardon. But mark, that is the work of the Spirit. Some preachers will tell their people, "Believe, only believe."

Yes, it is right they should tell them so. But they should remember it is also right to tell them that even this must be the work of the Spirit. For though we say, "Only believe," that is the greatest "only" in the world. And what some men say is so easy is just what those who want to believe find to be the hardest thing in all the world. It is simple enough for a man that has the Spirit in him to believe when he has the written Word before him and the witness of the Spirit in him. That is easy enough. But for the poor, tried sinner, who cannot see anything in the Word of God but thunder and threat—for him to believe—ah, my Brethren, it is not such a little matter as some make it to be. It needs the fullness of the power of God's Spirit to bring any man to such faith as that.

Well, when the sinner has thus believed, then the Holy Spirit brings all the precious things to him. There is the blood of Jesus. That can never save my soul unless God the Spirit takes that blood and sprinkles it upon my conscience. There is the perfect spotless righteousness of Jesus. It is a robe that will fit me and adorn me from head to foot, but it is no use to me till I have put it on. And I cannot put it on myself—God the Holy Spirit must put the robe of Jesus' righteousness on me. There is the Covenant of Adoption whereby God gives me the privileges of a son. But I cannot rejoice in my adoption until I receive the Spirit of adoption whereby I may be able to cry, "Abba, Father."

So, Beloved, you see–I might enlarge, but my time fails me–you see that every point that is brought out in the experience of the newborn Christian, every point in that part of salvation which we may call its beginning in the soul has to do with God the Holy Spirit. There is no step that can be taken without Him. There is nothing which can be accomplished aright without Him. Yes, though you had the best of means, the most correct of ceremonies, the most orthodox of truths and though you did exercise your minds upon all these things–and though the blood of Jesus Christ were shed for you and God Himself had ordained you from before the foundations of the world to be saved–yet still there must be that one link always inserted in the golden chain of the plan of salvation. For without that it were all incomplete. You must be quickened by the Spirit. You must be called out of darkness into light. You must be made a new creature in Christ Jesus.

Now, I wonder how many of you know anything about this. That is the practical part of it. Now my Hearer, do you understand this? Perhaps, Sir, you are exceedingly wise and you turn on your heel with a sneer and you say, "Supernaturalism in one of its phases. These Methodists are always talking about supernatural things." You are very wise, exceeding so, doubtless. But it seems to me that Nicodemus of old had gotten as far as you and you have gotten no farther than he. For he asked, "How could a man be born again when he is old?"

And though every Sunday-School child has had a smile at the expense of Nicodemus's ignorance, you are not wiser. And yet you are a Rabbi, Sir and you would teach us, would you? And you would teach us about these things and yet you sneer about supernaturalism? Well, the day may come–I pray it may come to you before the day of your death and your doom–when the Christ of the supernaturalists will be the only Christ for you. When you shall come into the floods of death–where you shall need something more than nature–then you will be crying for a work that is supernatural within your heart. And it may be that then, when you first of all awake to know that your wisdom was but one of the methods of madness, you may perhaps have to cry in vain, having for your only answer, "I called and you refused. I stretched out My hands and no man regarded. I also will mock at your calamity and laugh when your fear comes."

I hear another of you say, "Well, Sir, I know nothing of this work of God the Holy Spirit in my heart. I am just as good as other people. I never make a profession of religion. It is very rarely that I go into a place of worship at all, but I am as good as the saints, any of them. Look at some of them–very fine fellows certainly." Stop, now, religion is a thing between yourself and your Maker and you have nothing to do with those very fine fellows you have spoken of. Suppose I make a confession that a large number of those who are called saints deserve a great deal more to be called sinners double-dyed and then white-washed–suppose I make a confession of that, what has that to do with you?

Your religion must be for yourself and it must be between you and your God. If all the world were hypocrites that would not exonerate you before your God. When you came before the Master, if you were still at enmity to Him, could you venture to plead such an excuse as this–"All the world was full of hypocrites?" "Well," He would say, "what had that to do with you? So much the more reason why you should have been an honest man. If you say the Church was thus drifting away upon the quicksand through the evil conduct and folly of the members, so much the more reason why you should have helped to make it sound, if you thought you could have done so."

Another cries, "Well, I do not see that I need it. I am as moral a man as I can be. I never break the Sabbath. I am one of the most punctilious of Christians–I always go to Church twice a Sabbath. I hear a thoroughly evangelical minister and you would not find fault with him." Or perhaps says another, "I go to a Baptist Chapel, I am always found there, I am scrupulously correct in my conduct. I am a good father, a good husband. I do not know that any man can find fault with me in business." Well certainly that is very good and if you will be so good tomorrow morning as to go into Saint Paul's and wash one of those statues till you make it alive–then you will be saved by your morality.

But since you, even you, are dead in trespasses and sins–without the Spirit you may wash yourself ever so clean–but you cannot wash life into yourself any more than those statues. With all your washing those idols could never be made to walk, or think, or breathe. You must be quickened by the Holy Spirit, for you are dead in trespasses and sins.

Yes, my comely maiden, you that are everything excellent. You that are not to be blamed in anything. You that are affectionate, tender, kind and dutiful–whose very life seems to be so pure that all who see you think you are an angel. Even you, except you be born again, can not see the kingdom of God. The golden gate of Heaven must grind upon its hinges with a doleful sound and shut you out forever unless you are the "you must be born again." You, too, must be quickened by a Divine life. And it is comforting for you to recollect that the very same power which can awaken the moral man, which can save the man of rectitude and honesty, is able to work in you–is able to change you–to turn the lion to a lamb, the raven to a dove.

O my Hearers, ask yourselves–are you the subjects of this change? And if you are, rejoice with joy unspeakable, for happy is that mother's child and full of glory that can say, "I am born of God." Blessed is that man–God and the holy angels call him blessed who has received the quickening of the Spirit and is born of God. For him there may be many troubles, but there is "a far more exceeding and eternal weight of glory" to counterbalance all his woe. For him there may be wars and fights. But let him tarry, there are trumpets of victory, there are better wreaths than the laurels of conquerors. There is a crown of immortal glory, there is bliss unfading, there is acceptance in the breast of God forever and perpetual fellowship with Jehovah. But oh, if you are not born again this night I can but tremble for you and lift my heart in prayer to God and pray for you that He may now by His Divine Spirit make you alive, give you to know your need of Him and then direct you to the Cross of Jesus.

But if you know your need of a Savior tonight, if you are this night conscious of your death in sin, hear me preach the Gospel and I have done. The Lord Jesus Christ died for you. Do you know yourself to be guilty? Not as the hypocrite pretends to know it, but do you know it consciously, sensitively–do you weep over it? Do you lament it? Do you feel that you can not save yourself? Are you sick of all fleshly ways of saving? Can you say tonight, "Unless God shall put out the hand of His mercy, I know I deserve to be lost forever and I am"?

Then, as the Lord my God lives, before whom I stand, my Master bought you with His blood and those whom He bought with blood He will have. From the fangs of the lion and the jaws of the bear will He pluck them. He will save you–for you are a part of His bloody purchase. He has taken your sins upon His head. He suffered in your place. He has been punished for you. You shall not die–"your sins, which are many, are all forgiven." And I am the Master's glad herald to tell you tonight what His Word tells you also–that you may rejoice in the fullness of faith–for "Christ Jesus came into the world to save sinners," and "this is a faithful saying and worthy of all acceptation." May the Lord now be pleased to add his blessing for Jesus' sake.

THE POWER OF THE HOLY SPIRIT

"The power of the Holy Spirit."
Romans 15:13

A Sermon Delivered On Sunday Morning: 17 June 1855

POWER is the special and peculiar prerogative of God, and God alone. "Twice have I heard this, that power belongs unto God" (Psa. 62:11). God is God—and power belongs to Him. If He delegates a portion of it to His creatures, yet still it is His power. The sun, although he is "like a bridegroom coming out of his chamber and rejoices as a strong man to run his race," yet has no power to perform his motions except as God directs him. The stars, although they travel in their orbits and none could stay them, yet have neither might nor force except that which God daily infuses into them. The tall archangel, near His Throne, who outshines a comet in its blaze, though he is one of those who excel in strength and hearkens to the voice of the commands of God, yet has no might except that which his Maker gives to him.

As for Leviathan, who so makes the sea to boil like a pot that one would think the deep were hoary—as for Behemoth, who drinks up Jordan at a draught and boasts that he can snuff up rivers. As for those majestic creatures that are found on earth, they owe their strength to Him who fashioned their bones of steel and made their sinews of brass. And when we think of man—if he has might or power—it is so small and insignificant, that we can scarcely call it such. Yes, when it is at its greatest—when he sways his sceptre, when he commands hosts, when he rules nations—still the power belongs unto God. And it is true, "Twice have I heard this, that power belongs unto God."

This exclusive prerogative of God, is to be found in each of the three Persons of the glorious Trinity. The Father has power—for by His word were the heavens made and all the host of them. By His strength all things stand and through Him they fulfil their destiny. The Son has power—for like His Father, He is the Creator of all things—"Without Him was not anything made that was made," and "by Him all things consist." And the Holy Spirit has power. It is concerning the power of the Holy Spirit that I shall speak this morning. May you have a practical exemplification of that attribute in your own hearts—when you shall feel that the influence of the Holy Spirit is being poured out upon me–so that I am speaking the words of the living God to your souls. And may it be bestowed upon you when you are feeling the effects of it in your own spirits.

We shall look at the power of the Holy Spirit in three ways this morning. First, the outward and visible displays of it. Second, the inward and spiritual manifestations of it And third, the future and expected works thereof. The power of the Spirit will thus, I trust, be made clearly present to your souls.

First, then, we are to view the power of the Spirit in the OUTWARD AND VISIBLE DISPLAYS OF IT. The power of the Spirit has not been dormant–it has exerted itself. Much has been done by the Spirit of God already–more than could have been accomplished by any being except the Infinite, Eternal, Almighty Jehovah, of whom the Holy Spirit is one Person. There are four works which are the outward and manifest signs of the power of the Spirit– creation works, resurrection works, works of attestation or of witness and works of grace. Of each of the works I shall speak very briefly.

First, the Spirit has manifested the omnipotence of His power in creation works. For though not very frequently in Scripture, yet sometimes creation is ascribed to the Holy Spirit, as well as to the Father and the Son. The creation of the heavens above us is said to be the work of God's Spirit. This you will see at once by referring to the sacred Scriptures, Job 26:13–"By His Spirit He has garnished the heavens, His hand has formed the crooked serpent." All the stars of Heaven are said to have been placed aloft by the Spirit and one particular constellation called the "crooked serpent" is specially pointed out as His handiwork.

He looses the bands of Orion. He binds the sweet influences of the Pleiades and guides Aeturus with his sons. He made all those stars that shine in Heaven. The heavens were garnished by His hands and He formed the crooked serpent by His might. So also in those continued acts of creation which are still performed in the world. As the bringing forth of man and animals, their birth and generation. These are ascribed also to the Holy Spirit. If you look at the 104th Psalm, at the 29th verses, you will read, "You hide Your face, they are troubled. You take away their breath they die and return to their dust. You send forth Your Spirit, they are created and You renew the face of the earth."

So you see that the creation of every man is the work of the Spirit—and the creation of all life and all flesh—existence in this world is as much to be ascribed to the power of the Spirit as the first garnishing of the heavens, or the fashioning of the crooked serpent. And if you will look in the 1st chapter of Genesis, you will there see more particularly set forth that peculiar operation of power upon the universe which was put forth by the Holy Spirit. You will then discover what was His special work. In the 2nd verse of the 1st chapter of Genesis, we read, "And the earth was without form and void. And darkness was upon the face of the deep. And the Spirit of God moved upon the face of the waters."

We know not how remote the period of the creation of this globe may be—certainly many millions of years before the time of Adam. Our planet has passed through various stages of existence and different kinds of creatures have lived on its surface, all of which have been fashioned by God. But before that era came, wherein man should be its principal tenant and monarch, the Creator gave up the world to confusion. He allowed the inward fires to burst up from beneath and melt all the solid matter so that all kinds of substances were commingled in one vast mass of disorder. The only name you could give to the world then was that it was a chaotic mass of matter.

What it should be, you could not guess or define. It was entirely without form and void and darkness was upon the face of the deep. The Spirit came and stretching His broad wings, bade the darkness disperse and as He moved over it, all the different portions of matter came into their places and it was no longer "without form and void." It became round like its sister planets and moved, singing the high praises of God—not discordantly as it had done before—but as one great note in the vast scale of creation. Milton very beautifully describes this work of the Spirit in thus bringing order out confusion, when the King of Glory, in His powerful Word and Spirit, came to create new worlds—

"On heavenly ground they stood. And from the shore
They viewed the vast immeasurable abyss
Outrageous as a sea, dark, wasteful, wild,
Up from the bottom turned by furious winds
And surging waves, as mountains, to assault
Heaven's height and with the center mix the pole.
'Silence you troubled waves and you deep, peace,'

Said then the Omnificent Word. Your discord end.
Then on the watery calm
His brooding wings the Spirit of God outspread
And vital virtue infused and vital warmth
Throughout the fluid mass."

This, you see then is the power of the Spirit. Could we have seen that earth all in confusion, we should have said, "Who can make a world out of this?" The answer would have been, "The power of the Spirit can do it. By the simple spreading of His dove-like wings He can make all the things come together. Upon that there shall be order where there was nothing but confusion." Nor is this all the power of the Spirit. We have seen some of His works in creation. But there was one particular instance of creation in which the Holy Spirit was more especially concerned, viz., the formation of the body of our Lord Jesus Christ.

Though our Lord Jesus Christ was born of a woman and made in the likeness of sinful flesh, yet the power that begat Him was entirely in God the Holy Spirit–as the Scriptures express it, "The power of the Highest shall overshadow you." He was begotten as the Apostles' Creed says, of the Holy Spirit. "That holy Thing which is born of you shall be called the Son of the Highest." The corporeal frame of the Lord Jesus Christ was a masterpiece of the Holy Spirit. I suppose His body to have excelled all others in beauty. To have been like that of the first man, the very pattern of what the body is to be in Heaven, when it shall shine forth in all its glory.

That fabric, in all its beauty and perfection, was modelled by the Spirit. In His book were all the members written when as yet there were none of them. He fashioned and formed Him. And here again we have another instance of the creative energy of the Spirit.

A second manifestation of the Holy Spirit's power is to be found in the resurrection of the Lord Jesus Christ. If you have ever studied this subject, you have perhaps been rather perplexed to find that sometimes the resurrection of Christ is ascribed to Himself. By His own power and Godhead He could not be held by the bond of death, but as He willingly gave up His life He had power to take it again. In another portion of Scripture you find it ascribed to God the Father–"He raised Him up from the dead." "Him has God the Father exalted." And many other passages of similar import.

But, again, it is said in Scripture that Jesus Christ was raised by the Holy Spirit. Now all these things were true. He was raised by the Father because the Father said, "loose the prisoner—let Him go. Justice is satisfied. My Law requires no more satisfaction—vengeance has had its due—let Him go." Here He gave an official message which delivered Jesus from the grave. He was raised by His own majesty and power because He had a right to come out and He felt He had and therefore "burst the bonds of death—He could be no longer beholden of them."

But He was raised by the Spirit as to that energy which His mortal frame received, by which it rose again from the grave after having lain there for three days and nights. If you want proofs of this you must open your Bibles again, 1 Peter 3:18—"For Christ also has once suffered for sins, the Just for the unjust, that He might bring us to God, being put to death in the flesh but quickened by the Spirit."

And a further proof you may find in Romans, 8:11—(I love sometimes to be textual, for I believe the great fault of Christians is that they do not search the Scriptures enough and I will make them search them when they are here if they do not do so anywhere else)—"But if the Spirit of Him that raised up Jesus from the dead dwell in you, He that raised up Christ from the dead shall also quicken your mortal bodies by His Spirit that dwells in you."

The resurrection of Christ, then, was effected by the agency of the Spirit and here we have a noble illustration of His omnipotence. Could you have stepped, as angels did, into the grave of Jesus and seen His sleeping body, you would have found it cold as any other corpse. Lift up the hand, it falls by the side. Look at the eye—it is glazed. And there is a death thrust which must have annihilated life. See His hands. The blood distils not from them—they are cold and motionless. Can that body live? Can it start up?

Yes. And be an illustration of the might of the Spirit! For when the power of the Spirit came on Him, as it was when it fell upon the dry bones of the valley—"He arose in the majesty of His divinity and bright and shining, astonished the watchmen so that they fled away. Yes, He arose no more to die, but to live forever, King of kings and Prince of the kings of the earth."

The third of the works of the Holy Spirit which have so wonderfully demonstrated His power, are attestation works. I mean by this—works of witnessing. When Jesus Christ went into the stream of baptism in the river Jordan, the Holy Spirit descended upon Him like a dove and proclaimed Him God's Beloved Son. That is what I style an attestation work. And when afterwards Jesus Christ raised the dead, when He healed the leper, when He spoke to diseases and they fled, when demons rushed in thousands from those who were possessed of them, it was done by the power of the Spirit. The Spirit dwelt in Jesus without measure and by that power all those miracles were worked. These were attestation works.

And when Jesus Christ was gone, you will remember that master attestation of the Spirit when He came like a rushing mighty wind upon the assembled Apostles and cloven tongues sat upon them. And you will remember how He attested their ministry by giving them to speak with tongues as He gave them utterance. And how, also, miraculous deed's were wrought by them. How they taught, how Peter raised Dorcas, how he breathed life into Eutychus, how great deeds were wrought by the Apostles as well as their Master—so that "mighty signs and wonders were done by the Holy Spirit and many believed thereby."

Who will doubt the power of the Holy Spirit after that? Ah, those Socinians who deny the existence of the Holy Spirit and His absolute Personality—what will they do when we get them on creation, resurrection and attestation? They must rush in the very teeth of Scripture. But mark—it is a stone upon which if any man fall he shall be bruised. But if it fall upon him as it will do if he resists it, it shall grind him to powder. The Holy Spirit has power omnipotent, even the power of God, because He is God.

Once more, if we want another outward and visible sign of the power of the Spirit, we may look at the works of grace. Behold a city where a soothsayer has the power—who has given out himself to be some great one. A Philip enters it and preaches the Word of God—straightway a Simon Magus loses his power and himself seeks for the power of the Spirit to be given to him, fancying it might be purchased with money. See, in modern times, a country where the inhabitants live in miserable wigwams, feeding on reptiles and the meanest creatures.

Observe them bowing down before their idols and worshipping their false gods and so plunged in superstition, so degraded and debased, that it became a question whether they had souls or not. Behold a Moffat with the Word of God in his hand. Hear him preach as the Spirit gives him utterance and accompanies that Word with power. They cast aside their idols–they hate and abhor their former lusts. They build houses wherein they dwell. They become clothed and in their right mind. They break the bow and cut the spear in sunder. The uncivilized become civilized. The savage becomes polite. He who knew nothing begins to read the Scriptures. Thus out of the mouths of Hottentots God attests the power of His mighty Spirit.

Take a household in this city–and we could guide you to many such–the father is a drunkard. He has been the most desperate of characters. See him in his madness and you might just as well meet an unchained tiger as meet such a man. He seems as if he could rend a man to pieces who should offend him. Mark his wife. She, too, has a spirit in her and when he treats her ill she can resist him. Many broils have been seen in that house and often has the neighborhood been disturbed by the noise created there. As for the poor little children–see them in their rags and nakedness, poor untaught things.

Untaught, did I say? They are taught and well taught in the devil's school and are growing up to be the heirs of damnation. But someone whom God has blessed by His Spirit is guided to the house. He may be but a humble city missionary, perhaps, but he speaks to such a one. "O," says he, "come and listen to the voice of God." Whether it is by his own agency, or a minister's preaching, the Word, which is quick and powerful, cuts to the sinner's heart. The tears run down his cheeks–such as had never been seen before. He shakes and quivers. The strong man bows down–the mighty man trembles–and those knees that never shook begin to knock together.

That heart which never quailed before, now begins to shake before the power of the Spirit. He sits down on a humble bench by the penitent. He lets his knees bend, while his lips utter a child's prayer, but, while a child's prayer, a prayer of a child of God. He becomes a changed character. Mark the reformation in his house! That wife of his becomes the decent matron. Those children are the credit of the house and in due time they grow up like olive branches round his table, adorning his house like polished stones. Pass by the house–no noise or broils, but songs of Zion. See him–no drunken revelry. He has drained his last cup. And, now forswearing it, he comes to God and is

His servant. Now, you will not hear at midnight the bacchanalian shout. But should there be a noise, it will be the sound of the solemn hymn of praise to God. And, now, is there not such a thing as the power of the Spirit? Yes! And these must have witnessed it and seen it.

I know a village, once, perhaps, the most profane in England—a village inundated by drunkenness and debauchery of the worst kind, where it was impossible almost for an honest traveler to stop in the public house without being annoyed by blasphemy. A place noted for incendiaries and robbers. One man, the ringleader of all listened to the voice of God. That man's heart was broken. The whole gang came to hear the Gospel preached and they sat and seemed to reverence the preacher as if he were a God and not a man. These men became changed and reformed. And everyone who knows the place affirms that such a change had never been wrought but by the power of the Holy Spirit.

Let the Gospel be preached and the Spirit poured out and you will see that it has such power to change the conscience, to ameliorate the conduct, to raise the debased, to chastise and to curb the wickedness of the race, that you must glory in it. I say, there is nothing like the power of the Spirit. Only let that come and, indeed, everything can be accomplished.

II. Now, for the second point, THE INWARD AND SPIRITUAL POWER OF THE HOLY SPIRIT. What I have already spoken of may be seen. What I am about to speak of must be felt and no man will apprehend what I say with Truth unless he has felt it. The other, even the infidel, must confess. The other, the greatest blasphemer cannot deny it, he speaks the Truth. But this is what the one will laugh at as enthusiasm and what the other will say is but the invention of our fevered fancies. However, we have a more sure word of testimony than all that they may say. We have a witness within. We know it is the Truth and we are not afraid to speak of the inward spiritual power of the Holy Spirit. Let us notice two or three things wherein the inward and spiritual power of the Holy Spirit is very greatly to be seen and extolled.

First, in that the Holy Spirit has a power over men's hearts. Now, men's hearts are very hard to affect. If you want to get at them for any worldly object you can do it. A cheating world can win man's heart, a little gold can win man's heart, a trump of fame and a little clamor of applause can win man's heart. But there is not a minister breathing that can win man's heart himself. He can win his ears and make them listen. He can win his eyes and fix those eyes upon him. He can win the attention, but the heart is very slippery. Yes, the heart is a fish that troubles all Gospel fishermen to hold.

You may sometimes pull it almost all out of the water–but slimy as an eel, it slips between your fingers and you have not captured it after all. Many a man has fancied that he has caught the heart but has been disappointed. It would need a strong hunter to overtake the hart on the mountains. It is too fleet for human foot to approach. The Spirit alone has power over man's heart. Do you ever try your power on a heart? If any man thinks that a minister can convert the soul, I wish he would try. Let him go and be a Sabbath-School teacher. He shall take his class, he shall have the best books that can be obtained, he shall have the best rules, he shall draw his rampart about his spiritual Sebastopol.

He shall take the best boy in his class and if he is not tired in a week I shall be very much mistaken. Let him spend four or five Sabbaths in trying, but he will say, "The young fellow is incorrigible." Let him try another. And he will have to try another, another and another before he will manage to convert one. He will soon find, "It is not by might nor by power, but by My Spirit, says the Lord." Can a minister convert? Can he touch the heart? David said, "Your hearts are as fat as grease." Yes, that is quite true. And we cannot get through so much grease at all. Our sword cannot get at the heart–it is encased in so much fatness, it is harder than a nether millstone.

Many a good old Jerusalem blade has been blunted against the hard heart. Man, a piece of the true steel that God has put into the hands of His servants has had the edge turned by being set up against the sinner's heart. We cannot reach the soul. But the Holy Spirit can. "My Beloved can put in His hand by the hole in the door and my heart will move for sin." He can give a sense of blood-bought pardon that shall dissolve a heart of stone. He can–

"Speak with that voice which wakes the dead,
And bids the sinner rise–
And makes the guilty conscience dread
The death that never dies."

He can make Sinai's thunders audible. Yes and He can make the sweet whisperings of Calvary enter into the soul. He has power over the heart of man. Yes, the glorious proof of the omnipotence of the Spirit is that He has rule over the heart.

But if there is one thing more stubborn than the heart it is the will. "My Lord, Will-be-Will," as Bunyan calls him in his "Holy War," is a fellow who will not easily be bent. The will, especially in some men, is a very stubborn thing and in all men, if the will is once stirred up to opposition, there is nothing can be done with them. Free will somebody believes in. Free will many dream of. Free will! Wherever is that to be found? Once there was free will in Paradise and a terrible mess free will made there, for it spoiled all Paradise and drove Adam out of the garden. Free will was once in Heaven but it drove the glorious archangel out and a third part of the stars of Heaven fell into the abyss.

I want nothing to do with free will–but I will try to see whether I have got a free will within. And I find I have. Very free will to evil but very poor will to that which is good. Free will enough when I sin but when I would do good evil is present with me and how to do that which I would I find not. Yet some boast of free will. I wonder whether those who believe in it have any more power over persons' wills than I have. I know I have not any. I find the old proverb very true, "One man can bring a horse to the water, but a hundred cannot make him drink." I find that I can bring you all to the water and a great many more than can get into this chapel. But I cannot make you drink. And I don't think a hundred ministers could make you drink.

I have read old Rowland Hill, Whitfield and several others to see what they did. But I cannot discover a plan of turning your wills. I cannot coax you. And you will not yield by any manner of means. I do not think any man has power over his fellow creature's will–but the Spirit of God has. "I will make them willing in the day of My power." He makes the unwilling sinner so willing that he is impetuous after the Gospel. He who was obstinate, now hurries to the Cross. He who laughed at Jesus now hangs on His mercy. And he who would not believe, is now made by the Holy Spirit to do it, not only willingly, but eagerly. He is happy, is glad to do it, rejoices in the sound of Jesus' name and delights to run in the way of God's commandments. The Holy Spirit has power over the will.

And yet there is one thing more which I think is rather worse than the will. You will guess what I mean. The will I hope that my will is managed by Divine Grace. But I am afraid my imagination is not at times. Those who have a fair share of imagination know what a difficult thing it is to control. You cannot restrain it. It will break the reins. You will never be able to manage it. The imagination will sometimes fly up to God with such a power that eagles' wings cannot match it.

It sometimes has such might that it can almost see the King in His beauty and the land which is very far off. With regard to myself, my imagination will sometimes take me over the gates of iron, across that infinite unknown to the very gates of pearl and discovers the blessed Glorified. But if it is potent one way it is also another. For my imagination has taken me down to the vilest kennels and sewers of earth. It has given me thoughts so dreadful, that while I could not avoid them, yet I was thoroughly horrified at them.

These thoughts will come and when I feel in the holiest frame, the most devoted to God and the most earnest in prayer, it often happens that that is the very time when the plagues breaks out the worst. But I rejoice and think of one thing—that I can cry out when this imagination comes upon me. I know it is said in the Book of Leviticus when an act of evil was committed, if the maiden cried out against it, then her life was to be spared. So it is with the Christian. If he cries out, there is hope. Can you chain your imagination? No. But the power of the Holy Spirit can. Ah, it shall do it and it does do it at last. It does it even on earth.

III. But the last thing was, THE FUTURE AND DESIRED EFFECTS—for after all, though the Holy Spirit has done so much, He cannot say, "It is finished." Jesus Christ could exclaim concerning His own labor—"It is finished." But the Holy Spirit cannot say that. He has more to do yet—and until the consummation of all things, when the Son Himself becomes subject to the Father, it shall not be said by the Holy Spirit, "It is finished." What, then, has the Holy Spirit to do?

First, he has to perfect us in holiness. There are two kinds of perfection which a Christian needs—one is the perfection of justification in the Person of Jesus. And the other is the perfection of sanctification worked in him by the Holy Spirit. At present corruption still rests even in the breasts of the regenerate. At present the heart is partially impure. At present there are still lusts and evil imaginations. But, Oh, my soul rejoices to know that the day is coming when God shall finish the work which He has begun—and He shall present my soul, not only perfect in Christ, but, perfect in the Spirit, without spot or blemish, or any such thing.

And is it true that this poor depraved heart is to become as holy as that of God? And is it true that this poor spirit, which often cries, "O wretched man that I am, who shall deliver me from the body of this sin and death?" shall get rid of sin and death? I shall have no evil things to vex my ears and no unholy thoughts to disturb my peace? Oh, happy hour! may it be hastened! Just before I die, sanctification will be finished. But not till that moment shall I ever claim perfection in myself. But at that moment when I depart, my spirit shall have its last Baptism in the Holy Spirit's fire. It shall be put in the crucible for its last trying in the furnace.

And then, free from all dross and fine like a wedge of pure gold, it shall be presented at the feet of God without the least degree of dross or mixture. O glorious hour! O blessed moment! Methinks I long to die even if there were no Heaven–if I might but have that last purification and come up from Jordan's stream most white from the washing. Oh, to be washed white, clean, pure, perfect! Not an angel more pure than I shall be–yes, not God Himself more holy! And I shall be able to say, in a double sense, "Great God, I am clean– through Jesus' blood I am clean–through the Spirit's work I am clean, too!" Must we not extol the power of the Holy Spirit in thus making us fit to stand before our Father in Heaven?

Another great work of the Holy Spirit which is not accomplished is the bringing on of the latter-day glory. In a few more years–I know not when, I know not how–the Holy Spirit will be poured out in a far different style from the present. There are diversities of operations. And during the last few years it has been the case that the diversified operations have consisted in very little pouring out of the Spirit. Ministers have gone on in dull routine, continually preaching, preaching, preaching–and little good has been done. I do hope that perhaps a fresh era has dawned upon us and that there is a better pouring out of the Spirit even now.

For the hour is coming and it may be even now, when the Holy Spirit shall be poured out again in such a wonderful manner that many shall run to and fro and knowledge shall be increased–the knowledge of the Lord shall cover the earth as the waters cover the surface of the great deep! When His kingdom shall come and His will shall be done on earth even as it is in Heaven. We are not going to be dragging on forever like Pharaoh with the wheels off his chariot. My heart exults and my eyes flash with the thought that very likely I shall live to see the out-pouring of the Spirit when, "the sons and the daughters of God again shall prophecy and the young men shall see visions and the old men shall dream dreams."

Perhaps there shall be no miraculous gifts—for they will not be required. But yet there shall be such a miraculous amount of holiness, such an extraordinary fervor of prayer, such a real communion with God and so much vital religion and such a spread of the doctrines of the Cross that everyone will see that verily the Spirit is poured out like water and the rains are descending from above. For that let us pray—let us continually labor for it and seek it of God.

One more work of the Spirit which will especially manifest His power—the general resurrection. We have reason to believe from Scripture that the resurrection of the dead, while it will be effected by the voice of God and of His Word, (the Son), shall also be brought about by the Spirit. That same power which raised Jesus Christ from the dead shall also quicken your mortal bodies. The power of the resurrection is perhaps one of the finest proofs of the works of the Spirit. Ah, my Friends, if this earth could but have its mantle torn away for a little while, if the green sod could be cut from it and we could look about six feet deep into its bowels, what a world it would seem!

What should we see? Bones, carcasses, rottenness, worms, corruption. And you would say, "Can these dry bones live? Can they start up?" "Yes, in a moment! In the twinkling of an eye, at the last trump, the dead shall be raised." He speaks—they are alive! See them scattered—bone comes to his bone! See them naked—flesh comes upon them! See them still lifeless—"Come from the four winds, O breath and breathe upon these slain!" When the wind of the Holy Spirit comes, they live and they stand upon their feet an exceeding great army.

I have thus attempted to speak of the power of the Spirit and I trust I have shown it to you. We must now have a moment or two for practical inference. The Spirit is very powerful, Christian! What do you infer from that fact? Why, that you never need distrust the power of God to carry you to Heaven! O how that sweet verse was laid to my soul yesterday!—

"His tried Almighty arm
Is raised for your defense.
Where is the power can reach you there
Or what can pluck you thence?"

The power of the Holy Spirit is your bulwark and all His omnipotence defends you. Can your enemies overcome omnipotence? Then they can conquer you. Can they wrestle with Deity and hurl Him to the ground? Then they might conquer you. For the power of the Spirit is our power–the power of the Spirit is our might.

Once again, Christians, if this is the power of the Spirit, why should you doubt anything? There is your son. There is that wife of yours for whom you have supplicated so frequently–do not doubt the Spirit's power. "Though He tarry, wait for Him." There is your husband, O holy woman! And you have wrestled for his soul. And though he is ever so hardened and desperate a wretch and treats you ill, there is power in the Spirit. And, O you who have come from barren churches with scarcely a leaf upon the tree. Do not doubt the power of the Spirit to raise you up. For it shall be a "pasture for flocks, a den of wild asses," open, but deserted, until the Spirit is poured out from on high.

And then the parched ground shall be made a pool and the thirsty land springs of water. Then in the habitations of dragons, where each lay, shall be grass with reeds and rushes. And, O you members of Park Street! You who remember what your God has done for you especially–never distrust the power of the Spirit. You have seen the wilderness blossom like Carmel. You have seen the desert blossom like the rose. Trust Him for the future. Then go out and labor with this conviction–the power of the Holy Spirit is able to do anything! Go to your Sunday-School. Go to your tract distribution. Go to your missionary enterprise! Go to your preaching in your rooms, with the conviction that the power of the Spirit is our great help.

And now, lastly, to you sinners. What is there to be said to you about this power of the Spirit? Why, to me, there is some hope for some of you. I cannot save you–I cannot get at you. I make you cry sometimes–you wipe your eyes and it is all over. But I know my Master can. That is my consolation. Chief of sinners, there is hope for you! This power can save you as well as anybody else! It is able to break your heart, though it is an iron one. It can make your eyes run with tears though they have been like rocks before. His power is able this morning, if He will, to change your heart, to turn the current of all your ideas, to make you at once a child of God, to justify you in Christ.

There is power enough in the Holy Spirit. He is able to bring sinners to Jesus– He is able to make you willing in the day of His power. Are you willing this morning? Has He gone so far as to make you desire His name, to make you wish for Jesus? Then, O Sinner! while He draws you, say, "Draw me, I am wretched without You." Follow Him, follow Him and while He leads, tread in His footsteps and rejoice that He has begun a good work in you, for there is an evidence that He will continue it even unto the end.

And, O desponding one! Put your trust in the power of the Spirit. Rest on the blood of Jesus and your soul is safe, not only now, but throughout eternity. God bless you, my Hearers. Amen.

THE HOLY SPIRIT GLORIFYING CHRIST (Part 1)

"He shall glorify Me: for He shall take of Mine, and shall show it unto you."
John 16:14

A Sermon Delivered On Sunday Morning: 17 August 1862

WE always need the Spirit of God in our preaching. But I think we more especially require His Divine direction and instruction when the subject is Himself–for the Holy Spirit is so mysterious in His varied attributes and operations, that unless He Himself shall reveal Himself to us and give us the words in which to speak of Him, we shall surely fail either to understand for ourselves, or to enlighten others. In His light we see light, but without Him we grope like blind men in the dark.

Certain sins against the Holy Spirit continually exist in a degree in the Christian Church. Unholiness of life grieves the Holy Spirit. When Christian men walk not according to the Gospel. When their conversation is not ordered according to the pattern of Christ, then the Holy Spirit, who has no fellowship with unholiness, withdraws Himself in a measure from the Church. Discord, too, strife among Brethren, forgetfulness of the new commandment, that we love one another, grieves the sacred Dove–for as His nature is peaceable, as His office is to be the peace giver–so He tarries not where there is the din and noise of contending parties.

So, also, when He perceives His saints to be diseased with worldliness, when we prefer the treasures of Egypt to the reproach of Christ, and seek rather the things which are seen, which are temporal, than the things which are not seen, which are eternal–then again is the Holy Spirit quenched and departs from our midst. Above all, pride and that murmuring, rebellion, unbelief, obstinacy and self-seeking which pride leads to–all this grieves the Holy Spirit, for He dwells with those who are humble and of a contrite spirit. Where there is the voice of murmuring, where one man seeks to lift himself above another, and all to exalt themselves above their despised Lord, the Holy Spirit hides Himself and suffers barrenness to take the place of plenty, and death to reign where once life triumphed.

These are a few of the common and the constant infirmities of the Church, by which the Holy Spirit is much hindered in those marvelous manifestations which otherwise would be common and usual in the midst of our Israel.

But there are two faults of the Church which appear to me periodically to manifest themselves. The one is when men ascribe wrong things to the Holy Spirit, and make Him the Author of human novelties and delusions. In seasons when the minds of good men were anxiously alive to spiritual operations, certain weak-headed or designing persons have grown fanatical. Bewildered by their own confused feelings and puffed up by their fleshly minds, they have forsaken the true light which is in the Word, to follow after the will-o'-the-wisps of their own fancies, the absurdities of their own brains. Such vainglorious fools aspiring to be leaders, masters of sects, will boldly tell men of itching ears that fresh doctrines have been especially revealed to them.

They prate much of what they call the inner light (which is often an inner darkness), which dim candle they exalt above the light of the Word of God, and tell you that marvelous things have been taught to them in dreams and visions. Ah, this is a high and crying crime. What? Will you lay at the door of the Holy Spirit a deed which God has solemnly cursed? Do you not start back at such a thought? Is it not almost blasphemy to imagine it? And yet remember, he that adds a single word to the canon of inspiration is cursed. Give ear to the very words of the Lord our God, "If any man shall add unto these things, God shall add unto him the plagues that are written in this Book. And if any man shall take away from the Words of the Book of this prophecy, God shall take away his part out of the Book of Life and out of the holy city and from the things which are written in this Book."

And do you think the Holy Spirit would do that which involves a curse upon man? If I venture to add to God's Word, or to take from it, I do it with this as my penalty—that God shall blot my name out of the Book of Life and out of the holy city. And yet these base pretenders, who would lay their foolish notions at the door of God the Holy Spirit, will have it that He has taught them more than is in the Book, that He has removed that which God laid down as the grand landmark and added to the finished testimony of God. Let none of you have any sort of patience with men who talk thus.

Deny their very first principle. Tell them—whether it is the deceiver of Western America, or the false prophet of Arabia—tell them that they are all impostors, for they ascribe to the Holy Spirit that which is impossible for Him to commit—a violation of the revealed will of God in which it is declared that the canon of inspiration is shut up once and for all. A little of this evil I detect among godly people. I find that sometimes even gracious men think they have had revelations. Texts of Scripture are no doubt laid home by the Holy Spirit to the souls of men as much today as in Paul's time, and there can be no doubt whatever that the Spirit brings all things Christ has taught to our remembrance, and that He leads us into all Truth.

But when a man tells me that the Holy Spirit has revealed to him something that is not in the Bible, he lies! Is that a hard word? It does but express the Truth of God. The man may have dreamed his revelation, he may have fancied it—but the Holy Spirit goes never beyond the written Word. "He shall take of Mine and shall show it unto you." And beyond what Christ has spoken and what Christ has taught, the Holy Spirit goes in no sense and in no respect. You understand what Christ has taught through the Spirit's teaching. But anything beyond the teaching of Christ and His Apostles must be not of God but of man.

This is a most important principle to be held fast by all godly people, for the day may come when false prophets shall arise and delude the people, and by this shall we be able to discover them. If they claim anything beyond what Christ has taught, put them aside, for they are false prophets, wolves in sheep's clothing. The Spirit only teaches us that which Christ has taught beforehand either by Himself or by the inspired Apostles. "He shall take of Mine and shall show it unto you."

Just now we are in little danger from the excesses of fevered brains, for, as a rule, our sin is in being far too cold and dead to spiritual influences. I fear we are liable to another evil and are apt to forget the Person and work of the Comforter altogether. We fear some congregations might say, "We have not so much as heard whether there is any Holy Spirit." From how many modern sermons would you even know that there was a Holy Spirit? If it were not for the benediction, or the doxology, you might go in and out of many Churches and meeting houses in a year and scarcely know that there was such a Person as that blessed, blessed Giver of all good, the Holy Spirit.

Sometimes we hear a little about His influences, as if the Holy Spirit were not as truly a Person as even Jesus Christ Himself, who in flesh and blood trod this earth. Oh, dear Friends, I fear the first danger–that of running wild with whimsies and fancies about inner lights and new revelations. But I equally dread this last, this putting the Revelation above the Revealer, this taking the Book without the Author, this preaching of the Truth of God without the great Truth Applier–this going forth to work with the Sword, forgetting that it is the Sword of the Spirit and only as mighty as the Holy Spirit makes it "mighty to the pulling down of strongholds."

May this Church ever continue to reverence the Holy Spirit without exaggerating His work! May we prize Him, love Him, and adore Him because He so wondrously glorifies our blessed Lord! With this, by way of preface, I shall now come at once to our text, using it three ways–first, as a test to try various things by. Secondly, as a direction how to honor Jesus. And thirdly, as a stimulus, stirring us up to glorify Christ.

First, then, we shall use our text AS A TEST. There are a thousand things that claim to be of the Holy Spirit. How can we know whether they are or not? Here is a simple mode of discovering, "He shall glorify Me."

Let us, first of all, apply this test to ministers. There are crowds of preachers and reverend divines nowadays in the world. But all are not ministers of God. A true minister is a creation of the God of Heaven. It is no more in the power of the Church than it is in the power of the bishops to make ministers. Independency is as weak as Episcopacy on this point. God, alone, ordains ministers. All that the Church can do is to recognize them. We cannot make them at our colleges. We cannot make them by the laying on of hands, nor even by the choice of the Church. God must make them–God must ordain them. It is only for the Church to perceive God's work, and cheerfully to submit to His choice.

And, there are some churches which clearly are not of the Holy Spirit, because they glorify ceremonies. We could take you into certain places of worship where the general strain of ministry is a glorification of Baptism, the blessed Eucharist, confirmation, priesthood, and so on. There you hear much of the childish millinery with which they deck the altar, and much is said of those grotesque garments in which their priests disguise themselves. We could point to many places where the main object of teaching seems to be to exalt a rubric, to magnify a liturgy, to hold up a hierarchy, or to extol a ritual. All such churches we may at once sweepingly and unerringly condemn. They are not of the Holy Spirit, for the Holy Spirit teaches us not to magnify outward rites, but Christ. And that teaching is not of the Holy Spirit which does not glorify the Lord Jesus.

Into other places we might take you where very clearly the object is the extolling of doctrine. From the first of January to the last of December the minister bitterly contends for the favorite corners of his faith. Doctrine, with certain friends, is everything, and their rigid orthodoxy is the one care of their life. Now, against a sound creed and the Doctrines of Grace we have not a word to say. God be thanked that we love these things as much as those who exalt them above measure. We are not a whit behind the chief of these champions in our zeal for orthodoxy.

But still our Lord is, and must be, the leading theme of our ministry. We must continue to exalt Him rather than Calvinism, or any other system of theology. We are bold to say it, much as we love the Master's Throne, we still love the Master better. And dearly as we love battling for the walls of His vineyard, yet the clusters of His Eshcol are sweeter to our taste. We love Christ better than creed, and we think we would rather magnify our Master than any set of truths, however important they may be.

There are certain doctrinal Brethren, good enough in their way, but still you can evidently see that the doctrine of election is a thing that they contend more for than the doctrine of the redemption of Christ. Or if it is redemption, it is the specialty of redemption rather than the Divine sacrifice itself. I love to preach the distinguishing Grace of God, but I am far from thinking that some four or five points comprise all the truths which God has revealed. Be it ours to preach the doctrines as Dr. Hawker preached them—with Christ as their sum and substance. "A full Christ for empty sinners"—may this be our theme. To a great extent it is true of a church that seeks only to exalt doctrines, that it has not the fullness of the Holy Spirit in it, for of the Holy Spirit it is written, "He shall glorify Me."

Another class of ministers are well known to those of us who have looked upon the Church of God at large, whose ministry tends mainly to magnify a certain experience. If you have felt thus and thus, and so and so, no words of praise can be too strong for you. But if you have been led in another way, in a different path, then depend on it, according to the judgment of these divines, you never knew vital godliness at all. They are as intimate with the secrets of

Heaven as the pope himself, and are quite as infallible as he, in their small dominions. Some of these Brethren have, no doubt, gone through a very deep and awful experience—they have lived so much in sin, and have been so untrue to their Lord, that it is little marvel if they have to walk in darkness and see no light. These Brethren hold up that experience as a model and tell us that unless we know all they have learned, we are not Christ's.

Now, I say not a word against experimental preaching. I believe it to be the most soul-fattening preaching in the world—but it must be experience about Christ, it must be an experience that leads me out of self to Jesus—and if any ministry is experimental, yet does not exalt Christ, I have cause to suspect whether the Holy Spirit is with it, for this stands as an unchanging rule—"He shall glorify Me."

And, dear Brothers and Sisters, once again, we are cursed with some few men—would to God they were fewer—whose teaching constantly is, "morality." If we will do this, and do that and the other, we shall be saved—the old Law of Moses is toned down and then held up as the road to Heaven. Now, at once, you may forsake the synagogues where such men are in the chief places. If any man exalt the works of flesh, and not the finished work of Christ—if the doings, the willings, the prayers, the feelings of man, are put in the place of the blood and righteousness of our Lord Jesus Christ—that church is not of the Holy Spirit.

And what might I say of many who produce each Sunday their pretty little essays, their elaborate disquisitions, their high-sounding periods? What shall I say of all these, but that they are as "sounding brass and a tinkling cymbal," inasmuch as they forget Christ, the Person of Christ—God and man, the work of Christ—His Atonement and righteousness? The resurrection of Christ—the gift and joy of the saints, the intercession of Christ—our hope and our strength, and the second advent of Christ, which is as the bright morning star to every weary watcher in this world's darkness? That Church, and that Church only, is of the Holy Spirit which magnifies Christ Jesus.

And here, dear Brethren in the ministry—and there are some such present—how bitterly may you and I lament much of our ministry because it has not glorified Christ! When we shall lie stretched upon our dying beds, we shall look back with satisfaction to that poor stammering sermon in which we magnified the Master. We shall look with intense regret to that well-delivered oration in which we glorified a sect, or lifted up an ordinance at the expense of our Lord. Oh, what joy it shall be to remember that we did lift Him up, however feebly, yet we did extol Him. Though sometimes utterance would not come as our heart would have it, yet we did point to His flowing wounds and said, "Behold the way to God."

Oh, the sweet bliss of a Whitfield when he retires to his last couch, to feel that he did preach Jesus, whether it was at the market, or on the hill side, or in the Church, or in the barn! What a consolation to feel that he did cry faithfully, "Other foundation can no man lay than that which is laid!" Oh, the curse on the other hand, that shall rest on a man who, in his last moments, shall have to reflect–"I preached other men's sermons and talked of anything but Christ. I lifted up anything but the Lord"! Oh, how shall the howling of his eternal doom commence in his ear! How shall the judgments of God get hold upon him even before he passes to the dread tribunal of the Most High. We must, as preachers, come back more and more to this rule–to feel that if the Holy Spirit is in us, He will make us glorify Christ.

Having thus tried ministers, let us now take the same test with regard to doctrine. And very briefly here, lay it down as a self-evident truth that any teaching, whatever authority it may claim, which does not glorify Christ, is most assuredly false. And on the other hand, I think we shall seldom be wrong if we believe that when a teaching lifts Christ up and puts many crowns upon His head, it must be a doctrine according to godliness.

Dear Friends, Socinianism must be utterly abhorred of us, for it strikes at once at the Deity of our blessed Lord and Master. We cannot give to such persons even the name of Christians. Mohammedan they may be–it were well if they would join with those men–they may be good men, they may be moral men, they may be excellent citizens, but Christians they cannot be, if they deny our Lord to be very God of very God and worthy to be worshipped even as is the Father.

I marvel that sundry Dissenters should have fraternized with Arians and Socinians in attacking the Church of England, in the present sorrowfully mistaken onslaught called the Bicentenary. And I can only pray that the Lord may not visit them for this shameful confederacy with His enemies. In Arminianism, which is a mixture of truth and error, there is the doctrine of the saints falling from Divine Grace. This is a doctrine which is more dishonorable to Christ than I can tell you. To my mind, it seems to put its black and sooty finger right down the escutcheon of my Lord and Master, setting Him as a laughingstock to the whole world. It says He is One who begins to build and is not able to finish—there is a blot upon His power.

He loves, and yet He loves not to the end—there is a blot upon His faithfulness. He says, "I give unto My sheep eternal life and they shall never perish, neither shall any pluck them out of My hand." And yet, according to the Arminian, they do perish—according to that doctrine which is a stain upon His truthfulness. In fact, the doctrine of final falling away impugns the whole Character of Christ so much that it would render Him unworthy of our faith. When they shall prove that one who was once in Christ has fallen away and has been lost, I know not Christ, for He has violated His Word. He can no more be "the Truth," when He has thus put His own promises into the background and suffered His darlings to fall into the power of the dog.

If there is anything in Scripture as plain as noonday, it is the doctrine that, "He that believes in Him has everlasting life, and shall never perish, neither shall he come into condemnation." If the child of God can be disinherited, if Christ can divorce His spouse, if the Good Shepherd shall lose His sheep, if the limbs of Christ's mystical body can be cut off, or can be allowed to rot, then I know not what Scripture teaches, nor do I understand how Christ can be worthy of the Believer's trust. That doctrine, I think, must be reprobated, because it stains the honor and glory of Christ.

Without alluding to others, let that suffice as an instance. Examine well all doctrines. Look not at them with complacency because they are put in cunning language, or asserted in vigorous declamation. But if you perceive that any teaching dishonors Christ and makes much of human ability—if it exalts man and derogates from the Grace of God—it is false and dangerous. And if, on the other hand, it lays man in the dust and lifts up Christ as a Savior, the Alpha and Omega, the Beginning and the End of salvation, you may safely say that is the Holy Spirit's doctrine, for He shall glorify Christ.

Again, we may use our text as a means by which to try much of the conviction through which a sinner passes. In the first dawn of our spiritual life a mighty tempest of spiritual influence sweeps over the heart. The Holy Spirit is active, and the prince of the power of the air is active, too. There is more of God and more of Satan in a new convert, than perhaps in any other stage of human existence. For just then Satan rages with extraordinary fury to drag back the soul to destruction, and the Holy Spirit works in him mightily, with a power which only Omnipotence can wield.

How, in this confusion, can a man know what part of his conviction is of God, and what part of the devil? Young man, listen to me. You have a thought in your head that you are too great a sinner to be saved. That is not of the Holy Spirit, clearly, because it detracts from the power of Christ as a Savior. That cannot be of the Holy Spirit, for the Holy Spirit glorifies Christ. "Yes, Sir, but I feel myself to be a great sinner, utterly lost and ruined." That is of the Holy Spirit, because it lays you low in order that the greatness of Christ's salvation may be the more apparent.

"Oh but," you say, "I am not fit to come to Christ." Surely this feeling is not of the Holy Spirit, but of the devil, for it does not glorify Christ. What? Are you to make yourself fit to come to Christ? Why, that is making you a Christ—yes, it is making you an antichrist, which is no work of Heaven but a foul design of Hell. "But I heard old Mr. So-and-So say the other day, Sir, that when he was converted, he seemed to be dragged by the hair of his head to the very depths of Hell. He said his soul was full of blasphemy and his heart was in such an awful state that he cursed the day of his birth, because he thought he was shut out of the Covenant and was utterly lost beyond the reach of mercy."

Very well, no doubt what he has told you was his veritable experience. But do you want to experience every piece of devilry that a good man has known? Because a good man trips and falls into the gutter, must you trip and fall there, too? Because Jonah descends into the whale's belly, must we all dive into the sea? I tell you, Soul, that much of what your friend felt was not of God, but of his own corrupt heart and of the devil—and he knows it, and he will confess the same to you. Why, therefore, should you pant after that which is sinful and Satanic? Why should you desire to drink the poison of asps and sniff the fumes of Tophet?

If the Lord brings you, this morning, to put your soul just as it is into the hands of the Redeemer, honoring Him by a childlike trust, you have an experience infinitely more precious than the howling of devils, and the ravings of your proud heart could ever yield you. To be nothing, and to accept Christ as everything, is worked in us of the Holy Spirit—all the rest, those horrible insinuations, that terrible Hell-shaking—may be all dispensed with. Good men have felt these, but they are not good things. They come from Satan and are to be avoided and prayed against–not to be sought after.

I pray you, therefore, let the Holy Spirit lead you in His own way and ask not to be led in a way of your own choice. Why long for darkness when the Master wills to let you walk in the light? Into these balances, then, put all your convictions, and discover how far they are of God and how far of Satan. That which glorifies Christ is of the Holy Spirit. All the rest is of flesh, or of Hell.

Thus, we may test what is called experience. Very much of the experience of a Christian is not Christian experience. If any person should mount the platform and say, "I will tell you the experience of a man," and then inform us that he had been five times tried at the Old Bailey, you would say, "Well, you may have experienced that disgrace but it is not fair to call it human experience."

So, a Christian man may fall into great darkness and into sin, too. Let us mournfully confess it. But then, if he shall set up his darkness and his sin as being Christian experience, we say, "No. We do not judge you, you may be a Christian and know all this, but we cannot allow you to judge us and decide our spiritual state according to your peculiar method of feeling. I fear that many biographies have done as much mischief as service. While no doubt they comfort many who fall into the same state, yet a sufficient discrimination is not made between the man stirred by the powers of evil, and the same man when filled with the Holy Spirit.

When we get to that which comes from beneath we ought to write always in the spirit of our Apostle who cannot describe himself without an agony–"Oh, wretched man that I am! Who shall deliver me from the body of this death? I thank God through Jesus Christ my Lord." That which glorifies Christ is true Christian experience, and that which does anything but this, a Christian may experience–but it is not Christian experience.

Let us lift the scales of judgment once more. I think our text gives us an excellent test by which to try ourselves. My Hearer, are you saved or not, this morning? If you are saved, the bent, the tenor, the bias of your life is to glorify Christ. What do you say in looking back? Does the past glorify! "When I think of the love that cleansed me from such sin, of the Divine Grace that broke a heart so hard as mine, of the faithfulness that has kept me to this day, I can only glorify Christ." And what about the present? "Oh," can you say, "when I think of what I now am by the Grace of God and what I should have been now if the Holy Spirit had not prevented. When I look within and see so much blackness, I must magnify the Grace that keeps me. And when It look without and see so many temptations, I must and will speak well of His dear name. I must glorify my Lord Jesus"?

And what do you say about the future? Will you glorify Him then? I think I see even the timid ones with their eyes, a little brightening up when they say, "Yes! If He will but once bring me across the river, if I ever get beyond gunshot of the devil, and behold the face of Christ in Glory, I will sing loudest of all the crowd. I will magnify Him with all my powers, for I shall owe more to Him than anyone else before the Throne. I will never cease to sing with all the blood-washed throng, 'Bring forth the royal diadem, and crown him Lord of all.' "

Oh, if your heart is not so that Christ is ALL to you, and if your soul is not desiring this morning to honor Him, Him only, then indeed, I fear the Holy Spirit has had no dealing with your spirit, for where He has been at work, He must, He shall glorify Christ.

II. We are now to use our text as DIRECTION. How are we to glorify Christ?

The text tells us that we must have the Holy Spirit. Let our text, then, be sanctified to our humiliation. Here are we saved by the rich love of Christ, delivered from our sins, and made alive unto God. And yet we are such weak things that we cannot glorify Christ without the indwelling of the Holy Spirit. We may pant, and long, and pray that we may have helped to honor our Master, but we shall only dishonor Him and disgrace His cause, unless the Holy Spirit holds us up and strengthen us. Do you hear that, Christian Man and Woman? You have ten talents but those ten talents shall make you ten times a worse defaulter to your Master unless the Holy Spirit helps you.

You have eloquence, you have wit, you have wealth—with none of these can you glorify Christ, unless the Holy Spirit is with you. For, "He shall glorify Me." Man cannot, except as the Holy Spirit is with him. Bow your heads, then, O you saints of God, and ascribe glory unto the Holy Spirit, but unto yourselves shame and confusion of face. Let us employ this text as an excitement to earnest prayer. We as a Church, and I may speak freely for my own flock, we long to see Christ glorified. It is to this end we seek to train up our sons, young men in our much-loved college, that they may go forth as preachers of the Word.

We have agencies by which we hope to do something in our generation for our Master–but what is everything we can do without the Holy Spirit? Let us, therefore, pray without ceasing. Oh, without prayer, what are the Church's agencies but the stretching out of a dead man's arm, or the lifting up of the lid of a blind man's eye? Only when the Holy Spirit comes is there any life and force and power. Cry then mightily unto God, O you who seek to glorify Christ, for without the Holy Spirit you utterly fail.

And here what a lesson our text reads us of entire dependence upon the Holy Spirit. You can do nothing, you ministers of God! Nothing, you faithful watchmen of Jerusalem! You can do nothing, you teachers of youth, nothing you heralds of the Cross in foreign fields, nothing you ten thousands who are willing to give all your substance, your time and your talents–absolutely nothing can you accomplish until God the Holy Spirit comes.

We are by the seaside. There are a number of ships left high and dry by the ebb of the tide. A long tract of mud stretches out before us. What is to be done? Call the king's horses, bring the king's men, gather together the wise and the mighty. What can they all do? Nothing–their learning can only avail to prove most clearly that they can do nothing. But see, the tide rolls in, wave after wave rises from the deep, and lo, every ship floats and all the mud and sand is covered with the fullness of the sea. So is it with the Churches. We all lie high and dry upon the beach and there is nothing but the rock and mud of our own inability that is visible–and we can do nothing, absolutely nothing, till the holy tide comes.

The blessed spirit of revival, the Holy Spirit, is poured out, and now the heaviest Church is floating out to sea and that which was most inactive begins to move! Oh, what can we not do if we have the Holy Spirit? What can we do if we have Him not? See our utter and entire dependence upon Him. When we, as a Church, first came out into broader light and more public notice, I bear my witness, we had an entire dependence upon the Holy Spirit. What prayers have I heard, what striving and what groaning! We are reaping now the ripe fruits of the early sowing.

Lo, your minister but a stripling from the country–all untrained in academic lore, knowing nothing but just the doctrine of the Cross–came forth before the multitudes to proclaim simply the Word. How he felt his nothingness then, and how often he told you so! You cried to God, and the child, the lad, was helped. What mighty deeds were done in the conversion of hundreds! And now we have a name, and there is a great temptation to rest upon our success, and for men to think there is something in the preacher, that he can gather the crowd, can preach the Word, and it is sure to be blessed when he preaches it.

Brothers and Sisters, again I say we are nothing, we are less than nothing. Your minister is a fool, and nothing beyond. Unless the Holy Spirit is with him, he is able to do nothing except mischief. Nothing that shall be profitable to you, or make any heart glad but the heart of the Evil One, unless the Holy Spirit is with us still. Joyously would I receive again the jeer, the sneer, the constant slander that was heaped upon my devoted head, if I might have back again your entire dependence upon the Holy Spirit.

Oh, members of this Church, you who have been quickened under our word, let not your faith stand in the wisdom of man, but in the demonstration of the Spirit! And let us one and all feel that we are still as weak as water, and as vain as the whistling wind, unless He that was first with us is with us still. "He shall glorify Me." The Holy Spirit shall do it. None can do it if He is absent.

I know I am addressing some this morning who have seen the goings forth of the Holy One of Israel. In fact we as a Church have had to rejoice these nearly nine years in a blessed revival. But how diligent should we be while we have that revival, in order that we may retain it! All the farmers in England cannot make it leave off raining but when it does leave off and the sun shines, I know what they do–get their wheat in as quickly as they can. All the sailors on the ocean cannot make a capful of wind. When the sail flaps to and fro they cannot make it swell out as in the gale–but what can they do when the wind does blow? They can crowd on every yard of canvas.

So all the Christians in the world cannot make the Holy Spirit work. "The wind blows where it lists, and you hear the sound thereof, but can not tell from where it comes nor where it goes." But what we can do is this, when we have the Holy Spirit–we can use Him. When He is with us we can work. We must make hay while the sun shines. We must grind while the wind blows, we must be active and diligent for God when the visitation of the Holy Spirit is with us.

The revival has, to a great extent, ceased in many places. I fear it is because they did not diligently use its influence.

In Ireland how much of revival there was but the Holy Spirit withdrew necessarily because it was held up as a curiosity. Every newspaper reeked with the news of the revival. People went from England to see it. It could not last, then. God never does His great works to be stared at, to be held up as curiosities. The thing was ruined the moment men began curiously to talk of it, and spread abroad the news as of a phenomenon worthy of philosophical investigation.

These good things should never be made a subject of. "Come, see my zeal for the Lord of Hosts." While the good work goes on we should be so hard at work for the Master, that we have not time to put into every penny newspaper the tale of what God is doing. Let us then be up while the Master is with us, and doing His work, doing it in the Spirit's own way, seeking to glorify Jesus, and seeking to retain the Spirit in our midst.

III. And now, lastly, I am to take my text by way of A STIMULUS. Does the Holy Spirit glorify Christ? Ah, then, how should we aim to do it! Let us make, then, Beloved Brothers and Sisters in Christ, let us make this the one object of our life—to glorify Christ. You have been a man in a large way of business. Could you say while you were doing business so largely that your object was to honor Christ in it?

Well, you have come down in the world. You have a smaller shop now. Yes, and suppose you can glorify God more? Then you are in a better position than you used to be. I have seen many a man who prospered in his soul and honored his Master much, who has made a wrong step and has injured his usefulness and happiness. Wanting to get more business, he has launched into wide speculations and has had less time for serving his Lord. And he has thus really been in a worse position, for spirituals were under a decay.

You may have seen in the newspapers an instance of what sometimes comes through getting wealthy. A man and his wife were prospering in a little way of business, as hard-working people, near Birmingham. A friend died and left the wife some 1,300, no great sum but quite enough to ruin a man. They at once took a public house and you will remember that he now lies in prison on a charge of murdering his wife. Little marvel that when, tempted by what little they had, to seek after more they entered upon an ill occupation in order to increase their wealth. That evil trade soon led to vicious habits and to death.

Now I have seen Believers mournfully impoverish their souls by seeking after carnal wealth instead of seeking Christ. But let a man's only object be to glorify Christ, and he will feel very little concern where Providence places him, so long as he may still promote his one object and put crowns on the Redeemer's head.

This brings me to say, Brethren, while we make this our aim, let us take every opportunity of glorifying Christ. We throw thousands of opportunities away. Where we might do good, we neglect it. I chide my own self here very bitterly, and very often, but I fear I might chide many of you, too. You had an opportunity yesterday but you lost it. You might have spoken for Christ but you did not. No one can tell the good you might have done, but you did not do it. You were backward. Oh, as the Holy Spirit glorifies Christ everywhere, so do you! I pray you do this always, not merely at particular times, but make your whole life a glorifying of Christ.

As I sat on an omnibus yesterday, I heard a man saying behind me how greatly he admired the continental way of keeping Sundays–going to Church in the morning, and going to the theater at night. "Don't you see," he said, "it is irrational to think that the Almighty expects us to spend the whole day in praying. There is no man living who can pray for six hours together, let alone twelve." That was just putting in broad language what most ungodly people feel. I wonder what they would make of the Apostle Paul's admonition, "Pray without ceasing." Here was a man who thought that nobody could pray for six hours together, while the saints of God are to continue always in prayer.

No man comes up to the stature of the Christian, or such a man as he should be, unless he cannot only pray for six hours together but his whole life long. It was said of good old Rowland Hill that people did not so much notice his particular times of retirement, for he was a man who was always praying, wherever he might be. You would often find him alone talking to himself. And even in company his heart would be going away to the object of his best love– he would still be in communion with Christ.

Be always glorifying Christ, Christians, from the rising of the sun unto the going down thereof. Whether you work at a lap stone, or drive a plow, or lay the stones in a building–serve the Master in all these things. Whether you are diligent with the pen, or whether you buy and sell, or plow the sea–do all even to your eating or your drinking in the name of the Lord Jesus–and so like the Holy Spirit let it be said of you, "He shall glorify Me."

We conclude by endeavoring to magnify our Master ourselves. I want to say just two or three things to glorify Him and they shall be just these. I shall say this to the poor troubled doubting sinner, "Sinner, my Master is able to save you." "Oh but I am the biggest sinner out of Hell." Yes, and He is the greatest of all Saviors. "Yes, but I have gone over head and ears in iniquity." Yes, and He was baptized also in His agonies that He might save you. "Oh but He cannot save me!" Yes! He can! And if I am now addressing the scum of the earth, one of the devil's sweepings, one who is hardly fit for decent company, my Master is able to save you. Unto the uttermost He saves, and your sin, though black, He can cleanse and make you whiter than snow.

I would say something else to glorify Him. He is willing to save you. His generous heart desires you. Your perishing will not make Him glad, but He will weep over you as He did over Jerusalem. But your being saved will give Him to see of the travail of His soul. "Do you know who you are speaking to, Sir?" No I don't, but my Master does. For now He fixes His poor tearful eyes on you. Where is the sinner? Behind that pillar? Or in yonder corner? The Master looks at him, and He says, "Come unto Me all you that labor and are heavy laden and I will give you rest. Take My yoke upon you and learn of Me, for I am meek and lowly of heart and you shall find rest unto your souls."

What? Are you so far away? How loudly does He call you, "Come, Sinner, repent and come." Are you willing to come? Lo! He meets you! In the road He meets you–embracing you, He falls upon your neck to kiss you. He says, even this morning, He says it, "Take off his rags and clothe him in fine apparel. Wash him and make him clean, for I have put away his sins like a cloud, and like a thick cloud his iniquities."

That which glorifies Christ the most of all is the preaching of the Gospel to sinners, and therefore have I glorified Him now and would do so as long as I live. Believe in the Lord Jesus Christ and you shall be saved, for he that believes and is baptized shall be saved. He that believes not shall be damned. God give us to glorify Christ by trusting in Him! Amen.

THE HOLY SPIRIT GLORIFYING CHRIST (Part 2)

"He will glorify Me, for He will take of what is Mine and declare it to you."
John 16:14

A Sermon Delivered On Sunday Morning: 12 April 1891

THE needs of spiritual men are very great, but they cannot be greater than the power of the Divine Trinity is able to meet. We have one God–Father, Son and Holy Spirit–One in Three and Three in One. And that blessed Trinity in Unity gives Himself to sinners that they may be saved. In the first place, every good thing that a sinner needs is in the Father. The prodigal son was wise when he said, "I will arise and go to my father." Every good and perfect gift comes from God the Father, the first Person in the blessed Trinity, because every good gift and every perfect gift can only be found in Him. But the needy soul says, "How shall I get to the Father? He is infinitely above me. How shall I reach up to Him?" In order that you might obtain the blessings of Grace, God was in Christ Jesus, the second ever-blessed Person of the Sacred Trinity. Let me read you part of the verse that follows my text–"All things that the Father has are Mine." So you see, everything is in the Father, first, and the Father puts all things into Christ. "It pleased the Father that in Him should all fullness dwell." Now you can get to Christ because He is Man as well as God. He is "over all, God blessed forever," but He came into this world, was born of the Virgin Mary, lived a life of poverty, "suffered under Pontius Pilate, was crucified, dead and buried." He is the conduit conveying to us all blessings from the Father. In the Gospel of John we read, "Of His fullness have we all received and grace for grace." Thus you see the Father with every good thing in Himself putting all fullness into the Mediator, the Man Christ Jesus who is also the Son of God.

Now I hear a poor soul say, "But I cannot get to Christ. I am blind and lame. If I could get to Him, He would open my eyes, but I am so lame that I cannot run or even walk to Him. If I could get to Him, He would give me strength, but I lie as one dead. I cannot see Christ or tell where to find Him." Here comes in the work of the Holy Spirit, the third Person of the blessed Unity! It is His office to take of the things of Christ and show them unto saints and sinners, too. We cannot see them, but we shall see them quickly enough when He shows them to us! Our sin puts a veil between us and Christ. The Holy Spirit comes and takes the veil away from our heart and then we see Christ. It is the Holy Spirit's office to come between us and Christ, to lead us to Christ, even as the Son of God comes between us and the Father, to lead us to the Father so that we have the whole Trinity uniting to save a sinner–the Triune God bowing down out of Heaven for the salvation of rebellious men! Every time we dismiss you from this House of Prayer, we pronounce upon you the blessing of the Sacred Trinity–"May the Grace of our Lord Jesus Christ, and the love of God, and the communion of the Holy Spirit be with you!" And you need all that to make a sinner into a saint and to keep a saint from going back to being a sinner again! The whole blessed Godhead–Father, Son and Holy Spirit–must work upon every soul that is to be saved!

See how Divinely they work together–how the Father glorifies the Son, how the Holy Spirit glorifies Jesus, how both the Holy Spirit and the Lord Jesus glorify the Father! These Three are One, sweetly uniting in the salvation of the chosen seed.

Tonight our work is to speak of the Holy Spirit. Oh, what a blessed Person He is! He is not merely a sacred influence, but a Divine Person–"very God of very God." He is the Spirit of holiness to be reverenced, to be spoken of with delight, yet with trembling, for, remember, there is a sin against the Holy Spirit. A word spoken against the Son of Man may be forgiven, but blasphemy against the Holy Spirit (whatever that may be, I know not) is put down as a sin beyond the line of Divine Forgiveness! Therefore reverence, honor and worship God the Holy Spirit, in whom lies the only hope that any of us can ever have of seeing Jesus and so of seeing God the Father!

First, tonight, I shall try to speak of what the Holy Spirit does. " Secondly I shall seek to set forth what the Holy Spirit aims at. "He will glorify Me, for He will take of what is Mine and declare it to you." And, thirdly, I shall explain how in both these things He acts as the Comforter, for we read in the seventh verse, our Savior say, "If I go not away, the Comforter will not come unto you," and it is of the Comforter that He says, "He will glorify Me, for He will take of what is Mine and declare it to you."

First we are to consider WHAT THE HOLY SPIRIT DOES. Jesus says, "He will receive of Mine and show it to you."

The Holy Spirit, then, deals with the things of Christ. How I wish that all Christ's ministers would imitate the HolySpirit in this respect! When you are dealing with the things of Christ, you are on Holy Spirit ground—you are following the track of the Holy Spirit. Does the Holy Spirit deal with science? What is science? Another name for the ignorance of men. Does the Holy Spirit deal with politics? What are politics? Another name for every man getting as much as he can out of the nation. Does the Holy Spirit deal with these things? No, my Brothers, "He will receive of Mine." O my Brother, the Holy Spirit will leave you if you go gadding about after these insignificant trifles! He will leave you if you aim at magnifying yourself, your wisdom and your plans, for the Holy Spirit is taken up with the things of Christ! "He will glorify Me, for He will take of what is Mine and declare it to you." I like what Mr. Wesley said to his preachers. "Leave other things alone," he said, "you are called to win souls." So I believe it is with all true preachers. We may leave other things alone. The Holy Spirit, who is our Teacher, will acknowledge and bless us if we keep to His line of things. O preacher of the Gospel, what can you receive like the things of Christ? And what can you talk of so precious to the souls of men as the things of Christ? Therefore follow the Holy Spirit in dealing with the things of Christ.

Next, the Holy Spirit deals with feeble men. "He will glorify Me, for He will take of what is Mine and declare it to you." "To you." He is not above dealing with simple minds. He comes to those who have no training, no education and He takes the things of Christ and shows them to such minds. The greatest mind of man that was ever created was a poor puny thing compared with the infinite mind of God! We may boast about the great capacity of the human intellect, but what a narrow and contracted thing it is at its utmost width! So, for the Holy Spirit to come and teach the little mind of man is a great condescension. But we see the great condescension of the Holy Spirit even more when we read, "Not many wise men after the flesh, not many mighty, not many noble are called." And when we hear the Savior say, "I thank You, O Father, Lord of Heaven and earth, because You have hid these things from the wise and prudent, and has revealed them unto babes." The Holy Spirit takes of the things of Christ and shows them to those who are babes compared with the wise men of this world! The Lord Jesus might have selected princes to be His Apostles. He might have gathered together 12 of the greatest kings of the earth, or at least 12 senators from Rome—but he did not—He took fishermen and men belonging to that class to be the pioneers of His Kingdom! And God the Holy Spirit takes of the things of Christ, high and sublime as they are, and shows them to men like these Apostles were—men ready to follow where the Lord led them and to learn what the Lord taught them.

If you think of the condescension of the Holy Spirit in taking of the things of Christ and showing them to us, you will not talk any more about coming down to the level of children when you talk to them. I remember a young man who was a great fool, but did not know it and, therefore, was all the greater fool. Once, speaking to children, he said, "My dear children, it takes a great deal to bring a great mind down to your capacities." You cannot show me a word of Christ of that kind! Where does the Holy Spirit ever talk about its being a great come-down for Him to teach children, or to teach us? No, no! He glorifies Christ by taking of His things and showing them to us, even such poor ignorant scholars as we are.

If I understand what is meant here, I think that it means, first, that the Holy Spirit helps us to understand the words of Christ. If we will study the teaching of the Savior, it must be with the Holy Spirit as the Light of God to guide us. He will show us what Christ meant by the words He uttered. We shall not lose ourselves in the Savior's verbiage, but we shall get at the inner meaning of Christ's mind and be instructed therein, for the Lord Jesus says, "He will receive of Mine and show it to you." A sermon of Christ—even a single word of Christ—set in the Light of the Holy Spirit shines like a diamond! No, like a fixed star, with light that is never dim! Happy men and happy women who read the words of Christ in the Light shed upon them by the Holy Spirit! But I do not think that this is all that the text means.

It means this—"Not only shall He reveal My words, but My things," for Christ says, "All things that the Father has are Mine: therefore said I that He shall take of Mine, and shall show it to you."

The Holy Spirit takes the Nature of Christ and shows it to us. It is easy to say, "I believe Him to be God and Man," but the point is to apprehend that He is God and, therefore, able to save and even to work impossibilities. And to believe that He is Man and, therefore, feels for you, sympathizes with you and, therefore, is a Brother born to help you in your adversities. May the Holy Spirit make you see the God-Man tonight! May He show you the Humanity and the Deity of Christ as they are most blessedly united in His adorable Person—and you will be greatly comforted thereby.

The Holy Spirit shows to us the offices of Christ. He is Prophet, Priest, King. Especially to you, Sinner, Christ is a Savior. Now, if you know that He takes up the work of saving sinners and that it is His business to save men, why then, dear Friend, surely you will have confidence in Him and not be afraid to come to Him! If I wanted my shoes mended, I would not take my hat off when I went into a cobbler's shop and say, "Please excuse me. May I beg you to be so good as to mend my shoes?" No, it is his trade! It is his business. He is glad to see me. "What do you need, Sir?" he asks and he is glad for the work. And when Christ puts over His door, "Savior," I, needing to be saved, go to Him, for I believe that He knows His calling and that He can carry it out and that He will be glad to see me—and that I shall not be more glad to be saved than He will be to save me! I want you to catch that idea. If the Holy Spirit will show you that, it will bring you very near to joy and peace this very night!

May the Holy Spirit also show you Christ's engagements! He has come into the world engaged to save sinners. He pledged Himself to the Father to bring many sons and daughters to Glory and He must do it. He has bound Himself to His Father, as the Surety of the Covenant, that He will bring sinners into reconciliation with God. May the Holy Spirit show that fact to you—and right gladly you will leap into the Savior's arms!

It is very sweet when the Holy Spirit shows us the love of Christ—how intensely He loves men! How He loved them of old, for His delights were with the sons of men—not because He had redeemed them, but He redeemed them because He loved them and delighted in them! Christ has had an eternal love to His people—

"His heart is made of tenderness,
His heart melts with love."

It is His Heaven to bring men to Heaven! It is His Glory to bring sons and daughters to Glory! He is never so happy as when He is receiving sinners. And if the Holy Spirit will show you the depth and the height, the length and the breadth of the love of Christ to sinners, it will go a long way towards bringing all who are in this house, tonight, to accept the Savior.

And when the Holy Spirit shows you the mercy of Christ—how willingly He forgives, how He passes by iniquity, transgression and sin—how He casts your sins into the sea, throws them behind God's back, puts them away forever–ah, when you see this, then your hearts will be won to Him!

Specially I would desire the Holy Spirit to show you the blood of Christ. A Spirit-taught view of the blood of Christ is the most wonderful sight that ever weeping eyes beheld! There is your sin, your wicked, horrible, damnable sin–but Christ comes into the world and takes the sin and suffers in your place! And the blood of such an One as He, perfect Man and Infinite God–such blood as was poured out on Calvary's tree–must take away sin! Oh, for a sight of it! If any of you are now despairing and the Holy Spirit will take of the blood of Christ and show it to you, despair will have no place in you any longer! It will be gone, for "the blood of Jesus Christ His Son cleanses us from all sin," and He that believes in Him is forgiven all His iniquities!

And if the Holy Spirit will also take of the prayers of Christ and show them to you, what a sight you will have! Christ on earth, praying till He gets into a bloody sweat! Christ in Heaven, praying with all His glorious vestments on, accepted by the Father, glorified at the Father's right hand and making intercession for transgressor–praying for you, praying for all who come to God by Him and able, therefore, to save them to the uttermost! This is the sight you will have! A knowledge of the intercession of Christ for guilty men is enough to make despair flee away once and for all! I can only tell you these things, but if the Holy Spirit will take of them and show them to you, oh, Beloved, you will have joy and peace tonight through believing!

One thing I must add, however, and then I will leave this point upon which we could dilate for six months. I want you to remember that whatever the Holy Spirit shows you, you may have. Do you see that? He takes of the things of Christ and shows them to us. But why? Not as a boy at school does to one of his companions when he is teasing him. I remember often seeing it done. He pulls out of his pocket a beautiful apple and shows it to his schoolmate. "There," he says, "do you see that apple?" Is he going to say, "Now I am going to give you a piece of it"? No, not he! He only shows him the apple to tantalize him. Now, it would be blasphemy to imagine that the Holy Spirit would show you the things of Christ and then say, "You cannot have them." No, whatever He shows you, you may have! Whatever you see in Christ, you may have! Whatever the Holy Spirit makes you to see in the Person and work of the Lord Jesus, you may have it! And He shows it to you on purpose that you may have it, for He is no Tantalus to mock us with the sight of a blessing beyond our reach. He waits to bless us. Lay that thought up in your heart–it may help you some day, if not now. You remember what God said to Jacob, "The land where you lie, to you will I give it." If you find any promise in this Book and you dare to lie down upon it, it is yours! If you can just lie down and rest on it, it is yours–for it was not put there for you to rest on it without its being fulfilled to you! Only stretch yourself on any Covenant blessing and it is yours forever. God help us to do so!

II. But now, secondly, and very briefly, let us consider WHAT THE HOLY SPIRIT AIMS AT. Well, He aims at this–Jesus says, "He shall glorify Me." When He shows us the things of Christ, His objective is to glorify Christ. The Holy Spirit's objective is to make Christ appear to be great and glorious to you and to me. The Lord Jesus Christ is infinitely glorious and even the Holy Spirit cannot make Him glorious except to our apprehension–but His desire is that we may see and know more of Christ–that we may honor Him more and glorify Him more.

Well, how does the Holy Spirit go about this work? In this simple way, by showing us the things of Christ. Is not this a blessedly simple fact that when even the Holy Spirit intends to glorify Christ, all that He does is to show us Christ? Well, but does He not put fine words together and weave a spell of eloquence? No. He simply shows us Christ. Now, if you wanted to praise Jesus Christ tonight, what would you have to do? Why, you would only have to speak of Him as He is–holy, blessed, glorious! You would show Him, as it were, in order to praise Him, for there is no glorifying Christ except by making Him to be seen. Then He has the Glory that rightly belongs to Him. No words are needed, no descriptions are needed. "He will glorify Me, for He will take of what is Mine and declare it to you.

And is it not strange that Christ should be glorified by His being shown to you? To you, my dear Friend! Perhaps you are saying, "I am a nobody." Yes, but Christ is glorified by being shown to you! "Oh, but I am very poor, very illiterate and besides, very wicked!" Yes, but Christ is glorified by being shown to you! Now a great king or a great queen would not be rendered much more illustrious by being shown to a little Sunday school girl, or exhibited to a crossing sweeper boy. At least they would not think so–but Christ does not act as an earthly monarch might. He reckons it to be His Glory for the poorest pair of eyes that ever wept to look by faith upon Him. He reckons it to be His greatest honor for the poorest man, the poorest woman, or the poorest child that ever lived to see Him in the Light in which the Holy Spirit sets Him! Is not this a blessed Truth of God?

I put it very simply and briefly. The Holy Spirit, you see, glorifies Christ by showing Him to sinners. Therefore, if you want to glorify Christ, do the same! Do not go and write a ponderous book and put fine words together. Tell sinners, in simple language, what Christ is. "I cannot praise Him," says one. You do not need to praise Him. Say what He is. If a man says to me, "Show me the sun," do I say, "Well, you must wait till I strike a match and light a candle—and then I will show you the sun"? That would be ridiculous, would it not? And for our candles to be held up to show Christ is absurd. Tell what He did for sinners. That is all. "He will glorify Me, for He will take of what is Mine and declare it to you."

I will not say more on this point except that if any of us are to glorify Christ, we must talk much of Him. We must tell what the Holy Spirit has told us and we must pray the Holy Spirit to bless to the minds of men the Truths of God we speak by enabling them to see Christ as the Spirit reveals Him.

III. But now, thirdly, in both of these things—showing to us the things of Christ and glorifying Christ—THE HOLY SPIRIT IS A COMFORTER. Gracious Spirit, be a Comforter now to some poor struggling ones in the Tabernacle by showing them the things of Christ and by glorifying Him in their salvation!

First, in showing to men the things of Christ, the Holy Spirit is a Comforter. There is no comfort like a sight of Christ. Sinner, your only comfort must lie in your Savior, in His precious blood and in His Resurrection from the dead. Look that way, man! If you look inside, you will never find any comfort there. Look where the Holy Spirit looks. "He will receive of Mine and show it to you." When a thing is shown to you, it is meant for you to look at it. If you want real comfort, I will tell you where to look, namely, to the Person and work of the Lord Jesus Christ. "Oh," you say, "but I am a wretched sinner!" I know you are. You are a great deal worse than you think you are. "Oh, but I think myself the worst that ever lived." No, you are worse than that! You do not know half your depravity. You are worse than you ever dreamed you were! But that is not where to look for comfort. "I am brutish," one says. "I am proud. I am self-righteous. I am envious. I have everything in me that is bad, Sir, and if I have a little bit that is good, sometimes, it is gone before I can see it. I am just lost, ruined and undone!" That is quite true—but I never told you to look there. Your comfort lies in this, "He will receive of Mine"–that is, of Christ's–"and shall show it to you." Your hope of transformation, of gaining a new character altogether, of eternal life, lies in Christ who quickens the dead and makes all things new! Look away from self and look to Christ, for He alone can save you!

A sight of Christ is the destruction of despair. "Oh, but the devil tells me that I shall be cast into Hell! There is no hope for me." What does it matter what the devil tells you? He was a liar from the beginning. Let him say what he likes, but if you will look away to Christ, that will be the end of the devil's power over you! If the Holy Spirit shows you what Christ came to do on the Cross and what He is doing on His throne in Heaven, that will be the end of these troublous thoughts from Satan and you will be comforted.

Dear child of God, are you in sorrow tonight? May the Holy Spirit take of the things of Christ and show them to you! That is the end to sorrow when you see Jesus, for sorrow, itself, is so sweetly sanctified by the companionship of Christ which it brings you that you will be glad to drink of His cup and to be baptized with His Baptism!

Are you in need tonight, without even a place to lay your head? So, too, was He! "The Son of Man has not where to lay His head." Go to Him with your troubles. He will help you to bear your poverty. He will help you to get out of it for He is able to help you in temporal trials as well as in spiritual ones. Therefore go to Christ! All power is given unto Him in Heaven and in earth. Nothing is too hard for the Lord. Go your way to Him–and a sight of Him will give you comfort.

Are you persecuted? Well, a sight of the thorn-crowned brow will take the thorn out of persecution. Are you very,very low? I think that you have all heard the story I am about to tell you, but some of you have, perhaps, forgotten it. Many years ago when this great congregation first met in the Surrey Music Hall and the terrible tragedy occurred–when many persons were either killed or wounded in the panic–I did my best to hold the people together till I heard that some were dead. And then I broke down like a man stunned and for a fortnight or so I had little reason left. I felt so broken in heart that I thought that I would never be able to face a congregation again. And I went down to a friend's house, a few miles away, to be very quiet and still. I was walking round his garden and I well remember the spot and even the time when this passage came to me, "Him has God exalted with His right hand to be a Prince and a Savior." And this thought came into my mind at once, "You are only a soldier in the great King's army and you may die in a ditch. But it does not matter what becomes of you as long as your King is exalted. He—HE is glorious! God has highly exalted Him."You have heard of the old French soldiers when they lay dying. If the emperor came by when they were ready to expire, they would raise themselves up and give one more cheer for their beloved leader. " Viva l'Empereur!" would be their dying words. And so I thought, "He is exalted. What does it matters about me?"

And in a moment my reason was perfectly restored! I was as clear as possible. I went into the house, had family prayer and came back to preach to my congregation on the following Sabbath—restored only by having looked to Jesus and having seen that He was glorious! If He is to the front, what does it matter what happens to us? Rank on rank we will die in the battle if He wins the victory! Only let the Man on the White Horse win—Let the King who died for us and washed us in His precious blood be glorified—and it is enough for us!

But now, lastly, when Christ is glorified in the heart, He acts as a Comforter, too. I believe, Brothers and Sisters,that we would not have half the trouble that we have if we thought more of Christ. The fact is that we think so much of ourselves that we get troubled. But someone says, "But I have so many troubles." Why should you not have a great many troubles? Who are you that you should not have troubles? "Oh, but I have had loss after loss which you do not know of!" Very likely, dear Friend, I do not know of your losses, but is it any wonder that you should have them? "Oh," says one, "I seem to be kicked about like a football." Why should you not be? What are you? "Oh," said one poor penitent to me the other night, "for me to come to Christ, Sir, after my past life, seems so mean." I said, "Yes, so it is. But then, you are mean. It was a mean business of the prodigal son to come home and eat his father's bread and the fatted calf after he had spent his substance in riotous living." It was a mean thing, was it not? But then, the father did not think it mean! He clasped him to his bosom and welcomed him home. Come along, you mean sinners, you that have served the devil and now want to run away from him! Steal away from Satan at once, for my Lord is ready to receive you! You have no idea how willing He is to welcome you! He is so ready to forgive that you have not yet guessed how much sin He can forgive! "All manner of sin and blasphemy shall be forgiven unto men." Up to your necks in filth, in your very hearts saturated with the foulest iniquity—yet, if you come to Christ He will wash you whiter than snow! "Come now, and let us reason together, says the Lord: though your sins are as scarlet, they shall be as white as snow; though they are red like crimson, they shall be as wool." Come along and try my Lord!

Have exalted ideas of Christ! Oh, if a man will but have great thoughts of Christ, he shall then find his troubles lessening and his sins disappearing! I see you have been putting Christ on a wrong scale altogether! Perhaps even you people of God have not thought of Christ as you ought to do. I have heard of a certain commander who had led his troops into a rather difficult position. He knew what he was doing, but the soldiers did not all know—and there would be a battle in the morning. So he thought that he would go round from tent to tent and listen to what the soldiers said. He listened and there was one of them saying to his fellows, "See what a mess we are in now! Do you see, we have only so many cavalry, and so many infantry, and we have only a small quantity of artillery. And on the other side there are so many thousands against us! So strong, so mighty, that we shall be cut to pieces in the morning." And the general drew aside the canvas, and there they saw him standing and he said, "How many do you count me for?" He had won every battle that he had ever engaged in! He was the conqueror of conquerors. "How many do you count me for?"

O Souls, you have never counted Christ for what He is! You have put down your sins, but you have never counted what kind of a Christ He is who has come to save you! Rather do like Luther, who said that when the devil came to him, he brought him a long sheet containing a list of his sins, or of a great number of them and Luther said to him, "Is that all?" "No," said the devil. "Well go and fetch some more, then." Away went Satan to bring him another long list, as long as your arm. Said Luther, "Is that all?" "Oh, no," said the devil, "I have yet more." "Well go and bring them all," said Luther. "Fetch them all out, the whole list of them." Then it was a very long black list. I think that I have heard that it would have gone round the world twice. I know that mine would. Well, what did Luther say when he saw them all? He said, "Write at the bottom of them, 'The blood of Jesus Christ, His Son, cleanses us from all sin!'" It does not matter how long the list is when you write those blessed words at the end of it! Then the sins are all gone!

Did you ever take up from your table a bill for a large sum? You felt a kind of flush coming over your face. You looked down the list. It was a rather long list of items, perhaps from a lawyer or a builder. But when you looked at it, you saw that there was a penny stamp at the bottom and that the account was receipted. "Oh," you said, "I do not care how long it is, for it is all paid." So, though your sins are many, if you have a receipt at the bottom–if you have trusted Jesus–your sins are all gone, drowned in the Red Sea of your Savior's blood and Christ is glorified in Your salvation! May God the Holy Spirit bring every unsaved one here tonight to repentance and faith in our Lord Jesus Christ. The Lord bless every one of you, for His name's sake! Amen.

THE TEACHING OF THE HOLY SPIRIT

"But the Comforter, which is the Holy Spirit, whom the Father will send in My name, He shall teach you all things and bring all things to your remembrance, whatever I have said unto you."
John 14:26

A Sermon Delivered On Sunday Morning: 13 May 1860

THERE are many choice gifts comprehended in the Covenant of Grace, but the first and richest of them are these two–the gift of Jesus Christ for us and the gift of the Holy Spirit to us. The first of these I trust we are not likely to undervalue. We delight to hear of that "unspeakable gift"–the Son of God, who bare our sins and carried our sorrows and endured our punishment in His own body on the tree. There is something so tangible in the Cross, the nails, the vinegar, the spear, that we are not able to forget the Master, especially when so often we enjoy the delightful privilege of assembling round His table and breaking bread in remembrance of Him.

But the second great gift, by no means inferior to the first–the gift of the Holy Spirit to us–is so spiritual and we are so carnal–is so mysterious and we are so material–that we are very apt to forget its value, yes and even to forget the gift altogether. And yet, my Brethren, let us ever remember that Christ on the Cross is of no value to us apart from the Holy Spirit in us. In vain that blood is flowing, unless the finger of the Spirit applies the blood to our conscience. In vain is that garment of righteousness worked out, a garment without seam, woven from the top throughout–unless the Holy Spirit wraps it around us and arrays us in its costly folds.

The river of the water of life cannot quench our thirst till the Spirit presents the goblet and lifts it to our lip. All the things that are in the Paradise of God itself could never be blissful to us so long as we are dead Souls–and dead souls we are until that heavenly wind comes from the four corners of the earth and breathes upon us slain, that we may live. We do not hesitate to say that we owe as much to God the Holy Spirit as we do to God the Son. Indeed, it were a high sin and misdemeanour to attempt to put one Person of the Divine Trinity before another. You, O Father, are the source of all grace, all love and mercy towards us. You, O Son, are the channel of Your Father's mercy and without You Your Father's love could never flow to us. And you, O Spirit–You are He who enables us to receive that Divine virtue which flows from the Fountainhead, the Father, through Christ the Channel–and by Your means enters into our spirit and there abides and brings forth its glorious fruit. Magnify, then, the Spirit, you who are partakers of it–praise, laud and love His name always, for it is seemly to do so.

My work this morning is to set forth the work of the Holy Spirit, not as a Comforter, or as a Quickener, or as a Sanctifier, but principally as a Teacher, although we shall have to touch upon these other points in passing.

The Holy Spirit is the great Teacher of the Father's children. The Father begets us by His own will through the Word of Truth. Jesus Christ takes us into union with Himself, so that we become in a second sense the children of God. Then God the Holy Spirit breathes into us the "spirit of adoption, whereby we cry, Abba, Father." Having given us that spirit of adoption, He trains us, becomes our great Educator, cleanses away our ignorance and reveals one Truth of God after another–until at last we comprehend with all saints what are the heights and depths and lengths and breadths–and know the love of Christ which passes knowledge. And then the Spirit introduces the educated ones to the general assembly and Church of the firstborn whose names are written in Heaven.

Concerning this Teacher, these three things–first, what He teaches. Secondly, His methods of teaching. And thirdly, the nature and characteristics of that teaching.

First, then, WHAT THE HOLY SPIRIT TEACHES US. And here, indeed, we have a wide field spread before us, for He teaches to God's people all they do that is acceptable to the Father and all they know that is profitable to themselves.
I say that He teaches them all that they do. Now, there are some things which you and I can do naturally, when we are but children without any teaching. Who ever taught a child to cry? It is natural to it. The first sign of its life is its shrill feeble cry of pain. Ever afterwards you need never send it to school to teach it to utter the cry of its grief, the well known expression of its little sorrows. Ah, my Brethren, but you and I as spiritual infants, had to be taught to cry. For we could not even cry of ourselves, till we had received "the spirit of adoption, whereby we cry, Abba, Father." There are cries and groans which

cannot be uttered in words and speech–simple as this language of the new nature seems to be.

But even these feeblest groans, sighing, cries, and tears are marks of education. We must be taught to do this, or else we are not sufficient to do even these little things in and of ourselves. Children, as we know, have to be taught to speak and it is by degrees that they are able to pronounce first the shorter and afterwards the longer words. We, too, are taught to speak. We have none of us learned, as yet, the whole vocabulary of Canaan. I trust we are able to say some of the words. But we shall never be able to pronounce them all till we come into that land where we shall see Christ and "shall be like He; for we shall see Him as He is."

The sayings of the saints, when they are good and true, are the teachings of the Spirit. Marked you not that passage–"No man can say that Jesus is the Christ but by the Holy Spirit"? He may say as much in dead words, but the Spirit's saying, the saying of the soul, he can never attain to, except as he is taught by the Holy Spirit. Those first words which we ever used as Christians– "God be merciful to me, a sinner," were taught us by the Holy Spirit. And that song which we shall sing before the Throne–"Unto Him that loved us and washed us from our sins in His own blood, to Him be glory and dominion forever and ever," shall but be the ripe fruit of that same tree of knowledge of good and evil which the Holy Spirit has planted in the soil of our hearts.

Further, as we are taught to cry and taught to speak by the Holy Spirit, so are all God's people taught to walk and act by Him. "It is not in man that walks to direct his steps." We may take the best heed to our life, but we shall stumble or go astray unless He who first set us in the path shall guide us in it. "I taught Ephraim also to go, taking them by their arms." "He makes me to lie down in green pastures: He leads me beside the still waters." To stray is natural. To keep the path of right is spiritual. To err is human. To be holy is Divine. To fall is the natural effect of evil. But to stand is the glorious effect of the Holy Spirit working in us, both to will and to do of his own good pleasure.

There was never yet a heavenly thought, never yet a hallowed deed, never yet a consecrated act acceptable to God by Jesus Christ, which was not worked in us by the Holy Spirit. You have worked all our works in us. "For we are his workmanship, created in Christ Jesus unto good works, which God has before ordained that we should walk in them."

Now as it is with the simple deeds of the Christian, his crying, his speaking, his walking, his acting—all these are teachings of the Holy Spirit—so is it with the higher efforts of his nature. The preaching of the Gospel, when it is done right, is only accomplished through the power of the Holy Spirit. That sermon which is based upon human genius is worthless. That sermon which has been obtained through human knowledge and which has no other force in it than the force of logic or of oratory, is spent in vain. God works not by such tools as these. He cleans not spirits by the water from broken cisterns—neither does he save souls by thoughts which come from men's brains, apart from the Divine influence which goes with them.

We might have all the learning of the sages of Greece, no, better still, all the knowledge of the twelve Apostles put together—and then we might have the tongue of a seraph and the eyes and heart of a Savior—but apart from the Spirit of the living God, our preaching would yet be vain and our hearers and ourselves would still abide in our sins. To preach rightly can only be accomplished by the Holy Spirit. There may be a thing called preaching that is of human energy, but God's ministers are taught of the Holy One. And when their word is blessed, either to saint or sinner, the blessing comes not of them, but of the Holy Spirit and unto Him be all the glory, for it is not you that speak, but the Spirit of your Father which speaks in you.

So is it with sacred song. Whose are the wings with which I mount towards the skies in sacred harmony and joy? They are Your wings, O Holy Dove! Whose is the fire with which my spirit flames at times of hallowed consecration? Yours is the flame, O fiery Spirit! Yours. Whose is the tongue of fire which rested on the apostolic lips? Yours was that cleft tongue, You, Holy One of Israel! Whose is that dew which falls upon the withered blade and makes it smile and fire? Yours are those holy drops, You Dew of God. You are that womb of the morning from where these beauties of holiness proceed. You have worked an in us and unto You would we give well-deserved thanks. So, then, all the doings of the Christian, both the little and the major doings, are all the teachings of the Holy Spirit.

But now, farther—all that the Believer truly knows which is profitable to himself is taught him by the Holy Spirit. We may learn very much from the Word of God morally and mentally, but the Christian philosopher understands that there is a distinction between soul and spirit. He knows that the mere natural soul or intellect of man may instruct itself well enough out of the Word of God, but that spiritual things are only to be spiritually discerned. He knows that until that third, higher principle–the spirit–is infused into us in regeneration, we have not even the capability or the possibility of knowing spiritual things.

Now it is this third, higher principle, of which the Apostle speaks when he speaks of "body, soul and spirit." Mental philosophers declare there is no such thing as the third part–the spirit. They can find a body and a soul, but no spirit. They are quite right–there is no such thing in natural men. That third principle– the spirit–is an infusion of the Holy Spirit at regeneration and is not to be detected by mental philosophy. It is altogether a subtler thing–a thing too rare, too heavenly to be described by Dugald, Stewart, or Reid, or Brown or any of those mighty men who could dissect the mind, but who could not understand the spirit.

Now, the Spirit of God first gives us a spirit and then afterwards educates that spirit. All that our spirit knows is taught it by the Holy Spirit. Perhaps the first thing that we learn of is sin–He reproves us of sin. No man knows the exceeding sinfulness of sin but by the Holy Spirit. You may punish a man, you may tell him of the wrath of God and of sin–but you cannot make him know what an evil and a bitter thing sin is till the Holy Spirit has taught it to him.

'Tis an awful lesson, indeed, to learn–and when the Holy Spirit makes us sit down upon the stool of penitence and begins to drill this great Truth of God into us–that sin is damnation in the bud–that it is Hell in the germ–it is then when we begin to perceive it. Then we cry out, "Now I know how vile I am, my soul abhors itself in dust and ashes!" No man, I repeat it, will ever know the sinfulness of sin by argument, by punishment, by moral discipline, or by any means apart from the education of the Holy Spirit. It is a truth beyond the reach of human intellect to know how base a thing sin is. The spirit alone, engrafted and given by the Holy Spirit–that spirit alone can learn the lesson and only the Holy Spirit can teach it.

The next lesson the Spirit teaches us is the total ruin, depravity and helplessness of self. Men pretend to know this by nature, but they do not know it. They can only speak the words of experience as parrots speak like men. But to know myself utterly lost and ruined, to know myself so lost, "that in me (that is, in my flesh,) dwells no good thing," is a knowledge so distasteful, so hateful, so abominable to the carnal intellect, that man would not learn it if he

140

could. If he has learnt it, it is a clear proof that God the Holy Spirit has made him willing to see the Truth of God and willing to receive it.

We sometimes hear great preachers telling us that there is something grand left in man yet. They say that when Adam fell he might have broken his little finger, but did not ruin himself entirely–that man is a grand being–in fact a noble creature and that we are all wrong in telling men they are depraved and thundering out the Law of God at them–am I astonished that they should speak thus? No, my Brethren, it is the language of the carnal mind the whole world over and in every age. No wonder that a man is eloquent upon this point–every man needs to be eloquent when he has to defend a lie.

No wonder that glorious sentences have been uttered and flowery periods poured forth from a cornucopia of eloquence upon this subject. A man need exhaust all logic and all rhetoric to defend a falsehood–and it is no wonder that he seeks to do it, for man believes himself to be rich and increased in goods and to have need of nothing–till the Holy Spirit teaches him that he is naked and poor and miserable.

These lessons being learned, the Spirit proceeds to teach us further of the nature and character of God. God is to be heard in every wind and seen in every cloud. God's goodness and God's Omnipotence, the world clearly manifests to us in the works of creation, but where do I read of His grace, where do I read of His mercy, or of His justice? There are lines which I cannot read in creation. Those must have ears, indeed, who can hear the notes of mercy or of grace whispering in the evening gale.

No, Brethren, these parts of God's attributes are only revealed to us in this precious Book and there they are so revealed that we cannot know them until the Spirit opens our eyes to perceive them. Only He can enable us to understand the inflexibility of Divine justice and to see how God exacts punishment for every jot and tittle of sin. Only the Holy Spirit can enable us to know that that full justice does not eclipse His equally full mercy–but that the two move around each other, without for a single instant coming into contact, or conflict, or casting the slightest shadow one or the other. To see how God is just and yet the Justifier of the ungodly and so to know God that my spirit loves His nature, appreciates His attributes and desires to be like He–this is a knowledge which astronomy cannot teach–which all the researches of the sciences can never give to us.

We must be taught of God, if we ever learn of Him—we must be taught of God, by God the Holy Spirit. Oh, that we may learn this lesson well, that we may be able to sing of His faithfulness, of His covenant love, of His immutability, of His boundless mercy, of His inflexible justice. Oh, that we may be able to talk to one another concerning that incomprehensible One and may see Him even as a man sees His friend—and may come to walk with Him as Enoch did all the days of our life! This, indeed, must be an education given to us by the Holy Spirit.

But not to tarry on these points, though they are prolific of thought, let us observe that the Holy Spirit specially teaches us of Jesus Christ. It is the Holy Spirit who manifests the Savior to us in the glory of His Person—the complex Character of His Manhood and of His Deity. It is He who tells us of the love of His heart, of the power of His arms, of the clearness of His eyes, the preciousness of His blood and of the prevalence of His plea. To know that Christ is my Redeemer is to know more than Plato could have taught me. To know that I am a member of His body, of His flesh and of His bones—that my name is on His breast and engraved on the palms of his hands—is to know more than the Universities of Oxford or Cambridge could teach to all their scholars, learn they ever so well.

Not at the feet of Gamaliel did Paul learn to say, "He loved me and gave Himself for me." Not in the midst of the Rabbis, or at the feet of the members of the Sanhedrim, did Paul learn to cry—"Those things which I counted gain, I now count loss for Christ's sake." "God forbid that I should glory save in the Cross of our Lord Jesus Christ." No, this must have been taught as He Himself confesses—"not of flesh and blood, but of the Holy Spirit."

I need only hint that it is also the Spirit who teaches us our adoption. Indeed, all the privileges of the new covenant, beginning from regeneration, running through redemption, justification pardon, sanctification, adoption, preservation, continual safety, even unto an abundant entrance into the kingdom of our Lord and Savior Jesus Christ—all is the teaching of the Holy Spirit. Especially that last point, for "eye has not seen, nor ear heard, neither have entered into the heart of man, the things which God has prepared for them that love Him. But God has revealed them unto us by His Spirit, for the Spirit searches all things, yes, the deep things of God." He leads us into the truth of joys to come, carries our spirit upwards and gives us—

"That inward calm within the breast,
The surest pledge of glorious rest,
Which for the Church of God remains,
The end of cares, the end of pains."

II. And now I come to the second point, which is this–THE METHODS BY WHICH THE HOLY SPIRIT TEACHES GOD'S CHILDREN THESE PRECIOUS THINGS.

Here we must remark that we know nothing of the precise way of operation because the Spirit is mysterious. We know not from where He comes nor where He goes. But still let us describe what we can perceive. And first, in teaching God's people, one of the first things the Spirit does is to excite interest in their minds. I frequently find that when men are being educated for the ministry, the hardest thing is to set them going.

They are like bats on the ground. If once a bat gets on the earth he cannot fly until he creeps to the top of a stone and gets a little above the earth and then he gets wing and can fly well enough. So there are many who have not got their energies aroused–they have talent but it is asleep–and we want a kind of railway whistle to blow in their ears to make them start up and rub away the film from their eyes so that they may see.

Now it is just so with men–when the Spirit of God begins to teach them, He excites their interest in the things which He wishes them to learn. He shows them that these things here a personal bearing upon their soul's present and eternal welfare. He so brings precious Truths of God home, that what the man thought was utterly indifferent yesterday, he now begins to esteem inestimably precious "Oh," says he, "theology! Of what use can it be to me?" But now the knowledge of Christ and Him crucified has become to him the most desirable and excellent of all the sciences. The Holy

That done, He gives to the man a teachable spirit. There be men who will not learn. They profess that they want to know, but you never found the right way of teaching them. Teach them little by little and they say–"Do you think I am a child?" Tell them a great deal at once and they say–"You have not the power to make me comprehend!" I have been compelled sometimes to say to a man, when I have been trying to make him understand and he has said "I cannot understand you," "Well, Sir, I am thankful it is not my duty to give you an understanding if you have none."

Now, the Holy Spirit makes a man willing to learn in any shape. The disciple sits down at the feet of Christ. And let Christ speak as He may and teach Him as He will, whether with the rod, or with a smile, he is quite willing to learn. Distasteful the lessons are, but the regenerated pupil loves to learn best the very things he once hated. Cutting to his pride the doctrines of the Gospel, each one of them may be—but for this very reason he loves them. He cries, "Lord, humble me. Lord, bring me down. Teach me those things that will make me cover my head with dust and ashes. Show me my nothingness—teach me my emptiness. Reveal to me my filthiness." the Holy Spirit thus proceeds with His work awaking interest and enkindling a teachable spirit.

This done, the Holy Spirit in the next place puts the Truth of God in a dear light. How hard it is, sometimes, to state a fact which you perfectly understand yourself, in such a way that another man may see it. It is like the telescope. There are many persons who are disappointed with a telescope, because whenever they walk into an observatory and put their eye to the glass, expecting to see the rings of Saturn and the belts of Jupiter, they have said, "I can see nothing at all. A piece of glass and a grain or two of dust is all I can see!"

"But," says the astronomer, when he comes, "I can see Saturn in all her glory." Why cannot you? Because the focus does not suit the stranger's eye. By a little skill, the focus can be altered so that the observer may be able to see what he could not see before. So is it with language. It is a sort of telescope by which I enable another to see my thoughts, but I cannot always give him the right focus. Now the Holy Spirit always gives the right focus to every Truth of God. He sheds a light so strong and forcible upon the Word, that the spirit says. "Now I see it, now I understand it."

Even here, in this precious Book, there are words which I have looked at a hundred times, but I could not understand them, till at some favored hour, the key-word seemed as if it leaped up from the midst of the verse and said to me, "Look at the verse in my light," and at once I perceived—not always from a word in the verse itself, but sometimes in the context—I perceived the meaning which I could not see before. This, too, is a part of the Spirit's training—to shed a light upon the Truths of God.

144

But the Spirit not only enlightens the Truth of God, but He enlightens the understanding. 'Tis marvelous, too, how the Holy Spirit does teach men who seemed as if they never could learn. I would not wish to say anything which my brother might be grieved at. But I do know some Brethren, I won't say they are here today, but they are not out of the place–some Brethren whose opinion I would not take in anything worldly on any account. If it were anything to do with pounds, shillings and pence–anything where human judgment was concerned–I should not consult them. But those men have a deeper, truer and more experimental knowledge of the Word of God than many who preach it, because the Holy Spirit never tried to teach them grammar and never meant to teach them business. He never wanted to teach them astronomy. But He has taught them the Word of God and they understand it.

Other teachers have labored to beat the elements of science into them but without success, for they are as thick and addled in they brains as they can be. But the Holy Spirit has taught them the Word of God and they are clear enough there. I come in close contact with some young men. When we are taking our lessens for illustration out of the sciences, they seem to be all profound. But when I ask them a question to see if they have understood, they are lost. But, mark you, when we come to read a chapter out of some old Puritan book–come to theology–those Brethren give me the smartest and sharpest answers of the whole class.

When we once come to deal with things experimental and controversial, I find those men are able to double up their opponents and vanquish them at once, because they are deeply read in the Word of God. The Spirit has taught them the things of Christ, but He has not taught them anything else. I have perceived, also, that when the Spirit of God has enlarged the understanding to receive Bible truths, that understanding becomes more capable of receiving other truths.

I heard, some time ago, from a brother minister, when we were comparing notes, the story of a man who had been the dullest creature that was known. He was not more than one grade above an idiot, but when he was converted to God, one of the first things he wanted to do was to read the Bible. They had a long, long trek to teach him a verse, but he would learn it, he would master it. He stuck at it as hard as ever he could, till he was able to read, "In the beginning was the Word and the Word was with God and the Word was God."

That man was by-and-by asked to engage in prayer. At first he hardly put a sentence together. By-and-by he arrived at a considerable degree of fluency, because he would do it. He would not stand still, he said, in the Prayer Meeting and not have a word to say for his Master.

He began to read his Bible much and to pray with a great deal of profit and acceptableness to those that heard and after awhile, he actually began to speak in the villages and became sometime after an honored and acceptable pastor of one of our Baptist Churches. Had it not been for the Spirit of God first expanding the understanding to receive religious truth, that understanding might have been cramped and fettered and fast bolted to this very day. And the man might have been ever after an idiot and so have gone down to his grave—while now he stands up to tell to sinners round, in burning language, the story of the Cross of Christ. The Spirit teaches us by enlightening the understanding.

Lest I weary you, let me hurry on through the other points. He teaches us also by refreshing the memory. "He shall bring all things to your remembrance." He puts all those old treasures into the ark of our soul and when the time comes, He opens it and brings out these precious things in right good order and shows them to us again and again. He refreshes the memory and when this is done, He does better—He teaches us the Word, by making us feel its effect and that, after all, is the best way of learning. You may try to teach a child the meaning of the term "sweetness." But words will not avail. Give him some honey and he will never forget it.

You might seek to tell him of the glorious mountains and the Alps that pierce the clouds and send their peaks, like white-robed ambassadors up to the courts of Heaven. Take him there, let him see them and he will never forget them. You might seek to paint to him the grandeur of the American continent, with its hills and lakes and rivers, such as the world has never seen—let him go and view it and he will know more of the land than he could know by all your teaching, when he sits at home.

So the Holy Spirit does not only tell us of Christ's love—He sheds it abroad in the heart. He does not merely tell us of the sweetness of pardon—He gives us a sense of no condemnation and then we know all about it—better than we could have done by any teaching of words and thoughts. He takes us into the banqueting house and waves the banner of love over us. He bids us visit the garden of love and makes us lie among the lilies. He gives us that bundle of camphor, even our Beloved, and bids us place it all night betwixt our breasts. He takes us to the Cross of Christ and He bids us put our finger into the print of the nails and our hands into His side and tells us not to come "faithless, but believing," and so in the highest and most effectual manner He teaches us to profit.

III. But now I shall come to my third point. Although I feel as if I wished my subject were somewhat less comprehensive, but indeed it is a fault which does not often happen–to have too much rather than too little to speak of. But when we come upon a topic where God is to be glorified, then here, indeed, our tongue must be like the pen of a ready writer, as we speak of the things that we have made touching the King.

I am now to speak to you about the CHARACTERISTICS AND NATURE OF THE HOLY SPIRIT'S TEACHING. And first I would remark that the Holy Spirit teaches sovereignly. He teaches whom He pleases. He takes the fool and makes him know the wonders of the dying love of Christ, to bring aspiring wisdom low and make the pride of man humble and abase itself. And as the Spirit teaches whom He wills, He has His own hours of instruction and He will not be limited and bound by us.

And then again He teaches as He wills–some by affliction, some by communion. Some He teaches by the Word read, some by the Word spoken, some by neither, but directly by His own agency. And so also the Holy Spirit is a Sovereign in that He teaches in whatever degree He pleases. He will make one man learn much, while another comprehends but little. Some Christians wear their beards early–they come to a rapid and high degree of maturity and that on a sudden. Others creep but slowly to the goal and are very long in reaching it. Some Christians in early years understand more than others whose hairs have turned gray.

The Holy Spirit is a Sovereign. He doe not have all His pupils in one class and teach them all the same lesson by simultaneous instruction. But each man is in a separate class, each man learning a separate lesson. Some beginning at the end of the book, some at the beginning and some in the middle–some learning one doctrine and some another, some going backwards and some forwards. The Holy Spirit teaches sovereignly and gives to every man according as He wills. But then, wherever He teaches, He teaches effectually.

He never failed to make us learn yet. No scholar was ever turned out of the Spirit's school incorrigible. He teaches all His children, not some of them–"All your children shall be taught of the Lord and great shall be the peace of your children"–the last sentence being a proof that they have been effectually taught. Never once did the Spirit bring home the Truth of God to the heart and yet that heart fail to receive it. He has modes of touching the secret springs of life and putting the Truth of God into the very core of the being. He casts His healing mixtures into the fountain itself–not into the streams.

We instruct the ear and the ear is far removed from the heart. He teaches the heart itself and therefore his every word falls upon good soil and brings forth good and abundant fruit–he teaches effectually. Dear Brothers and Sisters, do you feel yourself to be a great fool sometimes? Your great Schoolmaster will make a good scholar of you yet. He will so teach you that you shall be able to enter the kingdom of Heaven knowing as much as the brightest saints. Teaching thus sovereignly and effectually, I may add, He teaches infallibly. We teach you errors through want of caution, sometimes through over zeal and again through the weakness of our own mind.

In the greatest preacher or teacher that ever lived there was some degree of error and hence our hearers should always bring what we say to the Law and the Testimony. But the Holy Spirit never teaches error–if you have learned anything by the Spirit of God, it is pure–unadulterated, undiluted Truth of God. Put yourself daily under His teaching and you shall never learn a word amiss, nor a thought awry, but become infallibly taught–well taught in the whole Truth of God as it is in Jesus.

Further, where the Spirit thus teaches infallibly He teaches continually. Whom once He teaches, He never leaves till He has completed our education. On and on and on, however dull the scholar, however frail the memory, however corrupt the mind, He still continues with His gracious work, till He has trained us up and made us "meet to be partakers of the inheritance of the saints in light."

Nor does He leave us till He has taught us completely. For as our text says, "He shall teach you all things." There is not a Truth of God so high that it shall not yet be mastered, nor a doctrine so hard that it shall not yet be received. High up, high up, tower the heights of the hill of knowledge–but there, when there–your feet shall stand. Weary may be the way and weak your knees, but up there you shall climb and one day with your forehead bathed in the sunlight of Heaven–your soul shall stand and look down on tempests, mists and all earth's clouds and smoke–and see the Master face to face and be like He and know Him as He is. This is the joy of the Christian, that he shall be completely taught and that the Holy Spirit will never give him up till He has taught him all truth.

I fear, however, that this morning I weary you. Such a theme as this will not be likely to be suitable to all minds. As I have already said, the spiritual mind alone receives spiritual things and the doctrine of the Spirit's agency will never be very interesting to those who are entire strangers to it. I could not make another man understand the force of an electric shock unless he has felt it. It would not be likely at all that he would believe in those secret energies which move the world, unless he had some means of testing for himself.

And those of you that never felt the Spirit's energy are as much strangers to it as a stone would be. You are out of your element when you hear of the Spirit. You know nothing of His Divine power. You have never been taught of Him and therefore how you should be careful to know what truths He teaches!

I close, therefore, with this sorrowful reflection. Alas, alas, a thousand times alas, that there should be so many who know not their danger, who feel not their load and in whose heart the light of the Holy Spirit has never shone! Is it your case, my dear Hearer, this morning? I do not ask you whether you have ever been educated in the school of learning. That you may be and you may have taken your degree and been first in honors–but you may still be as the wild ass's colt that knows nothing about these things.

Religion and the truth of it is not to be learnt by the head. Years of reading, hours of assiduous study, will never make a man a Christian. "It is the Spirit that quickens. The flesh profits nothing." Oh, are you destitute of the Spirit of the living God? For oh, I charge you to remember this, my Hearer–if in your soul mysterious and supernatural influences of the Holy Spirit have never been shed abroad, you are an utter stranger to all the things of God. The promises are not yours. Heaven is not yours. You are on your road to the land of the dead, to the region of the corpse–where their worm dies not and their fire is not quenched. Oh that the Spirit of God may rest upon you now!

Remember, you are absolutely dependent upon His influence. You are in God's hand today to be saved or to be lost—not in your own hands, but in His. You are dead in sins. Unless He quickens you, you must remain so. The moth beneath your finger is not more absolutely at your mercy than you are now at the mercy of God. Let Him but will to leave you as you are and you are lost. But oh, if mercy speaks and says, "Let that man live," you are saved. I would that you could feel the weight of this tremendous doctrine of sovereignty. It is like the hammer of Thor, it may shake your heart however stout it is and make your rocky soul tremble to its base—

"Life, death and Hell and worlds unknown,
Hang on His firm decree."

Your destiny hangs there now. And will you rebel against the God in whose hand your soul's eternal fate now rests? Will you lift the puny hand of your rebellion against Him who alone can quicken you—without whose gracious energy you are dead and must be destroyed? Will you go this day and sin against light and against knowledge? Will you go today and reject mercy which is proclaimed to you in Christ Jesus? If so, no fool was ever so mad as you are, to reject Him without whom you are dead and lost and ruined. O that instead thereof there may be the sweet whisper of the Spirit saying, "Obey the Divine command, believe on Christ and live!"

Hear the voice of Jehovah, who cries, "This is the commandment, that you believe in Jesus Christ whom he has sent!" Thus obedient, God says within Himself, "I have set My love upon him, therefore will I deliver him. I will set him on high because he has known My name." And you shall yet live to sing in Heaven of that sovereignty which, when your soul trembled in the balances, decided for your salvation and gave you light and joy unspeakable. Jesus Christ, the Son of God, died on Calvary's Cross, "and whoever believes on Him shall be saved."

"Unto you therefore which believe He is precious—but unto them which are disobedient the stone which the builders disallowed, the same is made the head of the corner and a stone of stumbling and a rock of offense." Believe that record true! Cast down your weapons. Yield to the sovereignly of the Holy Spirit. And He shall assuredly prove to you that, in that very yielding, there was a proof that He had loved you. For He made you yield. He made you willing to bow before Him in the day of His power.

May the Holy Spirit now rest on the word I have spoken, for Jesus' sake!

THE HOLY SPIRIT'S CHIEF OFFICE

"He shall glorify Me: for He shall take of Mine, and shall show it to you. All things that the Father has are Mine: therefore said I, that He shall take of Mine and shall show it to you."
John 16:14, 15

A Sermon Delivered On Sunday Morning: 26 July 1888

IT is the chief office of the Holy Spirit to glorify Christ. He does many things, but this is what He aims at in all of them—to glorify Christ. Brothers and Sisters, what the Holy Spirit does must be right for us to imitate! Therefore, let us endeavor to glorify Christ. To what higher ends can we devote ourselves, than to something to which God the Holy Spirit devotes Himself? Be this, then, your continual prayer, "Blessed Spirit, help me to always glorify the Lord Jesus Christ!"

Observe that the Holy Spirit glorifies Christ by showing to us the things of Christ. It is a great marvel that there should be any Glory given to Christ by showing Him to such poor creatures as we are! What? To make us see Christ—does that glorify Him? For our weak eyes to behold Him, for our trembling hearts to know Him and to love Him—does this glorify Him? It is even so, for the Holy Spirit chooses this as His principal way of glorifying the Lord Jesus. He takes of the things of Christ, not to show them to angels, not to write them in letters of fire across the brow of night, but to show them to us! Within the little temple of a sanctified heart, Christ is praised, not so much by what we do, or think, as by what we see. This puts great value upon meditation, upon the study of God's Word, and upon silent thought under the teaching of the Holy Spirit, for Jesus says, "He shall glorify Me: for He shall take of Mine, and shall show it to you."

Here is a Gospel word at the very outset of our sermon! Poor sinner, conscious of your sin, it is possible for Christ to be glorified by His being shown to you! If you look to Him, if you see Him to be a suitable Savior, an all-sufficient Savior. If your mind's eye takes Him in. If He is effectually shown to you by the Holy Spirit, He is thereby glorified! Sinner as you are, unworthy, apparently, to become the arena of Christ's Glory, yet shall you be a temple in which the King's Glory shall be revealed and your poor heart, like a mirror, shall reflect His Grace–

"Come, Holy Spirit, heavenly Dove,
With all Your quickening powers"

and show Christ to the sinner, that Christ may be glorified in the sinner's salvation!

If that great work of Grace is really done at the beginning of the sermon, I shall not mind, even, if I never finish it! God the Holy Spirit will have worked more without me than I could possibly have worked myself, and to the Triune Jehovah shall be all the praise! Oh, that the name of Christ may be glorified in every one of you! Has the Holy Spirit shown you Christ, the Sin-Bearer, the one Sacrifice for sin, exalted on high, to give repentance and remission? If so, then the Holy Spirit has glorified Christ, even in you!

Now, proceeding to examine the text a little in detail, my first observation upon it is this–the Holy Spirit is our Lord's Glorifier. "He shall glorify Me." Secondly, Christ's own things are His best Glory. "He shall glorify Me: for He shall take of Mine, and shall show it to you." And, thirdly, Christ's Glory is His Father's Glory. "All things that the Father has are Mine: therefore said I, that He shall take of Mine, and shall show it to you."

To begin, then, THE HOLY SPIRIT IS OUR LORD'S GLORIFIER. I want you to keep this Truth of God in your mind and never to forget it–that which does not glorify Christ is not of the Holy Spirit, and that which is of the Holy Spirit invariably glorifies our Lord Jesus Christ!
First, then, have an eye to this Truth in all comforts. If a comfort which you think you need and which appears to you to be very sweet, does not glorify Christ, look very suspiciously upon it. If, in conversing with an apparently religious man, he prates about truth which he says is comforting, but which does not honor Christ, do not have anything to do with it! It is a poisonous sweet–it may charm you for a moment, but it will ruin your soul forever if you partake of it. But blessed are those comforts which smell of Christ, those consolations In which there is a fragrance of myrrh, aloes and cassia, out of the King's palace–the comfort drawn from His Person, from His work, from His blood, from the Resurrection, from His Glory–the comfort directly fetched from

that sacred spot where He trod the winepress alone! This is wine of which you may drink, forget your misery and be unhappy no more!

But always look with great suspicion upon any comfort offered to you, either as a sinner or a saint, which does not come distinctly from Christ. Say, "I will not be comforted till Jesus comforts me. I will refuse to lay aside my despondency until He removes my sin. I will not go to Mr. Civility, or Mr. Legality, for the unloading of my burden. No hands shall ever lift the load of conscious sin from off my heart but those that were nailed to the Cross, when Jesus, Himself, bore my sins in His own body on the tree." Please carry this Truth of God with you wherever you go as a kind of spiritual litmus paper by which you may test everything that is presented to you as a cordial or comfort. If it does not glorify Christ, let it not console or please you!

In the next place, have an eye to this Truth of God in all ministries. There are many ministries in the world and they are very diverse from one another, but this Truth will enable you to judge which is right out of them all. That ministry which makes much of Christ, is of the Holy Spirit, but that ministry which decries Him, ignores Him, or puts Him in the background in any degree, is not of the Spirit of God! Any doctrine which magnifies man, but not man's Redeemer. Any doctrine which denies the depth of the Fall and, consequently, derogates from the greatness of salvation. Any doctrine which makes sin less and, therefore, makes Christ's work less—away with it, away with it! This shall be your infallible test as to whether it is of the Holy Spirit or not, for Jesus says, "He shall glorify Me." It were better to speak five words to the Glory of Christ, than to be the greatest orator who ever lived and to neglect or dishonor the Lord Jesus Christ!

We, my Brothers, who are preachers of the Word, have but a short time to live. Let us dedicate all that time to the glorious work of magnifying Christ! Longfellow says, in his Psalm of Life, that, "Art is long," but longer, still, is the great art of lifting up the Crucified before the eyes of the sin-bitten sons of men. Let us keep to that one employment! If we have but this one string upon which we can play, we may discourse such music on it as would ravish angels and will save men! Therefore, again I say, let us keep to that alone! Cornet, flute, harp, sackbut, psaltery, dulcimer and all kinds of music are for Nebuchadnezzar's golden image, but as for our God, our one harp is Christ Jesus! We will touch every string of that wondrous instrument, even though it is with trembling fingers—and marvelous shall be the music we shall evoke from it!

All ministries, therefore, must be subjected to this test—if they do not glorify Christ, they are not of the Holy Spirit.

We should also have an eye to this Truth in all religious movements and judge them by this standard. If they are of the Holy Spirit, they glorify Christ. There are great movements in the world, every now and then, and we are inclined to look upon them hopefully, for any stir is better than stagnation. But, by-and-by, we begin to fear, with a holy jealousy, what their effects will be. How shall we judge them? To what test shall we put them? Always to this test—does this movement glorify Christ? Is Christ preached? Then, therein, I rejoice, yes, and will rejoice! Are men pointed to Christ? Then this is the ministry of salvation! Is He preached as First and Last? Are men bid to be justified by faith in Him and then to follow Him, and copy His Divine example? It is well! I do not believe that any man ever lifted up the Cross of Christ in a hurtful way. If it is but the Cross that is seen, it is the sight of the Cross, not of the hands that lift it, that will bring salvation. Some modern movements are heralded with great noise and some come quietly, but if they glorify Christ, it is well.

But, dear Friends, if it is some new theory that is propounded. If it is some old error revived. If it is something very glittering and fascinating and, for a while it bears the multitudes away, think nothing of it. Unless it glorifies Christ, it is not for you and me. "Aliquid Christi," as one of the old fathers said, "Anything of Christ," and I love it! But nothing of Christ, or something against Christ—and it may be very fine and flowery, and it may be very fascinating and charming, highly poetical, and in consonance with the spirit of the age—but we say of it, "Vanity of vanities, all is vanity where there is no Christ!" Where He is lifted up there is all that is needed for the salvation of a guilty race! Judge every movement, then, not by those who adhere to it, nor by those who admire and praise it, but by this Word of our Lord, "He shall glorify Me." The Spirit of God is not in it if it does not glorify Christ!

Once again, Brothers, I pray you, eye this Truth of God when you are under a sense of great weakness—physical, mental, or spiritual. You have finished preaching a sermon, you have completed a round with your tracts, or you have ended your Sunday school work for another Sabbath. You say to yourself, "I fear that I have done very poorly." You groan as you go to your bed because you think that you have not glorified Christ. It is as well that you should groan if that is the case. I will not forbid it, but I will relieve the bitterness of your distress by reminding you that it is the Holy Spirit who is to glorify Christ—"He shall glorify Me." If I preach and the Holy Spirit is with me, Christ will be glorified! But if I were able to speak with the tongues of men and of angels, but without the power of the Holy Spirit, Christ would not be glorified. Sometimes our weakness may even help to make way for the greater display of the might of God. If so, we may glory in infirmity, that the power of Christ may rest upon us! It is not merely we, who speak, but the Spirit of the Lord who speaks by us.

There is a sound of abundance of rain outside the Tabernacle—would God that there were also the sound of abundance of rain within our hearts! May the Holy Spirit come at this moment and come at all times whenever His servants are trying to glorify Christ—and do, Himself, what must always be His own work! How can you and I glorify anybody, much less glorify Him who is infinitely glorious? But the Holy Spirit, being, Himself, the glorious God, can glorify the glorious Christ! It is a work worthy of God and it shows us, when we think of it, the absolute need of our crying to the Holy Spirit that He would take us in His hands and use us as a workman uses his hammer. What can a hammer do without the hand that grasps it? And what can we do without the Spirit of God?

I will make only one more observation upon this first point. If the Holy Spirit is to glorify Christ, I beg you to have an eye to the Truth of God amid all oppositions, controversies and contentions. If we, alone, had the task of glorifying Christ, we might be beaten. But as the Holy Spirit is the Glorifier of Christ, His Glory is in very safe hands. "Why do the heathen rage, and the people imagine a vain thing?" The Holy Spirit is still to the front! The eternal purpose of God to set His King upon the Throne and to make Jesus Christ reign forever and ever must be fulfilled, for the Holy Spirit has undertaken to see it accomplished! Amidst the surging tumults of the battle, the result of the conflict is never in doubt for a moment! It may seem as though the fate of Christ's cause hung in a balance and that the scales were in equilibrium, but it is not so. The glory of Christ never wanes—it must increase from day to day as it is made known in the hearts of men by the Holy Spirit! And the day shall come when Christ's praise shall go up from all human tongues. To Him every knee shall bow and every tongue shall confess that Jesus Christ is Lord, to the Glory of God the Father! Therefore, lift up the hands that hang down and confirm the feeble knees. If you have failed to glorify Christ by your speech as you should, there is Another who has done it and who will still do it, according to Christ's words, "He shall glorify Me." My text seems to be a silver bell, ringing sweet comfort into the dispirited worker's ears, "He shall glorify Me."

That is the first point–the Holy Spirit is our Lord's Glorifier. Keep that Truth of God before your mind's eye under all circumstances.

II. Now, secondly, CHRIST'S OWN THINGS ARE HIS BEST GLORY. When the Holy Spirit wants to glorify Christ, what does He do? He does not go abroad for anything–He comes to Christ, Himself, for that which will be for Christ's own Glory–"He shall glorify Me: for He shall take of Mine, and shall show it to you." There can be no Glory added to Christ! It must be His own Glory which He has, already, which is made more apparent to the hearts of God's chosen by the Holy Spirit!

First of all, Christ needs no new inventions to glorify Him. "We have struck out a new line of things," says one. Have you? "We have discovered something very wonderful." I dare say you have, but Christ, the same yesterday, today and forever, needs none of your inventions, or discoveries, or additions to His Truth. A plain Christ is always the loveliest Christ. Dress Him up and you have deformed Him and defamed Him. Bring Him out just as He is–the Christ of God, nothing else but Christ, unless you bring in His Cross–for we preach Christ Crucified! Indeed, you cannot have the Christ without the Cross, but preach Christ Crucified and you have given Him all the Glory that He wants. The Holy Spirit does not reveal in these last times any fresh ordinances, or any novel doctrines, or any new evolutions–He simply brings to mind the things which Christ, Himself, spoke, He brings Christ's own things to us and, in that was, glorifies Him!

Think for a minute of Christ's Person as revealed to us by the Holy Spirit. What can more glorify Him than for us to see His Person, very God of very God, and yet as truly Man? What a wondrous Being, as Human as ourselves, but as Divine as God! Was there ever another like He? Never!

Think of His Incarnation, His birth at Bethlehem. There was greater Glory among the oxen in the stall than ever was seen where those born in marble halls were swathed in purple and fine linen! Was there ever another Baby like Christ? Never! I wonder not that the wise men fell down to worship Him!

Look at His life, the standing wonder of all ages! Men who have not worshipped Him, have admired Him. His life is incomparable, unique–there is nothing like it in all the history of mankind! Imagination has never been able to invent anything approximating to the perfect beauty of the life of Jesus Christ!

Think of His death. There have been many heroic and martyr deaths, but there is not one that can be set side by side with Christ's death. He did not pay the debt of nature as others do, and yet He paid our nature's debt. He did not die because He must–He died because He would. The only "must" that came upon Him was a necessity of all-conquering love. The Cross of Christ is the greatest wonder of fact or of fiction! Fiction invents many marvelous things, but nothing that can be looked at for a moment in comparison with the Cross of Christ!

Think of our Lord's Resurrection. If this is one of the things that are taken and shown to you by the Holy Spirit, it will fill you with holy delight! I am sure that I could go into that sepulcher, where John and Peter went, and spend a lifetime in reverencing Him who broke down the barriers of the tomb and made it a passageway to Heaven. Instead of being a dungeon and a cul-de-sac into which all men seemed to go, but none could ever come out, Christ has, by His Resurrection, made a tunnel right through the grave! Jesus, by dying, has killed death for all Believers!

Then think of His Ascension. But why need I take you over all these scenes with which you are blessedly familiar? What a wondrous fact that when the cloud received Him out of the disciples' sight, the angels came to convoy Him to His heavenly Home!–

"They brought His chariot from above
To bear Him to His Throne!
Clapped their triumphant wings and cried,
'The glorious work is done.'"

Think of Him, now, at His Father's right hand, adored of all the heavenly host, and then let your mind fly forward to the glory of His Second Advent, the final judgment with its terrible terrors, the millennium with its indescribable bliss and the Heaven of heavens, with its endless and unparalleled splendor! If these things are shown to you by the Holy Spirit, the beatific visions will, indeed, glorify Christ, and you will sit down and sing with the blessed Virgin, "My soul does magnify the Lord, and my spirit has rejoiced in God, my Savior."

Thus you see that the things which glorify Christ are all in Christ–the Holy Spirit fetches nothing from abroad, but He takes of the things of Christ and shows them to us. The glory of kings lies in their silver and their gold, their silk and their gems, but the Glory of Christ lies in Himself! If we want to glorify a man, we bring him presents. If we wish to glorify Christ, we must accept presents from Him. Thus we take the cup of salvation, calling upon the name of the Lord, and in so doing we glorify Christ!

Notice, next, that these things of Christ are too bright for us to see till the Spirit shows them to us. We cannot see them because of their excessive Glory, until the Holy Spirit tenderly reveals them to us, until He takes of the things of Christ and shows them to us.

What does this mean? Does it not mean, first, that He enlightens our understandings? It is wonderful how the Holy Spirit can take a fool and make him know the wonders of Christ's dying love. And He does make him know it very quickly when He begins to teach him. Some of us have been very slow learners, yet the Holy Spirit has been able to teach something, even, to us! He opens the Scriptures and He also opens our minds–and when there are these two openings, together, what a wonderful opening it is! It becomes like a new revelation–the first is the revelation of the letter, which we have in the Book– the second is the revelation of the Spirit, which we get in our own spirit. O my dear Friend, if the Holy Spirit has ever enlightened your understanding, you know what it is for Him to show the things of Christ to you!

But next, He does this by a work upon the whole soul. I mean this. When the Holy Spirit convinces us of sin, we become fitted to see Christ and so the blessed Spirit shows Christ to us. When we are conscious of our feebleness, then we see Christ's strength, and thus the Holy Spirit shows Him to us. Often, the operations of the Spirit of God may seem not to be directly the showing of Christ to us, but as they prepare us for seeing Him, they are a part of the work.

The Holy Spirit sometimes shows Christ to us by His power of vivifying the Truth of God. I do not know whether I can quite tell you what I mean, but I have, sometimes, seen a Truth of God differently from what I have ever seen it before. I knew it long ago, I acknowledged it as part of the Divine Revelation, but now I realize it, grip it, grasp it, or, what is better, it seems to get a grip of me and hold me in its mighty hands! Have you not, sometimes, been overjoyed with a promise which never seemed anything to you before? Or a doctrine which you believed, but never fully appreciated, has suddenly become to you a gem of the first water, a very Kohinoor, or, "Fountain of Light"?

The Holy Spirit has a way of focusing the Light of God and, when it falls in this special way upon a certain point, then the Truth is revealed to us. He shall take of the things of Christ and show them to you. Have you ever felt ready to jump for joy, ready to jump from your seat, ready to sit up in your bed at night and sing praises to God through the overpowering influence of some grand old Truth which has seemed to be, at once, quite new to you? The Holy Spirit also shows to us the things of Christ in our experience. As we journey on in life, we pass up hill and down dale, through bright sunlight and through dark shadows—and in each of these conditions we learn a little more of Christ, a little more of His Grace, a little more of His Glory, a little more of His sin-bearing, a little more of His glorious righteousness! Blessed is the life which is just one long lesson upon the Glory of Christ! And I think that is what every Christian life should be. "Every dark and bending line" in our experience should meet in the center of Christ's Glory and should lead us nearer and nearer to the power of enjoying the bliss at His right hand forever and ever. Thus the Holy Spirit takes of the things of Christ and shows them to us, and so glorifies Christ.

Beloved, the practical lesson for us to learn is this—let us try to live under the influence of the Holy Spirit. To that end, let us think very reverently of Him. Some never think of Him at all. How many sermons there are without even an allusion to Him! Shame on the preachers of such discourses! If any hearers come without praying for the Holy Spirit, shame on such hearers! We know and we confess that He is everything to our spiritual life—then why do we not remember Him with greater love, worship Him with greater honor and think of Him continually with greater reverence? Beware of committing the sin against the Holy Spirit! If any of you feel any gentle touches of His power when you are hearing a sermon, beware lest you harden your heart against it! Whenever the sacred fire comes as but a spark, quench not the Holy Spirit, but pray that the spark may become a flame.

And you, Christian people, cry to Him that you may not read your Bibles without His light. Do not pray without being helped by the Spirit. Above all, may you never preach without the Holy Spirit! It seems a pity when a man asks to be guided of the Spirit in His preaching—and then pulls out a manuscript and reads it! The Holy Spirit may bless what he reads, but He cannot very well guide him when he has tied himself down to what he has written! And it will be the same with the speaker if he only repeats what he has learned and leaves no room for the Spirit to give him a new thought, a fresh Revelation of Christ! How can he hope for the Divine blessing under such circumstances? Oh, it were better for us to sit still until some of us were moved by the Spirit to get up and speak, than for us to prescribe the methods by which He should speak to us and even to write down the very words we mean to utter! What room is there for the Spirit's operations then—

"Come, Holy Spirit, heavenly Dove,"

I cannot help breaking out into that prayer, "Blessed Spirit, abide with us! Take of the things of Christ and show them to us that Christ may be glorified."

III. I am only going to speak a minute or two on the last point. It is a very deep one, much too deep for me. I am unable to take you into the depths of my text, I will not pretend to do so. I believe that there are meanings here which probably we shall never understand till we get to Heaven. "What you know not now, you shall know hereafter." But this is the point—CHRIST'S GLORY IS HIS FATHER'S GLORY—"All things that the Father has are Mine: therefore said I, that He shall take of Mine, and shall show it to you."

First, Christ has all that the Father has. Think of that! No mere man dares to say, "All things that the Father has are mine." All the Godhead is in Christ—not only all the attributes of it, but the essence of it. The Nicene Creed well puts it and it is not too strong in the expression: "Light of Light, very God of very God," for Christ has all that the Father has. When we come to Christ, we come to Omnipotent, Omnipresent Omniscience—we come to Almighty Immutability—we come, in fact, to the eternal Godhead! The Father has all things and all power Is given to Christ In Heaven and on earth, so that He has all that the Father has!

And, further, the Father is glorified in Christ's Glory. Never let us fall into the false notion that if we magnify Christ, we are depreciating the Father. If any lips have ever spoken concerning the Christ of God so as to depreciate the God of Christ, let those lips be covered with shame! We never preached Christ as merciful and the Father as only just, or Christ as moving the Father to be gracious. That is a slander which has been cast upon us, but there is not an atom of truth in it! We have known and believed what Christ, Himself, said, "I and My Father are One." The more glorious Christ is, the more glorious the Father is—and when men, professedly Christians, begin to cast off Christ, they cast off God the Father to a large extent. Irreverence to the Son of God soon becomes irreverence to God the Father, Himself! But, dear Friends, we delight to honor Christ, and we will continue to do so. Even when we stand in the Heaven of heavens, before the burning Throne of the Infinite Jehovah, we will sing praises unto Him and unto the Lamb, putting the two evermore in that Divine conjunction in which they are always to be found!

Thus, you see, Christ has all that the Father has, and when He is glorified, the Father, also, is glorified.

Next, the Holy Spirit must lead us to see this, and I am sure that He will. If we give ourselves up to His teaching, we shall fall into no errors. It will be a great mystery, but we shall know enough so that it will never trouble us. If you sit down and try to study the mystery of the Eternal—well, I believe that the longer you look, the more you will be like persons who look into the sea from a great height, until they grow dizzy, and are ready to fall and to be drowned. Believe what the Spirit teaches you and adore your Divine Teacher—then shall His instruction become easy to you. I believe that as we grow older, we come to worship God as Abraham did, as Jehovah, the great I AM. Jesus does not fade into the background, but the glorious Godhead seems to become more and more apparent to us. Our Lord's Word to His disciples, "You believe in God, believe also in Me," as we grow older, seems to turn into this, "You believe in Me, believe also in God." And as we come to a full confidence in the glorious Lord, the God of Nature, and of Providence, and of Redemption, and of Heaven, the Holy Spirit gives us to know more of the glories of Christ!

I have talked with you as well as I could upon this sublime theme and if I did not know that the Holy Spirit glorifies Christ, I would go home miserable, for I have not been able to glorify my Lord as I would. But I know that the Holy Spirit can take what I have said out of my very heart and can put it into your hearts—and He can add to it whatever I have omitted. Go, you who love the Lord, and glorify Him! Try to do it by your lips and by your lives. Go and preach Him, preach more of Him, and preach Him up higher, and higher, and higher!

An old lady, of whom I have heard, made a mistake in what she said, yet there was a Truth behind her blunder. She had been to a little Baptist Chapel where a high Calvinist preached and, on coming away she said that she liked "High Calvary" preachers best. So do I! Give me a "High Calvary" preacher— one who will make Calvary the highest of all the mountains! I suppose it was not a hill at all, but only a mound. Still, let us lift it higher and higher, and say to all other hills, "Why leap you, you high hills? This is the hill which God desires to dwell in! Yes, the Lord will dwell in it forever." The Crucified Christ is wiser than all the wisdom of the world! The Cross of Christ has more novelty in it than all the fresh things of the earth! O Believers and preachers of the Gospel, glorify Christ! May the Holy Spirit help you to do so!

And you, poor Sinners, who think that you cannot glorify Christ at all, come and trust Him—

"Come naked, come filthy, come just as you are,"
and believe that He will receive you, for that will glorify Him! Believe, even now, O Sinner at death's door, that Christ can make you live, and your faith will glorify Him! Look up out of the awful depths of Hell into which conscience has cast you and believe that He can pluck you out of the horrible pit, and out of the miry clay and set your feet upon a rock, and your trust will glorify Him! It is in the power of the sinner to give Christ the greatest Glory, if the Holy Spirit enables him to believe in the Lord Jesus Christ. You may come, you who are more leprous, more diseased, more corrupt than any other! And if you look to Him and He saves you, oh, then you will praise Him!

You will be of the mind of the one I have spoken of many times, who said to me, "Sir, you say that Christ can save me? Well, if He does, He shall never hear the last of it." No, and He never will hear the last of it! Blessed Jesus—

"I will love You in life, I will love You in death
And praise You as long as You lend me breath;
And say when the death-dew lies cold on my brow,
In mansions of glory and endless delight,
I'll ever adore You in Heaven so bright.
I'll sing with the glittering crown on my brow,

If ever I loved You, my Jesus, 'tis now."

We will do nothing else but praise Christ and glorify Him, if He will but save us from sin! God grant that it may be so with all of us, for the Lord Jesus Christ's sake! Amen.

THE HOLY SPIRIT'S INTERCESSION

"Likewise the Spirit also helps our infirmities: for we know not what we should pray for as we ought: but the Spirit itself makes intercession for us with groans which cannot be uttered. And He that searches the hearts knows what is the mind of the Spirit, because He makes intercession for the saints according to the will of God."
Romans 8:26, 27

A Sermon Delivered On Sunday Morning: 11 April 1880

THE Apostle Paul was writing to a tried and afflicted people and one of his objectives was to remind them of the rivers of comfort which were flowing near at hand. He first of all stirred up their pure minds by way of remembrance as to their sonship, for he says, "as many as are led by the Spirit of God, they are the sons of God." They were, therefore, encouraged to take part and lot with Christ, the elder Brother, with whom they had become joint heirs. And they were exhorted to suffer with Him that they might afterwards be glorified with Him. All that they endured came from a Father's hand and this should comfort them. A thousand sources of joy are opened in that one blessing of adoption. Blessed is the God and Father of our Lord Jesus Christ, by whom we have been begotten into the family of Grace!

When Paul had alluded to that consoling subject, he turned to the next ground of comfort, namely, that we are to be sustained under present trial by hope. There is an amazing glory in reserve for us and though as yet we cannot enter upon it, but in harmony with the whole creation must continue to groan and travail, yet the hope itself should minister strength to us and enable us to bear patiently "these light afflictions, which are but for a moment." This, also, is a Truth of God full of sacred refreshment–Hope sees a crown in reserve, mansions in readiness and Jesus, Himself, preparing a place for us–and by the rapturous sight she sustains the soul under the sorrows of the hour! Hope is the grand anchor by whose means we ride out the present storm.

The Apostle then turns to a third source of comfort, namely, the abiding of the Holy Spirit in and with the Lord's people. He uses the word, "likewise," to intimate that in the same manner as hope sustains the soul, so does the Holy Spirit strengthen us under trial. Hope operates spiritually upon our spiritual faculties and so does the Holy Spirit, in some mysterious way, Divinely operate upon the new-born faculties of the Believer so that he is sustained under his infirmities. In His light shall we see light–I pray, therefore, that we may be helped of the Spirit while we consider His mysterious operations–that we may not fall into error or miss precious Truths of God through blindness of heart.

The text speaks of "our infirmities," or as many translators put it in the singular–of "our infirmity"–by this is intended our affliction and the weakness which trouble discovers in us. The Holy Spirit helps us to bear the infirmity of our body and of our mind. He helps us to bear our cross, whether it is physical pain, mental depression, spiritual conflict, slander, poverty, or persecution. He helps our infirmity–and with a Helper so Divinely strong, we need not fear for the result! God's Grace will be sufficient for us! His strength will be made perfect in weakness! I think, dear Friends, you will all admit that if a man can pray, his trouble is at once lightened. When we feel that we have power with God and can obtain anything we ask for at His hands, then our difficulties cease to oppress us.

We take our burden to our heavenly Father and tell Him in the accents of childlike confidence and we come away quite content to bear whatever His holy will may lay upon us. Prayer is a great outlet for grief–it draws up the sluices and abates the swelling flood which, otherwise, might be too strong for us. We bathe our wounds in the lotion of prayer and the pain is lulled, the fever is removed. But the worst of it is that in certain conditions of heart we cannot pray. We may be brought into such perturbation of mind and perplexity of heart that we do not know how to pray. We see the Mercy Seat and we perceive that God will hear us. We have no doubt about that, for we know that we are His own favored children and yet we hardly know what to desire.

We fall into such heaviness of spirit and entanglement of thought that the one remedy of prayer, which we have always found to be unfailing, appears to be taken from us. Here, then, in the nick of time, as a very present help in time of trouble, comes in the Holy Spirit! He draws near to teach us how to pray and in this way He helps our infirmity, relieves our suffering and enables us to bear the heavy burden without fainting under the load. At this time our subjects for consideration shall be, first, the help which the Holy Spirit gives. Secondly, the prayers which He inspires. And thirdly, the success which such prayers are certain to obtain.

First, then, let us consider THE HELP WHICH THE HOLY SPIRIT GIVES. The help which the Holy Spirit renders to us meets the weakness which we deplore. As I have already said, if in time of trouble a man can pray, his burden loses its weight. If the Believer can take anything and everything to God, then he learns to glory in infirmity and to rejoice in tribulation. But sometimes we are in such confusion of mind that we know not what we should pray for as we ought to. In a measure, through our ignorance, we never know what we should pray for until we are taught of the Spirit of God, but there are times when this beclouding of the soul is dense, indeed, and we do not even know what would help us out of our trouble if we could obtain it.

We see the disease, but the name of the medicine is not known to us. We look over the many things which we might ask for of the Lord and we feel that each of them would be helpful, but none of them would precisely meet our case. For spiritual blessings which we know to be according to the Divine will, we could ask with confidence, but perhaps these would not meet our peculiar circumstances. There are other things for which we are allowed to ask, but we scarcely know whether, if we had them, they would really serve our turn and we also feel a diffidence as to praying for them. In praying for temporal things, we plead with measured voices, always referring our petition for revision to the will of the Lord.

Moses prayed that he might enter Canaan, but God denied him. The man that was healed asked our Lord that he might be with Him, but he received the answer," Go home to your friends." We pray on such matters with this reserve, "Nevertheless, not as I will, but as You will." At times this very spirit of resignation appears to increase our mental difficulty, for we do not wish to ask for anything that would be contrary to the mind of God and yet we must ask for something! We are reduced to such straits that we must pray, but what shall be the particular subject of prayer we cannot, for a while, make out. Even when ignorance and perplexity are removed, we know not what we should pray for "as we ought."

When we know the matter of prayer, yet we fail to pray in a right manner. We ask, but we are afraid that we shall not have, because we do not exercise the thought, or the faith which we judge to be essential to prayer. We cannot, at times, command even the earnestness which is the life of supplication. A torpor steals over us, our heart is chilled, our hands are numbed and we cannot wrestle with the angel. We know what to pray for as to objects, but we do not know what to pray for "as we ought." It is the manner of the prayer which perplexes us, even when the matter is decided upon! How can I pray? My mind wanders. I chatter like a crane. I roar like a beast in pain. I moan in the brokenness of my heart, but oh, my God, I know not what it is my inmost spirit needs, or if I know it, I know not how to frame my petition aright before You! I know not how to open my lips in Your majestic Presence—I am so troubled that I cannot speak! My spiritual distress robs me of the power to pour out my heart before my God!

Now, Beloved, it is in such a plight as this that the Holy Spirit aids us with His Divine help and hence He is "a very present help in time of trouble." Coming to our aid in our bewilderment, He instructs us. This is one of His frequent operations upon the mind of the Believer—"He shall teach you all things." He instructs us as to our need and as to the promises of God which refer to that need. He shows us where our deficiencies are; what our sins are and what our necessities are. He sheds a light upon our condition and makes us feel our helplessness, sinfulness and dire poverty very deeply. And then He casts the same light upon the promises of the Word and lays home to our heart that very text which was intended to meet the occasion—the precise promise which was framed with foresight of our present distress!

In that light He makes the promise shine in all its truthfulness, certainty, sweetness and suitability so that we, poor trembling sons of men, dare take that Word into our mouth which first came out of God's mouth and then come with it as an argument and plead it before the Throne of the heavenly Grace. Our prevalence in prayer lies in the plea, "Lord, do as You have said." How greatly we ought to value the Holy Spirit because when we are in the dark He gives us light! And when our perplexed spirit is so befogged and beclouded that it cannot see its own need and cannot find out the appropriate promise in the Scriptures, the Spirit of God comes in and teaches us all things and brings all things to our remembrance whatever our Lord has told us. He guides us in prayer and thus He helps our infirmity.

But the blessed Spirit does more than this! He will often direct the mind to the special subject of prayer. He dwells within us as a Counselor and points out to us what it is we should seek at the hands of God. We do not know why it is so, but we sometimes find our minds carried as by a strong undercurrent into a particular line of prayer for some one definite objective. It is not merely that our judgment leads us in that direction, though usually the Spirit of God acts upon us by enlightening our judgment, but we often feel an unaccountable and irresistible desire rising again and again within our heart and this so presses upon us that we not only utter the desire before God at our ordinary times for prayer, but we feel it crying in our hearts all day long–almost to the supplanting of all other considerations.

At such times we should thank God for direction and give our desire a clear road–the Holy Spirit is granting us inward direction as to how we should order our petitions before the Throne of Grace and we may now reckon upon good success in our pleading. Such guidance will the Spirit give to each of you if you will ask Him to illuminate you. He will guide you both negatively and positively. Negatively, He will forbid you to pray for such-and-such a thing, even as Paul essayed to go into Bithynia, but the Spirit would not allow him. And, on the other hand, He will cause you to hear a cry within your soul which shall guide your petitions, even as He made Paul hear the cry from Macedonia, saying, "Come over and help us." The Spirit teaches wisely, as no other teacher can. Those who obey His prompting shall not walk in darkness. He leads the spiritual eyes to take good and steady aim at the very center of the target and thus we hit the mark in our pleading.

Nor is this all, for the Spirit of God is not sent merely to guide and help our devotion, but He Himself "makes intercession for us" according to the will of God. By this expression it cannot be meant that the Holy Spirit ever groans or personally prays, but that He excites intense desire and creates unutterable groans in us and these are ascribed to Him. Even as Solomon built the temple because he superintended and ordained all, yet I know not that he ever fashioned a timber or prepared a stone, so does the Holy Spirit pray and plead within us by leading us to pray and plead. This He does by awakening our desires. The Holy Spirit has a wonderful power over renewed hearts–as much power as the skillful minstrel has over the strings among which he lays his accustomed hand.

The influences of the Holy Spirit, at times, pass through the soul like winds through an Aeolian harp, creating and inspiring sweet notes of gratitude and tones of desire to which we should have been strangers if it had not been for His Divine visitation. He knows how to create in our spirit hunger and thirst for good things. He can awaken us from our spiritual lethargy. He can warm us out of our lukewarmness. He can enable us, when we are on our knees, to rise above the ordinary routine of prayer into that victorious importunity against which nothing can stand! He can lay certain desires so pressingly upon our hearts that we can never rest till they are fulfilled! He can make the zeal for God's house to eat us up and the passion for God's Glory to be like a fire within our bones—this is one part of that process by which, in inspiring our prayers, He helps our infirmity. He is a true Advocate and most effectual Comforter. Blessed be His name!

The Holy Spirit also Divinely operates in the strengthening of the faith of Believers. That faith is at first of His creating and afterwards it is of His sustaining and increasing. And oh, Brothers and Sisters, have you not often felt your faith rise in proportion to your trials? Have you not, like Noah's ark, mounted towards Heaven as the flood deepened around you? You have felt as sure about the promise as you felt about the trial! The affliction was, as it were, in your very bones, but the promise was also in your very heart. You could not doubt the affliction, for you smarted under it, but you might almost as soon have doubted that you were afflicted as have doubted the Divine Help, for your confidence was firm and unmoved! The greatest faith is only what God has a right to expect from us, yet we never exhibit it except as the Holy Spirit strengthens our confidence and opens up before us the Covenant with all its seals and securities.

He it is that leads our soul to cry, "Though my house is not so with God, yet has He made with me an Everlasting Covenant ordered in all things and sure." Blessed be the Divine Spirit, then, that since faith is essential to prevailing prayer, He helps us in supplication by increasing our faith! Without faith, prayer cannot go anywhere, for he that wavers is like a wave of the sea driven and tossed by the wind and such an one may not expect anything of the Lord! Happy are we when the Holy Spirit removes our wavering and enables us, like Abraham, to believe without staggering, knowing full well that He who has promised is able, also, to perform!

By three figures I will endeavor to describe the work of the Spirit of God in this matter, though they all fall short and, indeed, all that I can say must fall infinitely short of the Glory of His work. The actual mode of His working upon the mind we may not attempt to explain—it remains a mystery and it would be an unholy intrusion to attempt to remove the veil. There is no difficulty in our believing that as one human mind operates upon another mind, so does the Holy Spirit influence our spirits. We are forced to use words if we would influence our fellow men, but the Spirit of God can operate upon the human mind more directly and communicate with it in silence. Into that matter, however, we will not dive lest we intrude where our knowledge would be drowned by our presumption.

My illustrations do not touch the mystery, but set forth the Grace. The Holy Spirit acts to His people somewhat as a prompter to a reciter. A man has to deliver a piece which he has learned, but his memory is treacherous and, therefore, somewhere out of sight there is a prompter so that when the speaker is at a loss and might use a wrong word, a whisper is heard which suggests the right one. When the speaker has almost lost the thread of his discourse, he turns his ear and the prompter gives him the catch-word and aids his memory. If I may be allowed the simile, I would say that this represents, in part, the work of the Spirit of God in us—suggesting to us the right desire and bringing all things to our remembrance whatever Christ has told us.

In prayer we should often come to a dead stand, but He incites, suggests and inspires—and so we go onward. In prayer we might grow weary, but the Comforter encourages and refreshes us with cheering thoughts. When, indeed, we are, in our bewilderment, almost driven to give up prayer, the whisper of His love drops a live coal from off the Altar into our soul and our hearts glow with greater ardor than before! Regard the Holy Spirit as your Prompter and let your ears be opened to His voice. But He is much more than this. Let me attempt a second simile—He is as an Advocate to one in peril at law. Suppose that a poor man had a great lawsuit touching his whole estate and he was forced, personally, to go into court and plead his own cause and speak up for his rights. If he were an uneducated man, he would be in a poor plight. An adversary in the court might plead against him and overthrow him, for he could not answer him. This poor man knows very little about the law and is quite unable to meet his cunning opponent.

Now, suppose one who was perfect in the law should take up his cause warmly and come and live with him and use all his knowledge so as to prepare his case for him, draw up his petitions for him and fill his mouth with arguments—would not that be a grand relief? This counselor would suggest the line of pleading, arrange the arguments and put them into right courtly language. When the poor man was baffled by a question asked in court, he would run home and ask his adviser and he would tell him exactly how to meet the objector. Suppose, too, that when he had to plead with the judge, this advocate at home should teach him how to behave and what to urge and encourage him to hope that he would prevail–would not this be a great gift?

Who would be the pleader in such a case? The poor client would plead, but still, when he won the suit, he would trace it all to the advocate who lived at home and gave him counsel. Indeed, it would be the advocate pleading for him, even while he pleaded himself! This is an instructive emblem of a great fact. Within this narrow house of my body, this tenement of clay, if I am a true Believer, there dwells the Holy Spirit and when I desire to pray I may ask Him what I should pray for as I ought and He will help me! He will write the prayers which I ought to offer upon the tablets of my heart and I shall see them there and so I shall be taught how to plead! It will be the Spirit's own self pleading in me and by me and through me before the Throne of Grace! What a happy man, in his lawsuit, would such a poor man be! And how happy are you and I that we have the Holy Spirit to be our Counselor!

Yet one more illustration. It is that of a father aiding his boy. Suppose it to is a time of war, centuries back. Old English warfare was then conducted by bowmen, to a great extent. Here is a youth who is to be initiated in the art of archery and, therefore, he carries a bow. It is a strong bow and, therefore, very hard to draw–indeed, it requires more strength than the urchin can summon to bend it. See how his father teaches him. "Put your right hand here, my Boy, and place your left hand so. Now pull"–and as the youth pulls, his father's hands are on his hands and the bow is drawn! The lad draws the bow, yes, but it is quite as much his father, too.

We cannot draw the bow of prayer alone. Sometimes a bow of steel is not broken by our hands, for we cannot even bend it. And then the Holy Spirit puts His mighty hand over ours and covers our weakness so that we draw, and lo, what splendid drawing of the bow it then is! The bow bends so easily we wonder how! Away flies the arrow and it pierces the very center of the target, for He who gives the strength, directs the aim! We rejoice to think that we have won the day, but it was His secret might that made us strong and to Him be the glory of it! Thus have I tried to set forth the cheering fact that the Spirit helps the people of God.

II. Our second subject is THE PRAYER WHICH THE HOLY SPIRIT INSPIRES, or that part of prayer which is especially and peculiarly the work of the Spirit of God. The text says, "The Spirit itself makes intercession for us with groans which cannot be uttered." It is not the Spirit that groans, but we that groan, but as I have shown you, the Spirit excites the emotion which causes us to groan. It is clear then the prayers which are indited in us by the Spirit of God are those which arise from our inmost soul. A man's heart is moved when he groans. A groan is a matter about which there is no hypocrisy. A groan comes not from the lips, but from the heart. A groan, then, is a part of prayer which we owe to the Holy Spirit and the same is true of all the prayer which wells up from the deep fountains of our inner life.

The Prophet cried, "My heart, my heart, I am pained at my very heart: my heart makes a noise in me." This deep ground-swell of desire, this tidal motion of the life-floods is caused by the Holy Spirit. His work is never superficial, but always deep and inward. Such prayers will rise within us when the mind is far too troubled to let us speak. We know not what we should pray for as we ought and then it is that we groan, or utter some other inarticulate sound. Hezekiah said, "like a crane or a swallow did I chatter." The Psalmist said, "I am so troubled that I cannot speak." In another place he said, "I am feeble and sorely broken: I have roared by reason of the disquietness of my heart." But he added, "Lord, all my desire is before You and my groaning is not hid from You."

The sighs of the prisoner surely come up into the ears of the Lord. There is real prayer in these "groans that cannot be uttered." It is the power of the Holy Spirit in us which creates all real prayer, even that which takes the form of a groan because the mind is incapable, by reason of its bewilderment and grief, of clothing its emotion in words. I pray you never think lightly of the supplications of your anguish. Rather judge that such prayers are like Jabez, of whom it is written, "He was more honorable than his brethren because his mother bore him with sorrow." That which is thrown up from the depth of the soul, when it is stirred with a terrible tempest, is more precious than pearl or coral, for it is the intercession of the Holy Spirit!

These prayers are sometimes "groans that cannot be uttered" because they concern such great things that they cannot be spoken. I need, my Lord! I need, I need; I cannot tell you what I need, but I seem to need all things! If it were some little thing, my narrow capacity could comprehend and describe it, but I need all Covenant blessings! You know what I have need of before I ask You and though I cannot go into each item of my need, I know it to be very great and such as I, myself, can never estimate. I groan, for I can do no more!

Prayers which are the offspring of great desires, sublime aspirations and elevated designs are surely the work of the Holy Spirit and their power within a man is frequently so great that he cannot find expression for them! Words fail and even the sighs which try to embody them cannot be uttered.

But it may be, Beloved, that we groan because we are conscious of the littleness of our desires and the narrowness of our faith. The trial, too, may seem too mean to pray about. I have known what it is to feel as if I could not pray about a certain matter and yet I have been obliged to groan about it. A thorn in the flesh may be as painful a thing as a sword in the bones and yet we may go and beseech the Lord thrice about it and, getting no answer, we may feel that we know not what to pray for as we ought—and so it makes us groan. Yes, and with that natural groan there may go up an unutterable groaning of the Holy Spirit! Beloved, what a different view of prayer God has from that which men think to be the correct one! You may have seen very beautiful prayers in print and you may have heard very charming compositions from the pulpit, but I trust you have not fallen in love with them. Judge these things rightly. I pray you never think well of fine prayers, for before the thrice holy God it ill becomes a sinful suppliant to play the orator! We heard of a certain clergyman who was said to have given forth "the finest prayer ever offered to a Boston audience." Just so! The Boston audience received the prayer and there it ended! We need the mind of the Spirit in prayer and not the mind of the flesh! The tail feathers of pride should be pulled out of our prayers, for they need only the wing feathers of faith—the peacock feathers of poetical expression are out of place before the Throne of God.

"Dear me, what remarkably beautiful language he uses in prayer!" "What an intellectual treat his prayers are!" Yes, yes. But God looks at the heart. To Him fine language is as sounding brass or a tinkling cymbal—while a groan has music in it! We do not like groans—our ears are much too delicate to tolerate such dreary sounds—but not so the great Father of Spirits. A Methodist Brother cries, "Amen," and you say, "I cannot bear such Methodistic noise!" No, but if it comes from the man's heart, God can bear it! When you get upstairs into your chamber this evening to pray and find you cannot pray, but have to moan, "Lord, I am too full of anguish and too perplexed to pray. Hear the voice of my roaring." Though you reach to nothing else, you will be really praying!

When, like David, we can say, "I opened my mouth and panted," we are by no means in an ill state of mind. All fine language in prayer and especially all intoning or performing of prayers must be abhorrent to God! It is little short of profanity to offer solemn supplication to God after the manner called, "intoning." The sighing of a true heart is infinitely more acceptable, for it is the work of the Spirit of God! We may say of the prayers which the Holy Spirit works in us that they are prayers of knowledge. Notice our difficulty is that we know not what we should pray for—but the Holy Spirit knows and, therefore, He helps us by enabling us to pray intelligently, knowing what we are asking for, so far as this knowledge is necessary to valid prayer.

The text speaks of the "mind of the Spirit." What a mind that must be! The mind of that Spirit who arranged all the order which now pervades this earth! There was once chaos and confusion, but the Holy Spirit brooded over all and His mind is the originator of that beautiful arrangement which we so admire in the visible creation! What a mind His must be! The Holy Spirit's mind is seen in our intercessions when, under His sacred influence, we order our case before the Lord and plead with holy wisdom for things convenient and necessary. What wise and admirable desires must those be which the Spirit of Wisdom, Himself, works in us!

Moreover, the Holy Spirit's intercession creates prayers offered in a proper manner. I showed you that the difficulty is that we know not what we should pray for "as we ought," and the Spirit meets that difficulty by making intercession for us in a right manner. The Holy Spirit works in us humility, earnestness, intensity, importunity, faith, resignation and all else that is acceptable to God in our supplications. We know not how to mingle these sacred spices in the incense of prayer. We, if left to ourselves, at our very best get too much of one ingredient or another and spoil the sacred compound. But the Holy Spirit's intercessions have in them such a blessed blending of all that is good that they come up as a sweet perfume before the Lord!

Spirit-taught prayers are offered as they ought to be. They are His own intercession in some respects, for we read that the Holy Spirit not only helps us to intercede but, "makes intercession." It is twice over declared in our text that He makes intercession for us and the meaning of this I tried to show when I described a father as putting his hands upon his child's hands. This is something more than helping us to pray, something more than encouraging us or directing us—but I venture no further except to say that He puts such force of His own mind into our poor weak thoughts and desires and hopes that He,

Himself, makes intercession for us, working in us to will and to pray according to His good pleasure!

I want you to notice, however, that these intercessions of the Holy Spirit are only in the saints. "He makes intercession for us" and, "He makes intercession for the saints." Does He do nothing for sinners, then? Yes, He quickens sinners into spiritual life and He strives with them to overcome their sinfulness and turn them into the right way. But in the saints He works with us and enables us to pray after His mind and according to the will of God! His intercession is not in or for the unregenerate. O, unbelievers you must first be made saints or you cannot feel the Spirit's intercession within you! What need we have to go to Christ for the blessing of the Holy Spirit which is peculiar to the children of God and can only be ours by faith in Christ Jesus!

"To as many as received Him, to them gave He power to become the sons of God." And to the sons of God, alone, comes the Spirit of adoption and all His helping Grace. Unless we are the sons of God, the Holy Spirit's indwelling shall not be ours–we are shut out from the intercession of the Holy Spirit. Yes, and from the intercession of Jesus, too, for He has said, "I pray not for the world, but for them which You have given Me." Thus I have tried to show you the kind of prayer which the Spirit inspires.

III. Our third and last point is THE SURE SUCCESS OF ALL SUCH PRAYERS. All the prayers which the Spirit of God inspires in us must succeed, because, first, there is a meaning in them which God reads and approves. When the Spirit of God writes a prayer upon a man's heart, the man himself may be in such a state of mind that he does not altogether know what it is! His interpretation of it is a groan and that is all. Perhaps he does not even get so far as that in expressing the mind of the Spirit, but he feels groans which he cannot utter. He cannot find a door of utterance for his inward grief.

Yet our heavenly Father, who looks immediately upon the heart, reads what the Spirit of God has indited there and does not need even our groans to explain the meaning! He reads the heart itself–"He knows," says the text, "what is the mind of the Spirit." The Spirit is one with the Father and the Father knows what the Spirit means! The desires which the Spirit prompts may be too spiritual for such babes in Grace as we are actually to describe or to express and yet they are within us. We feel desires for things that we should never have thought of if He had not made us long for them. We have aspirations for blessings which as to the understanding of them are still above us, yet the Spirit writes the desire on the renewed mind and the Father sees it!

Now that which God reads in the heart and approves of, for the word, "to know," in this case includes approval as well as the mere act of Omniscience– what God sees and approves of in the heart must succeed. Did not Jesus say, "Your heavenly Father knows that you have need of these things before you ask them"? Did He not tell us this as an encouragement to believe that we shall receive all necessary blessings? So it is with those prayers which are all broken up, wet with tears and discordant with sighs and inarticulate expressions and heaving of the bosom and sobbing of the heart and anguish and bitterness of spirit–our gracious Lord reads them as a man reads a book and they are written in a character which He fully understands!

To give a simple example–if I were to come into your house, I might find there a little child that cannot yet speak plainly. It cries for something and it makes very odd and objectionable noises, combined with signs and movements which are almost meaningless to a stranger. But his mother understands him and attends to his little pleas. A mother can translate baby talk. She comprehends incomprehensible noises! Even so does our Father in Heaven know all about our poor baby talk, for our prayers are not much better. He knows and comprehends the cries and moans and sighs and chattering of His bewildered children! Yes, a tender mother knows her child's needs before the child knows what it needs. Perhaps the little one stutters, stammers and cannot get its words out–but the mother senses what he would say and understands the meaning. Even so we know concerning our great Father–

"He knows the thoughts we mean to speak,
Before from our opening lips they break."

Rejoice in this because the prayers of the Spirit are known and understood of God and, therefore, they will be sure to reach Him!

The next argument for making us sure that they will reach Him is this–they are "the mind of the Spirit." God the Ever-Blessed is One and there can be no division between the Father, the Son and the Holy Spirit. These Divine Persons always work together and there is a common desire for the Glory of each blessed Person of the Divine Unity and, therefore, it cannot be conceived, without profanity, that anything could be the mind of the Holy Spirit and not be the mind of the Father and the mind of the Son! The mind of God is one and harmonious! If, therefore, the Holy Spirit dwells in you and He moves you to any desire, then His mind is in your prayer and it is not possible that the eternal Father should reject your petitions. That prayer which came from Heaven will certainly go back to Heaven! If the Holy Spirit prompts it, the Father must and will accept it, for it is not possible that He should put a slight upon the Ever-Blessed and adorable Spirit.

But one more word and that closes the argument, namely, that the work of the Spirit in the heart is not only the mind of the Spirit which God knows, but it is also according to the will or mind of God, for He never makes intercession in us other than is consistent with the Divine will. Now, the Divine will or mind may be viewed two ways. First, there is the will declared in the proclamations of holiness by the Ten Commandments. The Spirit of God never prompts us to ask for anything that is unholy or inconsistent with the precepts of the Lord. Then secondly, there is the secret mind of God, the will of His eternal predestination and decree of which we know nothing. But we do know this—that the Spirit of God never prompts us to ask anything which is contrary to the eternal purpose of God.

Reflect for a moment—the Holy Spirit knows all the purposes of God and when they are about to be fulfilled, He moves the children of God to pray about them and so their prayers keep touch and tally with the Divine decrees. Oh would you not pray confidently if you knew that your prayer corresponded with the sealed book of destiny? We may safely entreat the Lord to do what He has, Himself, ordained to do! A carnal man draws the inference that if God has ordained an event we need not pray about it, but faith obediently draws the inference that the God who secretly ordained to give the blessing has openly commanded that we should pray for it and, therefore, faith obediently prays!

Coming events cast their shadows before them and when God is about to bless His people, His coming favor casts the shadow of prayer over the Church. When He is about to favor an individual, He casts the shadow of hopeful expectation over His soul! Our prayers—let men laugh at them as they will and say there is no power in them—are the indicators of the movement of the wheels of Providence! Believing supplications are forecasts of the future! He who prays in faith is like the Seer of old—he sees that which is yet to be—his holy expectancy, like a telescope, brings distant objects near to him and things not seen as yet are visible to him! He is bold to declare that he has the petition which he has asked of God and he, therefore, begins to rejoice and to praise God before the blessing has actually arrived! So it is—prayer prompted by the Holy Spirit is the footfall of the Divine decree.

I conclude by saying, my dear Hearers, see the absolute necessity of the Holy Spirit, for if the saints know not what they should pray for as they ought—if consecrated men and women, with Christ suffering in them, still feel their need of the instruction of the Holy Spirit—how much more do you who are not saints and have never given yourselves up to God, require Divine teaching! Oh, that you would know and feel your dependence upon the Holy Spirit that He may prompt you this day to look to Jesus Christ for salvation! It is through the once crucified but now ascended Redeemer that this gift of the Spirit, this promise of the Father is shed abroad upon men! May He who comes from Jesus lead you to Jesus.

And, then, O you people of God, let this last thought abide with you—what condescension is this that this Divine Person should dwell in you forever and that He should be with you to help your prayers! Listen to me for a moment. If I read in the Scriptures that in the most heroic acts of faith, God the Holy Spirit, helps His people, I can understand it. If I read that in the sweetest music of their songs, when they worship best and chant their loftiest strains before the Most High God, the Spirit helps them, I can understand it. And even if I hear that in their wrestling prayers and prevalent intercessions God, the Holy Spirit helps them, I can understand it. But I bow with reverent amazement—my heart sinking into the dust with adoration—when I reflect that God, the Holy Spirit, helps us when we cannot speak but only groan!

Yes, and when we cannot even utter our groans He does not only help us but He claims as His own particular creation the "groans that cannot be uttered"! This is condescension, indeed! In deigning to help us in the grief that cannot even vent itself in groans He proves Himself to be a true Comforter! O God, my God! You have not forsaken me! You are not far from me, nor from the voice of my roaring. You did, for awhile, leave Your Firstborn when He was made a curse for us, so that He cried in agony, "Why have You forsaken Me?" But You will not leave one of the "many brethren" for whom He died—Your Spirit shall be with them and when they cannot so much as groan, He will make intercession for them with groans that cannot be uttered!

God bless you, my beloved Brothers and Sisters, and may you feel the Spirit of the Lord thus working in you and with you. Amen and amen.

THE HOLY SPIRIT'S THREEFOLD CONVICTION OF MEN

"And when He is come, He will reprove the world of sin, and of righteousness, and of judgment: of sin, because they believe not on Me; of righteousness, because I go to My Father, and you see Me no more; of judgment, because the prince of this world is judged."
John 16:8-11

A Sermon Delivered On Sunday Morning: 25 February 1883

THE Apostles had a stern task before them. They were to go into all nations and proclaim the Gospel to every creature, beginning at Jerusalem. Remember, only two or three years before they were simple fishermen engaged upon the Galilean Lake–men of little or no education, men of no rank or standing. At best they were but Jews and that nation was despised everywhere, while these peasants were not even men of repute among their own nation! Yet these men were to turn the world upside down! They were told by their Lord that they would be brought before rulers and kings for His sake and that they would be persecuted wherever they went. They were to proclaim the Gospel in the teeth of the imperial power of Rome, the ancient wisdom of Greece and the fierce cruelties of barbaric lands. And they were to set up the kingdom of peace and righteousness.

At the very time when they were about to receive their commission, they were also to lose the bodily Presence of their great Leader. While He was with them, they had felt no fear. If they were puzzled at any time by the Scribes and Pharisees, they resorted to Jesus, and they were rescued from bewilderment. Never man spoke like that Man! Never did such wisdom and prudence dwell in any mind as dwelt in the mind of Christ! His Presence was their protection, the broad shield behind which they securely stood, whatever shafts might be shot at them by their adversaries. But now that He was to depart out of the world unto the Father, they would be deprived of their fortress and high tower–they would be as children bereft of their father, or, at best, as soldiers without a general. Here was a sad case. Work given and power withdrawn–a battle beginning and the conquering Captain leaving.

How happy it was for these disciples that our blessed Lord could tell them that His going away would be for their gain rather than for their loss! For when He was gone, the Spirit of God would come to be an Advocate for them and with them, and by His power they would be able to silence all their enemies and achieve their mission! The Holy Spirit was to be their Comforter, that they might not be afraid, and their Advocate, that they might not be baffled. When they spoke, there would be a power within them suggesting their words, a power with those words convincing their hearers, and a power in their hearers causing the word spoken to abide in their memories–that power would be Divine, the power of the Holy Spirit, who is One God with the Father and the Son.

It is one thing for men to speak, and quite another thing for God to speak through men. The work of proclaiming the Gospel to the world was far too great for the 12, but it was by no means too great for the Spirit of God! Who can limit His power? Is anything too hard for the Lord? The Holy Spirit being their Helper, these feeble men were equal to the task which God had committed to their trust. The Presence of the Holy Spirit was better for them than the bodily Presence of the Lord Jesus. The Lord Jesus could only have been in one place as to His corporeal Presence, but the Holy Spirit could be everywhere! The sight of Jesus would but appeal to the senses, but the power of the Holy Spirit touched the heart and worked spiritual life and saving faith! Thus, by His own withdrawal and the sending of the Spirit, our Lord furnished His servants for the conflict.

We will, at this time, observe what the Holy Spirit did as an Advocate. The passage cannot be fully understood unless we give it three renderings. But I do not pretend that even then, we shall have pressed from this choice cluster, all the generous wine of its meaning! To my mind, it is a compendium of all the work of the Spirit of God. By our three readings we shall see much–first, the Spirit of God goes with the preaching of the Gospel to reprove men of sin–and so to embarrass them in the presence of the preacher of righteousness. Secondly (and this is a much more blessed result), to convict men of sin and so to lead them to repentance towards God and faith in our Lord Jesus Christ. And, thirdly, the ultimate result of the Holy Spirit's work will be to convict men before all intelligent beings of having been guilty of the grossest sin–having opposed the most perfect righteousness and of having defied the most glorious judgment. We shall try to see the meaning of the passage through these three windows.

First, we believe that a promise is here made to the servants of Christ that when they go forth to preach the Gospel the Holy Spirit will be with them TO REPROVE MEN. By this is meant, not so much to save them as to silence them. When the minister of Christ stands up to plead his Master's cause, another Advocate appears in court, whose pleadings would make it hard for men to resist the Truth of God. Observe how this reproof was given with regard to sin. On the day of Pentecost the disciples spoke with many different tongues, as the Spirit gave them utterance. Men from all countries under Heaven heard themselves addressed in their native tongues! This was a great marvel and all Jerusalem rang with it!

And when Peter stood up to preach to the assembled multitude and told the Jews that they had crucified the Holy One and the Just, the signs and wonders worked by the Spirit in the name of Jesus were a witness which they could not refute. The very fact that the Spirit of God had given to these unlettered men the gift of tongues was evidence that Jesus of Nazareth, of whom they spoke, was no impostor! It was laid down in the old Jewish Law that if a man prophesied and his prophecies did not come to pass, he was to be condemned as a false prophet. But if that which he said came to pass, then he was a true Prophet. Now, the Lord Jesus Christ had promised the outpouring of the Spirit, which had also been foretold in reference to the Messiah by the Prophet Joel. When, therefore, that mark of the true Messiah was set upon Jesus of Nazareth by the coming of the Holy Spirit and the working of miracles, men were reproved for having refused to believe in Jesus.

The evidence was brought home to them that they had, with wicked hands, crucified the Lord of Glory—and so they stood reproved. All the subsequent miracles went to prove the same thing, for when the Apostles worked miracles, the world was reproved of sin because it believed not on Christ. It was not that a few disciples testified to the sin of the race, but the Holy Spirit, Himself, made men tremble, as by His deeds of power, He bore witness to the Lord Jesus and exhibited the fact that in crucifying Jesus, the world had put to death the Incarnate Son of God! Do you not see the terrible power with which the first disciples were thus armed? It was more to them than the rod in the hand of Moses with which he smote Pharaoh with so many plagues. It needed all the willfulness of that stiff-necked generation to resist the Holy Spirit and refuse to bow before Him whom they had pierced—they were full of malice and obstinacy—but in their secret hearts they were sore put to it and felt that they were fighting against God.

Do you not see, too, dear Friends, how the working of the Holy Spirit with the Apostles and their immediate followers was a wonderful rebuke to the world concerning the matter of righteousness? Jesus was gone and His Divine example no longer stood out like clear light reproving their darkness–but the Holy Spirit attested that righteousness and compelled them to feel that Jesus was the Holy One and that His cause was righteous. The teaching of the Apostles, sealed by the Holy Spirit, made the world see what righteousness was as they had never seen it before! A fresh standard of morals was set up in the world and it has never been taken down–it stands in its place to rebuke, if not to improve! The world was then sunk in the uttermost depths of vice– even its good men were loathsome! But now another kind of righteousness was exhibited in the teachings of the Lord Jesus and the Spirit came to set the seal of Divine approval to it so that if men continued in sin, it might be against light and knowledge, for they now knew what was righteousness and could no longer be mistaken upon that point. God was with the preachers of a new righteousness and by many different signs and wonders He attested the cause of the Gospel.

Now, Brothers, we also rejoice in this, seeing that the witness of the Truth of God is for all time and we know of a surety that the Kingdom which our Lord Jesus has set up among men is Divinely sanctioned as the Kingdom of Righteousness which, in the end, shall grind to powder the powers of evil! We are the covenanted servants of a Lord whose righteousness was declared among men by the personal witness of God the Holy Spirit. Are you not glad to be enlisted in such a service? Oh, world, are you not embarrassed for resisting such a kingdom? These 12 fishermen could not, of themselves, have exhibited a new standard of righteousness among men! They could not, on their own, have set before all nations a higher ideal of moral excellence! But when the eternal power and majesty of the Godhead vouched for the righteousness of the Lord Jesus, the course of the Apostolic Church became like that of the sun in the heavens!

"Their line is gone out through all the earth, and their words to the end of the world." None could stand against them, for, as when the morning breaks, the darkness flies and the bats and the night birds hasten away, so when the messengers of mercy proclaimed the Righteousness of God, man's hypocrisy and self-glorying fled away! Then, too, they were made to feel that a judgment had come; that somehow the life and the death of Jesus of Nazareth had made a crisis in the world's history and condemned the way and manner of the ungodly. All historians must confess that the turning point of the race is the Cross of Christ. From that moment the power of evil received its mortal wound! It dies hard, but from that hour it was doomed. At the death of our Lord, the heathen oracles were struck dumb. There had been oracles all over the world, either the product of evil spirits or of crafty priests, but after the Christian era the world ceased to believe in these voices and they were no more heard.

Systems of false worship, so firmly rooted in prejudice and custom that it seemed impossible that they should ever be overthrown, were torn up by their roots by the breath of the Lord. The Apostles might have said to all the systems of falsehood, "as a bowing wall shall you be, and as a tottering fence." Men could not help perceiving that the Prince of Darkness had been cast down from his undivided power and that he spoke, from then on, with bated breath. The Seed of the woman had met the old serpent and, in the duel between them, He had gained such a victory that the cause of evil was henceforth hopeless. Moreover, the thought flashed upon humanity more clearly than ever–there would be a Day of Judgment! Men heard and felt the truth of the warning that God would judge the world, at the last, by the Man, Christ Jesus!

The dim forms of Rhadamanthus on a cloudy judgment seat and of the assembly before his throne, and of the crowds divided according to their lives, now began to assume another and far more definite shape. It was written on the heart of mankind that there is a judgment to come! Men will rise again! They shall stand before the Judgment Seat of Christ to give an account of the things done in the body, whether good or evil. The world heard this and the tidings have never been forgotten! The Holy Spirit has reproved men by the prospect of judgment! The Holy Spirit attested the life of Christ, the teaching of the Apostles and all the grand Truths of God that were contained therein, by what He did in the way of miracles and by what He did in the way of enlightening, impressing and subduing human hearts. Henceforth man is accused and rebuked by the great Advocate! And all who remain in opposition to the Lord Jesus, remain so in defiance of the clearest proofs of His mission. He who rejects human testimony when it is true is foolish, but he who despises the witness of the Holy Spirit is profane, for he calls the Spirit of Truth a liar! Let him beware lest he so sin against the Holy Spirit as to come under the most terrible of curses–for it is written of him that speaks against the Holy Spirit–"he has no forgiveness."

Brothers and Sisters, does not that put the Apostles in quite a different position from that in which they appeared to be? If we judge according to sense and carnal reason, their adventure was Quixotic, their success was impossible! Everybody would have said to them, "Go back to your nets and to your boats. What can you do against the established system of Judaism in your own country? And if that is too hard for you, what will you be able to do in other lands? There are nations that have been tutored in their own learning for thousands of years and have become adept in all the arts and sciences! They have brought all the charms of poetry, music and statuary to support their idolatrous systems–you are fools to think that you unlearned and ignorant men can ever overturn all this!"

Would not prudence agree with this? Yes, but if God is in these men–if He that dwelt in the bush at Horeb and made it burn, though it was not consumed–will dwell in them and each one of them shall be gifted with a tongue of fire, this is a different business altogether! Surely, He that made the world, could make it new! He that said, "Let there be light, and there was light," could command light to shine upon the moral and spiritual night. Thus much upon the first reading of the text. Let us advance to that which will more interest you.

II. The Holy Spirit was to go with the preaching of the Word of God TO CONVINCE MEN of three great prominent Truths of God. This was to be a saving Word–they are to be so convinced as to repent of sin, to accept of righteousness and yield themselves to the judgment of the Lord. Here we see as in a map, the work of the Spirit upon the hearts of those who are ordained unto eternal life! Those three effects are all necessary and each one is, in the highest degree, important to true conversion. First, the Holy Spirit is come to convince men of sin. It is absolutely necessary that men should be convinced of sin.

The fashionable theology of the day is–"Convince men of the goodness of God! Show them the universal fatherhood and assure them of unlimited mercy. Win them by God's love, but never mention His wrath against sin, or the need of an Atonement, or the possibility of there being a place of punishment! Do not censure poor creatures for their failings. Do not judge and condemn. Do not search the heart or lead men to be low-spirited and sorrowful. Comfort and encourage, but never accuse and threaten!" Yes, that is the way of man–but the way of the Spirit of God is very different! He comes on purpose to convince men of sin, to make them feel that they are guilty, greatly guilty–so guilty that they are lost, ruined and undone! He comes to remind them not only of God's loveliness, but of their own unloveliness–of their own enmity and hatred to this God of Love and, consequently, of their terrible sin in thus ill-using One so infinitely kind.

The Holy Spirit does not come to make sinners comfortable in their sins, but to cause them to grieve over their sins! He does not help them to forget their sin, or think little of it, but He comes to convince them of the horrible enormity of their iniquity! It is no work of the Spirit to pipe to men's dancing–He does not bring forth flute, harp, dulcimer and all kinds of music to charm the unbelieving into a good opinion of themselves–He comes to make sin appear sin and to let us see its fearful consequences! He comes to wound so that no human balm can heal! He comes to kill so that no earthly power can make us live! The flowers bedeck the meadows when the grass is green, but lo, a burning wind comes from the desert and the grass withers and the flowers fall away. What is it that makes the beauty and excellence of human righteousness to wither as the green herb? Isaiah says it is "because the Spirit of the Lord blows upon it."

There is a withering work of the Spirit of God which we must experience or we shall never know His quickening and restoring power. This withering is a most necessary experience and, just now, needs much to be insisted on. Today we have so many built up who were never pulled down; so many filled who were never emptied; so many exalted who were never humbled that I, the more earnestly, remind you that the Holy Spirit must convince us of sin or we cannot be saved! This work is most necessary because without it there is no leading men to receive the Gospel of the Grace of God. We cannot make headway with certain people because they profess faith very readily, but they are not convinced of anything. "Oh, yes, we are sinners, no doubt, and Christ died for sinners"–that is the free-and-easy way with which they handle heavenly mysteries–as if they were the nonsense verses of a boy's exercise, or the stories of Mother Goose!

This is all mockery and we are weary of it. But get near a real sinner and you have found a man you can deal with–I mean the man who is a sinner and there is no mistake about it—he mourns in his inmost soul that he is so. In such a man you find one who will welcome the Gospel, welcome Grace and welcome a Savior. To him the news of pardon will be as cold water to a thirsty soul—and the Doctrines of Grace will be as honey dropping from the comb! "A sinner," says one of our songsters, "is a sacred thing"—the Holy Spirit has made Him so. Your sham sinner is a horrid creature, but a man truly convinced of sin by the Spirit of God is a being to be sought after as a jewel that will adorn the crown of the Redeemer!

Note here, that the Spirit of God comes to convince men of sin because they never will be convinced of sin apart from His Divine advocacy. A natural conscience touched by the Spirit of God may do a good deal in the way of showing a man his faults. It may thus make him uneasy and may bring about a reformation of life. But it is only the Spirit of God that, to the full extent, convinces a man of sin so as to bring forth repentance, self-despair and faith in Jesus. For what is the sin that you and I are guilty of? Ah, Brothers and Sisters, it is not easy to tell, but this I know, that the extent of sin is never known till the Spirit of God reveals the secret chambers of the heart's abominations. We do a thousand things that we do not know to be sin till the Spirit of God enlightens us and pleads the cause of holiness in us.

What natural man, for instance, ever laments over evil thoughts or desires, or the imaginations which flit across his mind? Yet all these are sins and sins which cause a gracious heart the deepest distress! If we were never actually to commit evil, yet if we desire to do so, we have already sinned! And if we feel pleasure in thinking of evil, we have already sinned. This poison is in our nature and shows itself in a thousand ways. The fact that we not only sin, but are, by nature, sinful, is one which our pride kicks against—and we will not learn it till the Spirit of God teaches it to us. Neither does any man know the exceeding sinfulness of sin till the Light of God falls upon the black mass from the Holy Spirit. Every sin is, as it were, an assault upon God's Throne, Glory and life. Sin would dethrone the Most High and destroy Him if it could—but men do not see this. They talk of sin most lightly and know not that it scatters firebrands and death.

I tell you, when the Spirit of God makes a man see sin in its naked deformity, he is horrified! When I saw, or thought I saw, the heinousness of sin, it was intolerable and I had no rest in my spirit. Some such sight we must all have, or we shall never look to the Lord Jesus to take away our sin. None but those whose wounds smart are likely to apply for the heavenly balm. The Holy Spirit dwells upon one point in particular–"of sin, because they believe not on Me." None see the sin of unbelief except by His light. A man thinks, "Well, if I have not believed in Christ, that is a pity, perhaps, but still, I was never a thief, or a liar, or a drunk, or unchaste. Unbelief is a matter of very little consequence. I can set that right at any time." But the Holy Spirit makes a man see that not to believe in Christ is a crowning, damning sin, since, "he that believes not has made God a liar"–and what can be more atrocious than that?

He who believes not on Christ has rejected God's mercy and has done despite to the grandest display of God's love! He has despised God's unspeakable Gift and trampled on the blood of Christ! In this he has dishonored God on a very tender point. He has insulted Him concerning His only-begotten Son! How I wish that the Spirit of God would come upon unbelievers, here, and make them see what they are and where they are with regard to the one and only Savior! How shall they escape, who neglect so great a salvation? It will not matter how feebly I speak this morning if the Spirit of God will only work by the Truth of God on you–you will perceive the greatness of your crime and you will never rest until you have believed on the Lord Jesus–and found forgiveness for your high offense against the bleeding Lamb!

So far, then, upon the first operation of the Holy Spirit. The next work of the Spirit is to convince men of righteousness, that is to say, in Gospel terms, to show them that they have no righteousness of their own and no means of working righteousness–and that apart from Grace they are condemned! Thus He leads them to value the righteousness of God which is, upon all them that believe, a righteousness which covers sin and renders them acceptable with God. Lend me your ears a moment while I call your attention to a great wonder! Among men, if a person is convicted of wrong-doing, the next step is judgment. A young man, for instance, has been in the service of an employer and he has embezzled money–he is convicted of the theft by process of law and found guilty. What follows next?

Why, judgment is pronounced and he must suffer the penalty! But observe how our gracious God interpolates another process. Truly, His ways are not our ways! "He shall convince of sin." The next step would be judgment, but no, the Lord inserts an up to now unknown middle term and convinces "of righteousness." Be amazed at this! The Lord takes a man, even when he is sinful and conscious of that sin, and makes him righteous on the spot by putting away his sin and justifying him by the righteousness of faith, a righteousness which comes to him by the worthiness of Another who has worked out a righteousness for him! Can that be? Brothers and Sisters, this seems to be unthinkable–so impossible that it needs the Spirit of God to convince men of it!

I may now set forth the great plan whereby the Lord Jesus is made of God unto us righteousness! I may show how the Son of God became Man that He might fully keep the Law of God for us and, having done so, and having added His passive obedience to His active service, He presented to His Father a complete vindication of His injured Law so that every man that believes on Him shall be delivered from condemnation and accepted in the Beloved! I might also tell how Christ's righteousness is set to our account so that faith is reckoned unto us for righteousness, even as was the case with faithful Abraham. Yet all my labor will be in vain till the Spirit shall make it plain! Many hear the gladsome tidings, but they do not receive the Truth of God, for they are not convinced of it. They need to be persuaded of it before they will embrace it–and that persuasion is not in my power.

Did I hear one remark, "I cannot see this way of righteousness"? I answer, No, and you never will until the Spirit of God convinces you of it! Note well the great point of the Spirit's argument–"Of righteousness, because I go to My Father and you see Me no more." Our Lord was sent into the world to work out a righteousness and here, He says, "I go." But He would not go till He had done His work. He says, also, "I go to My Father." But He would not go back to His Father till He had fulfilled His Covenant engagements. "I go to My Father," that is, I go to receive a reward and to sit upon My Father's Throne. But He could not have received this Glory if He had not finished His appointed work! Behold, then, Christ has finished a righteousness which is freely given to all them that believe! And all those who trust in Christ are, for His sake, rewarded as righteous before God–and are, in fact, righteous, so that Paul says, "Who is he that condemns?"

His ground for asking that question is the same as that which the Spirit uses in my text. Paul says, "It is Christ that died, yes, rather, that is risen again, who is even at the right hand of God, who also makes intercession for us." He quotes, as the Holy Spirit does, the resurrection, ascension and enthronement of the great Intercessor as the proof positive that there is a perfect righteousness for all believing sinners! I know that many will say, "This is making people righteous who are not righteous" and, therefore, they will raise many objections. Just so! This is the Glory of God, that He justifies the ungodly and saves sinners by Christ. "Blessed is the man unto whom the Lord imputes not iniquity."

"I do not see it," cries one. And our answer is, "We know you do not! We are not in the least surprised that you reject our testimony—we never expected you to receive it unless the arm of the Lord should be revealed and the Holy Spirit should convince you of righteousness." No man comes to Christ who is not drawn of the Father and enlightened by the Spirit! But if the Spirit convinces you, we shall soon hear you sing—

"Jesus, Your blood and righteousness
My beauty are, my glorious dress!
Midst flaming worlds, in these arrayed,
With joy shall I lift up my head."

Dear people of God, pray hard that the Spirit of God may, even now, convince unbelievers that the only true righteousness for mortal men is that which comes not by the works of the Law, but by the hearing of faith!

But then comes a third point, the Spirit of God is to convince men of judgment. To whom is this judgment committed? "The Father has committed all judgment unto the Son." The true penitent feels that if he had all his sins forgiven him, yet it will not serve his turn so long as he lies wallowing in sin. He feels that the great enemy of his soul must be dethroned, or else forgiveness, itself, will afford him no rest of heart. He must be rescued from the power as well as from the guilt of sin, or else he abides in bondage. He must see the power of evil hewn in pieces before the Lord, as Samuel hewed Agag of old. Listen, O troubled one! You shall be set free, for, "the prince of this world is judged." Jesus came to destroy the works of the devil—and on the Cross, our Redeemer judged Satan, overcame him and cast him down!

Satan is now a condemned criminal, a vanquished rebel. His reigning power over all Believers is broken. He has great wrath, knowing that his time is short, but that wrath is held in check by his Conqueror! In His passion, our Lord fought Satan foot to foot and overcame him, spoiling principalities and powers and making a show of them openly, triumphing over them in it. Do you believe this? May the Spirit of God convince you of it! O tried Believer, the Lord Jesus overthrew the devil for you! He crushed the powers of darkness for you! Believing in Him, you shall find evil dethroned in you and all the forces of sin hurled from their high places! You shall overcome through the blood of the Lamb! Again, I ask, do you believe this? Christ is made of God unto us sanctification—He saves His people from their sins—He makes them holy and so breaks in pieces their enemy.

Though it will cost you many a conflict and the beaded sweat may, in the hour of temptation, stand upon your brow as you fear that you will fall from holiness, yet the Lord shall bruise Satan under your feet, shortly, for He has already bruised him under His own feet on your behalf! The Spirit of God is needed to convince our unbelieving hearts that it is so. Most men dream that they must overcome sin by their own strength. Alas, the strong armed man still keeps the house against our feebleness. You have a pretty piece of work before you if, in your own strength, you venture on this conflict. I can hear the devil laughing at you even now! This leviathan is not to be tamed by you. Job would say, "Will you play with him as with a bird?" Do you think the devil is as easily managed as a woman carries her pet bird on her finger and puts it to her lip to peck a seed?

Can you draw out leviathan with a hook? Will he speak soft words unto you? Will you take him to be a servant forever? Your arrows cannot come at him, nor your sword wound him! "Lay your hand upon him, remember the battle, do no more." A Divine power is needed and that power is ready to display itself if it is humbly sought! Many who are convinced of the righteousness of Christ are not yet fully convinced that evil is judged, condemned and cast down. They are haunted with the dread that they may yet perish by the hand of the enemy. Oh, my Brothers and Sisters, see the need of the Holy Spirit to advocate in your heart the cause of and Truth of God—and make you believe that the Lord Jesus has supreme power over every enemy!

I sometimes meet with a Christian who tells me the world is all going to the bad, the Gospel is being utterly defeated, Christ is routed, the devil is waving the black flag and shouting victory. I know how terrible is the conflict, but I believe that my Lord Jesus has judged the whole kingdom of evil and, in that fact I see Satan fall like lightning from Heaven! Our Lord must reign! His enemies must lick the dust! We shall judge the fallen angels at the Last Great Day and, mean mightier than error, love is stronger than hate and holiness is higher than sin, for the Lord's right hand and His holy arm have gotten Him the victory! Behold how the ascended Savior leads captivity captive! See how He comes from Edom with dyed garments from Bozrah, for He has trodden sin and Hell in the winepress and now He travels in the greatness of His strength, speaking in righteousness, mighty to save!

Let me run again over this ground, that we may not overlook anything. Dear Friends, those of us who are saved still need the Holy Spirit with us every day to convince us of sin! Good men do, at this hour, most complacently, things which, in clearer light, they would never think of doing! May the Holy Spirit continually show us layer after layer of sin, that we may remove it. May He reveal to us rank after rank of sin, that we may conquer all its forces. May He especially make known to us the sin of not believing in Christ, for even we have our doubts and fears. After a sermon concerning sin, the poor child of God cries out, "I dare not believe! I am afraid I shall be lost, after all." This unbelief is another sin. Strange way of escaping from sin by plunging into it!

To doubt the Lord is to add sin to sin! No sin is more pernicious than the sin of not believing. Whenever our heart distrusts the Lord, we grieve His Spirit–therefore we always need the Holy Spirit to convince us of this evil and bitter thing–and to lead us to trust after a child-like fashion. Any mistrust of God's promise; any fear of failure on God's part; any thought of His unfaithfulness is a crime against the honor of the Divine majesty! Oh, convincing Spirit, dwell with me from day to day convincing me of sin and especially making me to feel that the worst of all evils is to question my faithful Friend. So, also, may you always have the Spirit of God dwelling with you, convincing you of righteousness.

May those of you who are, indeed, Believers, never question but what you are righteous before God. We who believe are made the righteousness of God in Christ Jesus! Are we assured of this? If so, do not think and talk as if you were still under the curse of the Law, for you are no longer in any such condition. "Therefore being justified by faith, we have peace with God through our Lord Jesus Christ." "There is, therefore, now no condemnation to them which are in Christ Jesus," Oh, may the Spirit of God convince you of that every day–and convince you of it on the ground that Jesus is reigning yonder at the Father's right hand!. The interest of each Believer in His Lord is clear and sure. If Jesus is there, I am there. If the Father has accepted Him, He has accepted me!

Do you catch the logic of it? You are in Christ, you are one with Him–as He is, so are you in Him! Hold fast to the fact that you are not condemned. How can you be? You are at the right hand of God in Christ. You, condemned? Why, you are "accepted in the Beloved," for your Representative is accepted by God and made to sit upon His Throne! Jesus is exalted, not for Himself, alone, but for all those who believe in Him! May the blessed Spirit fully convince you of this grand Truth of God!

And, next, may He convince you of judgment–namely, that you have been judged and your enemy has been judged and condemned. The Day of Judgment is not a thing to be dreaded by a Believer. We have stood our trial, and have been acquitted. Our Representative has borne the penalty of our sin. Our chastisement is passed, for Jesus has borne it–He was numbered with transgressors. There is, now, no curse for us! There can be none– Heaven, earth, Hell cannot find a curse for those whom God has blessed– since the Lord Jesus "was made a curse for us." May the Spirit of God come on you afresh, my dearly Beloved, and make you confident and joyful in Him who is the Lord our righteousness, by whom evil has been judged, once and for all!

II. Last of all, let us read our text by rendering it, "convict"–"The Spirit of God will CONVICT the world of sin, of righteousness, and of judgment." There is the world. It stands a prisoner at the bar and the charge is that it is and has been full of sin. In courts of law you are often surprised with what comes out. You look at the prisoner and he seems to be a quiet, respectable person. And you say, "I should not think he is guilty." But the advocate who has engaged to plead the cause of righteousness stands up and gives an outline of the case– and you speedily change your mind, until, as the evidence proceeds, you say to yourself, "That is a villain if ever there was one."

Now hear the Spirit of God! The Spirit came into the world to make all men know that Jesus is the Christ. And He attested to that fact by miracles that could not be questioned, miracles without number! He has, moreover, attested the truth of the Gospel by the conversion of myriads, whose happy and holy lives have been a proof that Jesus Christ was, indeed, sent forth from God. But what did this wicked world do with Christ? They gave Him a felon's death! They nailed Him to a cross! By this, the world is condemned! We need no further evidence. The world is convicted–self-condemned by the slaughter of

Him who was Incarnate Goodness and unbounded Love! The world is base enough to desire to slay its God even when He comes on an errand of love!

Take the accused away! The world's guilt is proven beyond question. The wrath of God abides on it. What follows upon this? The trial is viewed from another point. The world has declared that the Gospel is not righteous, that the system which our Lord has come to establish is not true. Up to this day the world is continually raising objections, trying to confuse Believers and, if possible, to defeat our most holy cause. But the Spirit of God, by His teaching, proves that the Gospel is full of righteousness and, by all His operations through the Word of God, He proves that the Gospel is holy, just, good and tends to make men pure, godly, peaceable and holy. By sanctifying men through the Gospel so that they lead gracious lives, the Holy Spirit proves that the Gospel is righteous!

This process grows more and more complete as time rolls on. Were not the world unrighteous, it would, long ago, have yielded to the holy message and its holy Messenger. But it will be forced to acknowledge the Truth one day. The Holy Spirit makes the world know that Christ is righteous by flashing into its face the fact that Christ has gone–gone up to Glory, at the right hand of God–and this could not have been had He not been the Righteous One. When the world shall see Jesus enthroned, at the last, and all mankind shall behold the Son of Man on the clouds of Heaven, what conviction will seize on every mind! There will be no agnostics, then! Not a skeptic will be found in that day! Christ seen at the Father's right hand will end all unbelief!

And then the Spirit of God shall make men see the judgment. Before the day actually comes, they shall perceive that since Christ has judged the devil; since Christ has cast him down from his high places and his power over the world is already broken, assuredly He will smite all that are in the dominion of Satan and will not allow one of them to escape. The cause of evil is judged and its case is desperate. Oh, how the Spirit of God will convict men at that last day when they hear the Judge say, "Come, you blessed of My Father," or, "Depart, you cursed, into everlasting fire." Brothers and Sisters, will you be convinced by the Holy Spirit, now, or will you wait till then? Shall it be the convincement of Grace or the conviction of wrath? The Spirit still bears witness with us who preach the Gospel–will you yield to that Gospel and believe it, now? Or will you wait until the blaze of the last tremendous day? Which shall it be?

I think I hear you say, "The Gospel is true." Why, then, do you not believe it? If you confess "sin," why are you not washed from it? If there is "righteousness," why do you not seek it? If there is "judgment," why do you not ask to be so cleansed that you need not be afraid of it? Oh, Sirs, the most of men act as if they were born fools! If they were sick and we had a sure medicine for them, they would rush to us for it! If they were poor and we brought them gold, they would trample us down in their vehemence to snatch at wealth!

But when there is Christ to be had, the Divine remedy for sin—Christ to be had as a perfect Righteousness, Christ to make them stand securely at the last dread day—they turn their backs upon the heavenly Gift! Oh, Spirit of God, win these madmen! Bring back these fools and make them sane and wise, for Christ Jesus' sake! Amen.

PART III

KNOWING THE HOLY SPIRIT

RECEIVING THE HOLY SPIRIT

"He said unto them, Have you received the Holy Spirit since you believed?"
Acts 19:2

A Sermon Delivered On Sunday Morning: 13 July 1884

IT may be well to notice what question the Apostle did not put to these Ephesian disciples of John. He did not say to them, "Have you believed?" This would have been a very important question and it ought to be settled once and for all. Our faith must either be boldly affirmed or sorrowfully denied–it should not remain the subject of question. It is a great pity that so many Christians are always saying, "Have I believed?" and allowing that most vital point to be a matter of debate–for as long as the existence of faith within our souls is the subject of question, we must be unhappy. Faith is the cornerstone of the edifice of godliness–if it is not well laid and known to be well laid–there can be no sense of security to the inhabitant of the house. We not only ought to know that we believe, but to know Whom we believe! And it would be well for us to advance beyond common believing to assurance–and then to full assurance–the assurance of faith, the assurance of hope and the assurance of understanding.

Again, Paul does not put the question, "If you have believed, how came it about? By what agencies was faith created in your souls? When did you first become Believers?" These are very proper questions if we view them as points of interest, but they do not touch the essence of salvation. A man may be saved and yet know none of the details of his conversion. No doubt there are many strong Believers who could not point to any special agency as the means by which faith was begotten within them. In general, it was by the hearing of the Word of God and by the operation of the Holy Spirit–but they do not remember, as some do, a remarkable text, or a thrilling sermon, or a striking Providence, through which they were turned from darkness to the Light of God.

Thousands in the fold of Jesus come to the Good Shepherd by degrees. Many who now walk in the Light received daylight, not by the leaping of the sun above the horizon in a moment, but as our days mostly begin in this country–a little light tinged the eastern sky and then came a rosy hue, followed by a dim dawn—and afterwards came the actual rising of the sun which comes out of the chambers of the east and runs his course till he has created perfect day. Many are gradually brought to Christ and yet they are truly brought to Christ. I say we may ask about the when and the how of conversion if we wish to be interested, as we have a right to be, in the stories of the godly, but we must not ask such questions as if they were of vital importance and should stand first.

Paul does not enquire about ways, means and times, but he does ask—"Have you received the Holy Spirit since you believed?" Our Revised Version reads it, "Did you receive the Holy Spirit when you believed?" and others who are probably quite as accurate read it, "Are you receiving the Holy Spirit now that you have believed?" It does not matter one atom which way you read it—all the renderings come to this—"Do you see a connection between your believing and the Holy Spirit? Did you receive Him when you believed? Have you received Him since you believed? Are you daily receiving Him as you believe?"

That is the subject which is now before us—the Holy Spirit in our hearts as Believers. Has your faith been sealed by the impress of the Holy Spirit? This is a point of the utmost importance and upon it I desire to speak with deep and solemn earnestness in the power of the Holy Spirit, Himself. You know, dear Friends, when the Holy Spirit was given in the earliest ages, He showed His Presence by certain miraculous signs. Some of those who received the Holy Spirit spoke with tongues; others began to prophesy and a third class received the gifts of healing—so that wherever they laid their hands, disease fled before them. I am sure that if these powers were given now in connection with the reception of the Holy Spirit and your believing, you would all be anxious to possess them. I can hardly imagine a single Christian who would not put to himself the enquiry, "Have I received the Holy Spirit in that fashion?" You would want to be healing, or to be speaking with tongues, or to be working miracles by which you could benefit your fellow men and glorify God! Would you not?

Now, be it never forgotten that those works of the Holy Spirit which are permanent must assuredly be of greater value than those which were transitory. We cannot suppose that the Holy Spirit brought forth the best wine at first and that His operations gradually deteriorated. It is a rule of the Kingdom of God to keep the best wine for the last and, therefore, I conclude that you and I are not left to partake of the dregs, but that those works of the Holy Spirit which are at this time vouchsafed to the Church of God are, in every way, as valuable as those earlier miraculous gifts which have departed from us. The work of the Holy Spirit, by which men are quickened from their death in sin, is not inferior to the power which made men speak with tongues! The work of the Holy Spirit, when He comforts men and makes them glad in Christ, is by no means second to the opening of the eyes of the blind! Why, Sirs, men might have the gifts of the Spirit as to miracles and yet might perish, after all! But he that has the spiritual gifts of the Holy Spirit shall never perish– they are saving blessings and where they come, they lift the man out of his sinful state and make him to be a child of God!

I would, therefore, press it upon you, this morning, that as you would certainly enquire whether you had the gifts of healing and miracle-working, if such gifts were now given to Believers, much more should you enquire whether you have those more permanent gifts of the Spirit which are, this day, open to you all. By them you shall work no physical miracle, but shall achieve spiritual wonders of the grander sort! If we come to weigh spiritual operations, they are by no means secondary in the judgment of enlightened servants of God. Have you then received the Spirit since you believed? Beloved, are you now receiving the Spirit? Are you living under His Divine influence? Are you filled with His power?

Put the question personally. I am afraid some professors will have to admit that they hardly know whether there is any Holy Spirit. And others will have to confess that though they have enjoyed a little of His saving work, yet they do not know much of His ennobling and sanctifying influence. We have, none of us, participated in His operations as we might have done–we have sipped where we might have drunk! We have drunk where we might have bathed! We have bathed up to the ankles where we might have found rivers to swim in! Alas, of many Christians it must be affirmed that they have been naked, poor and miserable when they might, in the power of the Holy Spirit, have been clad in golden garments and have been rich and increased in goods.

He waits to be gracious, but we linger in indifference, like those of whom we read, "they could not enter in because of unbelief." There are many such cases and, therefore, it is not improper that I should, with all vehemence, press home upon you the question of the Apostle, "Have you received the Holy Spirit since you believed?" Did you receive Him when you believed? Are you receiving Him now that you are believing in Christ Jesus? We will, first, this morning, consider the question. And then we will listen to the lessons which it is calculated to teach.

I want you to consider THE QUESTION. In some respects it is a vital question. I shall not be playing around the outskirts of religion now, but plunging into its very center. This question has nothing to do with the sect to which you belong, nor with the particular condition in which your mind may happen to be for the present hour–it is an enquiry which touches the heart of the man and the inmost life of his spirit. "Have you received the Holy Spirit since you believed?" For, remember, the Holy Spirit is the Author of all spiritual life. Life does not lie latent in natural men for themselves to stir up– until the Holy Spirit visits them they are dead in trespasses and sins. If, when you believed, you had not a life imparted by the Holy Spirit, your believing was a dead believing, a mere counterfeit of living faith–and not the faith of God's elect!

If the Holy Spirit has not been with you since your conversion, every act of your religion has been formal, dead and unaccepted! In vain have you sung your formal songs! In vain have you attempted to adore! Your Hosannas have languished on your tongues and your devotion has fallen like a corpse before the altar. If the Holy Spirit is not there, life is not there–your many prayers have been mockeries! Your joys have been delusions and your griefs have been carnal! That which is born of the flesh is flesh and nothing better–let that flesh be washed and cleansed–yet all that comes of it is flesh! Only that which is born of the Spirit is spirit! There must, then, be a work from Heaven, a work of the Holy Spirit upon the heart, or else you have not believed unto life and you still abide in death.

As the Holy Spirit is the Author of our quickening, the Lord and Giver of life, so is He the Author of all true instruction. Brother, you have professed to be a Believer, but you know nothing at all unless the Holy Spirit has taught you. "All your children shall be taught of the Lord." To be taught of the minister is nothing–but to be taught of the Lord is everything! It is only the Spirit of God who can engrave the Truth of God upon the fleshy tablets of the heart. We speak to the ear, but only He can speak to the inmost soul. He that professes to be a Believer while he has never received the Truth of God in the power of it, as sent home by the Spirit of light and fire, has need to begin again and learn the first rudiments of the faith! He has learned nothing aright who has not been under the direct operation of the Holy Spirit. The knowledge of the letter only puffs up those who rest in it—and eventually the letter kills. But the inward whisper, the secret admonition, the silent operation of the Spirit of God which falls as the dew from Heaven upon the heart—this is quite another thing. He that has it not is blind and ignorant, though he has a Doctor of Divinity and is revered as a rabbi in Israel! Though he is a preacher to thousands, he is still in the dark unless the Spirit of God has shone upon his soul. See, then, how vital this question is! Both for life and for light we must have the Holy Spirit, or else we are dead and in the dark.

Furthermore, if we have believed in Christ aright, the Holy Spirit has come upon us to transform us altogether. By Divine Grace we are not now what we used to be—we have new thoughts, new wishes, new aspirations, new sorrows, new joys—and these are worked in us by the Spirit. A man's conversion is nothing. His believing is nothing. His profession is nothing unless he is made to be a new creature in Christ Jesus. But how can we be made new by any other power than the Holy Spirit? Only He that creates can new-create. "Except a man is born again, he cannot see the kingdom of God." We cannot hate evil and love right of ourselves, for the whole bent and bias of our spirit since the Fall are toward evil, only evil, and that continually! Neither can we renew ourselves. Who can bring a clean thing out of an unclean? Not one! Can an unclean thing bring forth itself clean out of uncleanness? Between the ribs of death there cannot be spontaneously formed the seeds of life. The Holy Spirit must transform us by the renewing of our minds—we must be begotten again unto a lively hope by the Resurrection of Jesus Christ from the dead, or else we are still in the flesh and cannot please God. If our faith has not brought with it the Holy Spirit. If, indeed, it is not the fruit of the Spirit and we are not changed in nature and in life, then our faith is presumption and our profession is a lie!

Furthermore, it is absolutely essential to all true religion that you and I should be sanctified. A faith which works not for purification will work for putrefaction. Unless our faith makes us pine after holiness and pant after conformity to God, it is no better than the faith of devils and, perhaps, it is not even as good as that! How can any man become holy except by the Spirit of Holiness? A holy man is the workmanship of the Holy Spirit! Through faith we are sanctified by the operation of the Holy Spirit so that we are delivered from the dominion of sin and set free to follow after that which is good and pure and right in the sight of God. Faith which does not bring holiness with it is a dead faith which will never bring us into communion with the living God! Oh, the absolute necessity that the Holy Spirit should rest upon us when we believe in Christ!

Beside that, remember, dear Friends, there is one mark of God's people which, if it is lacking, is fatal–and that is prayer. "Behold, he prays," is a true sign of the new birth! But can a man pray without the assistance of the Holy Spirit? Let him try to do so and, if he is honest and sincere, he will soon find the value of that text–"Likewise the Spirit also helps our infirmities: for we know not what we should pray for as we ought: but the Spirit itself makes intercession for us with groans which cannot be uttered." Pray without the Spirit of God? Oh, Sir, it will be a mechanical performance–the statue of prayer–not the living, prevailing supplication of an heir of Heaven! You may go to your chamber and kneel down at that particular chair where you have so often enjoyed communion with God, but unless you invoke the Spirit of God, the posture shall be a weariness, the exercise shall be heartless and the result shall be worthless!

What is the incense without the burning coals? What is the Mercy Seat without the Shekinah light? Prayer without the Spirit is as a bird without wings, or an arrow without a bow! As well hope to see a dead man sit up in his coffin and plead a case in a court of law, as hope to see a man prevail in prayer who is a stranger to the Holy Spirit, who is the Spirit of Grace and of supplications! You will leave your prayer closet unrefreshed if you have been in it without the Spirit. Even the desire to pray is not with us unless the Holy Spirit has worked it in the soul. No true word of supplication can arise from the heart unless the Spirit of God shall prompt it. Dear, dear Friends, you do see, do you not, how on all these points, contact with the Spirit of God becomes essential to our present spiritual life and to our eternal salvation? Look you to it; look you to it at once!

If all you have is what you have made yourself, you and your works must perish! If all your prayers have risen from no greater depth than your own heart and if they are the fruit of no better spirit than your own–they will never reach the ear of God, nor bring you blessings from the Throne of God. If there is not something supernatural about your religion, it will be a millstone about your neck to sink you into Hell! What comes from the dunghill and is of the dunghill will rot on the dunghill! That which comes from a man's heart, apart from the gracious operation of the Holy Spirit, will rise no higher than his own depraved nature and leave Him unblessed! But that which comes from above will elevate him to its own element and cause him to dwell with Christ at the right hand of God!

But now, while this is a vital question, I beg to say further that where it is not vital, it is, nevertheless, greatly important. I do not think we ought always to be asking the question, "Is this essential?" meaning thereby, "Is it essential to our salvation?" Those are miserable souls who would be stingy in obedience and love so that they would labor and love no more than is absolutely necessary to get to Heaven! They would be saved in the cheapest possible way and they would be content to crawl over the threshold of Glory, but not to go too far in! They want as much Grace as may be necessary to float them over the bar at the harbor's mouth, but they do not desire a grand entrance. O you miserly professors, stinting yourselves in the matter of the Grace of God—I have little to say to you!

But I turn to the children of God and joyfully remind them that there is, in the Holy Spirit, not only what they absolutely need to save them, but much more! Here is not only bread, but wine on the lees well refined. In the Holy Spirit there is comfort to gladden you, Grace to strengthen you, holiness to ennoble you and love to purify you. For, first, the Spirit of God is the Comforter and how important it is that you should be comforted! Why do you hang your heads? Why do you go mourning as if you were in the night and the dews were thick upon your eyelids? You are the children of the morning and the children of the day—rejoice in the Lord and walk in the light as He is in the light! "Have you received the Holy Spirit since you believed?" You whose brows are furrowed with care, whose hearts are distracted with anxiety, receive the Spirit of consolation and be glad in the Lord, for the joy of the Lord is your strength!

In the Holy Spirit there is also a spirit of enlightening. Do you read the Word of God understanding very little of it? Do you hear it as though you heard not? Why is this? Should you not seek more of the teaching of the Holy Spirit, that He may lead you into all Truths of God? How much happier you would be—and how much more useful—if you knew more of the things of God! The Holy Spirit can take of the things of Christ and can show them to you. Now you only see men as trees walking, but there is no need to be content with such dim vision, for the Comforter can anoint your eyes with eye salve that you may see—He can open your eyes that you may behold wondrous things out of His Law!

Why not seek to have the enlightening Spirit of God resting on you, to teach you in His Word and way?

The Spirit of God is, also, the Spirit of liberty, but some of God's children do not seem to have attained their freedom as yet. They have one fetter remaining on their feet and though they try to enter into the broad fields of heavenly enjoyment, they cannot escape from their prison. Of such we may well ask—Have you received the Spirit since you believed? If so, why are you the slaves of custom, the bandaged serfs of fashion? Why do you ask leave of your fellow men to breathe, or think? Why are you so cowardly that you dare not follow conscience, or speak of the things of God? The fear of man brings a snare to many and that snare is also a chain to their feet. It ought not be! Rather should they feel that, since the Son has made them free, they are free, indeed! The Holy Spirit is a free Spirit and makes men free—where the Spirit of the Lord is, there is liberty! Glory be to You, O God, "I am Your servant; You have loosed my bonds."

Many weak children of God have received the Spirit of bondage again to fear, but they have not yet received the Spirit of adoption by which we cry, "Abba, Father." Oh, the glory of the Spirit of God when He makes us feel that we are no more servants, but sons—not under the Law, but under Grace—not under wrath, but under love, not doomed to death, but endowed with life! He has brought us forth from prison and broken all our bonds asunder! He has set our feet in a large room and made us to walk at liberty because we keep His statutes! Ours is the freedom of no mean city, for our citizenship is in Heaven and the Spirit of God enables us to enjoy the citizenship of the New Jerusalem! It is important that we should know what this heavenly freedom means.

Some of God's people need to feel the Spirit of God as a power moving and impelling them to holy service. Do you ever hear, behind you, a voice saying, "This is the way; walk you in it"? Have you ever known holy impulses bidding you do this and that—impulses which did not come from human nature, for they impelled you to something which you would naturally have avoided? And do you ever follow after things unseen, driven onward as by a powerful wind, not to be resisted? Have you been made willing in the day of God's power to do the Divine bidding? I would we had more of it, for then we should be more ready for service and should do greater things than these. That same Spirit who moves the saints to work, also empowers them to achieve the purpose which is put into their souls. By His aid you shall go forth in your feebleness and put to flight the armies of the aliens! You shall be, in God's hands, as a sharp threshing instrument having teeth and shall thresh mountains–and beat them small–yes, fan them and the wind shall carry them away!

Does any man know what the Spirit of God can make of him? I believe the greatest, ablest, most faithful, most holy man of God might have been greater, abler, more faithful and more holy if he had put himself more completely at the Spirit's disposal. Wherever God has done great things by a man, He has had power to do more had the man been fit for it. We are straitened in ourselves, not in God! O Brothers and Sisters, the Church is weak today because the Holy Spirit is not upon her members as we would desire Him to be! You and I are tottering along like feeble babes, whereas, had we more of the Spirit, we might walk without fainting, run without weariness and even mount up with wings as eagles! Oh, for more of the anointing of the Holy Spirit whom Christ is prepared to give immeasurably unto us if we will but receive Him! "Have you received the Holy Spirit since you believed?" Is there not much Divine Power which has not, as yet, been manifested in you?

"Oh," says one, "I feel so dull today!" Do you? Is not the Holy Spirit the power to refresh you and to rekindle in your soul the dying flame of spiritual fervor? Oh, if you did but receive His power today, you would not mind the heaviness of the atmosphere, nor any other deadening surroundings, for the Spirit would triumph over the flesh. Do you know the power of the Spirit? Did He ever make you like the chariots of Amminadib? Did He ever carry you away with His supreme power? Did you ever run like Elijah before Ahab's chariot and feel that it was a little thing to do? Can you not say, "O my Soul, you have trodden down strength! By my God have I leaped over a wall and broken thorough a troop: I can do all things through Christ that strengthens me"? These are the expressions of souls familiar with the Holy Spirit–when He inspires them, they are divinely strong, even to omnipotence! Brothers and Sisters, we must have the Holy Spirit! Are you receiving His forces? Are you receiving His fullness even now?

Now I come to notice that this question is assuredly answerable. "Have you received the Holy Spirit?" The notion has sprung up that you cannot tell whether you have the Holy Spirit or not, but you can. Give a man an electric shock and I guarantee you he will know it! But if he has the Holy Spirit, he will know it much more. You may sometimes raise the question, "Did I ever feel the Holy Spirit in years gone by?" but you cannot ask the question, "Do I feel it now?" for if you feel it now you have the witness in yourself that the Lord is at work with you. You need not ask a question about present experience. If you do not feel the Holy Spirit at work distinctly and perceptibly, even now, then lift your heart to God for it and pray that you may now receive Him in all His fullness.

"Oh," says one, "I thought we must always say, 'I hope so. I trust so.'" I know that jargon, but men do not say, "I hope I have an estate," or, "I trust I have 20 shillings in the pound," or, "I think I have a wife and children." Some of us are quite clear about these matters, one way or the other! We should not live on guess-work as to daily life, much less as to eternal things. O Souls, live daily on what God gives you and you cannot doubt! Live near to Christ and you cannot doubt whether you love Him! Live in the Holy Spirit, give yourselves up fully to His Divine anointing and bedewing, and you will not have to say, "I hardly know whether there is any Holy Spirit," for He dwells with you and shall be in you!

Permit me to say here that there are many professors to whom this question is inevitable. I will pick out certain of them. There is the Brother with the long dreary face, the Knight of the Rueful Countenance. You know him and you pity him. His favorite hymn is–

"'Tis a point I long to know,
Oft it causes anxious thought."

Is there anything dreary? He delights in it as much as he can delight in anything! He is sure of nothing but the horrible–everything that is pleasant he is afraid of. His life is one protracted groan. Come along, Brother, and shake hands as cheerfully as you can. Please tell me, have you received the Holy Spirit since you believed? How he hesitates! Poor Soul, he is perplexed. He is not well acquainted with the Comforter. Here is a hymn for him–let us sing it to a gladsome tune–

"Why should the children of a King
Go mourning all their days?
Some tokens of Your Grace!
Do You not dwell in all the saints
And seal the heirs of Heaven?

When will You banish my complaints,
And show my sins forgiven?"

Surely, if we have the earnest of the Spirit, the first fruits of Heaven, we ought to rejoice in the Lord always! Brother, you look comfortless–how can this be when the Comforter has come to you?

Another Brother is a member of the Church and a very unpleasant neighbor, for he picks holes in everybody and everything. He is a born grumbler and since he has been new-born he has not given up the habit. When he goes home this morning, after dinner he will spend the afternoon in his growlery, complaining of the heat and, perhaps, of my sermon. Oh, my dear Brother, you who are so uneasy and unhappy–and so worrying and annoying to everybody–did you receive the Holy Spirit when you believed? Are you still receiving the Holy Spirit? I have sometimes thought that certain unfriendly friends must have been baptized in vinegar instead of water, from the sharp acid of their temperament. Surely the Spirit of God is a dove, full of peace, love and kindness–not a bird of prey! Let me put my hand on that Brother's shoulder, if he will allow such a rudeness, and say, "Have you received the Holy Spirit since you believed?"

Here comes another who flies out into great tempers and grows fiercely angry. A little thing puts him out–he finds fault readily enough and becomes excited in no time. He says that he is very sorry for it, afterwards, but this does not remove the wounds which he has inflicted. If you cut a person's head off, it is of small use to apologize to him afterwards. Many a man boils over with passion and scalds his friends and, then, in cooler moments expresses his regret. All very fine–but fine words cure no blisters! I would suggest to you, the next time you are in a great temper, that you ask yourself this question, "Have I received the Holy Spirit since I believed? Is He not the spirit of peace and gentleness?" I fancy anybody putting that question to you, when you are in an irritated state of mind, you would reply, "Pray do not mention such a subject here, for I am not acting as I ought to do." Then do act as you ought to do and ask for the Spirit of God to help you to be quiet, forgiving, humble and meek!

Here is a Brother who cannot be happy unless he indulges in worldly frivolities and useless amusements. When he gets into a grand frolic with worldly people, he finds himself at home–but the joys of godliness he despises! My Friend, the next time you are coming home from a party, I should like to meet you in the street and enquire, "Have you received the Holy Spirit since you believed?" You would think me almost blaspheming! Alas, the blasphemy is in your heart! You would feel awkward, would you not? Do not do things which make you feel awkward–keep out of those scenes which are unfit for a child of God! Do not play with the devil's children. Many people around this place are sore put to it to keep their children from bad company. There is no playground for their children but the streets–and it seems hard when they say that their children shall not associate with rude children in the road–yet they must do it. Our Lord does not love that His dear children should sport with heirs of wrath, or make them their intimates. Such evil communications will bring you misery sooner or later. You cannot expect the Holy Spirit to continue with you if you are joined with the adversaries of the Lord!

But there are certain persons who live solely to hoard and scrape and get money that they may grow rich and grind everybody else to pieces in the process. I would like, when the avaricious man is totaling up his gains, to put to him the question, "Have you received the Holy Spirit since you believed?" He would answer, "Don't, don't! It is terribly out of place to mention so serious a matter!" It is out of place, no doubt, for the man himself is out of place! But ought a Believer to be in a position in which it shall be out of place for a friend to speak to him about his eternal interests?

I know some to whom the question is needless. You never did put it to them and you never will. You meet them in the morning, soaring aloft, like the lark, in the praises of God. See them in trouble? They are patient and resigned to their heavenly Father's will. Mark how they spend their lives in hallowed service, seeking always to win sinners to Christ! Their common talk is sweet with the honey of the Holy Land–you cannot be with them 10 minutes without discovering that they have leaned on Jesus' bosom! There is an aroma about them which tells you that they dwell in the garden of the Lord. When they tell you their experience, it is even as if an angel shook his wings! You do not ask them if they have received the Holy Spirit–you stand still and admire the work of the Spirit of God in them!

Now, Beloved, be such yourselves. If our Church is to be strong and if it is to make a lasting impression upon its age but in His soul-enriching, heart-delighting, life-sanctifying power! Thus will He turn earth into Heaven and make us poor earth-born creatures meet to be partakers of the inheritance of the saints in light. So much upon the question. I cannot send it home–I can only pray that God the Holy Spirit, whom I desire to honor, may apply these thoughts with power to your souls.

II. One or two LESSONS can be gathered upon the very surface of this question. "Have you received the Holy Spirit since you believed?" The first lesson is, we are not to look for salvation to one single act of faith in the past, but to Jesus, in whom we continue to believe. I have read, very much to my grief, an assertion that whatever we may be, today, we are safe, if years ago we exercised a single act of faith. There may be truth in the statement, but it is so badly stated and so wretchedly distorted, that it looks like a lie–that which saves is a faith which does not spend itself in a single act, but continues to work and operate throughout the whole of life! It is not a question for me, today, "Did I believe in the Lord Jesus Christ in the year 1850, on a certain morning in the month of January?"

Oh, no–the question is, "Do I believe in the Lord Jesus at this hour?" For if my faith is "faith of the operation of God," it has continued to this hour and will continue to the end! All my troubles, all my temptations, all my sins have not killed my faith, but for every day, as the day has come, I have continued to receive the Holy Spirit's gracious aid since I believed and was brought into newness of life. "The just shall live by faith." It is a principle within, springing up unto everlasting life! It is a living well which never ceases to flow. It is not something I do in one five minutes and then have done with it–it is an holy act which I began to do at a certain time, but which I shall never leave off doing till there remains nothing more to be believed!

They say we do not believe in Heaven, but this is surely an error occasioned by lack of thought. Heaven is a fit sphere for faith, not faith for what we shall see there, but for things promised and not yet fulfilled. If I were to go to Heaven today, I would believe in my staying there; I would believe in the Lord's continuing to love me; I would believe in all the prophecies yet unfulfilled–in the ingathering of the redeemed, the perfecting of the Church– and the second Advent of the Lord. I would look for the resurrection, the new heavens and the new earth, the millennial glory, the binding of Satan and the eternal glory of the Triune God. Faith may be altogether lost in sight so far as things realized are concerned, but it will be grandly exercised upon blessings yet to come. We must live by faith, but it is not only our starting point, but the road along which we are to travel.

The next lesson of the text is that we must continue to live by receiving. We received Christ Jesus the Lord at the first, and now we receive the Holy Spirit. These disciples were questioned about their receiving rather than their expending, for at bottom everything depends upon what we receive. Nothing can come out of us if it does not first go into us. We are always charity children. It is our blessed lot to live upon the alms of Divine bounty. The question may still be asked of us, "What have you which you have not received?" We are always filled out of the fullness of the Lord, for we are not fountains but reservoirs, not creators but receivers! What shall we render unto the Lord for all His benefits towards us? We can only keep on receiving–take the cup of salvation and call upon the name of the Lord!

Again, let us learn that we may not despise the very lowest form of spiritual life–no, not even those who have not so much as heard whether there is a Holy Spirit. Paul, when he met these half-instructed disciples, did not say, "You see the door. Be off! You have nothing to do with me, for you are so desperately ignorant." On the contrary, he sat down and taught them more and then baptized them! God has some children who are mere babes and sucklings–and it is a fact for their comfort that He does not judge of their being His children by measuring their height. Babes in Grace are as much His children as those who have reached perfect manhood! Weaklings are dear to God–let them be dear to us. When you are considering some poor child of God who has no education and cannot read the Bible, do not judge him by his knowledge. The question is not whether he knows, "A" from "B," for if he knows, "J" from "I," he knows enough–that is to say, if he knows Jesus from himself, he has grasped the essential point. If He trusts Christ and not himself, he knows enough to take him to Heaven, and enough for you to take him into your heart.

Another lesson is that the Holy Spirit always keeps sweet company with Jesus Christ. As long as these good people only knew John the Baptist, they might know water baptism, but they could not know the Baptism of the Holy Spirit. It was only when they came to know Jesus, that the Spirit of God came upon them and they began to work those mighty things which are the fruits of the Spirit. Learn, then, to keep close to Christ both in your lives and in your teaching. The Spirit of God will not set His seal to what I say or what you say, but He will confirm the testimony of Jesus Christ! The things of God concerning Christ Jesus our Lord shall never be without the attesting power of the Holy Spirit.

Once more, the Holy Spirit can yet be more fully possessed by all Believers. If there should be a Brother or Sister here who has a notion that he cannot have any more Grace, I am afraid he is specially in need of it. The perfect Brother I must leave to the angels–he is above my reach, for I am sent to fallible men! I conceive that when a man is so good in his own esteem that he cannot be better, he is even then no better than he should be and is either cracked in his head or his honesty! However, I leave him to his own master. But as for you and for me, let us be certain that if we have been taught of the Spirit, there is yet more light for the Spirit to give us! If we have been quickened of the Spirit, there is yet more life for the Spirit to impart to us! If we have been comforted, there are greater consolations yet which the Spirit of God can apply to our hearts! If we have been made strong, we can be stronger, yet, to do yet greater exploits! If we have had communion with Christ, we can have closer communion and enter more thoroughly into the secret place of the tabernacle of the Most High! If it can be, then why should it not be?

Does not every man or woman here that is a Christian say, "I mean to realize all the possibilities of true religion"? Little religion is a miserable thing. He that has just enough to save him, at last, may not have enough to comfort him for the present. He that has much Grace and is filled with the Spirit of God, shall have two heavens–a Heaven here and a Heaven hereafter! I desire to make that true in my own case. I would find two heavens in Jesus; are there not many more? He who has the Spirit richly shall have the joy of the Lord, here, to be his strength, and the joy of the Lord hereafter to be his reward! Come, let us ask for all that God is willing to give! Does He not say, "Open your mouth wide, and I will fill it"? Come, you little ones! Why remain little?

Our prayer for you is that you may be as David and David as the angel of the Lord. Come! You are living on crumbs–why not eat abundantly of the Bread of Heaven? Do not be content with pennies, for a king's ransom is at your disposal! Poor Brother, rise out of your poverty! Sister, bowed down by reason of the little of the Spirit of God you have received, believe for more and pray upon a larger scale! May the Lord enlarge all our hearts and fill them! And then enlarge them again and fill them again–so that from day to day we may receive the Holy Spirit till, at the last, Jesus shall receive us into His Glory.

OUR URGENT NEED OF THE HOLY SPIRIT

"Through the power of the Holy Spirit."
Romans 15:13

A Sermon Delivered On Sunday Morning: 7 January 1877

I DESIRE to draw your attention, at this time, to the great necessity which exists for the continual manifestation of the power of the Holy Spirit in the Church of God if by her means the multitudes are to be gathered to the Lord Jesus. I did not know how I could much better do so than by first showing that the Spirit of God is necessary to the Church of God for its own internal growth in Grace. Hence my text in the 13th verse, "Now the God of hope fill you with all joy and peace in believing, that you may abound in hope, through the power of the Holy Spirit"–where it is evident that the Apostle attributes the power to be filled with joy and peace in believing, and the power to abound in hope, to the Holy Spirit.

But then, I also wanted to show you that the power of the Church outside, that with which she is to be aggressive and work upon the world for the gathering out of God's elect from among men, is also this same energy of the Holy Spirit. Hence I have taken the 19th verse, for the Apostle there says that God had through him made "the Gentiles obedient byword and deed, through mighty signs and wonders, by the power of the Spirit of God." So you see, dear Friends, that first of all, to keep the Church happy and holy within herself there must be a manifestation of the power of the Holy Spirit. And secondly, that the Church may invade the territories of the enemy and may conquer the world for Christ, but she must be clothed with the same sacred energy.

We may, then, go further and say that the power of the Church for external work will be proportionate to the power which dwells within her. Gauge the energy of the Holy Spirit in the hearts of Believers and you may fairly calculate their influence upon unbelievers. Only let the Church be illuminated by the Holy Spirit and she will reflect the light and become to onlookers "fair as the moon, clear as the sun and terrible as an army with banners." Let us, by two or three illustrations, show that the outward work must always depend upon the inward force.

On a cold winter's day when the snow has fallen and lies deep upon the ground, you go through a village. There is a row of cottages and you will notice that from one of the roofs the snow has nearly disappeared, while another cottage still bears a coating of snow. You do not stay to make enquiries as to the reason of the difference, for you know very well what is the cause. There is a fire burning inside the one cottage and the warmth glows through its roof, and so the snow speedily melts. In the other there is no tenant—it is a house to let and no fire burns on its hearth and no warm smoke ascends the chimney—therefore there lies the snow. Just as the warmth is inside so the melting will be outside.

I look at a number of Churches and where I see worldliness and formalism lying thick upon them, I am absolutely certain that there is not the warmth of Christian life within. But where the hearts of Believers are warm with Divine Love through the Spirit of God, we are sure to see evils vanish and beneficial consequences following. We need not look within—in such a case the exterior is sufficient index. Take an illustration from political life. Here is a trouble arising between different nations. There are angry spirits stirring and it seems very likely that the Gordian knot of difficulty will never be untied by diplomacy, but will need to be cut with the sword.

Everybody knows that one of the hopes of peace lies in the bankrupt condition of the nation which is likely to go to war, for if it is short of supplies, if it cannot pay its debts, if it cannot furnish the material for war, then it will not be likely to court a conflict. A country must be strong in internal resources before it can wisely venture upon foreign wars. Thus is it in the great battle of the Truth of God—a poor starving Church cannot combat the devil and his armies. Unless the Church is, herself, rich in the things of God and strong with Divine energy, she will generally cease to be aggressive and will content herself with going on with the regular routine of Christian work, crying, "Peace! Peace!" where peace should not be.

She will not dare to defy the world, or to send forth her legions to conquer its provinces for Christ when her own condition is pitiably weak. The strength or weakness of a nation's money supply affects its army in its every march. And in like manner, its measure of Grace influences the Church of God in all its actions. Suffer yet another illustration. If you lived in Egypt you would notice, once each year, the Nile rising. And you would watch its increase with anxiety, because the extent of the overflow of the Nile is very much the measure of the fertility of Egypt. Now the rising of the Nile must depend upon those far-off lakes in the center of Africa—whether they shall be well filled with the melting of the snows or not. If there is a scanty supply in the higher reservoirs, there cannot be much overflow into the Nile in its after-course through Egypt.

Let us translate the figure and say that, if the upper lakes of fellowship with God in the Christian Church are not well filled—if the soul's spiritual strength is not sustained by private prayer and communion with God—the Nile of practical Christian service will never rise to the flood. The one thing I want to say is this—you cannot get out of the Church what is not in it. The reservoir must be filled before it can pour forth a stream. We must, ourselves, drink of the living water till we are full—and then out of the midst of us shall flow rivers of living water—but not till then. Out of an empty basket you cannot distribute loaves and fishes, however hungry the crowd may be. Out of an empty heart you cannot speak full things, nor from a lean soul bring forth fat things full of marrow which shall feed the people of God.

Out of the fullness of the heart the mouth speaks, when it speaks to edification at all. So the first thing is to look well to home affairs and pray that God would bless us and cause His face to shine upon us, that His way may be known upon earth and His saving health among all people—

"To bless Your chosen race,
In mercy, Lord, incline,
And cause the brightness of Your face
On all Your saints to shine.
That so Your wondrous way
May through the world be known;
While distant lands their tribute pay,
And Your salvation own."

This morning, in trying to speak of the great necessity of the Church, namely, her being moved vigorously by the power of the Holy Spirit, I earnestly pray that we may enter upon this subject with the deepest conceivable reverence. Let us adore while we are meditating! Let us feel the condescension of this blessed Person of the Godhead in deigning to dwell in His people and to work in the human heart! Let us remember that this Divine Person is very sensitive. He is a jealous God.

We read of His being grieved and vexed and, therefore,, let us ask His forgiveness of the many provocations which He must have received from our hands. With lowly awe let us bow before Him, remembering that if there is a sin which is unpardonable, it has a reference to Him—the sin against the Holy Spirit which shall never be forgiven—neither in this world nor in that which is to come. In reference to the Holy Spirit we stand on very tender ground, indeed. And if ever we should veil our faces and rejoice with trembling, it is while we speak of the Spirit and of those mysterious works with which He blesses us.

In that lowly spirit and under the Divine overshadowing, follow me while I set before you seven works of the Holy Spirit which are most necessary to the Church—for its own good and equally necessary to her in her office of missionary from Christ to the outside world.

To begin, then, the power of the Holy Spirit is manifested in the QUICKENING of souls to spiritual life. All the spiritual life which exists in this world is the creation of the Holy Spirit, by whom the Lord Jesus quickens whomever He wills. You and I had not life enough to know our death till He visited us! We had not light enough to perceive that we were in darkness, nor sense enough to feel our misery! We were so utterly abandoned to our own folly that, though we were naked, poor and miserable, we dreamed that we were rich and increased in goods! We were under sentence of death as condemned criminals and yet we talked about merit and reward!
Yes, we were dead and yet we boasted that we were alive—counting our very death to be our life! The Spirit of God, in infinite mercy, came to us with His mysterious power and made us live. The first token of life was a consciousness of our being in the realm of death and an agony to escape from it. We began to perceive our insensibility and, if I may be pardoned such an expression, we saw our blindness. Every growth of spiritual life, from the first tender shoot until now, has also been the work of the Holy Spirit.

As the green blade was His production, so is the ripening corn! The increase of life, as much life as there is at the beginning, must still come by the operation of the Spirit of God who raised up Christ from the dead. You will never have more life, Brothers and Sisters, unless the Holy Spirit bestows it upon you. Yes, you will not even know that you need more, nor groan after more, unless He works in you to desire and to agonize according to His own good pleasure. See, then, our absolute dependence upon the Holy Spirit! If He were gone, we should relapse into spiritual death and the Church would become a morgue!

The Holy Spirit is absolutely necessary to make everything that we do to be alive. We are sowers, Brothers and Sisters, but if we take dead seed in our seed baskets there will never be a harvest! The preacher must preach living Truths of God in a living manner if he expects to obtain a hundred-fold harvest. Too much of Church work is nothing better than the movement of a galvanized corpse! Too much of religion is done as if it were performed by a robot, or ground off by machinery. Nowadays men care little about heart and soul—they only look at outward performances. Why, I hear they have now invented a machine which talks, though surely there was talk enough without this Parisian addition to the band of prattlers!

We can preach as machines, we can pray as machines and we can teach Sunday school as machines. Men can give mechanically and come to the Lord's Table mechanically—yes, and we, ourselves, shall do so unless the Spirit of God is with us! Most hearers know what it is to hear a live sermon which quivers all over with fullness of energy. You also know what it is to sing a hymn in a lively manner and you know what it is to unite in a live Prayer Meeting! But, ah, if the Spirit of God is absent, all that the Church does will be lifeless! It will be as the rustle of leaves above a tomb, the gliding of specters, the congregation of the dead turning over in their graves!

As the Spirit of God is the Quickener to make us alive and our work alive, so must He specially be with us to make those alive with whom we have to deal for Jesus. Imagine a dead preacher preaching a dead sermon to dead sinners—what can possibly come of it? Here is a beautiful essay which has been admirably elaborated and it is coldly read to the cold-hearted sinner. It smells of the midnight oil but it has no heavenly unction, no Divine power resting upon it, nor, perhaps, is that power even looked for! What good can come of such a production? As well may you try to calm the tempest with poetry or stay the hurricane with rhetoric as to bless a soul by mere learning and eloquence!

It is only as the Spirit of God shall come upon God's servant and shall make the Word which He preaches to drop as a living seed into the heart, that any result can follow his ministry! And it is only as the Spirit of God shall then follow that seed and keep it alive in the soul of the listener that we can expect those who profess to be converted to take root and grow to maturity of Grace and become our sheaves at the last! We are utterly dependent here and, for my part, I rejoice in this absolute dependence!

If I could have a stock of power to save souls which would be all my own, apart from the Spirit of God, I cannot suppose greater temptation to pride and to living at a distance from God! It is well to be weak in self and better, still, to be nothing–to simply be the pen in the hand of the Spirit of God–unable to write a single letter upon the tablets of the human heart except as the hand of the Holy Spirit shall use us for that propose. That is really our position and we ought practically to take it up! And doing so, we shall continually cry to the Spirit of God to quicken us in all things and quicken all that we do–and quicken the Word as it drops into the sinner's ears.

I am quite certain that a Church which is devoid of life cannot be the means of life-giving to the dead sinners around it. No! Everything acts after its kind and we must have a living Church for living work! O that God would quicken every member of this Church! "What," you ask, "do you think some of us are not alive unto God?" Brothers and Sisters, there are some of you, concerning whom I am certain, as far as one can judge of another, that you have life, for we can see it in all that you do! But there are some others of you, concerning whose spiritual life one has to exercise a good deal of faith and a great deal more charity, for we do not perceive in you much activity in God's cause, nor care for the souls of others, nor zeal for the Divine Glory! If we do not see any fruits, what can we do but earnestly pray that you may not turn out to be barren trees?

That is the first point and we think it is as clear as possible that we must have the quickening power of the Spirit for ourselves if we are to be the means in the hand of God of awakening dead souls.

II. Next, it is one of the peculiar offices of the Holy Spirit to ENLIGHTEN His people. He has done so by giving us His Word which He has inspired. But the Bible, inspired though it is, is never spiritually understood by any man apart from the personal teaching of its great Author. You may read it as much as you will and never discover the inner and vital sense unless your soul shall be led into it by the Holy Spirit Himself!

"What?" says one, "I have learned the Shorter Catechism and I have got the creed memorized by heart, and yet do I know nothing?" I answer, you have done well to learn the letter of the Truth of God, but you still need the Spirit of God to make it the light and power of God to your soul! The letter you may know, and know it better than some who know, also, the spirit, and I do not, for a moment, depreciate a knowledge of the letter—unless you suppose that there is something saving in mere head knowledge! But the Spirit of God must come and make the letter alive to you. He must transfer it to your heart, set it on fire and make it burn within you, or else its Divine force and majesty will be hid from your eyes.

No man knows the things of God save he to whom the Spirit of God has revealed them. No carnal mind can understand spiritual things. We may use language as plain as a pikestaff, but the man who has no spiritual understanding is a blind man and the clearest light will not enable him to see. You must be taught of the Lord, or you will die in ignorance! Now, my Brothers and Sisters, suppose that in a Church there should be many who have never been thus instructed—can you not see that evil must and will come of it? Error is sure to arise where the Truth of God is not experimentally known. If professors are not taught of the Spirit, their ignorance will breed conceit, pride, unbelief and a thousand other evils!

Oh, had you known more of the Truth of God, my Brother, you had not boasted so! Oh, had you seen that Truth of God which, as yet, has not been revealed to you because of your prejudice, you had not so fiercely condemned those who are better than yourself! With much zeal to do good, men have done a world of mischief through lack of instruction in Divine things! Sorrow, too, comes of ignorance. O, my Brother, had you known the Doctrines of Grace you had not been so long a time in bondage! Half of the heresy in the Church of God is not willful error, but error which springs of not knowing the Truth of God, not searching the Scriptures with a teachable heart, not submitting the mind to the light of the Holy Spirit!

We should, as a rule, treat heresy rather as ignorance to be enlightened than as a crime to be condemned. Unless, alas, that sometimes it becomes willful perversity when the mind is greedy after novelty, or puffed up with self confidence! Then other treatment may become painfully necessary. Beloved, if the Spirit of God will but enlighten the Church thoroughly, there will be an end to divisions! Schisms are generally occasioned by ignorance and the proud spirit which will not accept correction. On the other hand, real, lasting, practical unity within exists in proportion to the unity of men's minds in the Truth of God. Hence the necessity for the Spirit of God to conduct us into the whole Truth of God.

My dear Brother, if you think you know a doctrine, ask the Lord to make you sure that you know it, for much that we think we know turns out to be unknown when times of trial put us to the test. We really know nothing unless it is burnt into our souls as with a hot iron by an experience which only the Spirit of God can give! I think you will now see that the Spirit of God, being necessary for our instruction, we pre-eminently find, in His gracious operation, our strength for the instruction of others—for how shall those teach who have never been taught? How shall men declare a message which they have never learned?

"Son of man, eat this roll," for until you have eaten it yourself, your lips can never tell it to others. "The farmer that labors must first be a partaker of the fruits." It is the law of Christ's vineyard that none shall work there till, first of all, they know the flavor of the fruits which grow in the sacred enclosure. You must know Christ, Grace, love and the Truth of God, yourself, before you can ever be an instructor of babes for Christ. When we come to deal with others, earnestly longing to instruct them for Jesus, we perceive even more clearly our need of the Spirit of God.

Ah, my Brother, you think you will put the Gospel so clearly that they must see it—but their blind eyes overcome you. Ah, you think you will put it so zealously that they must feel it—but their clay-cold hearts defeat you! Old Adam is too strong for young Melancthon, depend upon it! You may think you are going to win souls by your pleading, but you might as well stand on the top of a mountain and whistle to the wind, unless the Holy Spirit is with you! After all your talking, your hearers will, perhaps, have caught your idea, but the mind of the Spirit, the real soul of the Gospel, you cannot impart to them—this remains, like creation itself, a work which only God can accomplish.

Daily, then, let us pray for the power of the Spirit as the Illuminator. Come, O blessed Light of God! You, alone, can break our personal darkness and only when You have enlightened us can we lead others in Your light! An ignorant Christian is disqualified for great usefulness, but he who is taught of God will teach transgressors God's ways and sinners shall be converted unto Christ! Both to burn within and shine without you must have the illuminating Spirit!

III. One work of the Spirit of God is to create in Believers the spirit of ADOPTION. "Because you are sons, God has sent forth the Spirit of His Son into your hearts, whereby you cry, Abba, Father!" "For you have not received the spirit of bondage again to fear, but you have received the Spirit of adoption, whereby we cry, Abba, Father!" We are regenerated by the Holy Spirit and so receive the nature of children–and that nature, which is given by Him, He continually prompts, excites, develops and matures–so that we receive day by day more and more of the childlike spirit.

Now, Beloved, this may not seem to you to be of very great importance at first sight, but it is, for the Church is never happy except all her members walk as dear children towards God. Sometimes the spirit of slaves creeps over us–we begin to talk of the service of God as though it were heavy and burdensome– and are discontent if we do not receive present wages and visible success, just as servants do when they are not happy. But the spirit of adoption works for love, without any hope of reward, and it is satisfied with the sweet fact of being in the Father's house and doing the Father's will.

This spirit gives peace, rest, joy, boldness and holy familiarity with God. A man who never received the spirit of a child towards God does not know the bliss of the Christian life! He misses its flower, its savor, its excellence and I should not wonder if the service of Christ should be a weariness to him because he has never, yet, got to the sweet things and does not enjoy the green pastures where the Good Shepherd makes His sheep to feed and to lie down. But when the Spirit of God makes us feel that we are sons and daughters, and we live in the House of God to go no more out forever, then the service of God is sweet and easy and we accept the delay of apparent success as a part of the trial we are called to bear.

Now, mark you, this will have a great effect upon the outside world! A body of professors performing religion as a task, groaning along the ways of godliness with faces full of misery, like slaves who dread the lash, can have but small effect upon the sinners around them. They say, "Those people serve, no doubt, a hard master, and they are denying themselves this and that. Why should we be like they?" But bring me a Church made up of children of God–a company of men and women whose faces shine with their heavenly Father's smile! Who are accustomed to take their cares and cast them on their Father as children should! Who know they are accepted and loved, and are perfectly content with the great Father's will! Put them down in the midst of a company of ungodly ones and I will guarantee you they will begin to envy them their peace and joy. Thus happy saints become most efficient operators upon the minds of the unsaved!

O blessed Spirit of God! Let us all, now, feel that we are the children of the great Father and let our childlike love be warm this morning! And so shall we be fit to go forth and proclaim the Lord's love to the prodigals who are in the far-off land among the swine! These three points are self-evident, I think. Now we pass to the fourth.

IV. The Holy Spirit is especially called the Spirit of HOLINESS. He never suggested sin nor approved of it, nor has He ever done otherwise than grieve over it–holiness is the Spirit's delight! The Church of God wears upon her brow the words, "Holiness to the Lord." Only in proportion as she is holy may she claim to be the Church of God at all. An unholy Church? Surely this cannot be her of whom we read, "Christ also loved the Church and gave Himself for it, that He might sanctify and cleanse it with the washing of water by the Word, that He might present it to Himself a glorious Church, not having spot, or wrinkle, or any such thing."

Holiness is not mere morality, not the outward keeping of Divine precepts out of a hard sense of duty while those Commandments, in themselves, are not delightful to us. Holiness is the entirety of our manhood fully consecrated to the Lord and molded to His will! This is the thing which the Church of God must have, but it can never have it apart from the Sanctifier, for there is not a grain of holiness beneath the sky but what is of the operation of the Holy Spirit! And, Brothers and Sisters, if a Church is destitute of holiness, what effect can it have upon the world? Scoffers utterly condemn and despise professors whose inconsistent lives contradict their verbal testimonies!

An unholy Church may pant and struggle after dominion and make what noise she can in pretense of work for Christ, but the kingdom comes not to the unholy, neither have they, themselves, entered it. The testimony of unholy men is no more acceptable to Christ than was the homage which the evil spirit gave to Him in the days of His flesh, to which He answered, "Hold your peace." "Unto the wicked," God says, "What have you to do to declare My statutes?" The dew is withheld and the rain comes not in its season to the tillage of those who profess to be the servants of God and yet sow iniquity.

After all, the acts of the Church preach more to the world than the words of the Church! Put an anointed man to preach the Gospel in the midst of a really godly people and his testimony will be marvelously supported by the Church with which he labors. But place the most faithful minister over an ungodly Church and he has such a weight upon him that he must first clear himself of it or he cannot succeed. He may preach his heart out! He may pray till his knees are weary, but conversions will be sorely hindered if, indeed, they occur at all. There is no likelihood of victory to Israel while Achan's curse is on the camp! An unholy Church makes Christ to say that He cannot do many mighty works there because of its iniquity.

Brethren, do you not see in this point our need of the Spirit of God? And when you get to grappling terms with sinners and have to talk to them about the necessity of holiness—a renewed heart and a godly life coming out of that renewed heart—do you expect ungodly men to be charmed with what you say? What does the unregenerate mind care for righteousness? Was a carnal man ever eager after holiness? Such a thing was never seen! As well expect the devil to be in love with God, as an unredeemed heart to be in love with holiness! But the sinner must love that which is pure and right, or he cannot enter Heaven! You cannot make him do so. Who can do it but that Holy Spirit who has made you to love what once you despised?

Go not out, therefore, to battle with sin until you have taken weapons out of the armory of the Eternal Spirit! Mountains of sin will not turn to plains at your bidding unless the Holy Spirit is pleased to make the Word effectual. So then, we see that as the Spirit of holiness we need the Holy Spirit.

Fifthly, the Church needs much PRAYER and the Holy Spirit is the Spirit of Grace and of supplications. The strength of a Church may pretty accurately be gauged by her prayerfulness. We cannot expect God to put forth His power unless we entreat Him to do so. But all acceptable supplication is worked in the soul by the Holy Spirit. The first desire which God accepts must be excited in the heart by the secret operations of the Holy One of Israel. And every subsequent pleading of every sort which contains in it a grain of living faith and, therefore,, comes up as a memorial before the Lord, must have been effectually worked in the soul by Him who makes intercession in the saints according to the will of God.

Our great High Priest will put into His censer no incense but that which the Spirit has compounded! Prayer is the creation of the Holy Spirit! We cannot do without prayer and we cannot pray without the Holy Spirit! And, therefore, our dependence on Him. Furthermore, when we come to deal with sinners, we know that they must pray. "Behold he prays," is one of the earliest signs of the new birth! But can we make the sinner pray? Can any persuasion of ours lead him to his knees to breathe the penitential sigh and look to Christ for mercy? If you have attempted the conversion of a soul in your own strength you know you have failed! And so you would have failed if you had attempted the creation of one single acceptable prayer in the heart of even a little child.

Oh then, dear Brothers and Sisters, let us cry to our heavenly Father to give the Holy Spirit to us! Let us ask Him to be in us more and more mightily as the Spirit of prayer, making intercession in us with groans that cannot be uttered, that the Church may not miss the Divine blessing for lack of asking for it! I do verily believe this to be her present weakness and one great cause why the kingdom of Christ does not more mightily spread—prayer is too much restrained— and, therefore,, the blessing is kept back! And it will always be restrained unless the Holy Spirit shall stimulate the desires of His people. O blessed Spirit, we pray You will make us pray, for Jesus' sake!

VI. Sixthly, the Spirit of God is in a very remarkable manner the giver of FELLOWSHIP. So often, as we pronounce the Apostolic benediction, we pray that we may receive the communion of the Holy Spirit. The Holy Spirit enables us to have communion with spiritual things. He, alone, can take the key and open up the secret mystery that we may know the things which are of God. He gives us fellowship with God, Himself, through Jesus Christ. By the Spirit we have access to the Father. Our fellowship is with the Father and with His Son, Jesus Christ, but it is the Spirit of God who brings us into communion with the Most High.

So, too, my dear Brothers and Sisters, our fellowship with one another, so far as it is Christian fellowship, is always produced by the Spirit of God. If we have continued together in peace and love these many years, I cannot attribute it to our constitutional good tempers, nor to wise management, nor to any natural causes, but only to the love into which the Spirit has baptized us so that rebellious natures have been still. If a dozen Christian people live together for 12 months in true spiritual union and unbroken affection, trace it to the love of the Spirit! And if 1,200, or four times that number shall be able to persevere in united service and find themselves loving each other better after many years than they did at the first, let it be regarded as a blessing from the Comforter, for which He is to be devoutly adored!

Fellowship can only come to us by the Spirit, but a Church without fellowship would be a disorderly mob, a kingdom divided against itself and, consequently, it could not prosper. You need fellowship for mutual strength, guidance, help and encouragement—without it your Church is a mere human society. If you are to make a good impression on the world, you must be united as one living body. A divided Church has long been the scorn of Antichrist. No sneer which comes from the Vatican has a greater sting in it than that which taunts Protestants with their divisions! And as it is with the great outward Church so it is with any one particular Church of Christ!

Divisions are our disgrace, our weakness, our hindrance! And as the gentle Spirit, alone, can prevent or heal these divisions by us, we are dependent upon Him for real loving fellowship with God and with one another. Let us daily cry to Him to work in us brotherly love and all the sweet Graces which make us one with Christ, that we all may be one even as the Father is One with the Son—and that the world may know that God has, indeed, sent Jesus and that we are His people.

VII. Seventhly, we need the Holy Spirit in that renowned office which is described by our Lord as THE PARACLETE or COMFORTER. The word bears another rendering, which our translators have given to it in that passage where we read, "If any man sins, we have an Advocate (or Paraclete) with the Father." The Holy Spirit is both Comforter and Advocate. The Holy Spirit, at this present moment, is our Friend and Comforter, sustaining the sinking spirits of Believers, applying the precious promises, revealing the love of Jesus Christ to the heart. Many a heart would break if the Spirit of God had not comforted it. Many of God's dear children would have utterly died by the way if He had not bestowed upon them His Divine consolations to cheer their pilgrimage.

That is His work and a very nooooaary work, for If Believers become unhappy they became weak In many points of service. I am certain that the joy of the Lord is our strength, for I have proved it so and proved also the opposite truth! There are on earth certain Christians who inculcate gloom as a Christian's proper state. I will not judge them, but this I will say, that in evangelistic work they do nothing and I do not wonder at it! Till snow in harvest ripens wheat. Till darkness makes flowers bloom. Till the salt sea yields clusters bursting with new wine, you will never find an unhappy religion promotive of the growth of the kingdom of Christ! You must have joy in the Lord, Brothers and Sisters, if you are to be strong in the Lord and strong for the Lord! Now, as the Comforter, alone, can bear you up amid the floods of tribulation which you are sure to meet with, you see your great need of His consoling Presence. We have said that the Spirit of God is the Advocate of the Church—not with God, for there, Christ is our sole Advocate—but with man! What is the grandest plea that the Church has against the world? I answer, the indwelling of the Holy Spirit, the standing miracle of the Church! External evidences are very excellent. You young men who are worried by skeptics, will do well to study those valuable works which learned and devout men have, with much labor, produced for us. But, mark you, all the evidences of the truth of Christianity which can be gathered from analogy, from history and from external facts are nothing whatever compared with the operations of the Spirit of God! These are the arguments which convince!

A man says to me, "I do not believe in sin, in righteousness, or in judgment." Well, Brothers and Sisters, the Holy Spirit can soon convince him! If he asks me for signs and evidences of the Truth of the Gospel, I reply, "Do you see this woman? She was a great sinner in the very worst sense and led others into sin. But now you cannot find more sweetness and light anywhere than in her. Do you hear this profane swearer, persecutor and blasphemer? He is speaking with purity, truth and humbleness of mind. Observe yon man who was, before, a miser, and see how he consecrates his substance! Notice that envious, malicious spirit and see how it becomes gentle, forgiving and amiable through conversion.

How do you account for these great changes? They are happening here everyday! Why? Is it a lie which produces truth, honesty and love? Does not every tree bear fruit after its kind? What, then, must that Grace be which produces such blessed transformations? The wonderful phenomena of ravens turned to doves and lions into lambs—the marvelous transformations of moral character which the minister of Christ rejoices to see worked by the Gospel— these are our witnesses and they are unanswerable!

Peter and John have gone up to the Temple and they have healed a lame man. They are soon seized and brought before the Sanhedrim. This is the charge against them—"You have been preaching in the name of Jesus and this Jesus is an impostor." What do Peter and John say? They need say nothing, for there stands the man that was healed! He has brought his crutch with him and he waves it in triumph! And he runs and leaps! He was their volume of evidences, their apology and proof. "When they saw the man that was healed standing with Peter and John, they could say nothing against them." If we have the Spirit of God among us and conversions are constantly being worked, the Holy Spirit is thus fulfilling His advocacy and refuting all accusers!

If the Spirit works in your own mind, it will always be to you the best evidence of the Gospel. I meet, sometimes, one piece of infidelity and then another, for there are new doubts and fresh infidelities spawned every hour—and unstable men expect us to read all the books they choose to produce. But the effect produced on our mind is less and less. This is our answer. "It is of no use your trying to stagger us, for we are already familiar with everything you suggest. Our own native unbelief has outstripped you! We have had doubts of a kind which even you would not dare to utter if you knew them! There is enough infidelity and devilry in our own nature to make us no strangers to Satan's devices.

"We have fought most of your suggested battles over and over again in the secret chamber of our meditation and have conquered, for we have been in personal contact with God! You sneer, but there is no argument in sneering. We are as honest as you are and our witness is as good as yours in any court of law—and we solemnly declare that we have felt the power of the Holy Spirit over our soul as much as any old ocean has felt the force of the north wind! We have been stirred to agony under a sense of sin and we have been lifted to ecstasy of delight by faith in the righteousness of Christ. We find that in the little world within our soul the Lord Jesus manifests Himself so that we know Him!

"There is a potency about the doctrines we have learned which could not belong to lies, for the Truths of God which we believe, we have tested in actual experience. Tell us there is no meat? Why, we have just been feasting! Tell us there is no water in the fountain? We have been quenching our thirst! Tell us there is no such thing as light? We do not know how we can prove its existence to you, for you are probably blind, but we can see! That is enough argument for us and our witness is true! Tell us there is no spiritual life! We feel it in our inmost souls. These are the answers with which the Spirit of God furnishes us and they are a part of His advocacy."

See, again, how entirely dependent we are on the Spirit of God for meeting all the various forms of unbelief which arise around us. You may have your societies for collecting evidence and you may enlist all your bishops and doctors of divinity and professors of apologetics—and they may write rolls of evidence long enough to girdle the globe—but the only Person who can savingly convince the world is the Advocate whom the Father has sent in the name of Jesus! When He reveals a man's sin and the sure result of it, the unbeliever takes to his knees! When He takes away the scales and sets forth the crucified Redeemer and the merit of the precious blood, all carnal reasonings are nailed to the Cross!

One blow of real conviction of sin will stagger the most obstinate unbeliever and afterwards, if his unbelief returns, the Holy Spirit's consolations will soon comfort it out of him. Therefore, as at the first, I say at the last—all this depends upon the Holy Spirit and upon Him let us wait in the name of Jesus, beseeching Him to manifest His power among us! Amen.

THE INDWELLING AND OUTFLOWING OF THE HOLY SPIRIT

"He that believes on Me, as the Scripture has said, out of his belly shall flow rivers of living water. (But this spoke He of the Spirit, which they that believe on Him should receive: for the Holy Spirit was not yet given; because that Jesus was not yet glorified)."
John 7:38, 39

A Sermon Delivered On Sunday Morning: 28 May 1882

IT is essential, dear Friends, that we should worship the living and true God. It will be ill for us if it can be said, "You worship you know not what." "You shall worship the Lord your God and Him only shall you serve." The heathens err from this command by multiplying gods and making this and that image to be the object of their adoration. Their excess runs to gross superstition and idolatry. I fear that sometimes we who, "profess and call ourselves Christians," err in exactly the opposite direction. Instead of worshipping more than God, I fear we worship less than God. This appears when we forget to pay due adoration to the Holy Spirit of God. The true God is triune–Father Son, and Holy Spirit–and though there is but one God, yet that one God has manifested Himself to us in the trinity of His sacred Persons.

If, then, I worship the Father and the Son, but forget or neglect to adore the Holy Spirit, I worship less than God. While the poor heathen, in his ignorance, goes far beyond and transgresses, I must take care lest I fall short and fail, also. What a grievous thing it will be if we do not pay that loving homage and reverence to the Holy Spirit which is so justly His due. May it not be the fact that we enjoy less of His power and see less of His working in the world because the Church of God has not been sufficiently mindful of Him? It is a blessed thing to preach the work of Jesus Christ, but it is an evil thing to omit the work of the Holy Spirit–for the work of the Lord Jesus, itself, is no blessing to that man who does not know the work of the Holy Spirit!

There is the ransom price, but it is only through the Spirit that we know the redemption! There is the precious blood, but it is as though the fountain had never been filled unless the Spirit of God leads us with repenting faith to wash therein! The bandage is soft and the ointment is effectual, but the wound will never be healed till the Holy Spirit shall apply that which the great Physician has provided. Let us not, therefore, be found neglectful of the work of the Divine Spirit, lest we incur guilt and inflict upon ourselves serious damage. You that are Believers have the most forcible reasons to hold the Holy Spirit in the highest esteem, for what are you now without Him? What were you and what would you still have been if it had not been for His gracious work upon you?

He quickened you, otherwise you had not been in the living family of God today. He gave you understanding that you might know the Truth of God, otherwise would you have been as ignorant as the carnal world is at this hour! It was He that awakened your conscience, convincing you of sin! It was He that gave you abhorrence of sin and led you to repent—it was He that taught you to believe and made you see that glorious Person who is to be believed, even Jesus, the Son of God! The Spirit has worked in you your faith, love, hope and every other Grace of God! There is not a jewel upon the neck of your soul which He did not place there—

"For every virtue we possess,
And every victory won,
And every thought of holiness,
Are His and His alone."

What have we learned, if we have learned aright, except by the teaching of the Holy Spirit? What can we say either in Brothers and Sisters, who is it that has comforted us in our distresses; directed us in our perplexities; strengthened us in our weaknesses and helped our infirmities in ten thousand ways? Is it not the Comforter whom the Father has sent in Jesus' name? Can I speak too highly of the riches of His Grace toward us? Can I too much extol the love of the Spirit? I know I cannot and you that know what He has worked in you delight to hear Him highly spoken of and His work and offices set forth! We are bound by a thousand ties to seek His honor who has worked in us our salvation! Let us never grieve Him by our ingratitude, but let us endeavor to extol Him.

For my part, it shall be the labor of this morning to impress upon you the necessity for His work and the superlative value of it. Beloved Brothers and Sisters, notwithstanding all that the Spirit of God has already done in us, it is very possible that we have missed a large part of the blessing which He is willing to give, for He is able to "do exceeding abundantly above all that we ask or think." We have already come to Jesus and we have drunk of the life-giving stream—our thirst is quenched and we are made to live in Him. Is this all? Now that we are living in Him and rejoicing to do so, have we come to the end of the matter?

Assuredly not! We have reached as far as that first exhortation of the Master, "If any man thirsts, let him come unto Me and drink." But do you think that the generality of the Church of God have ever advanced to the next—"He that believes on Me, as the Scripture has said, out of his belly shall flow rivers of living water"? I think I am not going beyond the grievous truth if I say that only here and there will you find men and women who have believed up to that point. Their thirst is quenched, as I have said, and they live—and because Jesus lives they shall live also—but health and vigor they have not! They have life, but they have not life more abundantly. They have little life with which to act upon others—they have no energy welling up and overflowing to go streaming out of them like rivers!

They have not thought it possible, perhaps, or thinking it possible, they have not imagined it possible to themselves. Or believing it possible to themselves they have not aspired to it, but they have stopped short of the fullest blessing. Their wading in to the sacred river has contented them and they know nothing of "waters to swim in." Like the Israelites of old, they are slow to possess all the land of promise, but rather sit down when the war has hardly begun! Brothers and Sisters, let us go in to get of God all that God will give us! Let us set our heart upon this, that we mean to have, by God's help, all that the infinite goodness of God is ready to bestow! Let us not be satisfied with the sip that saves, but let us go on to the Baptism which buries the flesh and raises us in the likeness of the risen Lord—even that Baptism into the Holy Spirit and into fire which makes us spiritual and sets us all on flame with zeal for the Glory of God and eagerness for usefulness by which that Glory may be increased among the sons of men!

Thus I introduce you to my texts and by their guidance we will enter upon the further consideration of the operations of the Holy Spirit, especially of those to which we would aspire.

We will commence with the remark that THE WORK OF THE SPIRIT IS INTIMATELY CONNECTED WITH THE WORK OF CHRIST. It is a great pity when persons preach the Holy Spirit's work so as to obscure the work of

Christ. I have known some do that, for they have held up before the sinner's eyes the inward experience of Believers, instead of lifting up, first and foremost, the crucified Savior to whom we must look and live! The Gospel is not, "Behold the Spirit of God," but, "Behold the Lamb of God." It is an equal pity when Christ is so preached that the Holy Spirit is ignored—as if faith in Jesus prevented the necessity of the new birth—and imputed righteousness rendered imparted righteousness needless.

Have I not often reminded you that in the third chapter of John, where Jesus taught Nicodemus the doctrine, "Except a man is born again of water and of the Spirit he cannot enter the kingdom of Heaven," we also read those blessed words, "And as Moses lifted up the serpent in the wilderness, even so must the Son of Man be lifted up: that whoever believes in Him should not perish, but have eternal life. For God so loved the world, that He gave His only begotten Son, that whoever believes in Him should not perish, but have everlasting life"? The necessity for regeneration by the Spirit is put very clearly, there, and so is the free promise that those who trust in Jesus shall be saved. This is what we ought to do—we must take care to let both these Truths of God stand out most distinctly with equal prominence!

They are intertwined with each other and are necessary each to each—what God has joined together let no man put asunder. They are so joined together that, first of all, the Holy Spirit was not given until Jesus had been glorified. Carefully note our first text—it is a very striking one—"This spoke He of the Spirit which they that believe on Him should receive: for the Holy Spirit was not yet." The word, "given," is not in the original—it is inserted by the translators to help explain the sense and they were, perhaps, wise in making such an addition, but the words are more forcible by themselves.

How strong the statement, "For the Holy Spirit was not yet." Of course, we, none of us, dream that the Holy Spirit was not yet existing, for He is eternal and self-existent, being most truly God. But He was not yet in fellowship with man to the full extent in which He now is since Jesus Christ is glorified. The near and dear communion of God with man which is expressed by the indwelling of the Spirit could not take place till the redeeming work was done and the Redeemer was exalted! As far as men and the fullness of the blessing were concerned, indicated by the outflowing rivers of living water, the Spirit of God was not yet.

"Oh," you say," but was not the Spirit of God in the Church in the wilderness and with the saints of God in all former ages?" I answer, Certainly, but not in the manner in which the Spirit of God now resides in the Church of Jesus Christ. You read of the Prophets and of one and another gracious man, that the Spirit of God came upon them, seized them, moved them, spoke by them– but He did not dwell in them. His operations upon men were a coming and a going–they were carried away by the Spirit of God and came under His power–but the Spirit of God did not rest upon them or abide in them.

Occasionally the sacred endowment of the Spirit of God came upon them, but they knew not "the communion of the Holy Spirit." As a French pastor very sweetly puts it, "He appeared unto men. He did not incarnate Himself in man. His action was intermittent–He went and came like the dove which Noah sent forth from the ark and which went to and fro, finding no rest–while in the new dispensation He dwells, He abides in the heart, as the dove, His emblem, which John the Baptist saw descending and alighting upon the head of Jesus. Affianced of the soul, the Spirit went off to see His betrothed, but was not yet one with her. The marriage was not consummated until Pentecost, after the glorification of Jesus Christ."

You know how our Lord puts it, "He dwells with you and shall be in you." That indwelling is another thing from being with us. The Holy Spirit was with the Apostles in the days when Jesus was with them, but He was not in them in the sense in which He filled them at and after the Day of Pentecost. The operations of the Spirit of God before our Lord's Ascension were not according to the full measure of the Gospel. But now the Spirit of God has been poured upon us from on high! Now He has descended and now He abides in the midst of the Church. And now we enter into Him and are baptized into the Holy Spirit, while He enters into us and makes our bodies to be His temples. Jesus said, "I will send you another Comforter which shall abide with you forever"–not coming and going–but remaining in the midst of the Church!

This shows how intimately the gift of the Holy Spirit is connected with our Lord Jesus Christ, inasmuch as in the fullest sense of His Indwelling, the Holy Spirit could not be with us until Christ had been glorified. It has been well observed that our Lord sent out 70 evangelists to preach the Gospel, even as He had before sent out the 12–and no doubt they preached with great zeal and produced much stir–but the Holy Spirit never took the trouble to preserve one of their sermons, or even the notes of one! I have not the slightest doubt that they were very crude and incomplete, showing more of human zeal than of Divine unction and, therefore, they are forgotten! But no sooner had the Holy Spirit fallen, than Peter's first sermon is recorded–and from then on we have frequent notes of the utterances of Apostles, deacons and evangelists! There was an abiding fullness and an overflowing of blessing out of the souls of the saints, after the Lord was glorified, which was not existing among men before that time!

Observe, too, that the Holy Spirit was given after the ascent of our Divine Lord into His Glory, partly to make that ascent the more renowned. When He ascended up on high, He led captivity captive and gave gifts to men. These gifts were men, in whom the Holy Spirit dwelt, who preached the Gospel unto the nations. The shedding of the Holy Spirit upon the assembled disciples on that memorable day was the glorification of the risen Christ upon the earth! I know not in what way the Father could have made the Glory of Heaven so effectually to flow from the heights of the New Jerusalem and to come streaming down among the sons of men as by giving that chief of all Gifts, the gift of the Holy Spirit when the Lord had risen and gone into His Glory!

With emphasis, may I say of the Spirit at Pentecost that He glorified Christ by descending at such a time. What grander celebration could there have been? Heaven rang with Hosannas and earth echoed the joy! The descending Spirit is the noblest testimony among men to the Glory of the ascended Redeemer! Was not the Spirit of God also sent at that time as an evidence of our Divine Master's acceptance? Did not the Father thus say to the Church, "My Son has finished the work and has fully entered into His Glory. Therefore I give you the Holy Spirit"? If you would know what a harvest is to come of the sowing of the bloody sweat and of the death wounds, see the first fruits! Behold how the Holy Spirit is given, Himself, to be the first fruits, the earnest of the Glory which shall yet be revealed in us! I need no better attestation from God of the finished work of Jesus than this blazing, flaming seal of tongues of fire upon the heads of the disciples! He must have done His work, or such a gift as this would not have come from it.

Moreover, if you desire to see how the work of the Spirit comes to us in connection with the work of Christ, recollect that it is the Spirit's work to bear witness of Jesus Christ. He does not take of a thousand different matters and show them to us, but He shall take, "of Mine," says Christ, "and He shall show them unto you." The Spirit of God is engaged in a service in which the Lord Jesus Christ is the beginning and the end. He comes to men that they may come to Jesus. Hence He comes to convince us of sin that He may reveal the great Sacrifice of sin—He comes to convince us of righteousness that we may see the Righteousness of Christ—and of judgment that we may be prepared to meet Him when He shall come to judge the quick and dead.

Do not think that the Spirit of God has come or ever will come among us to teach us a new Gospel, or something other than is written in the Scriptures. Men come to me with their stories and fancies and tell me that they were revealed to them by the Holy Spirit. I abhor their blasphemous impertinence and refuse to listen to them for a minute! They tell me this and that absurdity— and then father it upon the Spirit of Wisdom! It is enough to try our patience to hear their foolish ravings, but to find the Holy Spirit charged with them is more than we can bear! We have tests and judgments by which to know whether they who claim to speak by the Holy Spirit do so or not—for the testimony of the Spirit is always most honorable to our Lord Jesus Christ—and does not concern itself with the trifles of time and the follies of the flesh.

It is by the Gospel of Jesus Christ that the Spirit of God works in the hearts of men. "Faith comes by hearing and hearing by the Word of God"—the Holy Spirit uses the hearing of the Word of God for the conviction, conversion, consolation and sanctification of men. His usual and ordinary method of operation is to fasten upon the mind the things of God and to put life and force into the consideration of them. He revives in men's memories things that have long been forgotten and He frequently makes these the means of affecting the heart and conscience. The men can hardly remember hearing these Truths of God, but still, they were heard by them at some time or other! Saving Truths are such matters as are contained in their substance in the Word of God and lie within the range of the teaching, or the Person, or work, or offices of our Lord Jesus Christ. It is the Spirit's one business here below to reveal Christ to us and in us—and to that work He steadily adheres.

Moreover, the Holy Spirit's work is to conform us to the likeness of Jesus Christ. He is not working us to this or that human Ideal, but He is working us into the likeness of Christ that He may be the First-Born among many brethren. Jesus Christ is that standard and model to which the Spirit of God, by His sanctifying processes, is bringing us till Christ is formed in us the hope of Glory. It is for the Glory of Jesus that the Spirit of God always works. He works not for the Glory of a Church or of a community—He works not for the honor of a man or for the distinction of a sect—His one great objective is to glorify Christ! "He shall glorify Me," is our Savior's declaration, and when He takes of the things of Christ and shows them to us, we are led more and more to reverence and love and to adore our blessed Lord Jesus Christ.

I will not detain you longer with this. You will see how the works of Jesus and of the Spirit are joined together indissolubly, so that we may neither set the work of Jesus before the work of the Spirit nor the work of the Spirit before the work of Jesus. But we are glad to joy in both and to make much of them. As we delight in the Father's love and the Grace of our Lord Jesus, so do we equally rejoice in the communion of the Holy Spirit and, therefore, these Three agree in One.

II. We will now advance another step and here we shall need our second text. THE OPERATIONS OF THE HOLY SPIRIT ARE OF INCOMPARABLE VALUE. They are of such incomparable value that the very best things we can think of are not thought to be so precious as these are. Our Lord Himself says, "It is expedient for you that I go away: for if I go not away, the Comforter will not come unto you." Beloved Friends, the Presence of Jesus Christ was of inestimable value to His disciples and yet it was not such an advantage to His servants as the indwelling of the Holy Spirit! Is not this a wonderful statement? Well might our Lord preface it by saying, "Now I tell you the truth," as if He felt that they would find it a hard saying, for a hard saying it is!

Consider for a moment what Christ was to His disciples while He was here—and then see what must be the value of the Spirit's operations when it is expedient that they should lose all that blessing in order to receive the Spirit of God! Our Lord Jesus Christ was to them their Teacher. They had learned everything from His lips. He was their Leader—they had never to ask what to do—they had only to follow in His footsteps. He was their Defender—whenever the Pharisees or Sadducees assailed them, He was like a brazen wall to them! He was their Comforter—in all times of grief they resorted to Him and His dear sympathetic heart poured out floods of comfort at once. What if I were to say that the Lord Jesus Christ was everything to them, their All in All? What a father is to his children, yes, what a mother is to her suckling, that was Jesus Christ to His disciples! And yet the Spirit of God's abiding in the Church is better, even, than all this!

Now take another thought. What would you think if Jesus Christ were to come among us now, as in the days of His flesh? I mean not as He will come, but as He appeared at His first advent. What joy it would give you! Oh, the delights, the heavenly joys, to hear that Jesus Christ of Nazareth was on earth, again, a Man among men! Should we not clap our hands for joy? Our one question would be, "Master, where do You dwell?" for we should all long to live just where He lived. We could then sympathize with the Negroes when they flocked into Washington in large numbers to take up their residence there. Why, do you think, did they come to live in that city? Because Massa Abraham Lincoln, who had set them free, lived there! And they thought it would be glorious to live as near as possible to their great friend!

If Jesus lived anywhere, it would not matter where! If it were in the desert or on the bleakest of mountains, there would be a rush to the place! How would the spot be crowded! What rents they would pay for the worst of tenements if Jesus was but in the neighborhood! But don't you see the difficulty? We could not all get near Him in any literal or corporeal fashion. Now that the Church is multiplied into millions of Believers, some of the Lord's followers would never be able to see Him—and the most could only hope to speak with Him now and then! In the days of His flesh the 12 might see Him every day and so might the little company of disciples—but the case is altered, now that multitudes are trusting in His name.

If our Lord were at this time living in the United States, we should be much grieved to have an ocean between us and our Leader—all the companies that could be formed would not be able to run enough boats to carry us over. If the Master personally came here to this little island, it would not hold all the vast company of the faithful who would flock to it. It is much better to have the Holy Spirit, because He is dwelling with us and in us! The difficulties of the bodily Presence are too great and so, though we would be thankful, like the Apostles, if we had known Christ after the flesh, yet we do not marvel that they expressed little sorrow when they said that after the flesh they knew Him no more. The Comforter had filled the void caused by His absence and made them rejoice because the Lord had gone unto His Father!

Are we not apt to think that if our Lord Jesus were here it would give unspeakable strength to the Church? Would not the enemy be convinced if they saw Him? No, they would not! If they heard not Moses and the Prophets, neither would they be converted though one rose from the dead! Jesus rose, but they did not, therefore, believe. If our Lord had lingered here all this while, His Presence would not have converted unbelievers, for nothing can do that but the power of the Holy Spirit! "But," you say, "surely it would thrill the Church with enthusiasm. Fancy the Lord Himself standing on this platform this morning in the same garb as when He was upon earth. Oh, what rapturous worship! What burning zeal! What enthusiasm! We should go home in such a state of excitement as we never were in before!"

Yes, it is even so, but then the Lord is not going to carry on His Kingdom by the force of mere mental excitement—not even by such enthusiasm as would follow the sight of His Person. The work of the Holy Spirit is a truer work, a deeper work, a surer work and will more effectually achieve the purposes of God than even would the enthusiasm to which we should be stirred by the bodily Presence of our well-beloved Savior. The work is to be spiritual and, therefore, the visible Presence has departed. It is better that it should be so. We must walk by faith and by faith alone! How could we do this if we could see the Lord with these mortal eyes? This is the dispensation of the unseen Spirit, in which we render Glory to God by trusting in His Word and relying upon the unseen energy.

Now, faith works and faith triumphs though the world sees not the foundation upon which faith is built, for the Spirit who works in us cannot be discerned by carnal minds. The world sees Him not, neither knows Him. Thus, you see that the operations of the Holy Spirit must be inestimably precious. There is no calculating their value, since it is expedient that we lose the bodily Presence of Christ rather than remain without the indwelling of the Spirit of God.

III. Now go back to my first text, again, and follow me in the third head. Those operations of the Spirit of God, of which I am afraid some Christians are almost ignorant, are of wondrous power. The text says, "He that believes on Me, out of his belly shall flow rivers of living water." THESE OPERATIONS ARE OF MARVELOUS POWER. Brothers and Sisters, do you understand my text? Do rivers of living water flow out of you?

Notice, first, that this is to be an inward work—the rivers of living water are to flow out of the midst of the man. The words, are, according to our version, "Out of his belly"—that is, from his heart and soul. The rivers do not flow out of his mouth—the promised power is not oratory. We have had plenty of words, floods of words—but this is heart work. The source of the rivers is found in the inner life. It is an inward work at its fountainhead. It is not a work of talent and ability, show, glitter and glare—it is altogether an inward work. The life-flood is to come out of the man's inmost self—out of the heart and essential being of the man. Homage is shown too generally to outward form and external observance, though these soon lose their interest and power. But when the Spirit of God rests within a man, it exercises a home rule within him and he gives great attention to what an old divine was known to call, "the home department." Alas, many neglect the realm within which is the chief province under our care. O my Brothers and Sisters in Christ, if you would be useful, begin with yourself! It is out of your very soul that a blessing must come. It cannot come out of you if it is not in you! And it cannot be in you unless God the Holy Spirit places it there.

Next, it is life-giving work. Out of the heart of the man, out of the center of his life, are to flow rivers of living water. That is to say, he is instrumentally to communicate to others the Divine life. When he speaks; when he prays; when he acts, he shall so speak and pray and act that there shall be going out of him an emanation which is full of the life of Grace and godliness. He shall be a light by which others shall see! His life shall be the means of kindling life in other men's bosoms. "Out of his belly shall flow rivers of living water." Note the plenitude of it. The figure would have been a surprising one if it had said, "Out of him shall flow a river of living water." But it is not so—it says rivers.

Have you ever stood by the side of a very abundant spring? We have some such not far from London. You see the water bubbling up from many little mouths. Observe the sand dancing as the water forces its way from the bottom and there, just across the road, a mill is turned by the stream which has just been created by the spring! And when the waterwheel is turned, you see a veritable river flowing forward to supply Father Thames. Yet this is only one river! What would you think if you saw a spring yielding such supplies that a river flowed from it to the north and a river to the south, a river to the east and a river to the west? This is the figure before us—rivers of living water flowing out of the living man in all directions!

"Ah," you say, "I have not reached to that." A point is gained when you know, confess and deplore your failure. If you say, "I have all things and abound," I am afraid you will never reach the fullness of the blessing. But if you know something of your failure, the Lord will lead you further. It may be that the Spirit of Life which comes forth for you is but a trickling brooklet, or even a few tiny drops. Then be sure to confess it and you will be on the way to a fuller blessing! What a Word of God is this! Rivers of living water!! Oh that all professing Christians were such fountains! See how spontaneous it is—"Out of his belly shall flow." No pumping is required! Nothing is said about machinery and hydraulics! The man does not need exciting and stirring up, but, just as he is, influence of the best kind quietly flows out of him!

Did you ever hear a great hubbub in the morning, a great outcry, a sounding of trumpets and drums? And did you ever ask, "What is it?" Did a voice reply, "The sun is about to rise and he is making this noise that all may be aware of it"? No, he shines, but he has nothing to say about it! Even so, the genuine Christian just goes about flooding the world with blessings and, so far from claiming attention for himself, it may be that he is unconscious of what he is effecting! God so blesses him that his leaf does not wither and whatever he does is prospering, for he is like a tree planted by the rivers of water that bring forth its fruit in its season—his verdure and fruit are the natural outcome of his vigorous life. Oh, the blessed spontaneity of the work of Grace when a man gets into the fullness of it, for then he seems to eat and drink and sleep eternal life! And he spreads a savor of salvation all round! And this is to be perpetual—not like intermittent springs which burst forth and flow in torrents and then cease—but it is to be an everyday gushing out!

In summer and winter, by day and by night, wherever the man is, he shall be a blessing. As he breathes, he shall breathe benedictions! As he thinks, his mind shall be devising generous things. And when he acts, his acts shall be as though the hand of God were working by the hand of man! I hope I hear many sighs rising up in the place! I hope I hear friends saying, "Oh that I could get to that." I want you to attain the fullness of the favor! I pray that we may all get it because Jesus Christ is glorified! Therefore the Holy Spirit is given in this fashion, given more largely to those in the kingdom of Heaven than to all those holy men before the Lord's ascent to His Glory.

God gives no stinted blessing to celebrate the triumph of His Son! God gives not the Spirit by measure unto Him. On such an occasion Heaven's grandest liberality was displayed. Christ is glorified in Heaven above and God would have Him glorified in the Church below by vouchsafing a Baptism of the Holy Spirit to each of us. So I close by this, which I hope will be a very comforting and inspiriting reflection.

IV. THESE OPERATIONS OF THE SPIRIT OF GOD ARE EASILY TO BE
OBTAINED BY THE LORD'S CHILDREN. Did you say you had not received
them? They are to be had! They are to be had at once! First, they are to be
had by believing in Jesus. "This spoke He of the Spirit, which they that believe
on Him should receive." Do you not see that it is faith which gives us the first
drink and causes us to live? And this second, more abundant blessing of
being, ourselves, made fountains from which rivers flow, comes in the same
way! Believe in Christ, for the blessing is to be obtained not by the works of
the Law, nor by so much fasting, striving, or effort–but by belief in the Lord
Jesus!

With Him is the residue of the Spirit. He is prepared to give this to you, yes, to
every one of you who believe on His name. He will not, of course, make all of
you preachers–for who, then, would be hearers? If all were preachers, the
other works of the Church would be neglected. But He will give you this favor–
that out of you there shall stream a Divine influence all round you to bless your
children, to bless your servants, to bless the workmen in the house where you
are employed and to bless the street you live! In proportion as God gives you
opportunity, these rivers of living water will flow in this channel and in that–and
they will be pouring forth from you at all times–if you believe in Jesus for the
full blessing and can, by faith, receive it.

But there is another thing to be done as well, and that is to pray. And here I
want to remind you of those blessed Words of the Master, "Everyone that asks
receives; and he that seeks finds; and to him that knocks it shall be opened. If
a son shall ask bread of any of you that is a father, will he give him a stone?
Or if he ask for a fish, will he, for a fish give him a serpent? Or if he shall ask
for an egg, will he offer him a scorpion? If you, then, being evil, know how to
give good gifts unto your children: how much more shall your heavenly Father
give the Holy Spirit to them that ask Him?" You see, there is a distinct promise
to the children of God that their heavenly Father will give them the Holy Spirit
if they ask for His power–and that promise is made to be exceedingly strong
by the instances joined to it. If there is a promise that God can break (which
there is not), this is not the promise, for God has put it in the most forcible and
binding way.

I know not how to show you its wonderful force! Did you ever hear of a man
who, when his child asked for bread, gave him a stone? Go to the worst part
of London and will you find a man of that kind? You shall, if you like, get

among pirates and murderers, and when a little child cries, "Father, give me a bit of bread and meat," does the most wicked father fill his own little one's mouth with stones? Yet the Lord seems to say that this is what He would be doing if He were to deny us the Holy Spirit when we ask Him for His necessary working—He would be like one that gave his children stones instead of bread! Do you think the Lord will ever bring Himself down to that? He says, "How much more shall your heavenly Father give the Holy Spirit to them that ask Him?"

He makes it a stronger case than that of an ordinary parent! The Lord must give us the Spirit when we ask Him, for He has, herein, bound Himself by no ordinary pledge. He has used a simile which would bring dishonor on His name and that of the very grossest kind, if He did not give the Holy Spirit to them that ask Him! Oh, then, let us ask Him at once with all our hearts! Am I not so happy as to have in this audience some who will immediately ask? I pray that some who have never received the Holy Spirit at all may now be led, while I am speaking, to pray, "Blessed Spirit, visit me! Lead me to Jesus." But especially those of you that are the children of God—to you is this promise especially made! Ask God to make you all that the Spirit of God can make you—not only a satisfied Believer who has drunk for himself—but a useful Believer who overflows the neighborhood with blessing!

I see here a number of friends from the country who have come to spend their holiday in London. What a blessing it would be if they went back to their respective Churches overflowing! There are numbers of Churches that need flooding! They are dry as a barn floor and little dew falls on them. Oh that they might be flooded! What a wonderful thing a flood is! Go down to the river; look over the bridge and see the barges and other crafts lying in the mud. All the king's horses and all the king's men cannot tug them out to sea! There they lie, dead and motionless as the mud, itself! What shall we do with them? What machinery can move them? Have we a great engineer among us who will devise a scheme for lifting these vessels and bearing them down to the river's mouth? No, it cannot be done! Wait till the tide comes in! What a change! Each vessel walks the water like a thing of life! What a difference between the low tide and the high tide! You cannot stir the boats when the water is gone, but when the tide is at the full, see how readily they move—a little child may push them with his hand!

Oh, for a flood of Divine Grace! May the Lord send to all our Churches a great springtide! Then the indolent will be active enough and those who were half dead will be full of energy. I know that in this particular dock several vessels are lying that I should like to float, but I cannot stir them. They neither work for God nor come out to the Prayer Meetings! They do not give of their substance to spread the Gospel. If the flood would come, you would see what they are capable of—they would be active, fervent, generous, abounding in every good word and work! So may it be! So may it be! May springs begin to flow in all our Churches and may all of you who hear me this day get your share of the streams!

Oh that the Lord may now fill you and then send you home bearing a flood of Grace with you! It sounds odd to speak of a man's carrying home a flood within him and yet I hope it will be so—and that out of you shall flow rivers of living water! So may God grant it for Jesus' sake. Amen.

INTIMATE KNOWLEDGE OF THE HOLY SPIRIT

"The Spirit of Truth, whom the world cannot receive, because it sees Him not, neither knows Him; but you know Him, for He dwells with you and shall be in you."
John 14:17

A Sermon Delivered On Sunday Morning: 10 March 1889

THE part of the text on which we shall meditate is this–"The Spirit of Truth, you know Him, for He dwells with you and shall be in you." Observe that the Holy Spirit is here called the Spirit of Truth. There is much meaning in this expression. He is the Teacher of the Truth of God, unalloyed Truth, practical, divinely effective Truth of God. He never teaches anything but the Truth of God. If it comes from the Spirit of God, we may receive it from Him without any hesitation. It is He that takes of the things of Christ and shows them unto us. And these things are true and He thus proves Himself to be the Spirit of Truth.

He is the very Spirit and soul of Truth, the essence, the life and power of it. Divine Truth, when merely heard, takes no effect upon the mind until the Spirit of God enlivens it, and then it becomes a quickening force. He makes the Truth of God itself, in its reality and substance, to enter the soul and affect the heart. He is the Teacher of Truth and He is Himself the active power that makes Truth to be Truth to us in the assurance of our inmost souls. He is the Spirit of Truth in this sense, too, that He works truthfulness in His people. In those with whom the Holy Spirit works effectually "there is no deceit."

They are open-hearted, honest, sincere and true. They have an intense affection for the Truth of God and a zeal for it. They are by His truthful influence preserved from deadly error. If it were possible, false teachers would deceive even the elect. But where the Spirit of God dwells, He detects for us the false from the true and He gives us the spirit of a sound mind by which we reject that which is false and cleave only to that which is revealed of God. In this sense He is the Spirit of Truth. And as He works truthfulness in His people, so the work that He does is always true and real work.

You may get up an animal excitement and your converts will, in due time fail–but the Spirit of God works true conversion, sincere repentance and saving faith such as no sun of persecution can dry up and wither. He works deep conviction of sin and simple faith in the Lord Jesus. And these things abide in the heart. The new birth, as He works it, is not after the fancied manner of baptismal regeneration but after an effective spiritual manner so that a Divine life is imparted and the man becomes a child of God. He produces real sanctification–not the pretense of perfection but the reality of holiness. Everything the Spirit of God does is substance and not shadow. The baseless fabric of a vision is the work of man. But the eternal, abiding, everlasting work of Divine Grace is wrought by the Spirit of Truth alone.

As He is the Spirit of Truth, we may be sure that whatever He sets His seal upon, is true. He will only bear witness to the Truth of God. He will not assist in maintaining error. Mark this word–careful observation will show that in proportion as the nominal Church of the present day has departed from the truth of God, the Spirit of God has departed from her. He can never set His seal to a lie. The testimony of His sacred operation in "signs following," is borne only to the Truth of God. If I preach to you that which is not the Word of the Lord, it will not be followed by the work of the Spirit of Truth. There will be no conversions among sinners and there will be no edification for the people of God.

It is by the Truth of God as His instrument that the Spirit of God works. And we must be very careful that we do not bring forth any other instrument. Let us not talk, as some do, as if Scriptural doctrine were of little or no consequence. For where the doctrine is not of God, the Spirit of Truth is grieved and He will depart from such a ministry. Except we keep close to the Words of the Lord Jesus and the Revelation of the inspired Book, the Spirit of Truth will show His displeasure by refusing to use our utterances. In vain your music, your architecture, your learning and your "bright services" if the Truth of God is given up. Farewell to the witness of the Spirit in the hearts of men when men are taught the inventions of men in the place of the Revelation of God.

If the Holy Spirit is bearing witness in your spirit that you are the children of God, then you are truly born of God. The presence of the Divine Paraclete is the seal of your adoption. If He dwells in you, this is the token of your sonship. For He does not dwell in the unregenerate. If He helps, strengthens, comforts, guides, illuminates and sanctifies you, you have a seal which you need not question–the seal of God upon you–that you are His chosen and shall be His in the day when He makes up His jewels.

This brings me to the doctrine upon which I shall enlarge this morning. This is the distinction between the men of the world and the disciples of Christ. The world knows nothing of the Holy Spirit. But the disciples of Christ know Him. For the Lord Jesus says, "He dwells with you and shall be in you." There are a great many distinctions in the world of a religious kind–one man wears his phylacteries, another is girt with camel's hair. One man comes with multiplied ceremonies, another with none at all. You cannot judge who are the people of God by these external things.

Forms of Church government and modes of worship may be important in their own place–but before the Lord the infallible test is this–do you bear the fruit of the Spirit of God in you? Does He indwell you? "If any man has not the Spirit of Christ, he is none of His." But he that has the Spirit dwelling within his soul, he it is that is a true born heir of Heaven.

We have raised a solemn question to begin with, have we not? But, dear Friends, I do not desire it to remain a question. I pray that it may be no question with anyone of you but that you may know that it is so and may go on to enjoy the blessed privilege of being on intimate terms with the Holy Spirit–"But you know Him, for He dwells with you and shall be in you."

To come close up to my subject, the first head will be BELIEVERS IN JESUS CHRIST KNOW THE HOLY SPIRIT. They know Him, to begin with, by believing what has been taught them concerning the Comforter by the Lord Jesus Christ. When Jesus Christ had taught His people concerning the Holy Spirit and they had received His teaching, He said, "You know Him. For He dwells with you and shall be in you." If they had refused the sayings of Christ, if they had possessed no love, if they had not kept His Commandments, if they had arrogantly resolved to find out this mystery for themselves by their own thinking, apart from the instruction of their Master, they would not have known the Spirit of God. We must begin our acquaintance with the Spirit by sitting at the feet of Jesus and accepting His testimony as sure.

But more than this–we know the Holy Spirit by knowing our Lord Jesus and by Him knowing the Father. There is such an intimate union between the Holy Spirit, the Father, and the Son, that to know the Holy Spirit we must know the Son of God, and know the Father. If we know the Lord Jesus, we have the

Spirit of God. For by no one else could the things of Christ be revealed to us. Beginning then, at the very beginning–do you know the Lord Jesus Christ? You know something about Him–but do you know Him? Is He your friend, your acquaintance? Are you on personal terms of fellowship with Him?

If so, then you see the Father in His face. Jesus says, "He that has seen Me has seen the Father." And He tells His people, "From henceforth you know Him and have seen Him." You are, therefore, acquainted with God the Father through Jesus Christ the Son. And you have seen the glory of His Grace beaming in your Savior's face. In this way you have become acquainted with the Holy Spirit who is not divided from the Father and the Son. As you know the Son you know the Father, and in this way you come to know the Holy Spirit. No man comes to the Father but by the Son, and he that comes to the Father receives the Spirit.

We know the Holy Spirit, next, by His operations upon us. We not only know about His operations but we have been the subjects of them. All those who are true disciples of Christ have felt a divinely supernatural power working upon them. First, the Holy Spirit operates to our spiritual quickening. There was a time when we were dead in trespasses and in sins–holy feeling was unknown to us and the life of faith was far from us. At that time we did not desire nor even know spiritual things–we were carnally minded and the carnal mind knows not the things which are of God.

The Spirit of God came upon us and we were awakened and made to live. Do you remember that? Many of us can distinctly remember when we passed from death unto life. With others, the visible life may have been made manifest more gradually, but even in them there was a moment when the vital force entered the soul and they can now rejoice that they have been quickened who were once spiritually dead. You know the Spirit in measure when He breathes upon your dead heart and it begins to throb with the heavenly life. In connection with that quickening there was conviction of sin. In what a powerful light does the Holy Spirit set our sin!

In my discourses to you about sin I try to show you how heinous it is and how terrible are its consequences. But when a single beam from the Spirit of Truth shines upon sin, it makes it appear "exceeding sinful." I remember how Mr. Bunyan said, when under conviction, "I thought none but the devil himself could equal me for inward wickedness and pollution of mind." When the Spirit of God revealed him to himself he would have willingly changed places with toads and serpents for he esteemed the most loathsome objects to be better than himself. This revelation of darkness is the effect of light–the light of the Spirit of God. And when He convicts us of sin we begin to know Him.

After having convicted us of sin, He leads us to repentance and to faith in Jesus Christ–then we know Him! How many a promise did some of you hear but you could not receive it! How many a comforting discourse did you listen to and yet it did not comfort you! But when the Spirit of God came–in a moment you saw Jesus as the Consolation of Israel, the Friend of sinners, the atoning Sacrifice, the Surety of the Covenant of Grace–and sweet peace came streaming into your soul! At that time you did not only know that the Holy Spirit leads to Jesus Christ but you knew that He was leading you. In that respect you knew Him by an experimental acquaintance which is the best of knowledge.

Since that time, beloved Brethren, we have known the Holy Spirit in many ways–restraining from evil, stimulating to good, instructing, consoling, directing and enlivening. He has been to us the Spirit of reviving–we have grown dull and cold and sleepy, till that verse of the hymn has been verified–

"In vain we tune our formal songs,
In vain we strive to rise,
Hosannas languish on our tongues,
And our devotion dies."

But no sooner has the Spirit visited us than we have felt all alive–bright, cheerful and intense. Then our whole heart has run in the ways of God's commands and we have rejoiced in His name. How true is that word, "He restores my soul"! Thus have we known the Holy Spirit by His operations within us.

Oftentimes He has acted as an illuminator. A difficult Scripture or mysterious doctrine has been before me–I have looked at the original and I have examined what the best Biblical students have written upon it. And yet, when I have thus used all the helps within reach, the point has remained in the dark. My best aid has ever been to resort to the great Author of the sacred Word– even the Holy Spirit Himself. He can, by blessing the means which we are using, or by directly leading the mind in the right track put an end to all difficulty. He has the clue of every maze, the solution of every riddle. And to whom He wills, He can reveal the secret of the Lord.

Dear young Believers, you who wish to understand the Scriptures, seek this light from above for this is the true light. Other lights may mislead but this is clear and sure. To have the Spirit of God lighting up the inner chambers of truth is a great gift. Truth of the deeper sort is comparable to a cavern into which we cannot find our way except by a guide and a light. When the Spirit of Truth is come He pours daylight into the darkness and leads us into all Truth of God. He does not merely show the Truth but He leads us into it so that we stand within it and rejoice in the hidden treasure which it contains. Then we know Him as our sacred Illuminator.

I especially note that we also know Him as the Comforter. Alas for the disturbance of heart which we receive in the world–perhaps even in the family! Few things, it may be, are as we could wish and therefore we are sorely troubled. But when the Spirit of God comes, peace flows to us like a river and Jesus breathes on us and says, "Peace be unto you." Do you know that peace? Many saints of God have enjoyed a heavenly calm upon their sick beds–when pain should have distracted them. The Spirit of God has rested them in Jesus. I have heard of one saint, near his end, who asked, "Is this dying? Then I should like to keep on dying forever."

He felt so much comfort–such a flood of joy which the Holy Spirit creates–that death itself had not only lost its sting but had even become a joy to him! The comforts of the Holy Spirit take bitterness out of wormwood and gall and the sting out of the last enemy. May God give us His Grace to know the Holy Spirit as our Comforter! Happy knowledge! I trust that we have oftentimes known the Holy Spirit as guiding us in various ways. I will not speak largely on this for some might not understand it. But I know for sure that the Holy Spirit does give to His favored people hints as to things to come. I say not that any man is inspired to tell the future. But I do say that choice saints have received preparations for the future and foreshadowing of their coming experiences.

When Believers come into difficult circumstances they bow the knee and cry for guidance, even as David said, "Bring through life if we are willing to obey His monitions. Is it not written, "Your ears shall hear a word behind you saying, This is the way, walk you in it"? The Divine communications of the

Holy Spirit are the precious heritage of true saints. But they are a peculiar voice to their own souls and are not to be repeated in words.

If you know these Divine workings, as I am sure many of you do, then through His operations you are made to know the Holy Spirit—that deep calm—that peace which only He can give. That exhilaration, that superlative joy as of Heaven begun below which only the Lord can work. That steadfast courage, that holy patience, that fixedness of heart, that gentleness of manner and firmness of purpose which come only from above—these all introduce you to the wonderworking Spirit who takes pleasure thus to operate upon the minds of the heirs of eternal glory. Thus we know the Holy Spirit by His works and gifts and revelations.

But I do not think we have entered the center of the text even yet. "You know Him," says the text—you know not only His work but Himself. I may know the great achievements of an artist in marble but I may not know the sculptor himself. I may know a man's paintings and therefore I may guess somewhat of his character but yet I may not know the man himself. "You know Him," says our Lord. And truly we know the Holy Spirit as to His personality. If the Holy Spirit were a mere influence, we should read, "You know it." Let us always shun the mistake of calling the Holy Spirit "it." It cannot do anything. It is a dead thing—the Holy Spirit is a living, blessed Person and I hope we can say that we know Him as such. Others may doubt His personality. But we believe in the teaching of our Lord Jesus Christ and behold, in the names given to Him, the emotions ascribed to Him and the acts performed by Him, abundant proofs of His sacred personality. In our hearts we know HIM.

As we know His personality so we know also His Divinity because the Holy Spirit work in us effects which none but God could work. Who can give life to the spiritually dead? Who but the Lord and Giver of life? Who can instruct and illuminate as the Holy Spirit does? Only because He is Divine can He guide us into all Truth and purify us unto perfect holiness. There have been things worked in us—in our experience—in which we have beheld not only the finger of God but God Himself working in our hearts to will and to do of His own good pleasure. Oh, worship the Holy Spirit! The greatest crime of sinners is to blaspheme the Holy Spirit—and the greatest fault of saints is to neglect the Holy Spirit. Let us adore Him, yield to Him, confide in Him—and pray that we may know Him to the fullest.

So it comes to this—that as we know the Holy Spirit's personality and Godhead we come to know Him. I mean this—that there is now a personal relationship between the Believer and the Holy Spirit, a conscious and clear fellowship and communion. The communion of the Holy Spirit is one of the three choice blessings of the great Benediction. Do we not enjoy it? We speak with Him and He speaks with us. We trust Him and He puts us in trust with many a precious Truth of God. We are not strangers now. We do not talk of Him as a personage a long way off of whom we have heard—a Divine mystery with which Prophets and Apostles were acquainted in remote ages—but we know Him.

Come, let me look into your faces, my Beloved in the Lord, and let me ask you, Is this true or not? If you are obliged to say, "We do not know whether there is any Holy Spirit, for we are utter strangers to Him," then I pray the Lord to deal graciously with you and manifest His Son Jesus Christ to you by the power of that same Holy Spirit of whom we speak. The Spirit of Truth is to those of us who trust in the Lord Jesus our present help. He is more familiar with us than any other Person. For He enters within, where none else find admission. "You know Him. For He dwells with you and shall be in you." Thus much upon our first head. Now I will take you to another exceedingly important and interesting. May the Holy Spirit help me.

II. The second head is this—BELIEVERS KNOW THE HOLY SPIRIT THROUGH HIMSELF. Let us read the text again—"You know Him, for He dwells with you and shall be in you." It is not, "You know Him for you have heard gracious preaching." Nor, "You know Him for you have read about Him in the Scriptures." No—"You know Him, for He dwells with you and shall be in you." The moon cannot help us to see the sun nor can man reveal God. God can only be seen in His own light. No one can reveal the Holy Spirit but the Holy Spirit.

I thought this morning, coming along—I have to preach about the Holy Spirit. But what can I do without the Holy Spirit Himself? I can only preach aright concerning Him by His own Presence with me. And if He is not there, I shall only darken counsel by words without knowledge. Why is it that we know the Holy Spirit only by the Holy Spirit? I answer first, on account of the inadequacy of all means. By what methods can you make a man know the Holy Spirit? He is not to be discerned by the senses, nor perceived by eyes or ears. What if the preacher should be as eloquent as an angel—in what way would that make you know the Holy Spirit? You would probably remember more of the man than of his Subject. Nothing is more to be deplored than a hungering after mere oratory.

It would be infinitely better to speak with a stammer the Truth of God than to pour forth a flood of words in which the Truth is drowned. Words are nothing but air and wind and they cannot possibly reveal the Holy Spirit. No outward ordinances can reach the point any more than human speech. We greatly rejoice in the Baptism of Believers and in the breaking of bread in which the death of the Lord Jesus is set forth before us. But in what symbol could we fully see the Holy Spirit? If He were even to descend upon us as a dove we should see only the visible shape—we would not necessarily discern the Spirit. The Spirit Himself must reveal Himself.

Beloved, there is no chariot in which God can ride to us—the axles of creation itself would break beneath the enormous load of Deity. It is not possible for God to reveal Himself fully by His works—He is seen only by Himself. Therefore the Son of God, Himself, has come to us as "God with us." In Him we see God. The Holy Spirit must Himself come into the heart to which He would make Himself known.

This is even more clear from the inability of our nature to discover the Holy Spirit. We are dead by nature and how can we know anything until He makes us alive? Our eyes are spiritually blinded—how can we see Him until He opens our eyes? We are altogether without strength by nature—how can we run after Him until He first comes to us and gives us the power to do so? We are unable to perceive the Holy Spirit—the carnal man knows not the things which are of God for they are spiritual and must be spiritually discerned. We must be endowed with a spirit before we can discern the great Spirit. Flesh cannot transform itself into spirit. No, it is the Lord Himself who must come and breathe into us the Spirit of life and then we perceive Him who is the Spirit of Truth.

The Holy Spirit must reveal Himself to us if we are to know Him—this is clear from the nature of the case. How do I know a man but by the man himself appearing to me and speaking to me and manifesting himself to me? You cannot with accuracy judge of a man by his writings. It is a curious circumstance that Mr. Toplady, who wrote very bitterly on behalf of the Truth of God, was, in temper, the sweetest of men. On the other hand, Mr.

Romaine, of Blackfriars, who in their writings seem to be the gentlest of beings were by no means free from harshness. You must see a man. No, more–you must live with a man in order to know him. You must live with the Holy Spirit and He must dwell with you and be in you, before you can speak of knowing Him at all.

The facts of the case prove this. I shall put it to any Believer here who can humbly say, "I know Him, for He dwells with me and is in me." How do you know the Holy Spirit but by the Holy Spirit? Did you learn your religion from me? Then you have it all to unlearn. Did you learn it out of a book? You have need to begin again. Did you inherit it from your parents or borrow it from your friends? Then you are still ignorant of the vital point–God is only known through Himself. The Holy Spirit by the holy Spirit. Have you not found it so in your own case? Why, you have sat and heard a sermon which was in itself cheering, comforting and quickening, for your neighbor said, "What a happy time we have enjoyed!" Alas, you thought you had never felt more stupid and lifeless. Have you not gone down the Tabernacle steps and said to yourself, "I am as hard as stone and as cold as a winter's fog? What shall I do?"

Thus are you without the Spirit of God. But when the Divine Spirit comes upon you, such complaints are at an end. Then does the lame man leap as an hart and the tongue of the dumb is made to sing. Then are you full of living joy in listening to the Gospel–every word you hear seems to be on wheels. And towards you the cherubim fly swiftly bringing live coals from off the altar.

III. My third head is BELIEVERS ENJOY A SACRED INTIMACY WITH THE SPIRIT OF GOD. I am not going to withdraw that word intimacy. It is warranted by the language of our Lord. For He says, "You know Him, for He dwells with you and shall be in you."

First, He says, "He dwells with you." Is not that a wonderful sentence? The Holy Spirit is God, and therefore the Heaven of heavens cannot contain Him– and yet behold the condescending fact–"He dwells with you." The Holy Spirit is now upon earth, the vicar and representative of the Lord Jesus Christ who said, "I will send you another Comforter"–that is, another Helper and Advocate like I Iimself. Consider how our Lord dwelt with His disciples. After the same fashion, the Spirit of Truth dwells with us. Jesus permitted His disciples the most intimate communion with Himself–they ran to Him with their troubles, they told Him their difficulties, they confessed their doubts.

He was their Master and Lord, and yet He washed their feet. He ate and drank with them and permitted the freest conversation. You never find our Lord repelling their approaches or resenting their familiarities. He did not draw a ring round Himself and say, "Keep your distance." Now, in the same manner, the Spirit of Truth deals with Believers. "He dwells with you." You may go to Him at any time, you may ask what you will of Him, you may speak to Him as a man speaks with his friend. You cannot see Him, but He sees you, which is much better. You cannot hear His voice, but He hears yours. No, He hears your thoughts. He is most near to those who are in Christ. "He dwells with you."

Dwelling with us, He is in our assemblies. It is He who fulfils the promise of our Lord, "Lo, I am with you always, even unto the end of the world." It is by the Holy Spirit that the Lord Jesus is with us. That we might enjoy that sacred Presence, it was expedient for our Lord to go away. Beloved, what a mercy it is when the Holy Spirit is in our assembly! What a dreary business it is when the Holy Spirit is gone from the congregation! The people come and go and perhaps there may be fine music, splendid millinery, admirable eloquence, a vast crowd, or a wealthy congregation. But what of these things? They are a bag of wind! If the Holy Spirit is not in the congregation, it is gathered together in vain. Behold, the people spend themselves for very vanity if the Lord is not among them. But the Comforter does come into our assemblies. For it is written, "He dwells with you."

He also comes into our homes—"He dwells with you." Where do you dwell, O true Believer? Is it in a very poor lodging?—"He dwells with you." It may be, dear Friend, you live on board ship and are tossed upon the sea—"He dwells with you." Perhaps you go to work in a mine far beneath the surface of the earth—"He dwells with you." Many choice saints are bed-ridden but the Spirit dwells with them. I commend to all of you who love the Lord these gracious words—"He dwells with you." The first disciples said to the Lord Jesus, "Master, where do you dwell?" He answered, "Come and see." So I bid you note where the Divine Spirit chooses to dwell—behold and wonder—He dwells with His people wherever they are! He does not leave them alone but He abides with them as a shepherd with his flock.

Well may we know Him for He takes up His abode with us. And He does this, not as a latent, inoperative influence but He works in the place where He dwells. He makes our members instruments of His working and sanctifies the faculties of our nature as vessels of a temple wherein He dwells. He perfumes every chamber of the house of manhood and consecrates every corner of our being. O Believer, "He dwells with you" in all the might of His Godhead and you are made strong in the inner man by His strengthening! Fall back upon the Holy Spirit in the moment of your weakness.

Alas, my Brethren, are there any moments when we are not weak? Fall back, therefore, upon the Holy Spirit at all times. Even in the prayer in which you seek strength, ask that the Spirit may help your infirmities. Even for the faith which brings you all Divine Grace ask for the Spirit of God to work faith in you. "He dwells with you," for you are unable to live without His constant presence and you need not attempt the perilous experiment.

The second sentence runs, "He shall be in you." This is a greater marvel. "Know you not that your bodies are the temples of the Holy Spirit?" Take care of them, never defile them. Let not the idea of drunkenness, gluttony, or lust come near you. For it is written, "If any man defile the temple of God, him shall God destroy." With what reverence should we look upon the body now that it has been redeemed by the Lord Jesus and is indwelt by the Holy Spirit! The Spirit also dwells within your minds. We possess Him and He possesses us. "He shall be in you," as a king in his palace, or a soul in its body. I am afraid that many professors know nothing about this. I must be talking nonsense in the esteem of some of you–if it seems nonsense, let that fact condemn you. You cannot be right before God unless the Spirit of God is in you, in your mind, your heart, your desires, your fears, your hopes, your inmost life.

The Spirit must permeate your entire being, filling it full with His floods, even as the waters cover the channels of the deep. "He shall be in you." It is a wonderful fact. The Spirit shall be in you as the source of your life and the force of your life. What cannot a man do when the Holy Spirit is in him? His weakest endeavor will prosper when the Holy Spirit is pouring His life into him. For he shall be like a tree planted by the rivers of water that brings forth his fruit in his season. His leaf also shall not wither. And whatsoever he does, shall prosper. But without the Holy Spirit, what barren and withered trees we are! May we never know the awful drought which comes of the absence of the Spirit!

Brethren, when our Lord Jesus Christ came upon the earth and was beheld as God in human flesh, that was to us the pledge of the indwelling of the Holy Spirit in us—for as God dwelt in the human Person of the Lord Jesus Christ—even so does the Spirit abide in our humanity. Our Lord's life on earth was the picture of the Spirit's indwelling. As He was anointed of the Spirit, even so are we in our measure. "He went about doing good." He lived consecrated to God, loving the sons of men. And thus will the Spirit of God within us cause us to live—we shall imitate the Christ of God through the Spirit of God. The death of Christ was the way by which the Spirit was enabled to come to sinful men. By His great sacrifice the stone is rolled away which once blocked the road—

"It is through the purchase of His death,
Who hung upon the tree,
The Spirit is sent down to breathe
On such dry bones as we."

When our Lord rose from the dead, we had the guarantee that even so the Spirit of God would quicken our mortal bodies and renew us into newness of life. But it was when our Lord ascended up on high, leading captivity captive that the Holy Spirit was actually given. When our Redeemer returned to His Father's Throne, He scattered the largess of Heaven—He gave the Holy Spirit to men of various offices and to His whole Church. Then were the days of refreshing by Divine visitation. Your ascended Lord gives you this token of His love—the indwelling of the Holy Spirit in you—prize it above all things. Do you know it? It seems like an impertinence for me to put this question to some of you who are gray-headed, and yet there is need. I trust you knew the Holy Spirit before I was born. But yet I cannot help pressing the enquiry, for you may not know Him even now.

I have urged the question upon myself and therefore I urge it upon you. Does the Spirit of Truth dwell in you? If not, what will you do?

IV. I come to a conclusion with one more observation. BELIEVERS SHALL HAVE A CONTINUANCE AND AN INCREASE FOR THE SPIRIT'S INTIMACY. "He dwells with you and shall be in you."

Mark well the increase. Is it not a blessed step from "with" to "in"? "He dwells with you"—that is, a Friend in the same house. "And shall be in you," that is, a Spirit within yourself. This is nearer, dearer, more mysterious and more effective by far. The bread yonder is "with" me. I eat it and now it is "in" me. It could not nourish me until it advanced from "with" to "in." What a distinct advance it is for the child of God when he rises from the Spirit of God being with him to the Spirit of God being in him! When the Spirit of God helped the Apostles to work miracles, He was with them. But when they came to feel His spiritual work in their own souls and to rejoice in the comfort which He brought to them, then He was in them. Even if you could obtain miraculous gifts, you ought not to be satisfied to speak with tongues, nor to work miracles. But you should press on to know the Spirit with yourself—indwelling, communing, quickening you.

"He shall be in you." Notice that in consequence of this, we know Him. If a person dwells with us, we begin to know him. But if he dwells within us and has become intertwined with our being, then we know him, indeed. "He shall be in you" is a high degree of intimacy. As we have noticed the increase, so remark the continuance—"He shall be in you." There is no period in which the Holy Spirit will have finished His work so as to go away and leave the Believer to himself. Our Savior says of the Comforter, that He "shall abide with you forever." Grieve not the Spirit of God, I pray you—quench Him not, resist Him not—but carefully cherish in your hearts this Divine word, "He shall be in you." What comfort is here!

You dread the days of age and infirmity, but "He shall be in you." You tremble before that trial which threatens you, but "He shall be in you." You do not know how you will answer the gainsayer—take no thought what you shall speak—it shall be given you in the same hour what you shall speak, for He shall be in you. And when the last moment approaches, when you must breathe out your soul to God—the living Spirit who dwells with you, even as the nurse sits at your bedside—shall then be in you and by His living power within shall transform death into the gate of endless life. "He dwells with you and shall be in you." O child of God, your Comforter will not leave you! He will continue still to take up His residence within you until you shall be taken up to dwell where Jesus is forever and ever.

This is our great reliance for the future upholding of the Church as a whole and of each individual Believer—the Spirit of God dwells with us and shall be in us. The Church of God will never be destroyed. The gates of Hell shall not prevail against her. For the Holy Spirit dwells with us and shall be in us to the end of the world. This is the reliance of the child of God personally for his perseverance in Divine Grace. He knows that Jesus lives and therefore he shall live. And the Holy Spirit is within him, as the life of Christ, which can never die. The Believer pushes on despite a thousand obstacles, knowing that God gives him the victory through the Lord Jesus Christ—out of whose hand none can pluck him.

I have done. And yet I have done nothing unless the Spirit of God shall bless the word spoken. Oh, that some of you who have never known the Spirit of God may feel His power coming upon you at this moment! You may be sitting in the pew very careless, even now, and yet before you leave He may descend and soften your hard heart. The other day the ground was hard as iron and the water was turned to ice. But there came a breath from the south and soon a thaw set in, the snow vanished and the ice was gone—even so the Holy Spirit breathes on us and our inward frost disappears at once.

Come, Holy Spirit. Come even now. Let us implore His Presence and power. Pray for a closer, clearer knowledge of Him, O Children of God! Pray that sinners may be met with by His Grace. The first token of the Spirit's work will be that they will begin to feel their sin and cry for mercy—and when that is done, the glad tidings of pardon are for them. To them we say, "Believe on the Lord Jesus Christ and you shall be saved and your house." The Lord make the word effectual, for Jesus Christ's sake. Amen.

THE ENTREATY OF THE HOLY SPIRIT

"As the Holy Spirit says, Today if you will hear His voice, harden not your hearts."
Hebrews 3:7

A Sermon Delivered On Sunday Morning: 1 March 1874

THE peculiar circumstances in which we are now placed as a congregation demand of me that my discourses should be principally directed to the unconverted, that the awakened may be decided, that those may be awakened who as yet remain unmoved, and that a desire to seek the Lord may spread all around us. We may leave the 99 in the wilderness for a little while, just now, and go after that which has gone astray. It is our duty, usually, to feed the children, but for a while we may leave that to other agencies, and hand out food to those who are perishing of hunger. These seasons of revival do not last forever–they come and they go and, therefore–they must be taken advantage of while they are with us.

The farmer tells us that he must make hay while the sun shines and we, also, must attend, in the season, to the labor which it suggests–and that duty seems to me to look in the direction of the undecided. While God is speaking so mightily, we should plead with men to hear His voice! Clearly, it is our wisdom to say, "Amen," to what the Lord is saying, for as His Word cannot return unto Him void, ours will be sure to be fruitful when it tallies with the Lord's. Therefore the subject of my sermon this morning shall be that of our hymn writer–

"'Hear God while He speaks,' then hear Him today.
And pray while you hear, unceasingly pray!
Believe in His promise, rely on His Word,
And while He commands you, obey your great Lord."
I have taken this text with the earnest hope that God may bless it and I look to the Lord's people to baptize the text in floods of anxious tears for the unsaved.

The first point which it presents for serious consideration is this–THE SPECIAL VOICE OF THE HOLY SPIRIT. "As the Holy Spirit says, Today if you will hear His voice." The Apostle is continually quoting from the Old

Testament, but he does not often present his quotations in this peculiar fashion. In the very next chapter, when he is speaking of the same passage, he uses the expression, "Saying in David"–mentioning the human author of the Psalm. But in this case, to give full emphasis to the Truth of God, he quotes the Divine Author alone–"As the Holy Spirit says."

These words, it is true, are applicable to every passage of sacred Scripture, for we may say of all the Inspired Books–"As the Holy Spirit says." But it is designedly used here that the passage may have the greater weight with us. The Holy Spirit, in fact, not only speaks thus in the 95th Psalm, but it is His unvarying utterance. The Holy Spirit says, or continues, still, to say, "Hear you His voice today." He has a certain doctrine upon one occasion and a still deeper Truth of God at another period, according as there was need, or as His people were prepared for it. But this particular utterance is for all time and for every day of Divine Grace. The Holy Spirit, by Paul, as before by David, says, "Today."

Yes, that is still the burden which He lays upon His ministering servants–in every place they entreat and persuade men, saying, "Today if you will hear His voice, harden not your hearts." How does the Holy Spirit thus speak? He says this first, in the Scriptures. Every command of Scripture calls for immediate obedience. The Law of God is not given to us to be laid by upon the shelf to be obeyed at some future period of life! And the Gospel of our Lord and Savior Jesus Christ is not so intended for the 11 th hour as to be lightly trifled with during the first ten. Wherever the Holy Spirit exhorts, He speaks in the present tense, and bids us now repent, or now believe, or now seek the Lord!

I pray you always remember, whenever you read the Bible, that it is the Spirit of the living God who there admonishes you to immediate obedience! The calls of the Inspired Word are not those of Moses, or David, or Paul, or Peter, but the solemn utterances of the Holy Spirit speaking through them. With what a dignity does this Truth invest Holy Scripture and with what solemnity does it surround our reading of it! Quibbling with Scripture, trifling with it, disputing its doctrines, or neglecting its admonitions we grieve the Spirit of God! And this is very dangerous ground to trespass on, for although He is long-suffering and pitiful, yet remember it is of the sin against the Holy Spirit that it is said, "It shall never be forgiven."

Not every sin against the Holy Spirit is unpardonable—God be thanked for that! But there is a sin against the Holy Spirit which shall never be forgiven. Therefore do we tread, I say, on very delicate ground when we vex Him, as we do if at any time in reading His Word we count His teachings to be light matters. Beware, I say, you men of England, who have your Bibles in your houses among whom the Word of the Lord is common as wheat bread! Beware how you treat it, for in rejecting it you reject not only the voice of Apostles and Prophets, but the voice of the Holy Spirit Himself! The Holy Spirit says, "Today." He bids His people make haste and delay not to keep the commands of God! And He bids sinners seek the Lord while He may be found—and call upon Him while He is near. Oh, may you hear His warning voice and live!

Further, while the Holy Spirit speaks in Scripture in this way, He speaks in the same manner in the hearts of His people, for He is a living and active Agent. His work is not ended—He still speaks and writes—the pen is still in His hand! Not to write with ink upon paper, but upon the fleshy tablets of prepared hearts! Now the Spirit of God has been in this Church communicating with His people, and the tenor of the communication has been this—"Seek to win souls." And I will guarantee this assertion, that in no case has the Spirit said, "Seek the conversion of sinners at the end of the year—awake to earnestness about their souls when you have become more mature in years and judgment." But every man and woman here saved by Grace, who has felt the Holy Spirit within him, has felt an impulse to seek the conversion of sinners at once! He has felt a longing that they should no longer abide in sin, that they should now be awakened, should immediately lay hold of eternal life and find instantaneous peace in Christ.

I appeal to my Brothers and Sisters if it is not so. Have you not felt, "it is high time to awake out of sleep"? Have you not felt the force of the admonition, "Whatever your hand finds to do, do it with all your might"? At other times we have been satisfied to feel that there was a good work going on secretly, that the soil was being prepared for future harvests, that somehow or other God's Word would not return unto Him void. But now we are not so readily contented! We feel as if we must, during each service, see the Lord at work and we plead for immediate conversions! We are as eager for souls as misers are for money! I say not that all of you feel this, but I say that all who have been fully influenced by the Holy Spirit during this period of gracious visitation have been filled with agony for the immediate salvation of souls.

Like unto a woman in travail they have longed eagerly to hear the cry of new-born souls. Their prayer has been, "Today, good Lord, answer our entreaties and lead our fellow men to hear Your voice that they may be saved." I appeal to the people of God whether the Holy Spirit, when He stirs them up to soul-winning, does not say, "Today–today seek the salvation of men." The same is also true when the Holy Spirit speaks in the awakened. They are not yet numbered with the people of God, but they are under concern of soul–and I shall make my appeal to them, also.

You are now conscious that you have offended your God–you are alarmed to find yourselves in a condition of alienation from Him–you want to be reconciled and you pine for the assurance that you are really forgiven. Do you wish to wait for that assurance till six or seven years have passed away? Do you feel, this morning, that you could be perfectly satisfied to go out of this house in the state you are now in–and continue in it month by month? If such delay would satisfy you, the Spirit of God has not spoken with you in an effectual manner. You have been but partially influenced, like unhappy Felix, and having said, "When I have a more convenient season I will send for you," we shall hear no more of you.

If the Spirit of God is upon you, you are crying "Help, Lord, help me now! Save me now or I perish! Make haste to deliver me, make no tarrying, O my God. Hasten on wings of love to pluck me from the pit of destruction which yawns beneath my feet."–

"Come, Lord, Your fainting servant cheer,
Nor let Your chariot wheels delay.
Appear, in my poor heart appear,
My God, my Savior, come away!"

A truly awakened sinner pleads in the present tense and cries mightily for a present salvation! And it is certain that when

Once more, the Holy Spirit speaks, thus, by His deeds as well as by His words. We have a common proverb that actions speak more loudly than words. Now the acts of the Holy Spirit, in the leading of many in this place to the Savior, are so many practical invitations, encouragements and commands to others. The gate of Mercy stands open everyday of the year–and its very openness is an invitation and a command to enter—but when I see my fellow men go streaming through, when I see hundreds finding Christ as we have seen them, do not all these, as they enter the portal of Grace, call to others to come? Do they not say, "This way may be trod by such as you are, for we are treading it! This way assuredly leads to peace for we have found rest in it!"

It is surely so! This way of speaking from the Holy Spirit has come very closely home to some of you, for you have seen your children enter the kingdom, and yet you are not saved yourselves! Some of you have seen your sisters saved, but you still remain unconverted! There is a husband, yonder, whose wife has told him with sparkling eyes of the rest she has found in the Savior, but he himself refuses to seek the Lord! There are parents here who have found Jesus, but their children are a heavy burden to them, for their hearts are unrenewed! Did I see my brother pass the gate of salvation? May I not take that as an intimation from God's Spirit that He is waiting to be gracious to me, also? When I see others saved by faith, may I not be sure that faith will also save me?

Since I perceive that there is Grace in Christ for the sins of others exactly like myself, may I not hope that there is mercy, also, for me? I will venture to hope and dare to believe! Should not that be the resolve of each? And is not that the point to which the Holy Spirit would lead us? Is not the bringing of one sinner to Himself intended to allure others? "The Holy Spirit says, Today." But why so urgent, blessed Spirit, why so urgent? It is because the Holy Spirit is in sympathy with God—in sympathy with the Father who longs to press the prodigal to His bosom—in sympathy with the Son who is watching to see of the travail of His soul!

The Holy Spirit is urgent because He is grieved with sin and would not see it continued for an hour! And every moment that a sinner refuses to come to Christ is a moment spent in sin. Yes, that refusal to come is, in itself, the most wanton and cruel of offenses! The hardness of man's heart against the Gospel is the most grievous of all provocations! Therefore does the Holy Spirit long to see man rid of it, that he may yield himself to the Omnipotent power of love. The Holy Spirit desires to see men attentive to the voice of God because He delights in that which is right and good. It is to Him a personal pleasure. He is glad to behold His own work in the sinner carried on till salvation is secure. Besides, He waits to execute His favorite office of Comforter, and He cannot comfort an ungodly soul! He cannot comfort those who harden their hearts.

Comfort for unbelievers would be their destruction. As He delights to be the Comforter and has been sent forth from the Father to act specially in that capacity, that He may comfort the people of God, He watches with longing eyes for broken hearts and contrite spirits, that He may apply the balm of Gilead and heal their wounds. Therefore "the Holy Spirit says, Today." I leave this fact with you. The special voice of the text is not of man, but of the Holy Spirit Himself. He that has ears to hear let him hear–

"Then while 'tis called today,
Oh, hear the Gospel sound!
Come, Sinner, hurry, oh, hurry today,
While pardon may be found."

II. The text inculcates A SPECIAL DUTY. The duty is that we should hear the voice of God. If you so read it, the text bids us hear the voice of the Father saying, "Return unto Me, you backsliding children. Come now, and let us reason together: though your sins are as scarlet they shall be as wool." Or it may be the voice of Jesus Christ, for it is of Him that the Apostle is here speaking. It is Jesus who calls, "Come unto Me, all you that labor and are heavy laden, and I will give you rest." In fact, the voice to be heard is that of the Sacred Trinity, for with the Father, the Son and the Spirit also say, "Come." We are bid to hear and that, surely, is no hard duty. The grand evangelical precept is, "Incline your ear and come unto Me, hear and your soul shall live," for, "faith comes by hearing and hearing by the Word of God." Hear, then, the Lord's voice!

"Well," says one, "we do hear it. We read the Bible and whatever is preached on Sunday we are willing enough to hear." Ah, my dear Hearers, but there is hearing and hearing. Many have ears to hear, but they do not hear in reality. The kind of hearing which is demanded of us is the hearing with reverence. The Gospel is God's Word, not man's–the voice mon attention should be bestowed upon it. Listen to it devoutly, summoning all your powers to adoring attention. Angels veil their faces in Jehovah's Presence–and shall man trifle before Him? When God speaks do not regard it as the voice of merely a king, to whose message it might be treason to turn a deaf ear, but as the voice of your God, towards whom it is blasphemy to be inattentive!

Hear Him earnestly, with anxiety, to know the meaning of what He says, drinking in His doctrine, receiving with meekness the engrafted Word which is able to save your soul, bowing your understanding to it, longing to comprehend it, desirous to be influenced by it. "Hear His voice"–that is, hear it obediently, eager to do what He bids you, as He enables you. Do not hear and forget, as one that looks in a glass and sees his face, and afterwards forgets what manner of man he is? Retain the Word in your memories and, better still, practice it in your lives? To hear in this case is, in fact, to yield yourselves to the will of God, to let yourselves be as the elastic clay and His Word as the hand which molds you, or your tears as the molten metal and the Word as the mold into which you are delivered.

Hear the Lord when He instructs you. Be willing to know the Truth of God. How often are men's ears stopped up with the wax of prejudice, so that they are dull of hearing? They have made up their minds as to what the Gospel ought to be and will not hear what it is. They think themselves the judges of God's Word, instead of God's Word being their judge. Some men do not want to know too much–they might be uncomfortable in their sins if they did. And, therefore, they are not anxious to be instructed. When men are afraid of the Truth of God there is abundant reason to fear that the Truth of God is against them. It is one of the worst signs of a fallen condition when a son of Adam hides away from the voice of His Creator.

But, O dear Hearers, today hear His voice! Learn of Jesus! Sit as scholars at His feet, for, "Except you are converted and become as little children, you cannot enter into the kingdom of God." Hear Him as scholars hear their teacher, for all the children of Zion are taught of the Lord. But the Lord does more than instruct you–He commands. Let men say what they will, the Gospel to be preached to the ungodly is not merely warnings and teachings, it has its solemn, positive commands. Listen to this–"The times of this ignorance God winked at, but now commands all men everywhere to repent." As to faith, the Lord's Word does not come as a mere recommendation of its virtues, or as a promise to those who exercise it, but it speaks on this wise–"Believe on the Lord Jesus Christ and you shall be saved. He that believes and is baptized shall be saved; he that believes not shall be damned." The Lord puts the solemn sanction of a threat of condemnation upon the command to show that it is not to be trifled with!

"All power," says Christ, "is given unto Me in Heaven and in earth," and therefore clothed with that authority and that power, He sends out His disciples, saying to them, "Go you, therefore, and teach all nations, baptizing them in the name of the Father, and of the Son, and of the Holy Spirit." The Word goes forth with Divine authority, saying, "Repent you and believe the Gospel." This is as much God's command as that which says, "You shall love the Lord your God with all your heart," and there is this much the more of solemn obligation, that whereas the Law was given by Moses, the Gospel command was given by the Son of God Himself!

"He that despised Moses' Law died without mercy: of how much sorer punishment, suppose you, shall he be thought worthy, who has trod under foot the Son of God! Hear, then the commands of Jesus, for be sure of this–His Gospel comes to you with the imperial authority of the Lord of All! But the Lord does more than command, He graciously invites. With tenderness He bids sinners come to His banquet of mercy, for all things are ready. As though He pleaded with men and would gladly persuade where He might command, He cries, "Ho, everyone that thirsts, come you to the waters; and you that have no money, come buy wine and milk without money and without price."

Many of the Lord's invitations are remarkable for their extreme sympathy, as though it were rather He that would suffer than the sinner, if the sinner remained obstinate! He cries, "Turn you, turn you, why will you die, O house of Israel?" Like a father pleading with a beloved but disobedient son who is ruining himself, God, Himself, pleads as if the tears stood in His eyes–yes, the Incarnate God in very deed wept over sinners, and cried–"O Jerusalem, Jerusalem, how often would I have gathered your children together as a hen gathers her chickens under her wings, and you would not." Will you not listen, then, when God instructs? Shall He give light and your eyes be closed? Will you not obey when God commands? Do you intend to be rebels against Him? Will you turn your backs when God invites? Shall His love be slighted and His bounty treated with scorn? God grant it may not be so! The good Spirit asks no more than is just and right when He cries, "Hear you the voice of the Lord." But the Lord does more than invite, He adds His promises. He says, "Hear and your soul shall live; and I will make an Everlasting Covenant with you, even the sure mercies of David." He has told us that, "if we confess our sins, He is faithful and just to forgive us our sins, and to cleanse us from all unrighteousness." Glorious promises are there in His Word–exceedingly great and precious! Oh, do not, I beseech you, count yourselves unworthy of them, for if so, your blood will be on your own heads! The Lord also threatens as well as entreats. He warns you, "If you turn not, He will whet His sword: He has bent His bow and made it ready." He declares that the despisers shall wonder and perish. He asks, "How shall we escape if we neglect so great a salvation?"

He says, "The wicked shall be cast into Hell with all the nations that forget God." Though He has no pleasure in the death of him that dies, but had rather that he should turn unto Him and live, yet He will by no means clear the guilty, but every transgression and iniquity shall have its just recompense of reward. If Christ is rejected, eternal wrath is certain! By that door you enter Heaven, but if you pass it by, even He who at this hour stands with pierced hands to woo you, will, at the Last Great Day come with iron rod to break you. "Today, if you will hear His voice, harden not your hearts." I leave these thoughts with you. May God grant they may make impressions where His will designs they should.

III. There is, in our text, A SPECIAL TIME EMPHASIZE. "The Holy Spirit says, Today." Today is the set time for hearing God's voice. Today, that is, while God speaks. Oh, if we were as we should be, the moment God said, "Seek you My face," we should reply, "Your face, Lord, will I seek." As soon as the invitations of mercy were heard there would be an echo in our souls to them and we should say, "Behold, we come unto You that we may be saved."

Observe how in creation God's voice was heard in an instant. The Lord said, "Let there be light, and there was light." He said, "Let the waters bring forth abundantly the moving creature," and straightway it was so. There were no delays. God's fiat was immediately executed. Oh, you whom God has made men and endowed with reason, shall the insensible earth be more obedient than you? Shall the waves of the sea swarm with fish and the earth teem with grass as soon as Jehovah speaks—and will you sleep on when the heavenly voice cries, "Awake, you that sleep, and arise from the dead, and Christ shall give you life"? Hear God today, for today He speaks.

The Apostle says in the next chapter, "Today—after so long a time," and I will dwell upon that phrase—"after so long a time." I see that some of you have bald heads, or gray hairs lie thick upon them. If you are unconverted, well may the Holy Spirit say, "Today, after so long a time, hear His voice." Is it not long enough to have provoked your God these 60 years? Man, are not 70 years of sin enough? Perhaps you have almost fulfilled your fourscore years and still you hold out against the overtures of Divine mercy! Is not a graceless old age a standing provocation of the Lord? How long do you intend to provoke Him? How long will it be before you believe Him? You have had time enough to have found out that sin is folly and that their pleasures are vanity. Surely you have had time enough to see that if there is peace it is not to be found in the ways of sin! How long do you intend to linger on forbidden and dangerous ground? You may not have another day, O aged man, in which to consider your ways! O aged woman—you may not have another year granted you in which to provoke your God. "After so long a time," with sacred pressure would I urge you—"Today, if you will hear His voice."

I hope it is not only I pleading with you but, I trust, the Holy Spirit, also, says in your conscience, "Today attend the voice of God." "Today," that is, especially while the Holy Spirit is leading others to hear and to find mercy. Today, while the showers are falling. Today, receive the drops of Grace! Today, while there are prayers offered up for you. Today, while the hearts of the godly are earnest about you. Today, while the footstool of Heaven's Throne is wet with the tears of those who love you. Today, lest lethargy should seize the Church again. Today, lest the preaching of the Word of God should come to be a matter of routine and the preacher, himself, discouraged, should lose all zeal for your soul! Today, while everything is peculiarly propitious, hear the voice of God! While the wind blows, hoist the sail! While God is abroad on errands of love, go forth to meet Him!

Today, while yet you are not utterly hardened—while there is still a conscience left within you—today, while yet you are conscious of your danger in some degree, while yet there is a lingering look towards your Father's house—hear and live! Today, lest, slighting your present tenderness, it should never come again—and you should be abandoned to the shocking indifference which is the prelude of eternal death! Today, young people, while yet you are undefiled with the grosser vices. Today, you young men who are new to this polluting city, before you have steeped yourselves in its streams of lust. Today, while everything is helpful to you, hear the loving, tender, wooing voice of Jesus and harden not your hearts!

To me the text seems wonderfully Gospel-like when it says "Today," for what is it but another way of putting the doctrine of that blessed hymn—

"Just as I am, without one plea."

"Today"–that is, in the circumstances, sins and miseries in which you now are–hear the Gospel, and obey it! Today, since it finds you in yonder pew, hear God's voice of mercy in that pew! Today, you who have never been concerned before, while God speaks, let it concern you! "Ah," you say, "if I were living in another house." You are culled today, even if you are living with the worst of sinners! "I will hearken when I have enjoyed that sinful pleasure which I promised to myself next Wednesday" you say. Ah, if it is a sinful one, flee from it, or it may make a turning point in your history and seal your soul's ruin. "Today, if you will hear His voice."

"Ah, if I had attended a few more revival meetings, and felt in a better state, I would obey." It is not so written, Sinner! It is not so! I am not told to preach the Gospel to those of you who are ready to receive it and say, "He that believes and is baptized shall be saved, if he is already, in a measure, prepared to believe." No, but to every creature here I have the same message to deliver! In the name of Jesus of Nazareth, who is also God Almighty at the right hand of the Father, believe in Him and you shall live, for His message to you is for TODAY–it admits of no delay. "But I must reform, I must amend and then will I think about believing." That is to put the effect before the cause! If you will hear His voice, the reforming and the amending shall come to you. But you must not begin with them as the first matter.

The voice of God does not say that, but it says, "Believe in the Lord Jesus Christ." Oh, hear that voice! I must occupy a moment in showing you why the Lord in mercy says, "Today." Do you not know that other people die? Why may you not die, yourself? During these present services several have been taken from among us. I was surprised when I came home to find how many have died of late concerning whom I should have predicted a much longer life. Why may you not die speedily? "I am robust and healthy," says one. If you ever hear of a sudden death, does it not generally happen to the robust? It seems as if the storm swept over the sickly and they bowed before it like reeds–and so escaped its fury–while the vigorous in health, like powerful forest trees, resist the storm and are torn up by It. How often does sudden death come just where we least expected it! "Today, if you will hear His voice."

I will put a question to you which that holy man, Mr. Payson, puts to the awakened. He says, How would you like to arrange that you would find Christ at the end of the year and that your existence should depend upon the life of another person? Select the strongest man you know, and suppose that everything in reference to your eternal welfare is to depend upon whether he lives to see the next year. With what anxiety would you hear of his illness! How concerned you would be about his health! Well, Sinner, your salvation is risked by you upon your own life–is that any more secure? If you are procrastinating and putting off repentance, why should you be any more secure about your own life than you would be if all depended upon the life of another? Be not such fools as to trifle yourselves into your graves and trifle your souls into Hell.

"You would not stake your fortune on the cast of the dice, as the mad gambler does, and yet you are staking your soul's eternity upon what is quite as uncertain, for you do not know, when you fall asleep tonight, whether you shall awake tomorrow in your bed or in Hell! You do not know that the next breath you are expecting will ever come–and if it does not come you will be driven forever from God's presence." Oh, Sirs, if you want to play at hazards, hazard your gold, or hazard your reputations, but do not jeopardize your souls! The stakes are too heavy for any but those who are made mad by sin. Risk not your souls, I beg you, upon the hazard of your living another day, but listen to the voice of God today!

IV. I have little time for my last point, but I still must have space for it even if I detain you beyond the accustomed time of departure. The last point is this– The SPECIAL DANGER which is indicated in the text. "Today, if you will hear His voice, harden not your hearts." That is the special danger. And how is it incurred? When persons are under concern of soul their heart is, in a measure, softened–but they can readily harden it–first, by willingly relapsing into their former indifference– by shaking off all fear and saying in willful rebellion, "No, I will have none of it."

I once preached in a certain city and I was the guest of a gentleman who treated me with great kindness. But I noticed on the third occasion of my preaching that he suddenly left the room. One of my friends followed him out of the place and said to him, "Why have you left the service?" "Well," he said, "I believe I should have been converted altogether if I had stayed any longer, for I felt such an influence coming over me. But it would not pay–you know what I am–it would not pay." Many persons are of that kind. They are shaped, for a while, according to the earnest word they hear, but it is all in vain–the dog returns to his vomit and the sow that was washed to her wallowing in the mire. This is to harden your heart and provoke the Lord.

A common way of provoking God and hardening the heart is that indicated by the context. "Harden not your heart, as in the provocation, in the day of temptation in the wilderness"–that is to say, by unbelief–by saying, "God cannot save me, He is not able to forgive me. The blood of Christ cannot cleanse me. I am too black a sinner for God's mercy to deal with." That is a copy of what the Israelites said–"God cannot take us into Canaan; He cannot conquer the sons of Anak." Though you may look upon unbelief as a slight sin, it is the sin of sins! May the Holy Spirit convict you of it, for "when the Spirit of Truth is come He shall convince the world of sin," and especially of sin, "because they believe not on Jesus." "He that believes not is condemned already," says Christ, "because he has not believed on the Son of God," as if all other sins were inconsiderable in power to condemn in comparison with this sin of unbelief!

Oh, do not, therefore, doubt my Lord! Come, you blackest, filthiest sinner out of Hell! Jesus can cleanse you! Come, you granite-hearted sinner, you whose affections are frozen like an iceberg so that not one melting tear of penitence distils from your eyes! Jesus' love can soften your heart! Believe Him, believe Him, or else you harden your heart against Him! Some harden their hearts by asking for more signs. This, also, is after the manner of the Israelites. "God has given us manna. Can He give us water? He has given us water out of the Rock, can He give us meat, also? Can He furnish a table in the wilderness?" After all that God had done, they wanted Him to work miracles or they would not believe!

Let none of us harden our hearts in that way. God has already worked for men a miracle which transcends all others and is, indeed, the compendium of all wonders! He has given His own Son out of His bosom to be a Man and to die for sinners! The sinner who is not content with that display of the mercy of God will never be satisfied with any proof of it! Christ on the tree is the sum of all miracles under the Gospel dispensation. If you will not believe God, who "so loved the world, that He gave His only begotten Son, that whoever believes in Him should not perish, but have everlasting life," then you will never believe!

"Oh, but I want to feel! I want the influence that is abroad to come upon me in a strange manner! I want to dream at night, or to see visions by day." Do you? You are hardening your heart! You are rejecting what God gives and demanding Him to play the lackey to you—and to give you what your petulant pride demands. If you had these things you would still not believe! He who has Moses and the Prophets and rejects them, would not believe, even though one came to him from the dead! Christ on the Cross is before you—do not reject Him! For if you do, nothing else can convince you and there must you remain—hardening your heart in unbelief.

Those also harden their hearts who presume upon the mercy of God and say, "Well, we can turn when we please." Ah, how different will you find it. "We have only to believe and be saved." Yes, but you will find, "only believing," to be a very different thing from what you imagine! Salvation is no child's play, believe me. I have heard of one who woke up one morning and found himself famous—but you will not find salvation in that way. "He that seeks finds, and to him that knocks it shall be opened." You harden your hearts if you plunge into worldly pleasures—if you allow loose companions to talk with you—if on this holy day you indulge in idle talk, or listen to unhallowed mirth. Many a tender conscience is hardened by the company which surrounds it. A young woman hears a powerful sermon and God is blessing it to her, but she goes off tomorrow to spend the evening in a scene of gaiety—how can she expect that the Word of God will be blessed to her? It is a deliberate quenching of the Spirit and I wonder not that God should swear in His wrath that those who do so shall not enter into His rest. Oh, don't do these things, lest you harden your hearts against God!

Now, I must conclude, but I must put the matter fully before you. I want every sinner here to know his position this morning. God commands all men everywhere to repent! Christ commands men to believe in Him today. One of two things you have to do, you have no other choice—either you must say that you do not intend to obey God's command, or else you must yield to it. Like Pharaoh, you must say, "Who is the Lord that I should obey His voice?" Or else, like the prodigal son, you must resolve, "I will arise and go unto my Father." There is no other choice! Do not attempt to make excuses. God makes short work with sinners' excuses. Those who were invited to the great supper said, "We are going to our farm and our merchandise. We are about to try our yokes of oxen, or we have married a wife," but all the Lord said about it was, "None of the men which were bidden shall taste of My supper." That was the end of it.

There was a man, once, who had a talent, and he buried it in a napkin and said, "I knew that You were an austere man," and so on. What notice did his Master take of that speech? He merely said, "Out of your own mouth will I condemn you. You knew that I was an austere man, and therefore, for that very reason you ought to have been the more diligent in My service." The Lord sees through your excuses, therefore do not insult Him with them! I have you here, this morning, before me, and you shall say one thing or the other before the living God—and before Christ—who shall judge the quick and the dead. He bids you turn from your sin and seek His face now, and believe in His dear Son. Will you do it or not? Yes or no? And mark you, that, "Yes," or, "No," may be final.

This morning the last appeal may have been made to you! God commands and I charge you, if your heart intends rebellion, say, if you dare, "I will not obey." Then you will know where you are and you will understand your own position. If God is not God, fight it out with Him. If you do not believe in Him, if He really is not the Lord who made you and who can destroy you, or if you mean to be His enemy—take up your position and be as honest, even, if you are as proud as Pharaoh, and say—"I will not obey Him." But, oh, I pray you, do not thus rebel! God is gracious! Will you be rebellious? God is love! Will you, therefore, be hard-hearted? Jesus, by His wounds, invites you to come to Himself! And the Holy Spirit, Himself, is here and is saying in the text, "Today harden not your hearts."

Yield yourselves now to His love—

"Who round you now
The bands of a man would cast,
The cords of His love who was given to you
To His altar binding you fast."

At His altar may you be found safe in the day of His appearing! God bless you. I beg those of you who know how to pray to implore a blessing on this word, for Jesus' sake. Amen.

GRIEVING THE HOLY SPIRIT

"And grieve not the Holy Spirit of God, whereby you are sealed unto the day of redemption."
Ephesians 4:30

A Sermon Delivered On Sunday Morning: 9 October 1859

THERE is something very touching in this admonition, "Grieve not the Holy Spirit of God." It does not say, "Do not make Him angry." A more delicate and tender term is used–"Grieve Him not." There are some men of so hard a character that to make another angry does not give them much pain. And indeed, there are many of us who are scarcely to be moved by the information that another is angry with us. But where is the heart so hard that it is not moved when we know that we have caused others grief?–for grief is a sweet combination of anger and of love. It is anger, but all the gall is taken from it. Love sweetens the anger and turns the edge of it, not against the person, but against the offense. We all know how we use the two terms in contra-distinction, the one to the other.

When I commit any offense, some friend who has but little patience suddenly snaps asunder his forbearance and is angry with me. The same offense is observed by a loving father and he is grieved. There is anger in his bosom, but he is angry and sins not, for he is angry against my sin. And yet there is love to neutralize and modify the anger towards me. Instead of wishing me ill as the punishment of my sin, he looks upon my sin itself as being the ill. He grieves to think that I am already injured, from the fact that I have sinned. I say this is a heavenly compound, more precious than all the ointment of the merchants. There may be the bitterness of myrrh, but there is all the sweetness of frankincense in this sweet term "to grieve."

I am certain, my Hearers, I do not flatter you when I declare that I am sure that the most of you would grieve if you thought you were grieving anyone else. You, perhaps, would not care much if you had made anyone angry without a cause. But to grieve him, even though it were without a cause and without intention, would nevertheless cause you distress of heart and you would not rest until this grief had subsided–till you had made some explanation or apology and had done your best to allay the smart and take away the grief. When we see anger in another, we at once begin to feel hostility. Anger begets anger. But grief begets pity and pity is next akin to love. Now, is not this a very sweet expression–"Grieve not the Holy Spirit:? Of course the language is be to understood as speaking after the manner of men. The Holy Spirit of God knows no passion or suffering, but nevertheless His emotion is here described in human language as being that of grief. And is it not, I say, a tender and touching thing, that the Holy Spirit should direct His servant Paul to say to us, "Grieve not the Holy Spirit." Do not excite His loving anger, do not vex Him, do not cause Him to mourn. He is a dove–do not cause Him to mourn, because you have treated Him harshly and ungratefully.

Now, the purport of my sermon this morning will be to exhort you not to grieve the Spirit. But I shall divide it thus–first I shall discourse upon the love of the Spirit. Secondly, upon the seal of the Spirit. Then, thirdly, upon the grieving of the Spirit.

The few words I have to say UPON THE LOVE OF THE SPIRIT will all be pressing forward to my great mark–stirring you up not to grieve the Spirit. When we are persuaded that another loves us, we find at once a very potent reason why we should not grieve him. The love of the Spirit! How shall I explain it? Surely it needs a songster to sing it, for love is only to be spoken of in words of song. The love of the Spirit! Let me tell you of His early love to us. He loved us without beginning. In the Everlasting Covenant of Grace, as I told you last Sabbath, He was one of the high contracting parties in the Divine contract, whereby we are saved.
All that can be said of the love of the Father and of the love of the Son, may be said of the love of the Spirit–it is eternal, it is infinite, it is sovereign, it is everlasting–it is a love which cannot be dissolved, which cannot be decreased, a love which cannot be removed from those who are the objects of it. Permit me, however, to refer you to His acts, rather than His attributes. Let me tell you of the love of the Spirit to you and to me. Oh how early was that love which He manifested towards us, even in our childhood!

My Brethren, we can well remember how the Spirit was desirous to strive with us. We went astray from the womb speaking lies, but how early did the Spirit of God stir up our conscience and solemnly correct us on account of our youthful sins? How frequently since then has the Spirit wooed us! How often under the ministry has He compelled our hearts to melt and the tear has run down our cheeks and He has sweetly whispered in our ear, "My son, give Me your heart. Go to your chamber, shut your door about you, confess your sins and seek a Savior's love and blood." Oh—but let us blush to tell it—how often have we done despite to Him! When we were in a state of unregeneracy, how we were desirous to resist Him!

We quenched the Spirit. He strove with us but we strove against Him. But blessed be His dear name and let Him have everlasting songs for it, He would not let us go! We would not be saved, but He would save us. We sought to thrust ourselves into the fire, but He sought to pluck us from the burning. We would dash ourselves from the precipice, but He wrestled with us and held us fast. He would not let us destroy our souls. Oh, how we ill-treated Him, how we did set at nothing His counsel! How did we scorn and scoff Him. How did we despise the ordinance which would lead us to Christ! How did we violate that holy cord which was gently drawing us to Jesus and His Cross! I am sure, my Brothers and Sisters, at the recollections of the persevering struggles of the Spirit with you, you must be stirred up to love Him.

How often did He restrain you from sin when you were about to plunge headlong into a course of vice! How often did He constrain you to good, when you would have neglected it! You, perhaps, would not have been in the way at all—and the Lord would not have met you—if it had not been for that sweet Spirit, who would not let you become a blasphemer, who would not suffer you to forsake the House of God and would not permit you to become a regular attendant at the haunts of vice, but checked you and held you in, as it were, with bit and bridle. Though you were like a bullock, unaccustomed to the yoke, yet He would not let you have your way. Though you struggled against Him, yet He would not throw the reins upon your necks, but He said, "I will have him, I will have him against his will. I will change his heart, I will not let him go till I have made him a trophy of My mighty power to save." And then think, my Brethren, of the love of the Spirit after that—

"Do mind the time, the spot of land,
Where Jesus did you meet?
Where He first took you by the hand,
Your bridegroom's love—how sweet!"

Ah, then, in that blest hour, to memory dear, was it not the Holy Spirit who guided you to Jesus? Do you remember the love of the Spirit, when, after having quickened you, He took you aside and showed you Jesus on the tree?

Who was it that opened our blind eyes to see a dying Savior? Who was it that opened our deaf ears to hear the voice of pardoning love? Who opened our clasped and palsied hands to receive the tokens of a Savior's grace? Who was it that broke our hard hearts and made a way for the Savior to enter and dwell therein? Oh, it was that precious Spirit–that same Spirit–to whom you have done so much despite, whom in the days of your flesh you have resisted! What a mercy it was that He did not say, "I will swear in My wrath that they shall not enter into My rest, for they have vexed Me and I will take My everlasting flight from them." Or thus, "Ephraim is joined unto idols, I will let him alone!"

And since that time, my Brethren, how sweetly has the Spirit proved His love to you and to me. It is not only in His first striving and then His Divine quickening, but in all the sequel, how much have we owed to His instruction. We have been dull scholars with the Word before us, plain and simple, so that he that runs may read and he that reads may understand–yet how small a portion of His Word has our memory retained–how little progress have we made in the school of God's grace! We are but learners yet–unstable, weak and apt to slide–but what a blessed Instructor we have had! Has He not led us into many a Truth of God and taken of the things of Christ and applied them unto us?

Oh, when I think how stupid I have been, I wonder that He has not given me up. When I think what a dolt I have been, when He would have taught me the things of the kingdom of God, I marvel that He should have had such patience with me. Is it a wonder that Jesus should become a babe? Is it not an equal wonder that the Spirit of the living God should become a teacher of babes? It is a marvel that Jesus should lie in a manger–is it not an equal marvel that the Holy Spirit should become an Usher in the sacred school, to teach fools and make them wise? It was condescension that with stubborn unruly, wild asses' colts, to teach them the mystery of the kingdom and make them know the wonders of a Savior's love?

Furthermore, my Brethren, forget not how much we owe to the Spirit's consolation, how much has He manifested His love to you in cherishing you in all your sicknesses, assisting you in all your labors and comforting you in all your distresses. I can testify He has been a blessed Comforter to me. When every other comfort failed, when the promise itself seemed empty, when the ministry was void of power, it is then the Holy Spirit has proved a rich comfort unto my soul and filled my poor heart with peace and joy in believing. How many times would your heart have broken if the Spirit had not bound it up! How often has He who is your teacher become also your physician, closed the wounds of your poor bleeding spirit and has bound up those wounds with the plaster of the promise? And thus He has stanched the bleeding and has given you back your spiritual health once more.

It does seem to rise a marvel that the Holy Spirit should become a Comforter, for comforting is, to many minds, but an inferior work in the Church, though really it is not so. To teach, to preach, to command with authority—how many are willing to do this because this is honorable work. But to sit down and bear with the infirmities of the creature, to enter into all the stratagems of unbelief, to find the soul a way of peace in the midst of seas of trouble—this is compassion like a God, that the Holy Spirit should stoop from Heaven to become a Comforter of disconsolate spirits. What? Must He Himself bring the cordial? Must He wait upon His sick child and stand by his bed? Must He make his bed for him in his afflictions, must He carry him in his infirmity? Must He breathe continually into him his very breath? Does the Holy Spirit become a waiting servant of the Church? Does He become a lamp to enlighten? Does He become a staff on which we may lean? This, I say, should move us to love the Holy Spirit, for we have in all this, abundant proofs of His love to us.

Stop not here, Beloved—there are larger fields yet beyond—now that we are speaking of the love of the Spirit. Remember how much He loves us when He helps our infirmities. No, not only does He help our infirmities, but when we know not what to pray for as we ought He teaches us how to pray and when "we ourselves groan within ourselves," then the Spirit Himself makes intersession for us with groans which cannot be uttered—groans as we should groan, but more audibly—so that our prayers, which otherwise would have been silent, reach the ears of Christ and is then presented before His Father's face. To help our infirmities is a mighty instance of love. When God overcomes infirmity altogether, or removes it, there is something very noble and grand and sublime in the deed. When He permits the infirmity to remain and yet works with the infirmity, this is tender compassion indeed.

When the Savior heals the lame man you see His Godhead, but when He walks with the lame man, limping though his gait may be—when He sits with the beggar, when He talks with the publican, when He carries the babe in His bosom—then this helping of infirmities is a manifestation of love almost unequalled. Except for Christ's bearing our infirmities upon the tree and our sins in His own body, I know of no greater or more tender instance of Divine love than when it is written, "Likewise the Spirit also helps our infirmities." Oh how much you owe to the Spirit when you have been on your knees in prayer! You know, my Brethren, what it is to be dull and lifeless there. To groan for a word and yet you cannot find it. To wish for a word and yet the very wish is languid. To long to have desires and yet all the desire you have is a desire that you may be able to desire.

Oh, have you not sometimes, when your desires have been kindled, longed to get a grip at the promise by the hand of faith? "Oh," you have said, "if I could but plead the promise, all my necessities would be removed and all my sorrows would be allayed." But, alas, the promise was beyond your reach. If you touched it with the tip of your finger you could not grasp it as you desired, you could not plead it and therefore you came away without the blessing. But when the Spirit has helped our infirmities how have we prayed! Why, there have been times when you and I have so grasped the knocker at the Gate of Mercy and have let it fall with such tremendous force, that it seemed as if the very gate itself did shake and totter.

There have been seasons when we have laid hold upon the angel, have overcome Heaven by prayer, have declared we would not let Jehovah Himself go except He should bless us. We have and we say it without blasphemy, moved the arm that moves the world. We have brought down upon us the eyes that look upon the universe. All this we have done, not by our own strength, but by the might and by the power of the Spirit. He has so sweetly enabled us, though we have so often forgotten to thank Him. He has so graciously assisted us though we have often taken all the glory to ourselves instead of airing it to Him—must we not admire His love and must it not be a fearful sin, indeed, to grieve the Holy Spirit by whom we are sealed?

Another token of the Spirit's love remains, namely, His indwelling in the saints. We sing in one of our hymns—

"Do You not dwell in all the saints?"
We ask a question which can have but one answer. He does dwell in the heart of all God's redeemed and blood-washed people. And what a condescension is this, that He whom the Heaven of heavens cannot contain, dwells in your breast, my Brothers and Sisters! That breast often covered with

rags, may be a breast often agitated with anxious care and thought, a breast too often defiled with sin and yet He dwells there. The little narrow heart of man–the Holy Spirit has made His palace. Though it is but a cottage, a very hovel and all unholy and unclean–yet does the Holy Spirit condescend to make the heart of His people His continual abode.

Oh my Friends, when I think how often you and I have let the devil in, I wonder the Spirit has not withdrawn from us! The final perseverance of the saints is one of the greatest miracles on record. In fact, it is the sum total of miracles. The perseverance of a saint for a single day is a multitude of miracles of mercy. When you consider that the Spirit is of purer eyes than to behold iniquity and yet He dwells in the heart where sin often intrudes–a heart out of which comes blasphemies and murders and all manner of evil thoughts and concupiscence–what if sometimes He is grieved and retires and leaves us to ourselves for a season? It is a marvel that He is there at all, for He must be daily grieved with these evil guests, these false traitors, these base intruders who thrust themselves into that little temple which He has honored with His presence–the temple of the heart of man.

I am afraid, dear Friends, we are too much in the habit of talking of the love of Jesus, without thinking of the love of the Holy Spirit. Now I would not wish to exalt one Person of the Trinity above another, but I do feel this–that because Jesus Christ was a Man, bone of our bone and flesh of our flesh and therefore there was something tangible in Him that can be seen with the eyes and handled with the hands, therefore we more readily think of Him and fix our love on Him, than we do upon the Spirit. But why should it be? Let us love Jesus with all our hearts and let us love the Holy Spirit, too. Let us have songs for Him, gratitude for Him. We do not forget Christ's Cross, let us not forget the Spirit's operations. We do not forget what Jesus has done for us, let us always remember what the Spirit does in us.

Why do you talk of the love and grace and tenderness and faithfulness of Christ? Why do you not say the same of the Spirit? Was ever love like His, that He should visit us? Was ever mercy like His, that He should bear with our ill manners, though constantly repeated by us? Was ever faithfulness like His, that multitudes of sins cannot drive Him away? Was ever power like His, that overcomes all our iniquities and yet leads us safely on, though hosts of foes within and without would rob us of our Christian life?–

"Oh, the love of the Spirit I sing
By whom is redemption applied."

And unto His name be glory forever and ever.

II. This brings me to the second point. Here we have another reason why we should not grieve the Spirit. IT IS BY THE HOLY SPIRIT WE ARE SEALED. "BY whom we are sealed unto the day of redemption." I shall be very brief here. The Spirit Himself is expressed as the Seal, even as He Himself is directly said to be the Pledge of our inheritance. The sealing, I think, has a three-fold meaning. It is a sealing of attestation or confirmation. I want to know whether I am truly a child of God. The Spirit itself also bears witness with my spirit that I am born of God. I have the writings, the title-deeds of the inheritance that is to come—I want to know whether those are valid, whether they are true, or whether they are mere counterfeits written out by those old scribes of Hell, Master Presumption and Carnal Security.

How am I to know? I look for the Seal. After we have believed on the Son of God, the Father seals us as His children, by the gift of the Holy Spirit. "Now He which has anointed us is God, who also has sealed us and given the earnest of the Spirit in our hearts." No faith is genuine which does not bear the seal of the Spirit. No love, no hope can ever save us, except it is sealed with the Spirit of God, for whatever has not His seal upon it is spurious. Faith that is unsealed may be poison, it may be presumption. But faith that is sealed by the Spirit is true, real, genuine faith. Never be content, my dear Hearers, unless you are sealed, unless you are sure, by the inward witness and testimony of the Holy Spirit, that you have been begotten again unto a lively hope by the resurrection of Jesus Christ from the dead.

It is possible for a man to know infallibly that he is secure of Heaven. He may not only hope so, but he may know it beyond a doubt and he may know it thus—by being able with the eye of faith to see the seal, the broad stamp of the Holy Spirit set upon his own character and experience. It is a seal of attestation.

In the next place, it is a sealing of appropriation. When men put their mark upon an article, it is to show that it is their own. The farmer brands his tools that they may not be stolen. They are his. The shepherd marks his sheep that they may be recognized as belonging to his flock. The king himself puts his broad arrow upon everything that is his property. So the Holy Spirit puts the broad arm of God upon the hearts of all His people. He seals us. "You shall be Mine," says the Lord, "in the day when I make up my jewels." And then the Spirit puts God's seal upon us to signify that we are God's reserved inheritance–His peculiar people, the portion in which His soul delights.

But, again, by sealing is meant preservation. Men seal up that which they wish to have preserved and when a document is sealed it becomes valid. Now, it is by the Spirit of God that the Christian is sealed, that he is kept, he is preserved, sealed unto the day of redemption–sealed until Christ comes fully to redeem the bodies of His saints by raising them from the death and fully to redeem the world by purging it from sin and making it a kingdom unto Himself in righteousness. We shall hold on our way, we shall be saved. The chosen seed cannot be lost–they must be brought home at last–but how? By the sealing of the Spirit. Apart from that, they perish, they are undone. When the last general fire shall blaze out, everything that has not the seal of the Spirit on it shall be burned up. But the men upon whose forehead is the seal shall be preserved. They shall be safe "amid the wreck of matter and the crash of worlds." Their spirits, mounting above the flames, shall dwell with Christ eternally. And with that same seal on their forehead upon Mount Zion, they shall sing the everlasting song of gratitude and praise. I say this is the second reason why we should love the Spirit and why we should not grieve Him.

III. I come now to the third part of my discourse, namely, THE GRIEVING OF THE SPIRIT. How may we grieve Him–what will be the sad result of grieving Him–if we have grieved Him, how may we bring Him back again? How may we grieve the Spirit–I am now, mark you, speaking of those who love the Lord Jesus Christ. The Spirit of God is in your hearts and it is very, very easy, indeed, to grieve Him. Sin is as easy as it is wicked. You may grieve Him by impure thoughts. He cannot bear sin. If you indulge in lascivious expressions, or if even you allow imagination to coat upon any lascivious act, or if your heart goes after covetousness–if you set your heart upon anything that is evil– the Spirit of God will be grieved, for thus I hear Him speaking of Himself, "I love this man, I want to have his heart and yet he is entertaining these filthy lusts. His thoughts, instead of running after Me and after Christ and after the Father, are running after the temptations that are in the world through lust."

And then His Spirit is grieved. He sorrows in His soul because He knows what sorrow these things must bring to our souls. We grieve Him yet more if we indulge in outward acts of sin. Then is He sometimes so grieved that He takes His flight for a season, for the Dove will not dwell in our hearts if we take loathsome carrion in there. A clean being is the Dove and we must not strew the place which the Dove frequents with filth and mire–if we do, He will fly elsewhere. If we commit, sin if we openly bring disgrace upon our religion, if we tempt others to go into iniquity by our evil example, it is not long before the Holy Spirit will begin to grieve. Again, if we neglect prayer, if our closet door is cob-webbed, if we forget to read the Scriptures, if the leaves of our Bible are almost stuck together by neglect, if we never seek to do any good in the world, if we live merely for ourselves and not for Christ, then the Holy Spirit will be grieved, for thus He says, "They have forsaken Me, they have left the fountain of waters, they have hewn unto themselves broken cisterns."

I think I now see the Spirit of God grieving, when you are sitting down to read a novel and there is your Bible unread. Perhaps you take down some book of travels and you forget that you have got a more precious book of travels in the Acts of the Apostles and in the story of your blessed Lord and Master. You have no time for prayer, but the Spirit sees you very active about worldly things and having many hours to spare for relaxation and amusement. And then He is grieved because He sees that you love worldly things better than you love Him. His spirit is grieved within Him–take care that He does not go away from you–for it will be a pitiful thing for you if He leaves you to yourself.

Again–ingratitude tends to grieve Him. Nothing cuts a man to the heart more than after having done his utmost for another, he turns round and repays him with ingratitude or insult. If we do not want to be thanked, at least we do love to know that there is thankfulness in the heart upon which we have conferred a blessing. When the Holy Spirit looks into our soul and sees little love to Christ, no gratitude to Him for all He has done for us, then is He grieved.

Again–the Holy Spirit is exceedingly grieved by our unbelief. When we distrust the promise He has given and applied, when we doubt the power or the affection of our blessed Lord–then the Spirit says within Himself–"They doubt My fidelity, they distrust My power, they say Jesus is not able to save unto the uttermost"–thus again is the Spirit grieved. Oh, I wish the Spirit had an advocate here this morning that could speak in better terms than I can. I have a theme that overmasters me, I seem to grieve for Him. But I cannot make you grieve, nor explain the grief I feel. In my own soul I keep saying, "Oh, this is just what you have done–you have grieved Him." Let me make a full and frank confession even before you all. I know that too often, I, as well as you, have grieved the Holy Spirit. Much within us has made that sacred Dove to mourn and my marvel is that He has not taken His flight from us and left us utterly to ourselves.

Now suppose the Holy Spirit is grieved—what is the effect produced upon us? When the Spirit is grieved, He first bears with us. He is grieved again and again and again and again and still He bears with it all. But at last His grief becomes so excessive, that He says, "I will suspend My operations. I will leave life behind Me, but My own actual Presence I will take away." And when the Spirit of God goes away from the soul and suspends all His operations, what a miserable state we are in. He suspends His instructions. We read the Word, we cannot understand it. We go to our commentaries, they cannot tell us the meaning. We fall on our knees and ask to be taught, but we get no answer, we learn nothing. He suspends His comfort. We used to dance, like David before the ark and now we sit like Job in the ash pit and scrape our ulcers with a potsherd.

There was a time when His candle shone round about us, but now He is gone. He has left us in the black of darkness. Now He takes from us all spiritual power. Once we could do all things. Now we can do nothing. We could slay the Philistines and lay them heaps upon heaps, but now Delilah can deceive us and our eyes are put out and we are made to grind in the mill. We go preaching and there is no pleasure in preaching and no good follows it. We go to our tract distributing and our Sunday-School—we might almost as well be at home. There is the machinery there, but there is no love. There is the intention to do good, or perhaps not even that, but alas, there is no power to accomplish the intention. The Lord has withdrawn Himself, His light, His joy, His comfort, His spiritual power, all are gone.

And then all our graces flag. Our graces are much like the flower called the Hydrangea, when it has plenty of water it blooms, but as soon as moisture fails, the leaves drop down at once. And so when the Spirit goes away, faith shuts up its flowers—no perfume is exhaled. Then the fruit of our love begins to rot and drops from the tree. Then the sweet buds of our hope become frostbitten and they die. Oh, what a sad thing it is to lose the Spirit. Have you ever, my Brethren, been on your knees and have been conscious that the Spirit of God was not with you and what awful work it has been to groan and cry and sigh and yet go away again and no light to shine upon the promises, not so much as a ray of light through the chink of the dungeon? All forsaken, forgotten and forlorn, you are almost driven to despair. You sing with Cowper–

"What peaceful hours I once enjoyed,
How sweet their memory still!
But they have left an aching void,
The world can never fill.
Return, you sacred Dove, return,
Sweet messenger of rest,
I hate the sins that made You mourn,
And drove You from my breast.
The dearest idol I have known,
Whatever that idol be,
Help me to tear it from its throne,
And worship only You."

Ah, sad enough it is to have the Spirit drawn from us! But, my Brethren, I am about to say something with the utmost charity, which, perhaps, may look severe, but, nevertheless, I must say it. The Churches of the present day are very much in the position of those who have grieved the Spirit of God. For the Spirit deals with Churches just as it does with individuals. Of these late years how little has God worked in the midst of His Churches. Throughout England, at least some four or five years ago, an almost universal torpor had fallen upon the visible body of Christ. There was a little action, but it was spasmodic. There was no real vitality. Oh, how few sinners were brought to Christ, how empty had our places of worship become. Our Prayer Meetings were dwindling away to nothing and our Church meetings were mere matters of farce.

You know right well that this is the case with many London Churches to this day. And there are some that do not mourn about it. They go up to their accustomed places and the minister prays and the people either sleep with their eyes or else with their hearts and they go out and there is never a soul saved. The pool of Baptism is seldom stirred. But the saddest part of all is this–the Churches are willing to have it so. They are not earnest to get a revival of religion. We have been doing something, the Church at large has been doing something. I will not just now put my finger upon what the sin is, but there has been something done which has driven the Spirit of God from us. He is grieved and He is gone.

He is present with us here, I thank His name—He is still visible in our midst. He has not left us. Though we have been as unworthy as others, yet has He given us a long outpouring of His presence. These five years or more we have had a revival which is not to be exceeded by any revival upon the face of the earth. Without cries or shouts, without fallings down or swooning, steadily God adds to this Church numbers upon numbers, so that your minister's heart is ready to break with very joy when he thinks how manifestly the Spirit of God is with us.

But Brethren, we must not be content with this, we want to see the Spirit poured out on all Churches. Look at the great gatherings that there were in St. Paul's and Westminster Abbey and Exeter Hall and other places—how was it that no good was done—or so very little? I have watched with anxious eyes and I have never from that day forth heard but of one conversion and that in St. James' Hall, from all these services. Strange it seems. The blessing may have come in larger measure than we know, but not in so large a measure as we might have expected, if the Spirit of God had been present with all the ministers.

Oh would that we may live to see greater things than we have ever seen yet. Go home to your houses, humble yourselves before God, you members of Christ's Church and cry aloud that He will visit His Church and that He would open the windows of Heaven and pour out His Grace upon His thirsty hill of Zion, that nations may be born in a day, that sinners may be saved by thousands—that Zion may travail and may bring forth children. Oh, there are signs and tokens of a coming revival. We have heard but lately of a good work among the Ragged School boys of St. Giles's and our soul has been glad on account of that. And the news from Ireland comes to us like good tidings, not from a far country, but from a sister province of the kingdom. Let us cry aloud to the Holy Spirit, who is certainly grieved with His Church, and let us purge our Churches of everything that is contrary to His Word and to sound doctrine and then the Spirit will return and His power shall be manifest.

And now, in conclusion, there may be some of you here who have lost the visible presence of Christ with you—who have in fact so grieved the Spirit that He has gone. It is a mercy for you to know that the Spirit of God never leaves His people finally. He leaves them for chastisement, but not for damnation. He sometimes leaves them that they may get good by knowing their own weakness, but He will not leave them finally to perish. Are you in a state of backsliding, declension and coldness? Hearken to me for a moment and God bless the words. Brothers and Sisters, stay not a moment in a condition so perilous. Be not easy for a single second in the absence of the Holy Spirit. I beseech you use every means by which that Spirit may be brought back to you. Once more, let me tell you distinctly what the means are.

Search out for the sin that has grieved the Spirit. Give it up, slay that sin upon the spot. Repent with tears and sighs. Continue in prayer and never rest satisfied until the Holy Spirit comes back to you. Frequent an earnest ministry, get much with earnest saints–but above all, be much in prayer to God and let your daily cry be, "Return, return, O Holy Spirit return and dwell in my soul." Oh, I beseech you be not content till that prayer is heard, for you have become weak as water and faint and empty while the Spirit has been away from you.

Oh, it may be there are some here this morning with whom the Spirit has been striving during the past week. Oh yield to Him, resist Him not. Grieve Him not, but yield to Him. Is He saying to you now, "Turn to Christ"? Listen to Him, obey Him, He moves you. Oh I beseech you do not despise Him. Have you resisted Him many times? Then take care you do not again, for there may come a last time when the Spirit may say, "I will go unto My rest, I will not return unto him, the ground is accursed, it shall be given up to barrenness."

Oh, hear the word of the Gospel, before you separate, for the Spirit speaks effectually to you now in this short sentence–"Repent and be converted, every one of you, that your sins may be blotted out when the times of refreshing shall come from the presence of the Lord." And hear this solemn sentence, "He that believes in the Lord Jesus and is baptized, shall be saved. But he that believes not shall be damned." May the Lord grant that we may not grieve the Holy Spirit. Amen.

GRIEVE NOT THE HOLY SPIRIT

"And grieve not the Holy Spirit of God, whereby you are sealed unto the day of redemption."
Ephesians 4:30

A Sermon Delivered On Sunday Morning: 3 March 1867

IT is a very clear proof of the Personality of the Holy Spirit that He can be grieved. Now, it would be very difficult to imagine an influence, or a mere spiritual emanation being grieved. We can only grieve a person, and, inasmuch as the Holy Spirit may be grieved, we see that He is a distinct subsistence in the sacred Trinity. Rob Him not of the glory which is due to Him but be ever mindful to do Him homage. Our text, moreover, reveals to us the close connection between the Holy Spirit and the Believer. He must take a very tender and affectionate interest in us since He is grieved by our shortcomings and our sins. He is not a God who reigns in solitary isolation, divided by a great gulf, but He, the blessed Spirit, comes into such near contact with us, takes such minute observations, feels such tender regards that He can be grieved by our faults and follies.

Although the word, "grieve," is a painful one, yet there is honey in the rock! For it is an inexpressibly delightful thought that He who rules Heaven and earth, and is the creator of all things, and the infinite and ever blessed God, condescends to enter into such infinite relationships with His people that His Divine mind may be affected by their actions! What a marvel that Deity should be said to grieve over the faults of beings so utterly insignificant as we are! We may not understand the expression literally, as though the sacred Spirit could be affected with sorrow like to human sorrow, but we must not forego the consolatory assurance that He takes the same deep interest in us as a fond parent takes in a beloved but wayward child! Is not this a marvel? Let those who cannot feel, be unmoved. As for me, I shall not cease to wonder and adore!

The first point which we will consider this morning, is THE ASTOUNDING FACT that the Holy Spirit may be grieved. That loving, tender Spirit who, of His own accord, has taken upon Himself to quicken us from our death in sin and to be the Educator of the new life which He has implanted within us–that

Divine Instructor, Illuminator, Comforter, Remembrancer whom Jesus has sent forth to be our abiding Guide and Teacher—may be grieved! He whose Divine energy is life to our souls, dew to our graces, light to our understandings and comfort to our hearts may be vexed by us! The heavenly Dove may be disturbed! The celestial Fire may be dampened! The Divine Wind may be resisted! The blessed Paraclete may be treated with despite!

The loving grief of the Holy Spirit may be traced to His holy Character and perfect attributes. It is the nature of a holy being to be vexed with unholiness. There can be no concord between God and Belial. A Spirit immaculately pure cannot but take umbrage at uncleanness, and especially must He be grieved by the presence of evil in the objects of His affections. Sin everywhere must be displeasing to the Spirit of holiness, but sin in His own people is grievous to Him in the highest degree. He will not hate His people, but He does hate their sins—and hates them all the more because they nestle in His children's bosoms.

The Spirit would not be the Spirit of Truth if He could approve of that which is false in us. He would not be pure if that which is impure in us did not grieve Him. We could not believe Him to be holy if He could look with complacency upon our unholiness. Nor should we think of Him as being perfect if our imperfection could be regarded by Him without displeasure. No, because He is what He is—the Holy Spirit and the Spirit of holiness—therefore everything in us which falls short of His own Nature must be grievous to Him. He helps our infirmities, but He grieves over our sins. He is grieved with us mainly for our own sakes, for He knows what misery sin will cost us. He reads our sorrows in our sins.

"Ah, silly sheep," He seems to say, "I know the dark mountain upon which you will stumble. I see the thorns which will cut you, and the wounds which will pierce you! I know, O wayward child, the rod which you are making for your will, that quick temper, that love of self, that ardent pursuit of gain." He grieves over us because He sees how much chastisement we incur, and how much communion we lose.

When we might have been upon the mountain of fellowship, we are sighing in the dungeon of despondency, and all because, from motives of fleshy ease, we preferred to go down By-Path Meadow, and forsake the right way because it was rough. The Spirit is grieved that we should thus bring ourselves into the darkness of a loathsome dungeon, and subject ourselves to the blows of the crab tree club of giant Despair. He foresees how bitterly we shall rue the day in which we parted company with Jesus and so pierced ourselves through with many sorrows. He foresees that the backslider in heart will be filled with his own ways, and grieves because He foresees the backslider's grief. A mother's grief for the wrongdoing of her prodigal son is not so much the pain which he has directly occasioned her, as the sorrow which she knows that he will bring upon himself.

David did not so much lament his own loss of his child, as Absalom's death, with all its dread results, to Absalom himself. "O my son Absalom, my son, my son Absalom!" Here is deep sorrow. But the next sentence shows that it was by no means selfish, for he is willing to take a greater grief upon himself– "Would God I had died for you, O Absalom, my son, my son!" Such is the holy grief of the Spirit of God for those in whom He dwells. It is for their sakes that He is troubled.

Moreover, it is doubtless for Jesus Christ's sake that the Spirit is grieved. We are the purchase of Jesus' death upon the tree–He has bought us dearly and He should have us altogether for Himself–and when He does not have us completely as His own, you can well conceive that the Spirit of God is grieved. We ought to glorify Christ in these mortal bodies! It should be the one end and object of our desire to crown that head with gems which once was crowned with thorns. It is lamentable that we should so frequently fail in this reasonable service. Jesus deserves our best–every wound of His claims us, and every pang He bore, and every groan that escaped His lips is a fresh reason for perfect holiness and complete devotion to His cause! And, because the Holy Spirit sees us so traitorous to the love of Christ, so false to that redeeming blood, so forgetful of our solemn obligations, He grieves over us because we dishonor our Lord.

Shall I be wrong if I say that He grieves over us for the Church's sake? How might some of you be useful if you did but live up to your privileges! Ah, my Brethren, how the Comforter must surely grieve over those of us who are ministers, when He sets us as watchmen and we do not watch and the Church is invaded! When He commissions us as sowers of the good seed, and our hands are only half filled, or we scatter cockle and darnel instead of sowing the good wheat! How must He grieve over us because we have not that tenderness of heart, that melting of love, that vehemence of zeal, that earnestness of soul which we ought to exhibit! When the Church of God suffers damage through us–the Spirit loves the Church and cannot endure to see her robbed and despoiled, her children left to wander, her wounded sons unsuccored, and her broken hearts unhealed–because we are indifferent to our work, and careless in our labor for the Church, the Holy Spirit is much displeased.

But it is not only with ministers, but with all of you, for there is a niche that each of you should fill. And if that is vacant the Church loses by you–the kingdom of Christ suffers damage, the revenue which ought to come into Zion is cut short–and the Holy Spirit is grieved. Your lack of prayer, your lack of love, your deficiency in generosity–all these may be sad injuries to the Church of God–and therefore is the loving Spirit of God much disquieted once more. The Spirit of God mourns over the shortcomings of Christians for sinners' sakes, for it is the Spirit's office to convict the world of sin, of righteousness, and of judgment. But the course of many Believers is directly counter to this work of the Spirit. Their lives do not convict the world of sin, but rather tend to comfort transgressors in their iniquity.

We have heard the actions of professors quoted by worldlings as an excuse for their sins. Openly profane persons have said, "Look at those Christians! They do so-and-so, why may not we?" It is ill when Jerusalem comforts Sodom, and when the crimes of the heathens find precedents in the sins of Israel! It is the Spirit's work to convict the world of righteousness, but many a professor convicts the world of the opposite. "No," says the world, "there is no more righteousness to be had in Christ than anywhere else, for, look at those who follow Him, or pretend to do so–where is their righteousness? It does not exceed that of the scribes and Pharisees."

The Spirit of Truth convicts the world of judgment to come–but how few of us help Him in that great work! We live and act and talk as if there were no judgment to come–toiling for wealth as if this world were all careless of souls, as though Hell were a dream! Unmoved by eternal realities, unstirred by the terrors of the Lord, indifferent to the ruin of mankind, many professors live like worldlings and are as unchristian as infidels. This is an indisputable fact, but one to be lamented with tears of blood! Brothers and Sisters, I dare not think how much of the ruin of the world must be laid at the door of the Church! But I will dare to say this, that although the Divine purposes will be fulfilled, and God will not miss the number of His chosen, yet the fact that this London of ours is now rather a heathen than a Christian city can be laid at no one's door but that of the professing Church of God and her ministers!

Where else can it be? Is the city wrapped in darkness? It need not have been so. If we had been faithful it would not have been so! If we are faithful in the future it shall not long remain so. I cannot imagine an Apostolic Church, set down in the midst of London, and filled with the ardor of the first disciples, remaining long without influencing sensibly upon the masses. I know the increase of our population is immense—I know that we are adding every year a fresh town to this overgrown city. But I will not—I dare not tolerate the idea that the zeal of God's Church, if at its right pitch, is too feeble to meet the case! No, there is wealth enough among us, if it were consecrated, to build as many Houses of Prayer as shall be needed.

There is ability enough among us, if it were but given to the ministry of the Word, to yield a sufficiency of preachers of the Cross. We have all the pecuniary and mental strength that is needed. The point in which we fail is this—we are straitened in spiritual power! Poverty-stricken in Divine Grace! Lukewarm in zeal, meager in devotedness, staggering in faith. We are not straitened in our God, we are straitened in our own hearts. Brethren, I believe the Spirit of God is very greatly grieved with many Churches for the sake of the sinners in their congregations who are scarcely cared for, seldom prayed for, never wept for. Would that the thought of this might move us and our Brethren to mend our ways.

II. Secondly, let us refer to DEPLORABLE CAUSES which produce the grief of the Holy Spirit. The context is some assistance to us. We learn that sins of the flesh, filthiness, and evil speaking of every sort, are grievous to Him. Note the preceding verse: "Let no corrupt communication proceed out of your mouth." Let a Christian fall into the habit of talking in a loose, unchaste style. Let him delight in things that are indecorous, even if he shall not plunge into the commission of outward uncleanness, and the Spirit of God will not be pleased with him.

The Holy Spirit descended upon our Lord as a Dove. And a dove delights in the pure rivers of water and shuns all kinds of filthiness. In Noah's day the dove found no place for the sole of its feet on all the carcasses floating in the waste. And even so, the heavenly Dove finds no repose in the dead and corrupt things of the flesh. If we live in the Spirit, we shall not obey the desires of the flesh. They who walk after the flesh know nothing of the Spirit. It appears, from the thirty-first verse, that the Holy Spirit is grieved by any approach to bitterness, wrath, anger, clamor, evil speaking and malice.

If in a Christian Church there shall be dissension's and divisions. If Brother shall speak evil of Brother, and Sister of Sister, love is absent—and the Spirit of love will not long be present. The dove is the emblem of peace. One of the early fruits of the Spirit is peace. My dear Friends, I hope as a Church if there is any secret ill feeling among us, any hidden root of bitterness—even though it may not yet have sprung up to trouble us—it may be removed and destroyed at once! I do not know of any such abominable thing, and am happy to be able to say so. I trust we walk together in holy unity and concord of heart. If any of you are conscious of bitterness in ever so small a measure, purge it out lest the Spirit of God be grieved with you and grieved with the Church of God for your sake.

I have no doubt it greatly grieves the Spirit to see in Believers any degree of love of the world. His holy jealousy is excited by such unholy love. If a mother should see her child fonder of someone else than of her—if she should know that it was more happy in the company of a stranger than when in the bosom of its own parent—she would feel it a very hard trial to bear. Now the Spirit of God gives to Believers celestial joys and abounding comforts. And if He sees us turn our back upon all these to go into worldly company, to feed greedily upon the same empty joys which satisfy worldlings, He is a jealous God and He takes it as a great slight put upon Himself.

What? Does the Good Shepherd load the table with Heaven's own dainties, and do we prefer to devour the husks which the swine eat? When I think of a Christian man trying to find his enjoyment where the lowest of worldlings find theirs, I can scarcely imagine him to be a Christian! Or, if he is, he must very greatly grieve the Spirit of God. Why, you set the world, which you profess to have found empty, vain, and deceitful—you set that before the choice things of the kingdom of Grace! And while you profess to be, "raised up to sit together with Christ in heavenly places," you still grovel in the dust as others do!

What does the world say? "Ah, ah," they say, "Here is one of those Christian people coming after a little happiness! Poor soul! His religion gives him no joy and, therefore, he is looking for a little elsewhere. Make room for him, poor fellow, he has a hard time of it on Sundays." Then the notion goes abroad that

Christians have no joy in Christ! That we have to deny ourselves all true happiness and only get a little delight by stealth, when we do as others do. What a libel is this! And yet how many professors are responsible for it! If we live in communion with Jesus we shall not hanker after the world. We shall despise its mirth and trample on its treasures. Worldliness, in any shape, must be very grievous to the Spirit of God—not only the love of pleasure, but the love of gain.

Worldliness in Christian men and women in imitating the world in dress—worldliness in luxury, or in conversation—must displease the Spirit of God because He calls us a peculiar people, and He tells us to, "come out from among them and be separated, and touch not the unclean thing." And then He promises, "I will be a Father unto you, and you shall be My sons and daughters." And if we will not be separate how can we expect Him to be otherwise than grieved? Israel was constrained to quit Egypt for the wilderness, and God said, "I remember you, the love of your espousals, when you went after Me in the wilderness."

He seems to dote upon Israel's early separation to Himself! And so I believe the Lord delights to see His people severing fond connections, giving up carnal pleasures, and going outside the camp bearing the reproach of Christ. It ravishes the heart of Jesus to see His Church forsake the world! Here are His own words to His bride, "Hearken, O daughter, and consider, and incline your ear; forget also your own people, and your father's house; so shall the king greatly desire your beauty." He loves to have His saints entirely to Himself! He is a jealous Savior, and hence Paul says he labored that he might, "present the Church as a chaste virgin unto Christ."

Jesus wants to have our chastity to Himself maintained beyond suspicion that we may choose Him as our sole possession, and leave the base things of the earth to those who love them. Beware, my Brothers and Sisters, of grieving the Holy Spirit by worldliness! Moreover, the Spirit of God is greatly grieved by unbelief. What would grieve you more, dear Friend, than to have your child suspect your truthfulness? "Alas," cries the father, "Can it have come to this, that my own child will not believe me? Is my promise to be thrown in my teeth and am I to be told by my own son, 'My father, I cannot trust you'?"

It is not come to that with any of us, as parents, yet, and shall it be so with our God? Alas, it has been! We have done despite to the Spirit of Truth by doubting the promise and mistrusting the faithfulness of God! Of all sins, surely this must be one of the most provoking. If there is the virus of diabolical guilt in anything, it must be in the unbelief—not of sinners—but of God's own people! Sinners have never seen what saints have seen—never felt what we have felt, never known what we have known—and, therefore, if they should doubt, they do not sin against such light, nor do despite to such invincible arguments for confidence as we do. God forgive our unbelief, and may we never grieve His Spirit anymore!

Further, the Spirit is doubtless grieved by our ingratitude. When Jesus reveals His love to us, if we go away from the chamber of fellowship to talk lightly and forget that love. Or if, when we have been raised up from a sickbed we are no more consecrated than before. Or if, when our bread is given us and our water is sure, our heart never thanks the bounteous Giver. Or if, when preserved under temptation we fail to magnify the Lord—surely this, in each case, must be a God provoking sin! If we add pride to ingratitude we sorely grieve the blessed Spirit. When a saved sinner grows proud he insults the wisdom of the Spirit of God by his folly, for what can there be in us to be proud of?

Pride is a weed which will grow in any soil. Proud of the mercies of God? As well be proud of being in debt! Why, some of us are so foolish that God cannot exalt us, for if He did we should straightway grow dizzy in the brain, and should be sure to fall! If the Lord were to put so much as one gold piece of comfort into our pockets, we should think ourselves so rich that we should set up in business on our own account, and cease from dependence upon Him! He cannot indulge us with a little joy—He has to keep us as the father in the parable did the elder brother, who complained, "You never gave me a kid, that I might make merry with my friends."

Oh it is sad that we should be so foolish as to become proud of our graces! This is a great grief to the Spirit in a private person, and even more so when it becomes the fault of an entire Church. If you as a Church shall boast that you are numerous, or generous, or rich, it will be all over with you. God will abase those who exalt themselves! If your soul can make her boast in the Lord, you may boast as much as you will. But if you glory in anything else, God will hide His face, and you will be troubled though your mountain once stood so firm that you dreamed it could never be moved. I cannot give you a full list of all the evils which grieve the Spirit of God, but let me mention here, particularly, one—a lack of prayer.

This is grievous, either in the Church or in an individual. Does not this touch some of you? How little do some of us pray! Let each conscience now be its own accuser. My dear Brother, how about the Mercy Seat? How about the closet and secret communion with God? How about wrestling for your children? How about pleading for the pastor? Have you not been backward in interceding for the conversion of your neighbor? Could you read the story of Abraham's interceding for Sodom and say that you have interceded for London like that? Can you read of Jacob at the brook Jabbok, and say that you ever spent an hour, much less a night, in wrestling with the Angel? The prayerlessness of this age is one of its worst signs, and the prayerlessness of some of our Christian Churches looks as if God were about to withdraw Himself from the land!

In many Churches, as I am told, they have a difficulty in getting enough men to attend the Prayer Meetings to carry them on. I know of some–"Tell it not in Gath, publish it not in the streets of Askelon!"–I know of some Churches that have given up Prayer Meetings because nobody comes! Ah, if this case were a solitary one, it ought to be daily mourned over–but there are scores of Churches in the same condition–the Lord have mercy upon them and upon the land in which such Churches dwell!

To sum up many things which might be said, I think the Holy Spirit will be grieved with any one of us if we shall indulge any known sin, let it be what it may. And I will add to that, if any one of us shall neglect any known duty, let it be what it may. I cannot imagine the Spirit of God being pleased with a Brother who knows his Master's will, and does it not. I know the Word says that he shall be beaten with many stripes. Surely, beating with stripes must be the result of grief on the part of the hand that administers such stripes. Let any person or any Church know good and do it not, and to him or to it, it shall be sin! And that which might not be sin in the ignorant, will become sin to those blessed with light.

As soon as your conscience is enlightened and you know the path of duty, you need not say, "Others ought to do it," (so they should, but to their own Master they must stand or fall). If your judgment is enlightened, make haste and delay not to keep the Commandments of God. John Owen, in his treatise upon the Holy Spirit, makes a remark that he believes the Spirit of God was greatly grieved in England by the public affirmation in the articles of the doctrine that the Church of God has power to decree rites and ceremonies for herself. God's Word is the only rule of God's Church. Inasmuch as the Church of England, so called, claims to be her own lawmaker, she has grieved the Spirit!

When a Church claims to itself the right to judge what are to be its own ordinances instead of willingly and obediently acknowledging that she has no right of choice whatever–but is bound to obey the revealed will of her Great Head–she sins terribly! It is the duty of all Christians to search the Word as to what are the ordinances which God has fixed and commanded. And being once clear as to the rule of the Word, it is ours to obey it! If you see infant Baptism in the Word, do not neglect it! If it is not there, do not regard it!

Here I must give utterance to a thought which has long followed me. Perhaps the present sad condition of the Christian Church, and the prevalence of the dogma of "baptismal regeneration," may be traceable to the neglect that reigns in the Church almost universally with regard to the great Christian ordinance of Believers' Baptism. Men laugh at all talk about this as if the question were of no importance. But I take leave to say that whatever may be the Truth of God upon that ordinance, it is worth every Believer's while to find it out.

I meet constantly with people who have no sort of faith in infant Baptism, and have long ago given it up. And yet, though they admit that they ought to be baptized as Believers, they neglect the duty as unimportant. Now mark it– when the Last Great Day shall reveal all things, I am persuaded it will reveal this–that the Church's supplanting the Baptism of Believers by that of infants was not only a great means in the original establishment of Popery, but that the maintenance of the perverted ordinance in our Protestant Church is the chief root and cause of the present revival of Popery in this land.

If we would lay the axe to the roots of Sacramentarianism, we must go back to the old Scriptural method of giving ordinances to Believers only–the ordinances after faith–not before faith. We must give up baptizing in order to regenerate and administer it to those alone who profess to be already regenerate. When we all come to this we shall hear no more of "baptismal regeneration," and a thousand other false doctrines will vanish away. Lay down the rule that unbelievers have no right to Church ordinances, and you put it out of the power of men to establish the unhallowed institution of a State

Church! For, mark you, no National Church is possible on the principle of Believers' Baptism—a principle much too exclusive to suit the mixed multitude of a whole nation.

A State Church must hold to infant Baptism! Necessarily it must receive all the members of the State into its number—it must or else it cannot expect the pay of the State. Make the Church a body consisting only of professedly faithful men, believers in the Lord Jesus, and let the Church say to all others, "You have no part nor lot in this matter until you are converted," and there is the end of the unholy alliance between the Church and the world which is now a withering blight upon our land. Errors of doctrine, practice, and polity may cause the dew of Heaven to be withheld. You will say, "Such errors did not hinder revivals in other days!"

Perhaps not, but God does not always wink at our ignorance. In these days no one needs to be ignorant about the mystery of "baptismal regeneration"— the error has worked itself to its full development and reached such a climax that every Christian man ought to give it his most earnest consideration. Guilt will come upon us if we are not earnest in seeking out the roots of an evil which is the cause of such deadly mischief in the land. If, as a Church, we are clear in our testimony on this point, I entreat you to see if there is any other error with which you may be charged. Is there a part of Scripture which we have not attended to? Is there a Truth of God which we have neglected? Let us hold ourselves ready to relinquish our most cherished opinions at the commands of Scripture, whatever they may be.

I say to you what I say to others—if the form of our Church government, if the manner of our administration of Christian ordinances, if the doctrines we hold are unwarranted by the Word of God—let us be faithful to our consciences and to the Word and be ready to alter, according to our light. Let us give up the idea of stereotyping anything! Let us be ready at any moment and every moment to do just what the Spirit of God would have us do! For if not, we may not expect the Spirit of God to abide with us. O for a heart to serve God perfectly! O that such a heart were given to all His people so that they were ready to renounce authority, antiquity, taste, opinion, and bow before the Holy Spirit alone! May the Church yet come to walk by the simple rule of God's Book and by the light of God's Spirit, and then shall we cease to grieve the Holy Spirit!

III. Thirdly, and very briefly—much too briefly—THE LAMENTABLE RESULT of the Spirit's being grieved. In the child of God it will not lead to his utter destruction, for no heir of Heaven can perish. Neither will the Holy Spirit be utterly taken away from him, for the Spirit of God is given to abide with us forever. But the ill-effects are nevertheless most terrible. You will lose, my dear Friends, all sense of the Holy Spirit's Presence—He will be as one hidden from you—no beams of comfort, no words of peace, no thoughts of love.

There will be what Cowper calls, "an aching void which the world can never fill." Grieve the Holy Spirit and you will lose all Christian joy. The light shall be taken from you and you shall stumble in darkness. Those very means of Divine Grace which once were such a delight shall have no music in your ears. Your soul shall be no longer as a watered garden, but as a howling wilderness. Grieve the Spirit of God, and you will lose all power. If you pray, it will be a very weak prayer—you will not prevail with God. When you read the Scriptures you shall not be able to lift the latch and force your way into the inner mysteries of the Truth of God. When you go up to the House of God, there shall be none of that devout exhilaration, that running without weariness, that walking without fainting. You shall feel yourself like Samson when his hair was lost—weak, captive, and blind. Let the Holy Spirit depart and assurance is gone! Doubts follow, questions and suspicions are aroused—

"Do I love the Lord or no?
Am I His, or am I not?"

Grieve the Spirit of God, and usefulness will cease. The ministry shall yield no fruit. Your Sunday school work shall be barren. Your speaking to others and laboring for others souls shall be like sowing the wind. Let a Church grieve the Spirit of God, and oh, the blights that shall come and wither her fair garden! Then her days of solemn assembly shall have no acceptance with Heaven! Her sons, although all of them ordained as priests unto God, shall have no acceptable incense to offer.

Let the Church grieve the Spirit, and she shall fail to bless the age in which she lives. She shall cast no light into the surrounding darkness. No sinners shall be saved by her means. There shall be few additions to her number. Her missionaries shall cease to go forth. There shall be no marriage feasts of communion in her house. Darkness and death shall reign where all was joy and life. Brothers and Sisters, Beloved in the Lord, may the Lord prevent us from grieving His Spirit as a Church, but may we be earnest, zealous, truthful, united, and holy so that we may retain among us this heavenly Guest who will leave us if we grieve Him.

IV. Lastly, there is one PERSONAL ARGUMENT which is used in the text to forbid our grieving the Spirit–"Whereby you are sealed unto the day of redemption." What does this mean? There are many meanings assigned by different commentators. We shall be content with the following–A seal is set upon a thing to attest its authenticity and authority. By what can I know that I am truly what I profess to be– a Christian by profession? How do I know whether I am really a Christian or not? God sets a seal on every genuine Believer–what is it? It is the possession of the Holy Spirit of God!

If you have the Holy Spirit, my dear Friend, that is God's seal set upon you that you are His child! Do you not see, then, that if you grieve the Spirit you lose your seal, and you are like a commission with the seal torn away? You are like a note of hand without a signature! Your evidence of being God's child is the Spirit, for if "any man have not the Spirit of Christ, He is none of His." If you have not the Spirit in you, that will be decisive evidence for you that you do not belong to Christ, for you lack the groundwork of true assurance, which is the indwelling Presence, power, and enjoyment of the Spirit.

Moreover, I have said a seal is used for attestation, and so it is, not only to you, but to others. You say to the world around, "I am a child of God." How are they to know it? They can only judge as you must judge yourself, by looking for the seal. If you possess the Spirit of God, they will soon see you to be a Christian. If you have it not, whatever else you have, you will soon be discovered to be a forgery, for you lack the seal. Beloved, all Church history proves this, that when the Christian Church has been filled with the Spirit of God, the world has confessed her pedigree because it could not help doing so. But when the Church has lost her enthusiasm and fervor because she has lost the heavenly fire, then the world has asked, "What is this Christian Church more than the synagogue of the Jews, or the company of Mahomet?"

The world knows God's seal! And if it does not see it, it soon despises that society which pretends to be the Church of God and has not the mark and proof of it. The same truth holds good in all cases. For instance, in the matter of the Christian ministry. When I first came to minister in London there was some little talk about my being ordained. "If I am ordained of God, I do not need human ordination. And if, on the other band, God has not called me to the work, no man or set of men can do it." But it was said, "You must have a recognition service, that others may signify their approval!"

"No," I said, "if God is with me, they will recognize me quickly enough as a man of God. And if the Lord's Presence is denied me, human approval is of little worth." Brethren, if you profess to be called to any form of ministry, your only way of proving your call will be by showing the seal of the Spirit! When that seal is affixed to your labors, you will require no other recognition! The camp of Dan soon recognized Samson when the Spirit came upon him, and when he went among his enemies—the Philistines—with the jaw-bone of an ass, they soon recognized him as they saw him piling the slain heaps upon heaps!

This is how the Christian man or minister must compel the recognition of his status and call. Knights of the Cross must win their spurs upon the battlefield. The only way for a Christian to be discerned to be a Christian, or for a Church to be manifested as a Church of God is by having the Spirit of God, and in the name of the Spirit of God doing exploits for God and bringing glory to His holy name! Once more, a seal is used for preserving, as well as for attesting. The Easterner seals up his moneybags to secure the gold within, and we seal our letters to guard the enclosure. A seal is set for security.

Now, Beloved, as the only way by which you can be known to be a Christian is by really possessing the supernatural power of the Holy Spirit, so, also, the only way by which you can be kept a Christian, and preserved from going back to the world is by still possessing that same Holy Spirit. What are you if the Spirit of God is gone? Salt that has lost its savor. With what can you be salted? "Trees twice dead, plucked up by the roots...wandering stars, to whom is reserved the blackness of darkness forever." The Holy Spirit is not to you a luxury, but a necessity—you must have Him or you die—you must have Him, or you are damned! Yes, and with a double damnation.

Here comes in this choice promise that the Lord will not leave you, and will not forsake you—but if He did leave you forever, there would remain no more sacrifice for sin—it would be impossible to renew you again unto repentance, seeing that you would have crucified the Lord afresh, and put Him to an open shame. Grieve not, then, that Spirit upon whom you are so dependent! He is your credentials as a Christian! He is your life as a Believer! Prize Him beyond all price! Speak of Him with bowed head, with reverent awe! Rest upon Him with childlike, loving confidence! Obey His faintest monitions–neglect not His inward whispers. Turn not aside from His teachings in the Word, or by His ministers.

And be as ready to feel His power as the waves of the sea are to be moved by the wind, or a feather to be wafted by the gale. Hold yourselves ready to do His bidding. As the eyes of the handmaiden are to her mistress, so let your eyes be unto Him. When you know His will, ask no questions, count no costs, dare all hazards, defy all circumstances! Let the will of the Spirit be your absolute law, apart from gain or loss, apart from your own judgment or your own taste. Let the will of the Spirit, when once plainly perceived by you, be instantly obeyed, and try to perceive that will. Do not willfully shut your eyes to an unpleasant duty, or close your understanding to an unwelcome Truth. Lean not to your own understanding! Consider that the Holy Spirit alone can teach you, and that those who will not be taught of Him must remain hopelessly foolish.

Oh, if I might but live to see the Church of God recognize the power of the Holy Spirit! If I could but see her cast aside the grave clothes which she has so long persisted in wearing! If I could see her put no confidence in State or power–rely no longer upon eloquence and learning! If I could see her depend upon the Holy Spirit, even though her ministers should again be fishermen and her followers should again be the "base things of this world, and the things that are not"! Even though she should have to be baptized in blood. Even though the Man-Child should excite the dragon's wrath and he should pour floods out against her–yet the day of her final victory would have dawned–if she did but obey the Spirit!

If only her directories, creeds, rules, prayer books, rubrics, and canons were cast to the winds, and the free Spirit of the living God ruled everywhere! If, instead of the decrees of her councils and the slavish bondage of priestcraft and ritual, she would only embrace the liberty with which Christ has made her free, and walk according to His Word and the teachings of her heavenly Teacher–then might we hear the shout of the King in our midst, and the battlements of error would fall! God send it, and send it in our time, and His shall be praise!

I fear there are some here who do not grieve the Spirit, but do worse than that–they quench the Spirit–they resist the Spirit. May the Lord grant them forgiveness of this great sin, and may they be led to the Cross of Christ to find pardon for every sin! At the Cross, and there alone, can everlasting life be found. God bless you for Jesus' sake. Amen.

PART IV

HELP FROM THE HOLY SPIRIT

PRAYING IN THE HOLY SPIRIT

"Praying in the Holy Spirit."
Jude 1:20

A Sermon Delivered On Sunday Morning: 4 November 1866

THESE words occur in a passage where the Apostle is indicating the contrast between the ungodly and the godly. The ungodly are mocking, speaking great swelling words and walking after their ungodly lusts, while the righteous are building themselves up in their most holy faith, and keeping themselves in the love of God. The ungodly are showing the venom of their hearts by mourning and complaining, while the righteous are manifesting the new principle within them by "praying in the Holy Spirit." The ungodly man bears wormwood in his mouth, while the Christian's lips drop with the virgin honey of devotion. As the spider is said to find poison in the very flowers from which the bees suck honey, so do the wicked abuse to sin the same mercies which the godly use to the glory of God.

As far as light is removed from darkness, and life from death, so far does a Believer differ from the ungodly. Let us keep this contrast very vivid. While the wicked grow yet more wicked, let us become more holy, more prayerful, and more devout, saying with good old Joshua, "Let others do as they will, but as for me and my house, we will serve the Lord." Observe that the text comes in a certain order in the context. The righteous are described, first of all, as building themselves up in their most holy faith. Faith is the first Divine Grace, the root of piety, the foundation of holiness, the dawn of godliness—to this must the first care be given.

But we must not tarry at the first principles. Onward is our course! What, then, follows at the heels of faith? What is faith's first-born child? When the vine of faith becomes vigorous and produces fruit unto holiness, which is the first ripe cluster? Is it not prayer—"praying in the Holy Spirit"? That man has no faith who has no prayer, and the man who abounds in faith will soon abound in supplication. Faith tho mother, and prayer the child, are seldom apart from one another. Faith carries Prayer in her arms, and Prayer draws life from the breast of Faith. Edification in faith leads to fervency in supplication. Elijah first manifests his faith before the priests of Baal, and then retires to wrestle with God upon Carmel.

Study our text carefully and see what follows after "praying in the Holy Spirit." "Keep yourselves in the love of God." Next to prayer comes an abiding sense of the love of God to us and the flowing up of our love towards God. Prayer builds an altar and lays the sacrifice and the wood in order, and then Love, like the priest, brings holy fire from Heaven and sets the offering in a blaze! Faith is, as we have said, the root of Grace. Prayer is the lily's stalk, and love is the spotless flower. Faith sees the Savior, prayer follows Him into the house, but love breaks the alabaster box of precious ointment and pours it on His head.

There is, however, a step beyond even the hallowed enjoyments of love! There remains a topstone to complete the edifice—it is believing expectantly— "looking for the mercy of our Lord Jesus Christ unto eternal life." Far-seeing Hope climbs the staircase which Faith has built, and bowing upon the knees of Prayer looks through the window which Love has opened, and sees the Lord Jesus Christ coming in His glory and endowing all His people with the eternal life which is to be their portion. See, then, the value of prayer as indicating the possession of faith, and as foreshadowing and supporting the strength and growth of love.

Coming directly to the text, we remark that the Apostle speaks of prayer, but he mentions only one kind of praying. Viewed from a certain point, prayers are of many sorts. I suppose that no two genuine prayers from different men could be precisely alike. Master artists do not often multiply the same painting—they prefer to give expression to fresh ideas as often as they grasp the pencil. And so the Master Artist, the Holy Spirit, who is the Author of prayer, does not often produce two prayers that shall be precisely the same upon the tablets of His people's hearts.

Prayers may be divided into several different orders. There is deprecatory prayer in which we deprecate the wrath of God, and entreat Him to turn away His fierce anger, to withdraw His rod, to sheath His sword. Deprecatory prayers are to be offered in all times when calamity is to be feared, and when sin has provoked the Lord to jealousy. Then there are supplicatory prayers in which we supplicate blessings and implore mercies from the liberal hand of God, and entreat our heavenly Father to supply our needs out of His riches in glory by Christ Jesus. There are prayers which are personal in which the supplicant pleads mainly concerning himself. And there are pleadings which are intercessory, in which, like Abraham, the petitioner intercedes for Sodom, or entreats that Ishmael might live before God.

These prayers for others are to be multiplied as much as prayers for ourselves, lest we make the Mercy Seat to become a place for the exhibition of spiritual selfishness. The prayer may be public or private, vocal or mental, protracted or ejaculatory. Prayer may be salted with confession, or perfumed with thanksgiving. It may be sung to music, or wept out with groans. As many as are the flowers of summer, so many are the varieties of prayer! But while prayers are of these various orders, there is one respect in which they are all one if they are acceptable with God—they must be, every one of them, "in the Holy Spirit."

That prayer which is not in the Holy Spirit is in the flesh. That which is born of the flesh is flesh, and we are told that they which are in the flesh cannot please God. All that comes of our corrupt nature is defiled and marred, and cannot be acceptable with the most holy God. If the heavens are not pure in His sight, how shall those prayers which are born of the earth be acceptable with Him? The seed of acceptable devotion must come from Heaven's storehouse. Only the prayer which comes from God can go to God! The dove will only bear a letter to the cote from which it came, and so will prayer go back to Heaven if it came from Heaven. We must shoot the Lord's arrows back to Him.

That desire which He writes upon our heart will move His heart and bring down a blessing, but the desires of the flesh have no power with Him. Desirous to press this great Truth of God upon the minds of my Brothers and Sisters this morning, I shall use the few words of the text in five ways.

First we shall use the text as A CRUCIBLE to try our prayers in. I beseech you, examine yourselves with rigorous care! Use the text as a refining pot, a furnace, a touchstone or a crucible by which to discern whether your prayers have been true or not! This is the test—have they been in very deed—"praying in the Holy Spirit"? Brothers and Sisters, we need not judge those who pray unintelligible prayers, prayers in a foreign tongue, prayers which they do not understand. We know without a moment's discussion of the question that the prayer which is not understood cannot be a prayer in the Spirit, for even the man's own spirit does not enter into it–how then can the Spirit of God be there?

The mysterious words or Latin jargon of the priests cannot come up before God with acceptance! Let us, therefore, keep our judgment for ourselves. There may be those present who have been in the habit of using from their infancy a form of prayer. You perhaps would not dare to go out to your day's business without having repeated that form at the bedside. You would be afraid to fall asleep at night without going through the words which you have set yourselves to repeat. My dear Friends, may I put the question to you–will you try to answer it honestly? Have you prayed in the Holy Spirit? Has the Holy Spirit had anything to do with that form? Has He really made you to feel it in your heart? Is it not possible that you have mocked God with a solemn sound upon a thoughtless tongue? Is it not probable that from the random manner in which one comes to repeat a well-known form that there may be no heart whatever in it–and not an atom of sincerity?

Does not God abhor the sacrifice where the heart is not found? It would be a melancholy thing if we had increased our sins by our prayers! It would be a very unhappy fact if it should turn out that when we have bowed the knee in what we thought to be the service of God, we were actually insulting the God of Heaven by uttering words which could not but be disgusting to Him because our hearts did not go with our lips! Let us rest assured that if for seventy years we have punctually performed our devotions by the use of the book, or of the form which we have learned, we may, the whole seventy years, never once have prayed at all! And the whole of that period we may have been living in God's esteem an ungodly, prayerless life because we have never worshipped God, who is a Spirit, in spirit and in truth, and have never prayed in the Holy Spirit! Judge yourselves, Brothers and Sisters, that you be not judged!

But are there not others of us who never did use a written prayer? Who from our earliest childhood have eschewed and even abhorred forms of prayer, who nevertheless have good reason to try our prayer just as much as others? We have given forth extemporaneous utterances, and those extemporaneous utterances necessarily required some little exercise of the mind, some little attention–but still we may have been heartless in them. I suppose we are well aware that we can get into such a habit of extemporaneous prayer that it is really very little or no better than if we repeated what we had learned. There may be such a fluency acquired by practice that one's speech may ripple on for five or ten minutes, or a quarter of an hour, and yet the heart may be wandering in vanity or stagnant in indifference! The body may be on its knees, but the soul on its wings far away from the Mercy Seat.

Let us examine how far our public prayers have been in the Holy Spirit. The preacher standing here begs God to search him in that matter. If he has merely discharged the business of public prayer because it is his official duty to conduct the devotions of the congregation, he has much to account for before God–to lead the devotions of this vast throng without seeking the aid of the Holy Spirit is no light sin! And what shall be said of the prayers at Prayer Meetings? Are not many of them mere words? It were better if our friends would not speak at all rather than speak in the flesh!

I am sure that the only prayer in which the devout hearer can unite, and which is acceptable with God, is that which really is a heart prayer–a soul prayer, in fact–a prayer which the Holy Spirit moves us to pray. All else is beating the air and occupying time in vain. My Brethren, I thank God that there are so many of you in connection with this Church who are gifted in prayer, and I wish that every member of every Christian Church could pray in public. You should all try to do so, and none of you should give it up unless it becomes an absolute impossibility. But oh, my Brethren who pray in public, may it not be sometimes with you as with others of us–the exercise of gift and not the outflow of Divine Grace? And if so, ask the Lord to forgive you of such praying and enable you to wait upon Him in the power of the Holy Spirit.

We may not forget to scrutinize our more private prayers, our supplications at the family altar, and above all, our prayers in that little room which we have dedicated to communion with God. O Brothers and Sisters, we might well be sick of our prayers if we did but see what poor things they are! There are times when it is a sweet and blessed thing to lay hold of the horns of the altar and to feel that the blood which sprinkles the altar has sprinkled you–that you have spoken to God and prevailed! Oh it is a blessed thing to grasp the Angel of the Covenant, and to wrestle with Him even hour after hour, saying, "I will not let You go except You bless me"! But I fear these are not constant things. We may say of them that they are angels' visits, few and far between.

Come, my Brethren, put your prayers into this crucible of "praying in the Holy Spirit." You will cast in much metal, but there will come out little of fine gold. Come and lay your prayers upon this threshing floor, and thresh them with this text, "praying in the Holy Spirit." And oh, how much of straw and of chaff will there be, and how little of the well winnowed grain! Come and look through this window at the fields of our devotions, overgrown with nettles, and briars, and thistles–a wilderness of merely outward performances! And how small that little spot, enclosed by Grace, which God the Holy Spirit Himself has cleared, and dug, and planted–from which the fruit of prayer has been brought forth unto perfection!

May our heavenly Father teach us to be humble in His Presence as we reflect how little even of our best things will stand the test of His searching eyes, and may those of us who are His saints come to Him afresh, and ask Him to fill us with His Spirit, and to accept us in His Son!

II. We shall next use the text as A CORDIAL. It is a very delightful reflection to the Christian mind that God observes His people and does not sit as an indifferent spectator of their conflicts and difficulties. For instance, He closely observes us in our prayers. He knows that prayer, while it should be the easiest thing in the world, is not so. He knows that we erring ones find it not always easy to approach Him in the true spirit of supplication and He observes this with condescending compassion. That is a precious verse for those hearts which are very weak and broken, "He knows our frame: He remembers that we are dust." And that other, "Like as a father pities his children, so the Lord pities them that fear Him."

He takes notice of our frailties and of our failures in the work of supplication. He sees His child fall as it tries to walk and marks the tears with which it bemoans its weakness. "The eyes of the Lord are upon the righteous, and His ears are open unto their cry." A sweeter thought remains in the text, namely, that having considered these failures of ours, which are many of them sinful, our Lord is not angry with us on account of them. And instead of being turned to wrath, He is moved to pity for us and love towards us. Instead of saying, "If you cannot pray, you shall not have. If you have not Grace enough even to ask aright, I will shut the gates of mercy against you." No, He devises means by which to bring the lame and the banished into His Presence! He teaches the ignorant how to pray and strengthens the weak with His own strength!

Herein He also does wonders, for the means whereby He helps our infirmity are exceedingly to be marveled at. That help is not to be found in a book or in the dictation of certain words in certain consecrated places, but in the condescending assistance of God Himself, for who is He that is spoken of in the text but God? The Holy Spirit, the third Person of the adorable Trinity, helps our infirmities, making intercession for us with groans that cannot be uttered! It is a mark of wondrous condescension that God should not only answer our prayers when they are made, but should make our prayers for us! That the King should say to the petitioner, "Bring your case before me and I will grant your desire," is kindness. But for him to say, "I will be your secretary. I will write out your petition for you. I will put it into proper words and use fitting phrases so that your petition shall be framed acceptably"–this is goodness at its utmost stretch!

And this is precisely what the Holy Spirit does for us poor, ignorant, wavering, weak sons of men. I am to understand from the expression, "praying in the Holy Spirit," that the Holy Spirit is actually willing to help me to pray–that He will tell me how to pray! And that when I get to a point where I am at a pause and cannot express my desires, He will appear in my extremity and make intercession in me with groans which cannot be uttered. Jesus in His agony was strengthened by an angel–you are to be succored by God Himself! Aaron and Hur held up the hands of Moses, but the Holy Spirit Himself helps your infirmities!

My beloved Brothers and Sisters in Christ, the thought needs no garnishing of oratorical expressions! Take it as a wedge of gold of Ophir and value it. It is priceless, beyond all price. God Himself, the Holy Spirit, condescends to assist you when you are on your knees, and if you cannot put two words together in common speech to men, yet He will help you to speak with God! Ah, and if at the Mercy Seat you fail in words, you shall not fail in reality, for your heart shall conquer. God needs not words. He never reads our petitions according to the outward utterance, but according to the inward groaning. He notices the longing, the desiring, the sighing, the crying.

Remember that the outward of prayer is but the shell–the inward of prayer is its true kernel and essence. If prayer is wafted to Heaven in the song of the multitude, with the swell of glorious music, it is not one whit more acceptable to God than when it is wailed forth in the bitter cry of anguish from a desolate spirit. That cry so discordant to human ears is music to the ears of God–

"To Him there's music in a sigh,
And beauty in a tear."

Notice this, then, and be comforted.

III. The text may further serve as A CHART to direct us in the way of prayer. Here I shall need to speak at greater length. Praying how? By the book? Without a book? In public? In private? By the way? In the house? On your knees? Standing? Sitting? Kneeling? Nothing is said about these! Posture, place, and time are all left open. There is no rubric except one—"in the Holy Spirit."

That is indispensable. That granted, nothing else matters one whit. If it is praying in the Holy Spirit, all else may be as you will. What does praying in the Holy Spirit mean? The word may be translated, "by the Holy Spirit," or, "through the Holy Spirit," as well as, "in the Holy Spirit." And the phrase means, first, praying in the Holy Spirit's power. The carnal mind knows nothing about this. I might as well express myself in high Dutch as in English upon this point to an unregenerate man. But regenerate men who are born of the Spirit and live in the Spirit world are cognizant of communications between their spirits and the Holy Spirit who is now resident in the midst of the Church of God.

We know that the Divine Spirit, without the use of sounds, speaks in our hearts. We know that without an utterance which the ears can hear He can make our soul know His Presence and understand His meaning. He casts the spiritual shadow of His influence over us, coloring our thoughts and feelings according to His own design and will. It is a great spiritual fact which the Christian knows for certain that the Holy Spirit, the Divine Spirit, has frequent dealings with spiritual minds and imparts to them His power. Our new-born spirit has a certain degree of power in it, but the power is never fully manifested or drawn out except when the Spirit of God quickens our spirit and excites it to activity.

Our spirit prays, but it is because it is overshadowed and filled with the power of the Holy Spirit. I cannot just now explain myself, but I mean this, that if I, as a man, could go to the Throne of Grace and only pray as my fleshy nature would pray, that prayer would be unacceptable. But when I go to the Mercy Seat and my new nature prays as the Holy Spirit enables me to pray, then my prayer will succeed with God. If I do before God at the throne what flesh and blood can do and no more, I have done nothing–for that which is of the flesh still mounts no higher than flesh.

But if, in coming before the Throne of the heavenly Grace, God's eternal Spirit speaks to my soul and lifts it out of the dead level of fallen humanity. And if He brings it up to be filled with Divine force–if that Spirit is in me a well of water springing up unto everlasting life, if I receive that Divine light and power of the Holy Spirit–and if in His power I fervently draw near to God, my prayer must be prevalent with God! This power may be possessed by every Christian. May God grant it to all of His people now, that they may all pray in the Spirit!

That, I think, is one meaning of the text–praying in the power of the Spirit. No doubt the principal sense of the text is praying in the Spirit as to matter. We do not know always what to pray for, and, Brothers and Sisters, if we were to refrain from prayer for a few minutes till we did know, it would be a good and wise rule. The habit into which we have fallen, in extemporaneous praying, of always praying directly what we are asking–without an instant's pause in which to think of what we are going to ask–is very prejudicial to the spirit of prayer. I would like, when I am alone, to take a few minutes to consider what I am going to ask of God, for otherwise it seems to me to be like seeking an interview with one of the officers of State to ask for something which might occur to us at the moment.

How would you like to have an audience with Lord Derby, and then consider all of a sudden what it was you had come for? Surely common sense would say, Tarry awhile till you have your case mapped out in your own mind, and then when you clearly know yourself what it is you want, you will be able to ask for what you need. Should we not wait upon God in prayer, asking Him to reveal to us what those matters are concerning which we should plead with Him? Beware of hit-or-miss prayers! Never make hap-hazard work of supplication. Come to the Throne of Grace intelligently understanding what it is that you require.

It is well with us in prayer when the Holy Spirit guides the mind. Are not all spiritual men conscious of this, that they feel themselves shut up as to certain matters, and only free in another direction? Then let them obey the Holy Spirit and pray as He directs, for He knows what should be our petition. Well, then what? My dear Brothers and Sisters, pray for that which God the Spirit moves you to pray for, and be very sensitive of the Holy Spirit's influence. I like a metaphor used by Thomas Shillitoe in his Life, when he says he wished his own mind to be like a cork upon the water, conscious of every motion of the Spirit of God. It were well to be so sensitive of the Spirit of God that His faintest breath should cause a ripple upon the sea of our soul and make it move as the Spirit would have it.

We have reached a high state of sanctification when God the Spirit and our own inward spirit are perfectly in accord. May we be led into that unspeakably blessed state! We do not pray aright if we think what it is we want and we wish for, and then ask for it in selfish willfulness. We pray aright when we consent to that which is the mind of the Spirit, and speak as He moves us to speak. We shall be surely enriched with good things when we wait for the very matter of our supplications to have it all from Him. Lord, teach us to pray! Put the thoughts into our minds, the desires into our hearts, and the very words into our lips, if it is Your will, so that all our prayers may be praying in the Spirit and not in the flesh.

The main part of praying in the Spirit must lie not merely in the Spirit's power, or in the Spirit's teaching us the matter, but in the Spirit's assisting us in the manner. Observe, Brothers and Sisters, the many ways there are of praying which are obnoxious to God—observe them and avoid them! There is but one manner of praying which the Lord accepts. You know what it is. I will briefly describe its attributes. He that comes to God must remember that He is "a Spirit, and that they who worship Him must worship Him in spirit and in truth, for the Father seeks such to worship Him." The very first essential of prayer is to pray in truth, and we do not pray in truth unless the Spirit of God leads our vain minds into the sincerity and reality of devotion.

To pray in truth is this—it is not to use the empty expression of prayer, but to mean what we say. It is for the heart to agonize with God and heave with strong desires. And where will you obtain such a manner of prayer except in the spiritual man, when moved by the Holy Spirit? The carnal man, if he is foolish enough, can intone a prayer. The carnal man can "read the office," and "do duty" as well as anybody else who can read a book, but he is not praying! No prayer can come from him. Only the spiritual man can sigh and long, and cry in his inmost heart, and in the chamber of his soul before God—but he will not do it except as the Spirit of Truth leads him in sincerity into the secret of heart prayer.

Praying in the Holy Spirit is praying in fervency. Cold prayers, my Brothers and Sisters, ask the Lord not to hear them! Those who do not plead with fervency, plead not at all. As well speak of lukewarm fire as of lukewarm prayer! It is essential that it be red hot. Real prayer is burnt as with hot iron into a man's soul, and then comes forth from the man's soul like coals of juniper which have a most vehement heat. Such prayers none but the Holy Spirit can give. I have heard from this spot prayers which I never can forget, nor will you ever forget them either.

Last January and February there were times when certain of our Brethren were helped to pray with such power that we were bowed down in humiliation, and afterwards borne up as on the wings of eagles in the power of supplication! There is a way of praying with power in which a man seems to get hold of the posts of Heaven's gate, as Samson grasped the pillars of the temple, and appears as though he would pull all down upon himself sooner than miss the blessing. It is a brave thing for the heart to vow, "I will not let You go except You bless me." That is praying in the Holy Spirit. May we be tutored in the art of offering effectual fervent prayer!

Next to that, it is essential in prayer that we should pray perseveringly. Any man can run fast at a spurt, but to keep it up mile after mile—there is the battle! And so, certain hot spirits can pray very fervently every now and then, but to continue in prayer—who shall do this except the Spirit of God sustains him? Mortal spirits flag and tire. The course of mere fleshly devotion is as the course of a snail which melts as it crawls. Carnal minds go onward and their devotion grows small by degrees and miserably less, as they cry out, "What a weariness it is!" But when the Holy Spirit fills a man and leads him into prayer, he gathers force as he proceeds—and grows more fervent even when God delays to answer! The longer the gate is closed the more vehemently does he use the knocker till he thunders in his prayer! And the longer the Angel lingers, the more resolved is he that if he grasps Him with a death grip he will never let Him go without the blessing.

Beautiful in God's sight is tearful and yet unconquerable importunity. Jesus delights to be laid hold of by one who says, "I cannot take No for an answer, this blessing I must have, for You have promised it and You have taught me to ask for it, and I will not believe that You can belie yourself." Surely we must have the Holy Spirit to help us thus to pray. Praying in the Spirit we shall be sure to pray in a holy frame of mind. Brothers and Sisters, do you ever get distracted in your minds? "Ah," you say, "I wonder when I am not." I will venture to say that you have come into this house burdened, and yet on the road you were saying, "This is a blessed Sunday, I feel I have God's Presence."

Then some silly gossip met you on the steps and told you an idle tale which distracted you. You may even get quietly seated here, and then the recollection of a child at home, or the remembrance of what somebody said about six weeks ago will perplex your mind so that you cannot pray. But when the Holy Spirit comes, He takes a scourge of small cords and drives these buyers and sellers out of the temple and leaves it clear for God. And then you can come with a holy, devout frame of mind, fixed and settled in your great object of approach to God. This is to approach Him in the Spirit. Oh for more of this blessed, undisturbed devotion!

I could not, however, finish the description of praying in the Spirit if I did not say that it means praying humbly, for the Holy Spirit never puffs us up with pride. He is the Spirit that convicts of sin and so bows us down in contrition and brokenness of spirit. We must pray before God like the humble publican, or we shall never go forth justified as he was. We shall never sing Gloria in Excelsis except we pray to God De Profundis—out of the depths must we cry, or we shall never see the glory in the highest! True prayer must be loving prayer if it is praying in the Holy Spirit. Prayer should be perfumed with love, saturated with love—love to our fellow saints, and love to Christ. Moreover, it must be a prayer full of faith. The effectual fervent prayer of a man prevails only as he believes in God, and the Holy Spirit is the Author of faith in us, and nurtures and strengthens it so that we pray believing God's promises.

Oh that this blessed combination of excellent Graces, priceless and sweet as the spices of the merchant, might be fragrant within us because the Holy Spirit's power is shed abroad in our hearts! Time fails me, therefore I must dispense with a full description of what praying in the Holy Spirit is, but I hope you will possess it and so understand it.

IV. Fourthly, I shall use the text as A CHERUB to proclaim our success in prayer. Praying in the Spirit—blessed words! Then with such prayer it is an absolute certainty that I must succeed with God in prayer. If my prayer were my own prayer, I might not be so sure of it. But if the prayer which I utter is God's own prayer written on my soul, God is always One with Himself—and what He writes on the heart is only written there because it is written in His purposes.

It is said by an old Divine that prayer is the shadow of Omnipotence. Our will, when God the Holy Spirit influences it, is the indicator of God's will. When God's people pray, it is because the blessing is coming and their prayers are the shadow of the coming blessing! Rest assured of this, Brothers and Sisters, God never did belie Himself! He never contradicted in one place what He said in another. You and I may contradict ourselves, not only through untruthfulness, but even through infirmity.

We may not be able to stand up to our word, and we may forget what we said—and so in another place may say something that contradicts it—but God is neither infirm as to memory, nor yet changeable as to will. What He promised yesterday He fulfils today. What He said in one place, He declares in another. Then if God said in my heart, "Pray for So-and-So," it is because He has said it in the book of His decrees. The Spirit of God's writing in the heart always tallies with the writing of destiny in the book of God's eternal purpose. Rest assured that you cannot but succeed when you have laid your soul like a sheet of paper before the Lord and asked Him to write upon it! Then it is no more your own prayer, merely, but the Spirit making intercession in you according to the will of God.

At such time you need not say, "I hope God will answer the prayer." He will do it—He is pledged to do it. It is a kind of infidelity to say, "I do not know whether the Lord is true to His promise or not, but I hope He is." He is true! Let God be true and every man a liar. Oh, if more of you tried Him as some of us have been compelled to do, you would have to hold up your hands in astonishment, and say, "Truly, whatever else is not a fact, it is a fact that God, who sits in the highest heavens, listens to the cries of His people, and gives them according to the desire of their hearts." If the Spirit teaches you to pray, it is as certain as two times two make four that God will give you what you are seeking for.

Then I will use the text in conclusion as A CHARIOT in which to convey our own souls onward in the delightful exercise of prayer. The exercise allotted to us today and tomorrow is that of praying in the Spirit. Brothers and Sisters, it is delightful to some of us to believe that the Spirit of God is the Author of the great wave of prayer now breaking over the Churches to which we belong. It was not of our devising or planning, but it was the motion of God's Holy Spirit upon a few Brethren who desired to spend a day in solemn prayer and found such blessing in it that they could not but tell others of it!

That, then, others spontaneously moved, and without a word of opposition or difference of opinion all said, "Amen. Let us also meet together for prayer." The spirit of brotherly kindness, unanimity, and love was given to our denomination, and then a spirit of earnest desire to bring down a blessing from God. We have known the time when it was not so. We have known the time when a day of fasting and prayer, if not despised, at any rate would not have been appreciated as it will be now. We are of one heart in this matter and I know from communications with many Christian men that many of God's people already feel as if they were peculiarly in prayer–as if it were no effort now to pray, but as if it were their very breath now to breathe out longing desires for the revival of saints and the ingathering of sinners.

Brothers and Sisters of this Church, you have had God's Presence. For many years you have been favored with much of "praying in the Holy Spirit," and seen with your own eyes the great things God has done in answer to supplication. Will one of you draw back now? Will there be one man today or tomorrow who will not be earnest in prayer? Will one man, or even one child in union with this Church, be lukewarm in prayer? I would say, Sin not against the Lord by abstaining from going up to the Mercy Seat with your Brothers and Sisters. Offend not the Lord so that He deprive you of the blessing because you deprive yourself of joining in the exercise.

My dear Friends, it was when they were all met together with one accord in one place that suddenly they heard the sound as of a rushing, mighty wind. We cannot be all in one place, but, at any rate, let us be all with one accord. What? Do you say you have nothing to pray for? What? No children unconverted, no friends unsaved, no neighbors who are still in darkness? What? Live in London and not pray for sinners? Where do you live? Is it in some vast wilderness, amidst "some boundless contiguity of shade," where rumor of sin and of ignorance has never reached your ear? No, you are living in the midst of millions of ungodly millions! Millions that despise the God who made them! Millions that despise the Gospel of Christ!

Millions, not thousands! Hear that word and see if you can tell its meaning! Millions who are living without God and without hope, and are going down to Hell! We have, throughout the realm, too, dangerous mischiefs spreading. Need I continually remind you of them? Infidelity wearing the miter, and

Popery usurping the place of Protestantism! You are assailed by the wolf and the lion, the serpent and the bear! All forms of mischief are coming forth to attack the Church. Not pray? If you pray not, shall I say, May you smart for your negligence? No I dare not in the slightest shade speak as though I imprecated a woe upon you, but the woe will come upon you, depend upon it! If I say it not, yet will God say it at this present hour. "Curse you Meroz, said the Lord, because they came not up to the help of the Lord, to the help of the Lord against the mighty."

We are not asking you to contribute of your wealth in this case. If we did, the Lord Jesus has a right to it, and you should freely give it. Neither are we asking you all this day to preach. If we did, some of you might be excused for lack of ability. But we claim your prayers, and must not be denied! Not able to pray? Then are you graceless, Christless, hopeless, lost, and I will not ask you to join with us! But I ask you first to go to God for yourselves. And if you are a Christian you can pray. Poverty does not make you poor in prayer. Lack of education need not hinder you upon your knees. Lack of position and rank in society will be no encumbrance to you when you deal with God who hears the poor man when he cries and answers him with a largess of Divine Grace!

Brothers and Sisters, if you love Christ, if you ever felt His love shed abroad in your heart. If you have been washed in His blood. If you have been saved from wrath through Him. If you are new creatures in Him. If you hope to see His face with acceptance at the last, I might put it to you as a demand! But I press it upon you as a brotherly entreaty–join with us in praying in the Holy Spirit! Shall one start back? Take heed, then, if you refuse to unite with your Brethren in prayer, lest when you choose to cry you should find yourself straitened and shut up in prison! Beware, lest by refusing to pray now, that the Spirit of God has come, you afterwards feel yourself deprived of the comfortable Presence of the Holy Spirit and find the sweetness of devotion to have departed from you.

The Lord send a blessing. He must send it–our hearts will break if He does not! We feel that it is coming. We have grasped the promise. We have pleaded with Jehovah! We have pleaded the blood of Jesus! We are pleading it now! We mean to continue in such pleading till the blessing comes, and we may rely upon it that the heavenly shower will soon descend! He has not said to the seed of Jacob, "Seek you My face in vain." Brothers and Sisters, be hopeful, and let us unanimously join in praying in the Holy Spirit!

May the Lord bless you, dear Friends, in this respect for Jesus' sake.

THE HOLY SPIRIT—THE NEED OF THE AGE

"O you that are named the House of Jacob, is the Spirit of the Lord straitened? are these His doings? Do not My words do good to him that walks uprightly?"
Micah 2:7

A Sermon Delivered On Sunday Morning: 13 March 1887

BROTHERS AND SISTERS, what a stern rebuke to the people of Israel is contained in the title with which the Prophet addressed them—"O you that are named the House of Jacob"! It is as much as to say to them—"You wear the name, but you do not bear the character of Jacob." It is the Old Testament version of the New Testament saying, "You have a name to live and are dead." They gloried that they were the seed of Israel! They vaunted the peculiar privileges which came to them as the descendants of God's honored and chosen servant Jacob! But they did not act in the same way as Jacob would have acted—they were devoid of Jacob's faith in Jehovah, they knew nothing of Jacob's power of prayer—and nothing of his reliance upon the Covenant.

The words of Micah imply that the descendants of Jacob in his day were proud of the name, "House of Jacob," but that they were not worthy of it. Nothing is more mischievous than to cling to a name when the thing for which it stands has disappeared. May we never come to such a stage of declension that even the Spirit of God will be compelled, in speaking to us, to say, "O you that are called the Church of God!" To be named Christians, but not to be Christians, is to be deceivers or deceived! The name brings with it great responsibility and if it is a name, only, it brings with it terrible condemnation! It is a crime against the Truth of God if we dare to take the name of His people when we are not His people. It is a robbery of honor from those to whom it is due. It is a practical lie against the Holy Spirit! It is a defamation of the character of the bride of Christ to take the name of Christian when the Spirit of Christ is not among us! This is to honor Christ with our lips and disgrace Him by our lives!

What is this but to repeat the crime of Judas and betray the Son of Man with a kiss? Brothers and Sisters, I say again, may we never come to this! Truths, not names, facts, not professions, are to be the first consideration! Better to be true to God and bear the names of reproach which the adversary is so apt to coin, than to be false to our Lord and yet to be decorated with the names of saints and regarded as the most orthodox of Believers. Whether named, "the House of Jacob," or not, let us be wrestlers like Jacob and like he, may we come off as prevailing princes—the true Israel of God!

When the Lord found His chosen people to be in such a state that they had rather the name than the character of His people, He spoke to them by the Spirit of the Lord. Was not this because their restoration must come from that direction? Was not their evil spirit to be removed by the Lord's good Spirit? "O you that are named the House of Jacob, is the Spirit of the Lord straitened?" I believe, Brothers and Sisters, that whenever the Church of God declines, one of the most effectual ways of reviving her is to preach much Truth concerning the Holy Spirit. After all, He is the very breath of the Church. Where the Spirit of God is, there is power! If the Spirit is withdrawn, then the vitality of godliness begins to decline and the energy thereof is near to dying out. If we, ourselves, feel that we are backsliding, let us turn to the Spirit of God, crying, "Quicken me in Your way."

If we sorrowfully perceive that any Church is growing lukewarm, be it our prayer that the Holy Spirit may work graciously for its revival. Let us direct the attention of our fellow Christians under declension to the Spirit of God. They are not straitened in Him, but in themselves! Let them turn to Him for enlargement. It is He alone who can quicken us and strengthen the things which remain which are ready to die. I admire the wisdom of God here, that when speaking by the Prophet, He rebukes the backsliding of the people and He immediately directs their minds to the Holy Spirit who can bring them back from their wanderings and cause them to walk worthy of the vocation wherewith they were called. Let us learn from this Divine Wisdom and, in lowly reverence and earnest faith, let us look to the Spirit of the Lord.

In speaking to Israel upon the Spirit of God, the Prophet Micah uses the remarkable language in our text, upon which I would now speak to you. "O you that are named the House of Jacob, is the Spirit of the Lord straitened? Are these His doings? Do not My words do good to him that walks uprightly?" May the Holy Spirit help me to speak and you to hear!

And, first, I think we may consider these words to have been spoken TO DENOUNCE THOSE WHO WOULD CONTROL THE SPIRIT OF GOD. "Is the Spirit of the Lord straitened?" Can you hold Him a captive and make Him speak at your dictation?

On turning to the connection you will find that there were certain Prophets sent of God to Israel who were unpopular. The message which they brought was not acceptable—the people could not endure it and so we read in the sixth verse—"Prophesy you not, say they to them that prophesy: they shall not prophesy to them, that they shall not take shame." The words of these Prophets came so home to their consciences and made them so ashamed of themselves, that they said, "Do not prophesy! We wish not to hear you." To these Micah replies, "Is the Spirit of the Lord to be straitened by you?"

There were some in those days who would altogether have silenced the Spirit. They would banish all spiritual teaching from the earth, that the voice of human wisdom might be not contradicted. But can they silence the Spirit of God? Has He not continually spoken according to His own will and will He not continue to do so? Is He not the free Spirit who, like the wind, blows where He wishes? If the adversaries could have slain with the sword all the messengers of God, would He not have found others? And if these, also, had been killed, could He not, out of stones, have raised up heralds of His Truth? While the Scriptures remain, the Holy Spirit will never be without a voice to the sons of men! And while He remains, those Scriptures will not be left without honest hearts and tongues to expound and enforce them! Is it possible for men anywhere to silence the Spirit of God? They may be guilty of the crime because they desire to commit it and attempt to do so, but yet, its accomplishment is beyond their reach. They may "quench the Spirit" in this and that man, but not in those in whom He effectually works. The Almighty Spirit may be resisted, but He will not be defeated! As well might men attempt to stop the shining of the sun, or seal up the winds, or still the pulsing of the tides, as effectually to straiten the Spirit of the Lord—

"When God makes bare His arm,
Who can His work withstand?"

Jehovah speaks and it is done—who shall resist His Word? When His Spirit attends that Word, shall it fall to the ground? "My Word," says He, "shall not return unto Me void"—and all the sinners on earth and all the devils in Hell cannot alter that grand decree! Every now and then there seems to be a lull in the history of holy work, a silence from God, as if He were wearying of men and would speak no longer to them. But before long, in some unexpected quarter, the voice of the Lord is heard once more—some earnest soul breaks the awful silence of spiritual death and again the adversary is defeated! Outbursts of the great Spirit of Life, and Light, and Truth comes at the Divine will—when men least look for it or desire it! When Jesus has been crucified, even then the Holy Spirit descends, and the victories of the Cross begin. No, my Brethren, the Spirit of the Lord is not silenced—the voice of the Lord is heard above the tumults of the people!

The apostate Israelites also tried to straiten the Spirit of God by only allowing certain persons to speak in His name. They would have a choice of their Prophets—and a bad choice, too. See in the 11th verse—"If a man should walk in a false spirit and speak a lie, saying, I will prophesy unto you of wine and of strong drink, even he shall be the prophet of this people." They had a liking for preachers who would indulge their lusts, pander to their passions and swell their pride with windy flatteries! This age also inclines greatly to those who have cast off the restraints of God's Revelation and utter the flattering inventions of their own boasted "thought." Your liberal spirits, your large-hearted men, your despisers of the old and hunters after the new—these are the idols of many! As for those who would urge upon men separation from the world and holiness to the Lord, they are Puritans and out of date! In Micah's days, Israel would only hear false prophets—the rest they would not listen to. "What?" asks Micah, "is the Spirit of the Lord then to be shut up to speak to you by such men as you would choose? Is He not to speak by whomever He pleases?"

It is the tendency of churches in all ages to fetter the free Spirit. Now they are afraid that we shall have too many preachers and they would restrain their number by a sort of trades-union! In certain churches none must speak in God's name unless they have gone through a certain humanly-prescribed preparation and have been ordained after a regulation manner—the Spirit of God may speak by the ordained, but He must not speak by others! In my inmost soul I treasure the liberty of prophesying. Not the right of every man to speak in the name of the Spirit, but the right of the Spirit to speak by whomever He pleases! He will rest on some rather than on others and God forbid that we should straiten His Sovereignty! Lord, send by whomever You will send! Choose whom You will to the sacred office of ministers of God!

Among the poor and illiterate the Spirit of God has had voices as clear and bold as among the educated and refined—and He will have them still, for He is not straitened—and it is the way of Him to use instruments which pour contempt upon all the vain-glory of men! He anoints His own to bear witness for His Truth by life and lips—these the professing church may criticize and even reject, saying, "The Lord has not spoken by these," but the Word of the Lord will stand, notwithstanding the judgment of men! God's true ministers shall be acknowledged of Him—wisdom is justified of her children. The Lord's Spirit will not be straitened or shut up by all the rules, modes and methods which even good men may devise. The wind blows where it wishes and the power of the Spirit waits not for man, neither tarries for the sons of men!

Further, this people tried to straiten the Spirit of God by changing His testimony. They did not wish the Prophets to speak upon subjects which caused shame to them. They bade them prophesy smooth things. Tell us that we may sin with safety! Tell us that the punishment of sin is not so overwhelming as we have feared! Stand up and be advocates for the devil by flattering us with "a larger hope!" Hint to us that, after all, man is a poor, inoffensive creature who does wrong because he cannot help it and that God will wink at his sins! And if He does punish us for a while, He will soon set it all right! That was the style of teaching which Israel desired and, no doubt, they found prophets to speak in that manner, for the demand soon creates the supply! But Micah boldly asks, "Is the Spirit of the Lord straitened?" Do you think that He will have His utterances toned down and His Revelation shaped to suit your tastes?

Brothers and Sisters, let me ask you, do you imagine that the Gospel is a nose of wax which can be shaped to suit the face of each succeeding age? Is the Revelation, once given by the Spirit of God, to be interpreted according to the fashion of the period? Is "advanced thought" to be the cord with which the Spirit of the Lord is to be straitened? Is the old Truth of God that saved men hundreds of years ago to be banished because something fresh has been hatched in the nests of the wise? Do you think that the witness of the Holy Spirit can be shaped and molded at our will? Is the Divine Spirit to be the pupil rather than the Teacher of the ages? "Is the Spirit of the Lord straitened?" My very soul boils within me when I think of the impudent arrogance of certain willful spirits from whom all reverence for Revelation has departed! They would teach Jehovah wisdom! They criticize His Word and amend His Truth. Certain Scriptural doctrines are, indeed, discarded as dogmas of the medieval period! Others are denounced as gloomy because they cannot be called untrue. Paul is questioned and quibbled out of court and the Lord Jesus is first praised and then explained away. We are told that the teaching of God's ministers must be conformed to the spirit of the age. We shall have nothing to do with such treason to the Truth of God! "Is the Spirit of the Lord straitened?" Shall His ministers speak as if He were? Verily, that same treasure of Truth which the Lord has committed unto us we will keep inviolate so long as we live, God helping us. We are not so unmindful of the words of the Apostle, "Hold fast the form of sound words," as to change a syllable of what we believe to be the Word of the Lord!

Certain of these backsliding Israelites went so far as to oppose the testimony of God. Note in the eighth verse—"Even of late My people have risen up as an enemy." It is sad when God's own people become the enemies of God's own Spirit, yet those who professed to be of the House of Jacob, instead of listening to the voice of the living God, began to sit in judgment upon His Word and even to contradict the same! The worst foes of the Truth of God are not infidels, but false professors! These men called themselves God's people and yet fought against His Spirit. "What then," asks Micah, "is the Spirit of the Lord straitened?" Will the Spirit of God fail? Will His operations on the hearts of men come to nothing? Will the Truth of God be put to shame and have no influence over human minds? Shall the Gospel be driven out of the world? Will there be none to believe it? None to proclaim it? None to live for it? None to die for it? We ask, with scorn, "Is the Spirit of the Lord straitened?"

Brothers and Sisters, my confidence in the success of the old faith is not lessened because so many forsake it! "For all flesh is as grass, and all the glory of man as the flower of grass. The grass withers and the flower thereof falls away: but the Word of the Lord endures forever. And this is the Word which, by the Gospel, is preached to you." If all the confessors of the faith could be martyred—even from their ashes, like a heavenly phoenix—the Truth of God would rise again! The Spirit of the Lord lives and, therefore, the Truth of God must also live. Is not all Truth of God immortal? How much more that which is the shrine of God! The Spirit's witness concerning the sin of man, the Grace of God, the mission of Jesus, the power of His blood, the glory of His Resurrection, reign and advent—this witness, I say, cannot cease or fail! It is to be greatly lamented that so many have turned aside unto vanities and are now the enemies of the Cross, but fear not, for the victory is in sure hands! O you that would control the Spirit of God, remember who He is and bite your lips in despair! What can you do against Him? Go bit the tempest and bridle the north wind—and then dream that the Spirit of the Lord is to be straitened by you! He will speak when He pleases, by whom He pleases and as He pleases—and His Word shall be with power! None can stay His hand, nor say unto Him, "What are You doing?" Thus much upon the first use of our text.

II. The second use of it is this, TO SILENCE THOSE WHO WOULD CENSURE THE SPIRIT. Some even dare to bring accusations against the Holy Spirit of God! Read the text again—"O you that are named the House of Jacob, is the Spirit of the Lord straitened? Are these His doings?" If anything is amiss, is He to be blamed for it?

The low estate of the Church—is that to be laid at God's door? It is true that the Church is not so full of life and energy and power and spirituality and holiness as she was in her first days and, therefore, some insinuate that the Gospel is an antique and an effete thing—in other words, that the Spirit of God is not so mighty as in past ages. To which the answer is, "Is the Spirit of the Lord straitened? Are these His doings?" If we are lukewarm, is that the fault of the Spirit of Fire? If we are feeble in our testimony, is that the fault of the Spirit of Power? If we are weak in prayer, is that the fault of the Spirit who helps our infirmities? Are these His doings? Instead of blaming the Holy Spirit, would it not be better for us to smite upon our breasts and chasten our hearts? What if the Church is not "fair as the moon, clear as the sun, and terrible as an army with banners," as once she was? Is not this because the Gospel has not been fully and faithfully preached and because those who believe it have not lived up to it with the earnestness and holiness which they ought to have exhibited? Is not that the reason? In any case, are these His doings? Can you lay the blame of defection and backsliding, of lack of strength, of lack of faith—at the door of the Holy Spirit? God forbid! We cannot blame the Holy One of Israel!

Then it is said, "Look at the condition of the world. After the Gospel has been in it nearly 2,000 years, see how small a part of it is enlightened, how many cling to their idols, how much of vice, error, poverty and misery are to be found in the world!" We know all these sad facts, but are these His doings? Tell me, when has the Holy Spirit created darkness or sin? Where has He been the Author of vice or oppression? From where come wars and strife? Come they from Him? Come they not from our own lusts? What if the world is still an Augean stable, greatly needing cleansing—has the Spirit of God in any degree or sense rendered it so? Where the Gospel has been fully preached, have not the Words of the Lord done good to them that walk uprightly? Have not cannibals, even during the last few years, been reclaimed and civilized? Has not the slave trade and other evils been ended by the power of Christian influence? How, then, can the Spirit of Christ, the spirit of the Gospel, be blamed?

Will you attribute the darkness to the sun? Will you charge the filthiness of swine to the account of the crystal stream? Will you blame the pest upon the fresh breeze from the sea? It were quite as just and quite as sensible. No, we admit the darkness and the sin and the misery of men. Oh, that our head were waters and our eyes a fountain of tears that we might weep day and night concerning these things! But these are not the work of the Spirit of God! These come of the spirit from beneath. He that is from above would heal them. He is not straitened. These are not His doings. Where His Gospel has been preached and men have believed it and lived according to it, they have been enlightened, sanctified and blessed. Life and love, light and liberty and all other good things come of the Spirit of the Lord—

"Blessings abound wherever He reigns;
The prisoner leaps to lose his chains,
The weary find eternal rest,
And all the sons of need are blessed."

But some have said, "Yes, but then see how few the conversions are nowadays! We have many places of worship badly attended. We have others where there are scarcely any conversions from the beginning of the year to the end of it." This is find some other reason far more near the truth? O Sirs, if there are no conversions, we cannot fall back upon the Spirit of God and blame Him! Has Christ been preached? Has faith been exercised? The preacher must take his share of blame; the Church with which he is connected must also inquire whether there has been that measure of prayer for a blessing on the Word that there ought to have been. Christians must begin to look into their own hearts to find the reason for defeat. If the work of God is hindered in our midst, may there not be some secret sin with us which hinders the operation of the Spirit of God? May He not be compelled, by the very holiness of His Character, to refuse to work with an unholy or an unbelieving people? Have you never read, "He did not many mighty works there because of their unbelief"? May not unbelief be turning a fruitful land into barrenness? The Spirit Himself is not straitened in His power—but our sin has made Him hide Himself from us! The lack of conversions is not His doing—we have not gone forth in His strength. We shake off with detestation the least trace of a thought that should lay any blame to the Spirit of the Most High. Unto us be shame and confusion of face as at this day!

But it is also said that there is a lack of power largely manifested by individual saints. Where are now the men who can go up to the top of Carmel and cover the heavens with clouds? Where are the apostolic men who convert nations? Where are the heroes and martyr spirits of the better days? Have we not fallen upon an age of little men who little dare and little do? It may be so, but this is no fault of the great Spirit! Our degeneracy is not His doing. We have destroyed ourselves and only in Him is our help found! Instead of crying today, "Awake, awake, O arm of the Lord," we ought to listen to the cry from Heaven which says, "Awake, awake, O Zion! Shake yourself from the dust, and put on your beautiful garments." Many of us might have done great exploits if we had but given our hearts to it. The weakest of us might have rivaled David and the strongest among us might have been as angels of God! We are straitened in ourselves—we have not reached out to the possibilities of strength which lie within our grasp. Let us not wickedly insinuate a charge against the good Spirit of our God, but let us in truthful humility blame ourselves.

If we have not lived in the Light of God, can we marvel that we are in great part, dark? If we have not fed upon the Bread of Heaven, can we wonder that we are faint? Let us return unto the Lord! Let us seek again to be baptized into the Holy Spirit and into fire—and we shall yet again behold the wonderful works of the Lord! He sets before us an open door, but if we enter not, we are, ourselves, to blame. He gives liberally and upbraids not, but if we are still impoverished, we have not because we ask not, or because we ask amiss! Thus much, then, have I spoken, using the text to silence those who would censure the Spirit of God.

III. In the third place, our subject enters a more pleasing phase while I use it TO ENCOURAGE THOSE WHO TRUST IN THE SPIRIT OF THE LORD. My Brothers and Sisters, let us this morning with joy remember that the Spirit of the Lord is not straitened!

Let this meet our trouble about our own straitness. What narrow and shallow vessels we are! How soon we are empty! We wake up on Sunday morning and wonder where we shall find strength for the day. Do you not sigh, "Alas, I cannot take my Sunday school class today with any hope of teaching with power! I am so dreadfully dull and heavy. I feel stupid and devoid of thought and feeling"? In such a case, say to yourself, "Is the Spirit of the Lord straitened?" He will help you. You purpose to speak to someone about his soul and you fear that the right words will not come? You forget that He has promised to give you what you shall speak. "Is the Spirit of the Lord straitened?" Cannot He prepare your heart and tongue?

As a minister of Christ I have constantly to feel my own straitness. Perhaps more than any other man I am faced by my own inefficiency and inability to address such an audience so often and to print all that is spoken. Who is sufficient for these things? I do not feel half as capable of addressing you now as I did 20 years ago. I sink as to conscious personal power, though I have a firmer faith than ever in the all-sufficiency of God. No, the Spirit of the Lord is not straitened! That promise is still our delight–"My Grace is sufficient for you." It is a joy to become weak that we may say with the Apostle, "When I am weak then am I strong." Behold, the strength of the Lord is gloriously revealed– revealed to perfection in our weakness! Come, you feeble workers, you fainting laborers, come and rejoice in the unstraitened Spirit! Come, you that seem to plow the rock and till the sand, come and lay hold of this fact that the Spirit of the Lord is Omnipotent! No rock will remain unbroken when He wields the hammer! No metal will be unmelted when He is the fire! Still will our Lord put His Spirit within us and gird us with His power, according to His promise, "As your days, so shall your strength be."

This also meets another matter, namely, the lack of honored leaders. We cry at this time, "Where are the eminent teachers of years gone by?" The Lord has made a man more precious than the gold of Ophir. Good and great men were the pillars of the Church in former times, but where are they now? Renowned ministers have died and where are their successors? It is not an infrequent thing with the older Brothers and Sisters, for them to say, one to the other, "Do you see the young men springing up who will equal those whom we have lost?" I am not among those who despair for the good old cause, but certainly I would be glad to see the Elishas who are to succeed the Elijahs who have gone up! Oh, for another Calvin or Luther! Oh, for a Knox or a Latimer, a Whitefield or a Wesley! Our fathers told us of Romaine and Newton, Toplady and Rowland Hill–where are the like of these? When we have said, "where?" echo has answered, "where?" But herein is our hope–the Spirit of the Lord is not straitened! He can raise up standard-bearers for His hosts! He can give to His Church stars in her firmament as bright as any that ever gladdened our fathers' eyes! He that walks among the golden candlesticks can so trim the lamps that those which are dim shall burn with sevenfold splendor! He who found a Moses to face Pharaoh and Elijah to face Jezebel, can find a man to confront the adversaries today! To equip an army of apostolic men would be a small matter to the Creator of Heaven and earth! Let us have no fear about this. He that ascended on high, leading captivity captive, gave such large gifts unto men that unto the end of the dispensation they will not be exhausted! Still does He give evangelists, pastors and teachers according as the need of the Church may be. Let us cast away all fear as to a break in the succession of witnesses, for the Word of the Lord endures forever and it shall never lack a man to declare it!

Brethren, the great Truth of God now before us may prevent our being dismayed by the peculiar character of the age in which we live. It is full of a terrible unrest. The earthquake in the Riviera is only typical of a far greater disturbance which is going on everywhere. The foundations of society are quivering. The cornerstones are starting. No man can foretell what the close of this century may see. The age is growing more and more irreverent, unbelieving, indifferent. The men of this generation are even more greedy of gain, more in haste after their ambitions than those that preceded them. They are fickle, exacting, hungering after excitement and sensation. Here comes in the Truth of God—"The Spirit of the Lord is not straitened." Was not the Gospel intended for every age and for every condition of human society? Will it not meet the case of London and Ireland as well as the case of the old Roman empire in the midst of which it first began its course? It is even so, O Lord! Our fathers trusted in You; they trusted in You and You did deliver them! And we with joyful confidence fall back upon the same delivering power, saying in our hearts, "The Spirit of the Lord is not straitened, He will bear us through!"

But, then, sometimes we are troubled because of the hardness of men's hearts. You that work for the Lord know most about this. If anybody thinks that he can change a heart by his own power, let him try with anyone he pleases and he will soon be at a nonplus. Old Adam is too strong for young Melancthon—our trembling arm cannot roll away the stone of natural depravity! Well, what then? The Spirit of the Lord is not straitened! Did I hear you cry, "Alas, I have tried to reclaim a drunk and he has gone back to his degradation"? Yes, he has beaten you, but is the Spirit of the Lord straitened? Do you cry, "But he signed the pledge and yet he broke it"? Very likely your bonds are broken, but is the Spirit of the Lord straitened? Cannot He renew the heart and cast out the love of sin? When the Spirit of God works with your persuasions, your convert will keep his pledge.

"Alas!" cries another, "I hoped I had rescued a fallen woman, but she has returned to her iniquity." No unusual thing is this with those who exercise themselves in that form of service. But is the Spirit of the Lord straitened? Cannot He save the woman that was a sinner? Cannot He create a surpassing love to Jesus in her forgiven spirit? We are baffled, but the Spirit is not! "But it is my own boy," cries a mother. "Alas, I brought him up tenderly from his youth, but he has gone astray. I cannot persuade him to hear the Word of God—I cannot do anything with him!" Dear mother, register that confession of inability and then, by faith, write at the bottom of it, "But the Spirit of the Lord is not straitened." Have faith in God and never let your discovery of your own weakness shake your firm conviction that with God all things are possible! It seems to me to be a fountain of comfort, a storehouse of strength. Do not limit the Holy One of Israel, nor conceive of the Holy Spirit as bound and checked by the difficulties which crop up in fallen human nature! No case which you bring to Him with affectionate tears and with an earnest faith in Jesus shall ever be dismissed as incurable. Despair of no man since the Lord of Hosts is with us!

"Ah well," says one, "but I am oppressed with the great problem which lies before the Church. London is to be rescued, the world is to be enlightened. Think of India, China and the vast multitudes of Africa. Is the Gospel to be preached to all these? Are the kingdoms of this world to become the Kingdoms of our Lord? How can these things be! Why, Sirs, when I think of London, alone, a world of poverty and misery, I see the sheer impossibility of delivering this world from the power of darkness." Do you prefer a theory which holds out no hope of a converted world? I do not wonder! Judge after the sight of the eyes and the hearing of the ears and the thing is quite beyond all hope. But is the Spirit of the Lord straitened? Surely the good Lord means to convince the Church of her own powerlessness, that she may cast herself upon the Divine might! Looking around she can see no help for her in her great enterprise—let her look up and watch for His coming who will bring her deliverance! Amid apparent helplessness the Church is rich in secret succors. If the Spirit of God shall anoint our eyes, we shall see the mountain full of horses of fire and chariots of fire round about the servants of the Lord. Behold, the stars in their courses fight against our adversaries! The earth shall yet help the woman and the abundance of the seas shall yield their strength unto God. When the time comes for the Lord to make bare His arm, we shall see greater things than these–and then we shall wrap our faces in a veil of blushing confusion to think that we ever doubted the Most High! Behold, the Son of Man comes! Shall He find faith among us? Shall He find it anywhere on the earth? The Lord help us to feel in our darkest hour that His arm is not shortened!

IV. I must close by remarking that this text may be used TO DIRECT THOSE WHO ARE SEEKING AFTER BETTER THINGS. I hope that in this audience there are many who are desiring to be at peace with God through Jesus Christ. You are already convinced of sin, but you are, by that conviction, driven to despondency and almost to despair. Now notice this–whatever Grace you need in order to salvation, the Holy Spirit can work it in you. You need a more tender sense of sin. Is the Spirit of the Lord straitened? Can He not give it to you? You need to be able to perceive the way of salvation–can He not instruct you? You need to be able to take the first step to Christ–you need, in fact, to trust Him wholly and alone and so find peace in Him. Is the Spirit of the Lord straitened? Can He not give you faith? Do you cry, "I would believe, but I cannot tell how"? The Spirit will help you to believe! He can shed such light into your mind that faith in Christ shall become an easy and a simple thing with you. The Spirit of God is not straitened! He can bring you out of darkness into His marvelous light! If you are quite driven from all reliance on your own natural power, then cry unto Him, "Lord, help me!" The Holy Spirit has come on purpose to work all our works in us. It is His office to take of the things of Christ and to show them to us. Yield yourself to His gracious direction! Be willing and obedient–and He will lead you into all Truth!

Notice again–although you are under deep depression of spirit and you feel shut up so that you cannot come forth–yet the Spirit of the Lord is not straitened. He is not weighed down nor discouraged. His name is The Comforter and He can comfort to purpose. Though you are, today, ready to lay violent hands upon yourself by reason of the trouble of your restless thoughts, yet is the Spirit of the Lord straitened? Look to the strong for strength, even to your God. Does not the Lord cry to you, "Look unto Me and be you saved, all you ends of the earth; for I am God, and there is none else"? Your strength as well as your salvation lies in Him! When we were yet without strength, in due time Christ died for the ungodly. Trust in the Lord forever, for in the Lord Jehovah there is everlasting strength. Trust, implicitly trust, for the

Spirit of God is not straitened! Your despondency and unbelief are not His doings, they are your own. He has not driven you into this misery. He invites you to come forth from it and trust the Son of God—and rest in the finished righteousness of Christ—and you shall come at once into light and peace!

May I invite you to remember how many persons have already found joy, peace and salvation by believing the teaching of the Spirit of God? In the text the question is asked, "Do not My Words do good to him that walks uprightly?" Many of us can bear testimony today that the Word of the Lord is not word only, but power! It has done good to us. The Gospel has not only been much to us, it has been everything to us. Personally, I do not believe and preach the Gospel because I have made a choice and have preferred it to any other theory of religion out of many others which might have been accepted. No. There is no other Truth to me! I believe it because I am a saved man by the power of it! The Truths of God revealed by the Spirit has new-created me! I am born again by this living and incorruptible Seed. My only hope of holiness in this life and of happiness in the life to come is found in the life and death, the Person and merit of the Lord Jesus Christ, the Son of God!

Give up the Gospel? I may when it gives me up, but not while it grasps my very soul! I am not perplexed with doubt, because the Truth of God which I believe has worked a miracle in me. By its means I have received and still retain a new life to which I was once a stranger. I am like the good man and his wife who had kept a lighthouse for years. A visitor who came to see the lighthouse, looking out from the window over the waste of waters, asked the good woman, "Are you not afraid of a night when the storm is out and the big waves dash right over the lantern? Do you not fear that the lighthouse and all that is in it will be carried away?" The woman remarked that the idea never occurred to her. She had lived there so long that she felt as safe on the lone rock as ever she did when she lived on the mainland. As for her husband, when asked if he did not feel anxious when the wind blew a hurricane, he answered, "Yes, I feel anxious to keep the lamps well trimmed and the light burning, lest any vessel should be wrecked." As to anxiety about the safety of the lighthouse, or his own personal security in it, he had outlived all that.

Even so it is with me! "I know whom I have believed, and am persuaded that He is able to keep that which I have committed to Him against that day." From henceforth let no man trouble me with doubts and questionings! I bear in my soul the proofs of the Spirit's truth and power and I will have none of your artful reasoning. The Gospel to me is TRUTH–I am content to perish if it is not true. I risk my soul's eternal fate upon the truth of the Gospel and I know no risk in it. My one concern is to keep the lamps burning, that I may thereby enlighten others. Only let the Lord give me oil enough to feed my lamp so that I may cast a ray across the dark and treacherous sea of life, and I am well content. Now, troubled Seeker, if it is so, that your minister and many others in whom you confide have found perfect peace and rest in the Gospel, why should not you? Is the Spirit of the Lord straitened? Do not His Words do good to them that walk uprightly? Will not you also try their saving virtue?

In conclusion, just a hint to you. The Words of God do good to those who walk uprightly. If they do no good to you, may it not be that you are walking crookedly? Have you given up all secret sin? How can you hope to get peace with God if you live according to your own lusts? Give up the hopeless hope! You must come right out from the love of sin if you would be delivered from the guilt of sin. You cannot have your sin and go to Heaven–you must either give up sin or give up hope. "Repent" is a constant exhortation of the Word of God. Quit the sin which you confess. Flee the evil which crucified your Lord! Sin forsaken is, through the blood of Jesus, turned into sin forgiven! If you cannot find freedom in the Lord, the straitness is not with the Spirit of God, but your sin lies at the door blocking up the gangway of Grace. Is the Spirit of God straitened? No, His Words "do good to them that walk uprightly." And if you, in sincerity of heart, will quit your sin and believe in Christ, you, also, shall find peace, hope and rest. Try it and see if it is not so. Amen.

THE HOLY SPIRIT—THE GREAT TEACHER

"Howbeit when He, the Spirit of Truth, is come, He will guide you into all Truth: for He shall not speak of Himself; but whatever He shall hear, that shall He speak: and He will show you things to come."
John 16:13

A Sermon Delivered On Sunday Morning: 18 November 1855

THIS generation has gradually, and almost imperceptibly, become to a great extent a godless generation. One of the diseases of the present generation of mankind is their secret but deep-seated godlessness by which they have so far departed from the knowledge of God. Science has discovered to us second causes. And hence, many have too much forgotten the first Great Cause, the Author of all—they have been able so far to pry into secrets that the great axiom of the existence of a God has been too much neglected. Even among professing Christians, while there is a great amount of religion, there is too little godliness—there is much external formalism but too little inward acknowledgment of God. Too little living on God, living with God and relying upon God.

Hence arises the sad fact that when you enter many of our places of worship you will certainly hear the name of God mentioned—but except in the benediction, you would scarcely know there was a Trinity. In many places dedicated to Jehovah the name of Jesus is too often kept in the background. The Holy Spirit is almost entirely neglected. And very little is said concerning His sacred influence. Even religious men have become to a large degree godless in this age. We sadly require more preaching regarding God—more preaching of those things which look not so much at the creature to be saved, as at God the Great One to be extolled.

My firm conviction is that in proportion as we have more regard for the sacred godhead, the wondrous Trinity in Unity, shall we see a greater display of God's power and a more glorious manifestation of His might in our churches. May God send us a Christ-exalting, Spirit-loving ministry—men who shall proclaim God the Holy Spirit in all His offices and shall extol God the Savior as the Author and Finisher of our faith. Men who shall not neglect that Great God, the Father of His people, who, before all worlds, elected us in Christ His Son, justified us through His righteousness, and will inevitably preserve us and gather us together in one, in the consummation of all things at the last great day.

Our text has regard to God the Holy Spirit. Of Him we shall speak and Him only, if His sweet influence shall rest upon us.

The disciples had been instructed by Christ concerning certain elementary doctrines but Jesus did not teach His disciples more than what we should call the A B Cs of religion. He gives His reasons for this in the 12th verse—"I have yet many things to say unto you, but you cannot bear them now." His disciples were not possessors of the Spirit. They had the Spirit so far as the work of conversion was concerned, but not as to the matters of bright illumination, profound instruction, prophecy and inspiration. Jesus says, "I am now about to depart and when I go from you I will send the Comforter unto you. You cannot bear these things now. Howbeit, when He, the Spirit of Truth is come, He will guide you into all Truth."

The same promise that He made to His Apostles stands good to all His children. And in reviewing it, we shall take it as our portion and heritage and shall not consider ourselves intruders upon the manor of the Apostles, or upon their exclusive rights and prerogatives. For we conceive that Jesus says even to us, "When He, the Spirit of Truth is come, He will guide you into all Truth."

Dwelling exclusively upon our text, we have five things to say. First of all, here is an attainment mentioned—a knowledge of all Truth. Secondly, here is a difficulty suggested, a Person provided a manner hinted at—we may know whether He works, by His "guiding us into all.

Here is AN ATTAINMENT MENTIONED, which is a knowledge of all Truth. We know that some conceive doctrinal knowledge to be of very little importance and of no practical use. We do not think so. We believe the science of Christ crucified not only be arousing but instructing. Not merely awakening, but enlightening—that it should appeal not only to the passions but to the understanding We are far from thinking doctrinal knowledge to be of secondary importance. We believe it to be one of the first things in the Christian life, to know the Truth and then to practice it. We scarcely need this morning tell you how desirable it is for us to be well taught in things of the kingdom.

First of all, nature itself. The natural man separates himself and inter meddles with all knowledge. God has put an instinct in him by which he is rendered unsatisfied if he cannot probe mystery to its bottom. He can never be content until he can solve secrets. What we call curiosity is something given us of God impelling us to search into the knowledge of natural things. That curiosity, sanctified by the Spirit, is also brought to bear in matters of heavenly science and celestial wisdom. "Bless the Lord," said David, "O my soul, and all that is within me bless His holy name!"

If there is a curiosity within us, it ought to be employed and developed in a search after Truth. "All that is within me," sanctified by the Spirit should be developed, And, verily, the Christian man feels an intense longing to bury his ignorance and receive wisdom. If he, when in his natural estate panted for terrestrial knowledge, how much more ardent is the wish to unravel, if possible, the sacred mysteries of God's Word? A true Christian is always intently reading and searching the Scripture that he may be able to certify himself as to its main and cardinal truths.

I do not think much of that man who does not wish to understand doctrines. I cannot conceive him to be in a right position when he thinks it is no matter whether he believes a lie or truth, whether he is heretic or orthodox, whether he received the Word of God as it is written, or as it is diluted and misconstrued by man. God's Word will ever be to a Christian a source of great anxiety. A sacred instinct within will lead him to pry into it. He will seek to understand it. Oh! there are some who forget this, men who purposely abstain from mentioning what are called high doctrines because they think if they should mention high doctrines they would be dangerous. So they keep them back.

Foolish men! They do not know anything of human nature. For if they did understand a grain's worth of humanity, they would know that the hiding of these things impels men to search them out. From the fact that they do not mention them, they drive men to places where these and these only, are preached. They say, "If I preach election and predestination and these dark things, people will all go straight away, and become Antinomians." I am not so sure if they were to be called Antinomians it would hurt them much–but hear me, oh, you ministers that conceal these Truths–that is the way to make them Antinomians, by silencing these doctrines.

338

Curiosity is strong–if you tell them they must not pluck the Truth, they will be sure to do it. But if you give it to them as you find it in God's Word, they will not seek to "wrest" it. Enlightened men will have the Truth and if they see election inScripture they will say, " it is there, and I will find it out. If I cannot get it in one place, I will get it in another." The trueChristian has an inward longing and anxiety after it. He is hungry and thirsty after the Word of Righteousness and he must and will feed on this Bread of Heaven, or at all hazards he will leave the husks which unsound divines would offer him.

Not only is this attainment to be desired because nature teaches us so, but a knowledge of all Truth is very essential for our comfort. I do believe that many persons have been distressed half their lives from the fact that they had not clear views of Truth. Many poor souls, for instance, under conviction, abide three or four times as long in sorrow of mind as they would require to do if they had someone to instruct them in the great matter of justification.

So there are believers who are often troubling themselves about falling away. But if they knew in their soul the great consolation that we are kept by the grace of God through faith unto salvation, they would be no more troubled about it. So have I found some distressed about the unpardonable sin. But God instructs us in that doctrine and shows us that no conscience that is really awakened ever can commit that sin. He shows us that we need never fear or tremble–all that distress is for nothing. Depend on this, the more you know of God's Truth–all things else being equal–the more comfortable you will be as a Christian.

Nothing can give a greater light on your path than a clear understanding of divine things. It is a mingle-mangled Gospel too commonly preached which causes the downcast faces of Christians. Give me the congregation whose faces are bright with joy, let their eyes glisten at the sound of the Gospel, then will I believe that it is God's own Words they are receiving. Instead thereof you will often see melancholy congregations whose visages are not much different from the bitter countenance of poor creatures swallowing medicine because the Word spoken terrifies them by its legality, instead of comforting them by its grace. We love a cheerful Gospel and we think "all the Truth" will tend to comfort the Christian.

"Comfort again?" says another, "always comfort." Ah, but there is another reason why we prize Truth–because we believe that a true knowledge of all the Truth will keep us very much out of danger. No doctrine is so calculated to preserve a man from sin as the doctrine of the grace of God. Those who have called it a licentious doctrine did not know anything at all about it. Poor ignorant things, they little knew that their own vile stuff was the most licentious doctrine under Heaven. If they knew the grace of God in Truth, they would soon see that there was no preservative from lying like a knowledge that we are elect of God from the foundation of the world.

There is nothing like a belief in my eternal perseverance and the immutability of my Father's affection which can keep me near to Him from a motive of simple gratitude. Nothing makes a man so virtuous as belief of Truth. A lying doctrine will soon beget a lying practice. A man cannot have an erroneous belief without by-and-bye having an erroneous life. I believe the one thing naturally begets the other. Keep near God's Truth. Keep near His Word–keep the head right and especially keep your heart right with regard to Truth–and your feet will not go far astray.

Again–I hold also that this attainment to the knowledge of all Truth is very desirable for the usefulness which it will give us in the world at large. We should not be selfish–we should always consider whether a thing will be beneficial to others. A knowledge of all Truth will make us very serviceable in this world. We shall be skillful physicians who know how to take the poor distressed soul aside, to put the finger on his eye and take the scale off for him–that Heaven's light may comfort him. There will be no character, however perplexing may be its peculiar phase, but we shall be able to speak to it and comfort it. He who holds the Truth is usually the most useful man.

As a good Presbyterian brother said to me the other day–"I know God has blessed you exceedingly in gathering in souls but it is an extraordinary fact that nearly all the men I know–with scarcely an exception–who have been made useful in gathering in souls, have held the great doctrines of the grace of God." Almost every man whom God has blessed to the building up of the church in prosperity and around whom the people have rallied, has been a man who has held firmly to free grace from first to last, through the finished salvation of Christ. Do not you think you need have errors in your doctrine to make you useful? We have some who preach Calvinism all the first part of the sermon and finish up with Arminianism, because they think that will make them useful.

Useful? Nonsense!—That is all it is. A man, if he cannot be useful with the Truth, cannot be useful with an error. There is enough in the pure doctrine of God without introducing heresies to preach to sinners. As far as I know, I never felt hampered or cramped in addressing the ungodly in my life. I can speak with as much fervency and yet not in the same style as those who hold the contrary views of God's Truth. Those who hold God's Word, never need add something untrue in speaking to men. The sturdy Truth of God touches every chord in every man's heart. If we can, by God's grace, put our hand inside a man's heart, we want nothing but that whole Truth to move him thoroughly and to stir him up. There is nothing like the real Truth and the whole Truth, to make a man useful.

II. Now, again—here is a DIFFICULTY SUGGESTED, and that is that we require a Guide to conduct us into all Truth. The difficulty is that Truth is not so easy to discover. There is no man born in this world by nature who has the Truth in his heart. There is no creature that ever was fashioned, since the Fall, who has a knowledge of Truth innate and natural. It has been disputed by many philosophers whether there are such things as innate ideas at all. But it is of no use disputing as to whether there are any innate ideas of Truth. There are none such. There are ideas of everything that is wrong and evil. But in us— that is, our flesh—there dwells no good thing.

We are born in sin and shapened in iniquity. In sin did our mother conceive us. There is nothing in us good and no tendency to righteousness. Then since we are not born with the Truth, we have the task of searching for it. If we are to be blest by being eminently useful as Christian men, we must be well instructed in matters of Revelation. But here is the difficulty—that we cannot follow without a Guide the winding paths of Truth. Why is this?

First, because of the very great intricacy of Truth itself—Truth itself is no easy thing to discover. Those who fancy they know everything and constantly dogmatize with the spirit of, "We are the men, and wisdom will die with us," of course see no difficulties whatever in the system they hold. But I believe the most earnest student of Scripture will find things in the Bible which puzzle him. However earnestly he reads it, he will see some mysteries too deep for him to understand. He will cry out, "Truth! I cannot find you. I know not where you are, you are beyond me. I cannot fully view you." Truth is a path so narrow that two can scarce walk together in it. We usually tread the narrow way in single file, two men can seldom walk arm in arm in the Truth.

We believe the same Truth in the main but we cannot walk together in the path, it is too narrow. The way of Truth is very difficult. If you step an inch aside on the right you are in a dangerous error. If you swerve a little to the left you are equally in the mire. On the one hand there is a huge precipice and on the other a deep morass. Unless you keep to the true line, to the breadth of a hair, you will go astray. Truth is a narrow path indeed. It is a path the eagle's eye has not seen and a depth the diver has not visited.

It is like the veins of metal in a mine, it is often of excessive thinness and moreover it runs not in one continued layer. Lose it once and you may dig for miles and not discover it again. The eye must watch perpetually the direction of the lode. Grains of Truth are like the grains of gold in the rivers of Australia– they must be shaken by the hand of patience and washed in the stream of honesty, or the fine gold will be mingled with sand. Truth is often mingled with error and it is hard to distinguish it. But we bless God it is said, "When the Spirit of Truth is come, He will guide you into all Truth"

Another reason why we need a guide is the invidiousness of error. It busily steals upon us and, if I may so describe our position, we are often like we were on Thursday night in that tremendous fog. Most of us were feeling for ourselves and wondering where on earth we were. We could scarcely see an inch before us. We came to a place where there were three turnings. We thought we knew the old spot. There was the lamp-post and now we must take a sharp turn to the left. But not so. We ought to have gone a little to the right. We have been so often to the same place that we think we know every flag-stone and there's our friend's shop over the way.

It is dark, but we think we must be quite right and all the while we are quite wrong and find ourselves half-a-mile out of the way. So it is with matters of Truth. We think, surely this is the right path. And the voice of the Evil One whispers, "That is the way, walk in it." You do so and you find to your great dismay that instead of the path of Truth, you have been walking in the paths of unrighteousness and erroneous doctrines. The way of life is a labyrinth. The grassiest paths and the most bewitching are the farthest away from right. The most enticing are those which are garnished with wrested Truths. I believe there is not a counterfeit coin in the world so much like a genuine one, as some errors are like the Truth. One is base metal, the other is true gold. Still in externals they differ very little.

We also need a Guide, because we are so prone to go astray. Why, if the path of Heaven were as straight as Bunyan pictures it, with no turning to the right hand or left–and no doubt it is–still, we are so prone to go astray that we should go to the right to the Mountains of Destruction, or to the left in the dark Wood of Desolation. David says, "I have gone astray like a lost sheep." That means very often–for if a sheep is put into a field twenty times, if it does not get out twenty-one times, it will be because it cannot find a hole in the hedge. If grace did not guide a man, he would go astray though there were hand-posts all the way to Heaven.

Let it be written, "Miklat, Miklat, the way to refuge," he would turn aside and the avenger of blood would overtake him. If some guide did not, like the angels in Sodom, put his hand on his shoulders and cry, "Escape, escape for your life! Look not behind you! Stay not in all the plain." These, then, are the reasons why we need a Guide.

III. In the third place, here is A PERSON PROVIDED. This is none other than God and this God is none other than a Person. This Person is "He, the Spirit," the "Spirit of Truth." Not an influence or an emanation but actually a Person. "When the Spirit of Truth is come, He shall guide you into all Truth." Now, we wish you to look at this Guide to consider how adapted He is to us.

In the first place, He is infallible. He knows everything and cannot lead us astray. If I pin my sleeve to another man's coat,he may lead me part of the way rightly, but by-and-bye he will go wrong himself and I shall be led astray with him. But if I give myself to the Holy Spirit and ask His guidance, there is no fear of my wandering.

Again–we rejoice in this Spirit because He is ever-present. We fall into a difficulty sometimes. We say, "Oh, if I could take this to my minister, he would explain it. But I live so far off and am not able to see him." That perplexes us and we turn the text round and round and cannot make anything out of it. We look at the commentators. We take down pious Thomas Scott and, as usual he says nothing about it if it is a dark passage. Then we go to holy Matthew Henry and if it is an easy Scripture, he is sure to explain it. But if it is a text hard to be understood, it is likely enough, of course, left in its own gloom. And even Dr. Gill himself, the most consistent of commentators, when he comes to a hard passage manifestly avoids it in some degree.

But when we have no commentator or minister, we have still the Holy Spirit. And let me tell you a little secret—whenever you cannot understand a text, open your Bible, bend your knee and pray over that text. And if it does not split into atoms and open itself, try again. If prayer does not explain it, it is one of the things God did not intend you to know and you may be content to be ignorant of it. Prayer is the key that opens the cabinets of mystery. Prayer and faith are sacred picklocks that can open secrets and obtain great treasures. There is no college for holy education like that of the blessed Spirit, for He is an ever present Tutor to whom we have only to bend the knee, and He is at our side, the great Expositor of Truth.

But there is one thing about the suitability of this Guide which is remarkable. I do not know whether it has struck you—the Holy Spirit can "guide us into a Truth but it is only the Holy Spirit who can "guide us into mark that word—"all Truth." Now, for instance, it is a long while before you can lead some people to election. But when you have made them see its correctness, you have not led them "into" it. You may show them that it is plainly stated in Scripture but they will turn away and hate it.

You take them to another great Truth but they have been brought up in a different fashion and though they cannot answer your arguments, they say, "The man is right, perhaps," and they whisper—but so low that conscience itself cannot hear—"but it is so contrary to my prejudices, that I cannot receive it." After you have led them to the Truth and they see it is true, how hard it is to lead them into the Truth of their depravity but they are not brought into it and made to feel it. Some of you are brought to know the Truth that God keeps us from day today. But you rarely get into it, so as to live in continual dependence upon God the Holy Spirit and draw fresh supplies from Him.

The thing is to get inside it. A Christian should do with Truth as a snail does with his shell—live inside it, as well as carry it on his back and bear it perpetually about with him. The Holy Spirit, it is said, shall lead us into all Truth. You may be brought to a chamber where there is an abundance of gold and silver but you will be no richer unless you effect an entrance. It is the Spirit's work to unbar the two-leaved gates and bring us into a Truth, so that we may get inside it and, as dear old Rowland Hill said, "Not only hold the Truth, but have the Truth hold us."

IV. Fourthly, here is METHOD SUGGESTED–"He shall guide you into all Truth." Now I must have an illustration. I must compare Truth to some cave or grotto that you have heard of, with wondrous stalactites hanging from the roof and others starting from the floor. A cavern, glittering with spar and abounding in marvels. Before entering the cavern you inquire for a guide, who comes with his lighted flambeau. He conducts you down to a considerable depth and you find yourself in the midst of the cave. He leads you through different chambers. Here he points to a little stream rushing from amid the rocks and indicates its rise and progress.

There he points to some peculiar rock and tells you its name. Then he takes you into a large natural hall, tells you how many persons once feasted in it, and so on. Truth is a grand series of caverns. It is our glory to have so great and wise a Conductor. Imagine that we are coming to the darkness of it. He is a light shining in the midst of us to guide us. And by the light He shows us wondrous things. In three ways the Holy Spirit teaches us–by suggestion, direction, and illumination.

First, he guides us into all Truth by suggesting it. There are thoughts that dwell in our minds that were not born there but which were exotics brought from Heaven and put there by the Spirit. It is not a fancy that angels whisper into our ears and that devils do the same–both good and evil spirits hold converse with men. And some of us have known it. We have had strange thoughts which were not the offspring of our souls but which came from angelic visitors. And direct temptations and evil insinuations have we had which were not brewed in our own souls but which came from the pestilential cauldron of Hell.

So the Spirit does speak in men's ears, sometimes in the darkness of the night. In ages gone by He spoke in dreams and visions but now He speaks by His Word. Have you not at times had unaccountably in the middle of your business a thought concerning God and heavenly things and could not tell from where it came? Have you not been reading or studying the Scripture but a text came across your mind and you could not help it? Though you even put it down, it was like cork in water and would swim up again to the top of your mind. Well, that good thought was put there by the Spirit.

He often guides His people into all Truth by suggesting, just as the guide in the grotto does with his flambeau. He does not say a word, perhaps, but He walks into a passage Himself and you follow Him. So the Spirit suggests a thought and your heart follows it up. Well can I remember the manner in which I learned the doctrines of grace in a single instant. Born, as all of us are by nature, an Arminian, I still believed the old things I had heard continually from the pulpit and did not see the grace of God. I remember sitting one day in the house of God and hearing a sermon as dry as possible and as worthless as all such sermons are, when a thought struck my mind—how came I to be converted?

I prayed, thought I. Then I thought how came I to pray? I was induced to pray by reading the Scriptures. How came I to read the Scriptures? Why did I read them and what led me to that? And then, in a moment, I saw that God was at the bottom of all and that He was the Author of faith. And then the whole doctrine opened up to me, from which, by God's grace, I have not departed.

But sometimes he leads us by direction. The guide points and says—"There, gentlemen, go along that particular path,that is the way." So the Spirit gives a direction and tendency to our thoughts. Not suggesting a new one but letting a particular thought, when it starts, take such-and-such a direction. Not so much putting a boat on the stream as steering it when it is there. When our thoughts are considering sacred things He leads us into a more excellent channel from that in which we started. Time after time have you commenced a meditation on a certain doctrine and, unaccountably, you were gradually led away into another. And then you saw how one doctrine leaned on another, as is the case with the stones in the arch of a bridge—all hanging on the keystone of Jesus Christ crucified. You were brought to see these things not by a new idea suggested but by direction given to your thoughts.

But perhaps the best way in which the Holy Spirit leads us into all Truth is by illumination. He illuminates the Bible.Now, have any of you an illuminated Bible at home? "No," says one, "I have a Morocco Bible. I have a Polyglot Bible. I have a Marginal Reference Bible." Ah! that is all very well—but have you an illuminated Bible? "Yes, I have a large family Bible with pictures in it." There is a picture of John the Baptist baptizing Christ by pouring water on His head and many other nonsensical things. But that is not what I mean—have you an illuminated Bible?

"Yes, I have a Bible with splendid engravings in it." Yes. I know you may have. But have you an illuminated Bible? "I don't understand what you mean by an 'illuminated Bible.' " Well, it is the Christian man who has an illuminated Bible. He does not buy it illuminated originally, but when he reads it–

"A glory gilds the sacred page,
Majestic like the sun
Which gives a light to every age,
It gives, but burrows none."

There is nothing like reading an illuminated Bible! Beloved, you may read to all eternity and never learn anything by it, unless it is illuminated by the Holy Spirit.

And then the words shine forth like stars. The book seems made of gold leaf. Every single letter glitters like a diamond. Oh, it is a blessed thing to read an illuminated Bible lit up by the radiance of the Holy Spirit! Have you read the Bible and studied it, my Brother, and yet have your eyes been unenlightened? Go and say, "O Lord gild the Bible for me. I want an expounded Bible. Illuminate it. Shine upon it. For I cannot read it to profit unless You enlighten me." Blind men may read the Bible with their fingers, but blind souls cannot. We want a light to read the Bible by, there is no reading it in the dark. Thus the Holy Spirit leads us into all Truth, by suggesting ideas, by directing our thoughts, and by illuminating the Scriptures when we read them.

The last thing is AN EVIDENCE. The question arises, How may I know whether I am enlightened by the Spirit's influence and led into all Truth? First, you may know the Spirit's influence by its unity secondly, by its universalityTruth.

If you are judging a minister, whether he has the Holy Spirit in him or not, you may know him in the first place by the constant unity of his testimony. A man cannot be enlightened by the Holy Spirit who preaches yes and no. The Spirit never says one thing at one time and another thing at another time. There are indeed many good men who say both yes and no but still their contrary testimonies are not both from God the Spirit, for God the Spirit cannot witness to black and white, to a falsehood and Truth. It has been always held as a first principle that Truth is one thing.

But some persons say, "I find one thing in one part of the Bible and another thing in another and though it contradicts itself must I believe it?" All quite right, Brother, if it did contradict itself. But the fault is not in the wood but in the carpenter. Many carpenters do not understand dove-tailing, so there are many preachers who do not understand dove-tailing. It is very nice work and it is not easily learned–it takes some apprenticeship to make all doctrines square together. Some preachers preach very good Calvinism for half-an-hour and the next quarter-of-an hour Arminianism. If they are Calvinists, let them stick to it. If they are Arminians, let them stick to it–let their preaching be all of a piece.

Don't let them pile up things only to kick them all down again. Let us have one thing woven from the top throughout, and let us not rend it. How did Solomon know the true mother of the child. "Cut it in halves," said he. The woman who was not the mother did not care so long as the other did not get the whole and she consented. "Ah," said the true mother, "give her the living child. Let her have it, rather than cut it in halves." So the true child of God would say, "I give it up, let my opponent conquer. I do not want to have the Truth cut in halves. I would rather be all wrong than have the Word altered to my taste."

We do not want to have a divided Bible. No, we claim the whole living child or none at all. We may rest assured of this, that until we get rid of our linsey-woolsey doctrine and cease to sow mingled seed, we shall not have a blessing. An enlightened mind cannot believe a Gospel which denies itself. It must be one thing or the other. One thing cannot contradict another and yet it and its opposite be equally true. You may know the Spirit's influence then, by the unity of its testimony.

And you may know it by its universalityTruth. When first he starts he will not know half the Truth. He will believe it but not understand it. He will have the germ of it but not the sum total in all its breadth and length. There is nothing like learning by experience. A man cannot set up for a theologian in a week. Certain doctrines take years to develop themselves. Like the aloe that takes a hundred years to be dressed, there are some Truths that must lie long in the heart before they really come out and make themselves appear so that we can speak of them as that we do know and testify of that which we have seen.

The Spirit will gradually lead us into all Truth. For instance if it is true that Jesus Christ is to reign upon the earth personally for a thousand years, as I am inclined to believe it is, if I be under the Spirit, that will be more and more opened to me, until I with confidence declare it. Some men begin very timidly. A man says, at first, "I know we are justified by faith and have peace with God. But so many have cried out against eternal justification that I am afraid of it." But he is gradually enlightened and led to see that in the same hour when all his debts were paid, a full discharge was given. That in the moment when his sin was cancelled, every elect soul was justified in God's mind, though they were not justified in their own minds till afterwards. The Spirit shall lead you into all Truth.

Now, what are the practical inferences from this great doctrine? The first is with reference to the Christian who is afraid of his own ignorance. How many are there who are just enlightened and have tasted of heavenly things, who are afraid they are too ignorant to be saved? Beloved, God the Holy Spirit can teach anyone, however illiterate, however uninstructed. I have known some men who were almost idiots before conversion, but they afterwards had their faculties wonderfully developed. Some time ago there was a man who was so ignorant that he could not read and he never spoke anything like grammar in his life, unless by mistake.

And moreover, he was considered to be what the people in his neighborhood called "daft." But when he was converted, the first thing he did was to pray. He stammered out a few words and in a little time his powers of speaking began to develop themselves. Then he thought he would like to read the Scriptures and after long, long months of labor, he learned to read. And what was the next thing? He thought he could preach. And he did preach a little in his own homely way, in his house. Then he thought, "I must read a few more books." And so his mind expanded, until, I believe he is at the present day a useful minister, settled in a country village, laboring for God.

It needs but little intellect to be taught of God. If you feel your ignorance, do not despair. Go to the Spirit–the great Teacher–and ask His sacred influence and it shall come to pass that He "shall guide you into all Truth."

Another inference is this—whenever any of our Brethren do not understand the Truth, let us take a hint as to the best way of dealing with them. Do not let us controvert with them. I have heard many controversies but never heard of any good from one of them. We have had controversies with certain men called Secularists and very strong arguments have been brought against them. But I believe that the Day of Judgment shall declare that a very small amount of good was ever done by contending with these men. Better let them alone—where there is no fuel the fire goes out. And he that debates with them puts wood upon the fire.

So with regard to Baptism. It is of no avail to quarrel with our Paedo-Baptist friends. If we simply pray for them that the God of Truth may lead them to see the true doctrine, they will come to it far more easily than by discussions. Few men are taught by controversy, for–

"A man convinced against his will, is of the same opinion still."
Pray for them that the Spirit of Truth may lead them "into all Truth." Do not be angry with your brother, but pray for him. Cry, "Lord! open his eyes that he may behold wondrous things out of Your Law."

Lastly, we speak to some of you who know nothing about the Spirit of Truth, nor about the Truth itself. It may be that some of you are saying, "We care not much which of you are right, we are happily indifferent to it." Ah! but, poor Sinner, if you knew the gift of God and who it was that spoke the Truth, you would not say, "I care not for it." If you knew how essential the Truth is to your salvation, you would not talk so. If you knew that the Truth of God is that you are a worthless sinner, but if you believe, then God from all eternity, apart from all your merits, loved you. If you knew that He bought you with the Redeemer's blood and justified you in the forum of Heaven—and will by-and-bye justify you in the forum of your conscience through the Holy Spirit by faith.

If you knew that there is a Heaven for you beyond the chance of a failure, a crown for you, the luster of which can never be dimmed—then you would say, "Indeed the Truth is precious to my soul!" Why, my ungodly Hearers, these men of error want to take away the Truth which alone can save you, the only Gospel that can deliver you from Hell. They deny the great truths of free grace, those fundamental doctrines which alone can snatch a sinner from Hell. And even though you do not feel interest in them now I still would say you ought to desire to see them promoted.

May God give you grace to know the Truth in your hearts! May the Spirit "guide you into all Truth!" For if you do not know the Truth here, recollect there will be a sorrowful learning of it in the dark chambers of the pit where the only light shall be the flames of Hell! May you here know the Truth! And the Truth shall make you free–and if the Son shall make you free, you shall be free indeed, for He says, "I am the Way, the Truth, the Life."

Believe on Jesus, you chief of sinners! Trust His love and mercy and you are saved, for God the Spirit gives faith and eternal life.

THE HOLY SPIRIT AND THE ONE CHURCH

"These are they who separate themselves, sensual, having not the Spirit."
Jude 1:19

A Sermon Delivered On Sunday Morning: 13 December 1855

WHEN a farmer comes to thrash out his wheat and get it ready for the market there are two things that he desires–that there may be plenty of it, of the right sort–and that when he takes it to market, he may be able to carry a clean sample there. He does not look upon the quantity alone–for what is the chaff to the wheat? He would rather have a little clean than he would have a great heap containing a vast quantity of chaff, but less of the precious corn. On the other hand, he would not so winnow his wheat as to drive away any of the good grain and so make the quantity less than it need to be. He wants to have as much as possible–to have as little loss as possible in the winnowing and yet to have it as well winnowed as may be.

Now, that is what I desire for Christ's Church and what every Christian will desire. We wish Christ's Church to be as large as possible. God forbid that by any of our winnowing, we should ever cast away one of the precious sons of Zion. When we rebuke sharply, we would be anxious lest the rebuke should fall where it is not needed and should bruise and hurt the feelings of any who God has chosen. But on the other hand, we have no wish to see the Church multiplied at the expense of its purity. We do not wish to have a charity so large that it takes in chaff as well as wheat. We wish to be just charitable enough to use the fan thoroughly to purge God's floor–but yet charitable enough to pick up the most shriveled ear of wheat, to preserve it for the Master's sake, who is the Husbandman.

I trust, in preaching this morning, God may help me so to discern between the precious and the vile. And, that, I may say nothing uncharitable which would cut off any of God's people from being part of His true and living and visible Church. And yet at the same time I pray that I may not speak so loosely and so without God's direction as to embrace any in the arms of Christian affection whom the Lord has not received in the Everlasting Covenant of His love.

Our text suggests to us three things. First, an inquiry–have we the Spirit? Secondly, a caution–if we have not the Spirit we are sensual. Thirdly, a suspicion–there are many persons that separate themselves. Our suspicion concerning them is that notwithstanding their superfine profession, they are sensual, not having the Spirit–for our text says, "These are they who separate themselves, sensual, having not the Spirit."

First, then, our text suggests AN INQUIRY–Have we the Spirit? This is an inquiry so important that the philosopher may well suspend all his investigations to find an answer to this question on his own personal account. All the great debates of politics, all the most engrossing subjects of human discussion may well stop today and give us pause to ask ourselves the solemn question–"Have I the Spirit?" For this question does not deal with any externals of religion, but it deals with religion in its most vital point. He that has the Spirit, although he is wrong in fifty things, being right in this, is saved. He that has not the Spirit, be he ever so orthodox, be his creed as correct as Scripture–yes, and his morals outwardly as pure as the Law–is still unsaved. He is destitute of the essential part of salvation–the Spirit of God dwelling in him.

To help us to answer this question, I shall try to set forth the effects of the Spirit in our hearts under sundry Scriptural metaphors. Have I the Spirit? I reply, "and what is the operation of the Spirit? How am I to discern it?" Now the Spirit operates in many ways, all of them mysterious and supernatural, all of them bearing the real marks of His own power and having certain signs following whereby they may be discovered and recognized.

The first work of the Spirit in the heart is a work during which the Spirit is compared to the wind. You remember that when our Savior spoke to Nicodemus He represented the first work of the Spirit in the heart as being like the wind, "which blows where it lists." "Even so," says He, "is everyone that is born of the Spirit." Now you know that the wind is a most mysterious thing. And although there are certain definitions of it which pretend to be explanations of the phenomenon, yet they certainly leave the great question of how the wind blows and what is the cause of its blowing in a certain direction, where It was before. Breath within us, wind without us–all motions of air–are to us mysterious. And the renewing work of the Spirit in the heart is exceedingly mysterious. It is possible that at this moment the Spirit of God may be breathing into some of the thousand hearts before me. Yet it would be

353

blasphemous if anyone should ask, "Which way went the Spirit from God to such a heart? How entered it there?"

And it would be foolish for a person who is under the operation of the Spirit to ask how it operates–you know not where is the storehouse of the thunder. You know not where the clouds are balanced. Neither can you know how the Spirit goes forth from the Most High and enters into the heart of man. It may be that during a sermon two men are listening to the same Truth. One of them hears as attentively as the other and remembers as much of it. The other is melted to tears or moved with solemn thoughts. But the one though equally attentive, sees nothing in the sermon, except, maybe, certain important truths well set forth. As for the other, his heart is broken within him and his soul is melted. Ask me how it is that the same Truth has an effect upon the one and not upon his fellow. I reply, because the mysterious Spirit of the living God goes with the Truth to one heart and not to the other.

The one only feels the force of Truth and that may be strong enough to make him tremble, like Felix. But the other feels the Spirit going with the Truth and that renews the man, regenerates him and causes him to pass into that gracious condition which is called the state of salvation. This change takes place instantaneously. It is as miraculous a change as any miracle of which we read in Scripture. It is supremely supernatural. It may be mimicked, but no imitation of it can be true and real. Men may pretend to be regenerated without the Spirit, but regenerated they cannot be. It is a change so marvelous that the highest attempts of man can never reach it. We may reason as long as we please but we cannot reason ourselves into regeneration. We may meditate till our hairs are gray with study. But we cannot meditate ourselves into the new birth. That is worked in us by the sovereign will of God alone–

"The Spirit, like some heavenly wind,
Blows on the sons of flesh,
Inspires us with a heavenly mind,
And forms the man afresh."

But ask the man how–he cannot tell you. Ask him when–he may recognize the time, but as to the manner thereof he knows no more of it than you do. It is to him a mystery.

You remember the story of the valley of vision. Ezekiel saw dry bones lying scattered here and there in the valley. The command came to Ezekiel, "Say to these dry bones, live." He said, "Live," and the bones came together, "bone to his bone and flesh came upon them." But as yet they did not live. "Prophesy, son of man. Say to the Wind, breathe upon these slain, that they may live." They looked just like life. There was flesh and blood there. There were the eyes and hands and feet. But when Ezekiel had spoken there was a mysterious something given which men call life and it was given in a mysterious way, like the blowing of the wind. It is even so today. Unconverted and ungodly persons may be very moral and excellent—they are like the dry bones, when they are put together and clothed with flesh and blood.

But to make them live spiritually it needs the Divine Inspiration from the breath of the Almighty, the Divine Spirit, the Divine Wind should blow on them and then they would live. Say, my Hearer, have you ever had any supernatural influence on your heart? For if not I may seem to be harsh with you. But I am faithful. If you have never had more than nature in your heart, you are "in the gall of bitterness and in the bonds of iniquity." No, Sir, sneer not at that utterance. It is as true as this Bible, for it is from this Bible it was taken and for proof thereof hear me. "Except a man be born again (from above) of water and of the Spirit, he cannot see the kingdom of God." What say you to that? It is in vain for you to talk of making yourself to be born again. You can not be born again except by the Spirit and you must perish unless you are. You see, then, the first effect of the Spirit and by that you may answer the question.

In the next place, the Spirit in the Word of God is often compared to fire. After the Spirit, like the wind has made the dead sinner live, then comes the Spirit like fire. Now fire has a searching and tormenting power. It is purifying, but it purifies by a terrible process. Now after the Holy Spirit has given us the life of Christianity, there immediately begins a burning in our heart—the Lord searches and tries our reins and lights a candle within our spirits which discovers the in your heart? For if not, you have not yet received the Spirit. To explain what I mean, let me just tell a piece of my own experience by way of illustrating the fiery effects of the Spirit.

I lived careless and thoughtless. I could indulge in sin as well as others and did do so. Sometimes my conscience pricked me, but not enough to make me cease from vice. I could indulge in transgression and I could love it—not so much as others loved it—my early training would not let me do that—but still enough to prove that my heart was debased and corrupt. One time something more than conscience pricked me. I knew not then what it was. I was like Samuel, when the Lord called him. I heard the voice, but I knew not from where it came. A stirring began in my heart and I began to feel that in the sight of God I was a lost, ruined and condemned sinner. That conviction I could not shake off. Do what I might it followed me. If I sought to amuse my mind and take it off from serious thoughts it was of no use. I was obliged still to carry about with me a heavy burden on my back.

I went to my bed and there I dreamed about Hell and about "the wrath to come." I woke up and this dreary nightmare, this incubus, still brooded on me. What could I do? I renounced first one vicious habit–then another–it mattered not. All this was like pulling one firebrand from a flame that fed itself with blazing forests. Do what I might, my conscience found no rest. Up to the house of God I went to hear the Gospel. There was no Gospel for me. The fire burned but the more fiercely and the very breath of the Gospel seemed to fan the flame. Away I went to my chamber and my closet to pray–the heavens were like brass and the windows of the sky were barred against me. No answer could I get. The fire burned more vehemently. Then I thought, "I would not live always. Would God I had never been born!" But I dared not die, for there was Hell when I was dead. And I dared not live, for life had become intolerable. Still the fire blazed right vehemently till at last I came to this resolve–"If there is salvation in Christ, I will have it. I have nothing of my own to trust to. I do this hour, O God, renounce my sin and renounce my own righteousness, too."

And the fire blazed again and burned up all my good works, yes–and my sins with them. And then I saw that all this burning was to bring me to Christ. And oh, the joy and gladness of my heart when Jesus came and sprinkled water on the flame and said, "I have bought you with My blood. Put your trust in Me. I will do for you what you can not do for yourself. I will take your sins away. I will clothe you with a spotless robe of righteousness. I will guide you all your journey through and land you at last in Heaven." Say, my dear Hearer, do you know anything about the Spirit of burning? For if not, again I say, I am not harsh, I am but true–if you have never felt this, you know not the Spirit.

To proceed a little further. When the Spirit has thus quickened the soul and convicted it of sin, then He comes under another metaphor. He comes under the metaphor of oil. The Holy Spirit is very frequently in Scripture compared to oil. "You anoint my head with oil, my cup runs over." Ah, Brethren, though the beginning of the Spirit is by fire, it does not end there. We may be first of all convicted and brought to Christ by misery. But when we get to Christ there is no misery in Him and our sorrow results from not getting close enough to Him. The Holy Spirit comes, like the good Samaritan and pours in the oil and the wine. And oh, what oil it is with which He anoints our head and with which He heals our wounds! How soft the liniments which He binds round our bruises! How blessed the eye salve with which He anoints our eyes! How heavenly the ointment with which He binds up our sores and wounds and bruises and makes us whole and sets our feet upon a Rock and establishes our goings!

The Spirit, after He has convicted, begins to comfort. And you that have felt the comforting power of the Holy Spirit will bear me witness there is no Comforter like He that is the Paraclete. Oh, bring the music, the voice of song and the sound of harps! They are both as vinegar upon niter to him that has a heavy heart. Bring me the enchantments of the magic world and all the enjoyments of its pleasures. They do but torment the soul and prick it with many thorns. But oh, Spirit of the living God, when You blow upon the heart there is not a wave of that tempestuous sea which does not sleep forever when You bid it be still! There is not one single breath of the proud hurricane and tempest which does not cease to howl and which does not lie still, when You say to it, "Peace be unto you. Your sins are forgiven you." Say, do you know the Spirit under the figure of oil? Have you felt Him at work in your spirits, comforting you, anointing your head, making you glad and causing you to rejoice?

There are many people that never felt this. They hope they are religious. But their religion never makes them happy. There are scores of professors who have just enough religion to make them miserable. Let them be afraid that they have any religion at all. For religion makes people happy. When it has its full sway with man it makes him glad. It may begin in agony, but it does not end there. Say, have you ever had your heart leaping for joy? Have your lips ever warbled songs of ecstatic praise? Do your eyes ever flash the fire of joy? If these things are not so, I fear lest you are still without God and without Christ. For where the Spirit comes, His fruits are—joy, peace, love, confidence and assurance forever.

Bear with me once more. I have to show you one more figure of the Spirit and by that also you will be able to ascertain whether you are under His operation.

When the Spirit has acted as wind, as fire and as oil, He then acts like water. We are told that we are "born again of water and of the Spirit." Now I do not think you foolish enough to need that I should say that no water, either of immersion or of sprinkling, can in the least degree operate in the salvation of a soul. There may be some few poor creatures, whose heads were put on their shoulders the wrong way, who still believe that a few drops of water from a priest's hands can regenerate souls. There may be such a few, but I hope the race will soon die out. We trust that the day will come when all those gentry will have no "other Gospel" to preach in our Churches but will have clean gone over to Rome and when that terrible spot upon the Protestant Church, called Puseyism, will have been cut out like a cancer and torn out by its very roots. The sooner we get rid of that the better. And whenever we hear of any of them going over to Rome, let them go—I wish we could as easily get rid of the devil—they may go together—we do not want either of them in the Protestant Church.

But the Holy Spirit, when He comes in the heart, comes like water. That is to say, He comes to purify the soul. He that today lives as foul as he did before his pretended conversion is a hypocrite and a liar. He that this day loves sin and lives in it just as he was likely to do, let him know that the Truth is not in him, but he has received the strong delusion to believe a lie. God's people are a holy people. God's Spirit works by love and purifies the soul. Once let it get into our hearts and it will have no rest till it has turned every sin out. God's Holy Spirit and man's sin cannot live together peaceably—they may both be in the same heart—but they cannot both reign there, nor can they both be quiet there. For "the Spirit lusts against the flesh and the flesh lusts against the Spirit." They cannot rest, but there will be a perpetual warring in the soul, so that the Christian will have to cry, "O wretched man that I am! Who shall deliver me from the body of this death?" But in due time the Spirit will drive out all sin and will present us blameless before the Throne of His Majesty with exceeding great joy.

Now, my Hearer, answer you this question for yourself and not for another man. Have you received this Spirit? Answer me, anyhow—if it is with a scoff, answer me. If you sneer and say, "I know nothing of your enthusiastic rant," be it so, Sir—say "no," then. It may be you care not to reply at all. I beseech you do not put away my entreaty. Yes or no? Have you received the Spirit? "Sir, no man can find fault with my character. I believe I shall enter Heaven through my own virtues." That is not the question, Sir. Have you received the Spirit? All that you say you may have done. But if you have left the other undone and have not received the Spirit, it will go ill with you at last. Have you had a supernatural operation upon your own heart? Have you been made a new man in Christ Jesus! For if not, depend on it, as God's Word is true, you are out of Christ and dying as you are. You will be shut out of Heaven, be you who you may and what you may.

II. Thus, I have tried to help you to answer the first question—the inquiry—have we received the Spirit? And this brings me to the CAUTION. He that has not received the Spirit is said to be sensual. Oh, what a gulf there is between the least Christian and the greatest moralist! What a wide distinction there is between the greatest professor destitute of grace and the least of God's Believers who has grace in His heart. As great a difference as there is between light and darkness, between death and life, between Heaven and Hell is there between a saint and a sinner. For mark, my text says—in no very polite phrase—that if we have not the Spirit we are sensual. "Sensual!" says one. "Well, I am not a converted man—I don't pretend to be—but I am not sensual." Well, Friend and it is very likely that you are not—not in the common acceptation of the term sensual. But understand that this Word, in the Greek, really means what an English word like this would mean, if we had such a one—soulish.

We have not such a word—we want such a one. There is a great distinction between mere animals and men—man has a soul and the mere animal has none. There is another distinction between mere men and a converted man. The converted man has the Spirit—the unconverted man has none. He is a soulish man—not a spiritual man. He has got no further than mere nature and has no inheritance in the spiritual kingdom of grace. Strange it is that soulish and sensual should after all mean the same! Friend, you have not the Spirit. Then you are nothing better—be you what you are, or whatsoever you may be—than the Fall of Adam left you. That is to say, you are a fallen creature, having only capacities to live here in sin and to live forever in torment. But you have not the capacity to live in Heaven at all, for you have no Spirit. And therefore you are unable to know or enjoy spiritual things. And mark you, a man may be in this state and be a sensual man and yet he may have all the virtues that could grace a Christian. But with all these—if he has not the Spirit—he has got not an inch further than where Adam's fall left him—that is, condemned and under the curse.

Yes, and he may attend to religion with all his might—he may take the sacrament and be baptized and may be the most devout professor. But if he has not the Spirit he has not started a solitary inch from where he was, for he is still in "the bonds of iniquity," a lost soul. No, further, he may pick up religious phrases till he may talk very fast about religion. He may read biographies till he seems to be a deep taught child of God. He may be able to write an article upon the deep experience of a Believer—but if this experience is not his own, if he has not received it by the Spirit of the living God, he is still nothing more than a carnal man and Heaven is to him a place to which there is no entrance. No, further—he might go so far as to become a minister of the Gospel and a successful minister, too. And God may bless the word that he preaches to the salvation of sinners. But unless he has received the Spirit—be he as eloquent as Apollos and as earnest as Paul—he is nothing more than a mere soulish man, without capacity for spiritual things.

No, to crown all, he might even have the power of working miracles as Judas had—he might even be received into the Church as a Believer as was Simon Magus and after all that—though he had cast out devils, though he had healed the sick, though he had worked miracles—he will have the gates of Heaven shut in his teeth if he has not received the Spirit. For this is the essential thing—without which all others are in vain—the reception of the Spirit of the living God. It is a searching Truth, is it not, my Friends? Do not run away from it. If I am preaching to you falsehood, reject it. But if this is a Truth which I can substantiate by Scripture, I beseech you, rest not till you have answered this question—Have you the Spirit, living, dwelling, working in your heart?

III. This brings me, in the third place, to THE SUSPICION. How singular that "separation" should be the opposite of having the Spirit. Hark, I hear a gentleman saying, "Oh, I like to hear you preach smartly and sharply. I am persuaded, Sir, there are a great many people in the Church that ought not to be there. And so I, because there is such a corrupt mixture in the Church, have determined not to join anywhere at all. I do not think that the Church of Christ nowadays is at all clean and pure enough to allow of my joining with it. At least, Sir, I did join a Church once, but I made such a deal of noise in it they were very glad when I went away. And now I am just like David's men—I am one that is in debt and discontented and I go round to hear all new preachers that arise. I have heard you now these three months—I mean to go and hear someone else in a very little time if you do not say something to flatter me. But I am quite sure I am one of God's special elect. I don't join any Church because a Church is not good enough for me. I don't become a member of any denomination, because they are all wrong, everyone of them."

Hark, Brother, I have something to tell you, that will not please you. "These are they that separate themselves, sensual, having not the Spirit." I hope you enjoy the text. It certainly belongs to you, above every man in the world. "These are they who separate themselves, sensual, having not the Spirit." When I read this over I thought to myself, there are some who say, "Well, you are a Dissenter, how do you make this agreeable with the text, 'These are they who separate themselves.' " You are separated from the Church of England. Ah, my Friends, that a man may be and be all the better for it. But the separation here intended is separation from the one universal Church of Christ. The Church of England was not known in Jude's day–so the Apostle did not allude to that. "These are they who separate themselves"–that is from the Church of Christ–from the great universal body of the elect. Moreover, let us just say one thing. We did not separate ourselves–we were turned out. Dissenters did not separate themselves from the Church of England, from the Episcopal Church. But when the Act of Uniformity was passed they were forcibly turned out of their pulpits.

Our forefathers were as sound Churchmen as any in the world–but they could not take in all the errors of the Prayer Book and they were therefore hounded to their graves by the intolerance of the conforming professors. So they did not separate themselves. Moreover, we do not separate ourselves. There is not a Christian beneath the scope of God's Heaven from whom I am separated. At the Lord's Table I always invite all Churches to come and sit down and commune with us. If any man were to tell me that I am separate from the Episcopalian, the Presbyterian, or the Methodist, I would tell him he did not know me, for I love them with a pure heart fervently and I am not separate from them. I may hold different views from them and in that point truly I may be said to be separate. But I am not separate in heart, I will work with them–I will work with them heartily. No, though my Church of England brother sends me, as he has done, a summons to pay a Church tax that I cannot in conscience pay, I will love him still. And if he takes chairs and tables it matters not–I will love him for all that. And if there is a ragged-school or anything else for which I can work with him to promote the glory of God, therein will I unite with him with all my heart.

I think this bears rather hard on our friends–the Strict Communion Baptists. I should not like to say anything hard against them for they are about the best people in the world. But they really do separate themselves from the great body of Christ's people. The Spirit of the living God will not let them do this really, but they do it professedly. They separate themselves from the great Universal Church. They say they will not commune with it. And if anyone comes to their table who has not been baptized, they turn him away. They "separate," certainly. I do not believe it is willful schism that makes them thus act. But at the same time I think the old man within has some hand in it.

Oh, how my heart loves the doctrine of the one Church. The nearer I get to my Master in prayer and communion, the closer am I knit to all His disciples. The more I see of my own errors and failings, the more ready am I to deal gently with them that I believe to be erring. The pulse of Christ's body is communion. And woe to the Church that seeks to cure the ills of Christ's body by stopping its pulse. I think it sin to refuse to commune with anyone who is a member of the Church of our Lord Jesus Christ. I desire this morning to preach the unity of Christ's Church. I have sought to use the fan to blow away the chaff. I have said no man belongs to Christ's Church unless he has the Spirit. But, if he has the Spirit, woe be to the man that separates himself from him.

Oh, I should think myself grossly in fault if at the foot of these stairs I should meet a truly converted child of God, who called himself a Primitive Methodist, or a Wesleyan, or a Churchman, or an Independent and I should say, "No, Sir, you do not agree with me on certain points. I believe you are a child of God, but I will have nothing to do with you." I should then think that this text would bear very hard on me. "These are they who separate themselves, sensual, having not the Spirit." But would we do so, Beloved? No, we would give them both our hands and say, God speed to you in your journey to Heaven. So long as you have got the Spirit we are one family and we will not be separate from one another. God grant the day may come when every wall of separation shall be beaten down! See how to this day we are separate. There! You will find a Baptist who could not say a good word to a Paedo-Baptist if you were to give him a world. You find to this day Episcopalians who hate that ugly word, "Dissent." And it is enough for them that a Dissenter has done a thing–they will not do it then–be it ever so good.

Ah, and furthermore, there are some to be found in the Church of England that will not only hate Dissenters, but hate one another into the bargain. Men are to be found that cannot let brother ministers of their own Church preach in their parish. What an anachronism such men are! They would seem to have been sent into the world in our time purely by mistake. Their proper era would have been the time of the dark ages. If they had lived then, what fine Bonners they would have made! What splendid fellows they would have been to have helped to poke the fire in Smithfield! But they are quite out of date in these times and I look upon such a curious clergyman in the same way that I do upon a Dodo—as an extraordinary animal whose race is almost, if not quite extinct.

Well, you may look and look and wonder. The animal will be extinct soon. It will not be long, I trust, before not only the Church of England shall love itself, but when all who love the Lord Jesus shall be ready to preach in each other's pulpits, preaching the same Truth, holding the same faith and mightily contending for it. Then shall the world "see how these Christians love one another." And then shall it be known in Heaven that Christ's kingdom has come and that His will is about to be done on earth as it is in Heaven.

My Hearer, do you belong to the Church? For out of the Church there is no salvation. But mark what the Church is. It is not the Episcopalian, Baptist, or Presbyterian—the Church is a company of men who have received the Spirit. If you can not say you have the Spirit, go your way and tremble. Go your way and think of your lost condition. And may Jesus by His Spirit so bless you that you may be led to renounce your works and ways with grief and fly to Him who died upon the Cross and find a shelter there from the wrath of God.

I may have said some rough things this morning, but I am not given much to cutting and trimming and I do not suppose I shall begin to learn that art now. If the thing is untrue, it is with you to reject it. If it is true, at your own peril reject what God stamps with Divine authority. May the blessing of the Father, the Son and the Holy Spirit rest upon the one Church of Israel's one Jehovah. Amen and Amen.

A MOST NEEDFUL PRAYER CONCERNING THE HOLY SPIRIT

"Cast me not away from Your Presence. And take not Your Holy Spirit from me."
Psalm 51:11

A Sermon Delivered On Sunday Morning: 9 October 1870

THIS Psalm is beyond all others a photograph of penitent David. You have probably seen that interesting slab of stone which bears on its surface indications of the fall of raindrops in a primeval shower–this Psalm preserves the marks of David's teardrops for the inspection and instruction of succeeding generations. Or what if I change the figure and borrow another from an Oriental fable? They said of old that pearls were formed by drops of spring rain falling into shells upon the shores of the sea. So here, the drops of David's repentance are preserved in inspired Scripture as precious, priceless pearls.

This Psalm is as full of meaning as of tenderness. I know not how large a literature has gathered around it, but certainly writers of all creeds and ages have used their pens to illustrate it–and there is room for as many more. It is a perfectly inexhaustible Psalm. Its deep shaft of sorrowful humiliation leads to veins of golden ore. The stones of it are the place of sapphires.

We shall confine ourselves, this morning, to this one verse–not with any prospect of being able to bring out all its meaning, but rather hoping to make use of it–and to find produced in ourselves a measure of the feeling which it so solemnly expresses. If we should be made to drink into its spirit, and then to pour out our hearts at the feet of our Redeemer, it will be an unspeakable blessing. We shall use the text, first, in its evident sense as the utterance of a penitent saint. Secondly, we shall employ it, as I think it may be used, as the cry of an anxious Church. And then, thirdly, but in a very modified sense, we shall put it into the mouths of awakened, but as yet unsaved souls.

First, then, in its largest, widest, and primitive sense, we must regard this verse as THE CRY OF A PENITENT CHILD OF GOD. "Cast me not away from Your Presence. And take not Your Holy Spirit from me." This will certainly be fit language for any child of God here who has fallen into gross sin. I trust, my Brothers and Sisters, this may not be your case, but if it should be, hesitate not when you have fallen into David's sin, if you feel David's repentance, to offer David's prayer, "Cast me not away from Your Presence. And take not Your Holy Spirit from me."

Backsliding Christian, you may yet return—there are pardons for sins of deepest dye. The Lord will heal your broken bones, and restore unto you the joy of His salvation. But probably far more of us will have an equal necessity to utter this supplication on account of gradual inward backsliding from the former closeness of our walk with God. One great sin, when committed, startles the soul into repentance.

But a continuation of sin will be found to be even more dangerous. Though no one of the company of our transgressions may be a peculiarly striking iniquity, yet the whole together may produce an equally lamentable result upon the soul. White ants will devour a carcass as surely and as speedily as a lion. Many threads of silk twisted together may hold a man as fast as one band of iron.

Come, let us consider. Many of us have been saved by Divine Grace, and not barely saved, but we have been made to walk in the light of God's Countenance. We have been somewhat like Daniel, men greatly beloved and highly favored. Now, have we acted in conformity with such distinguishing mercy? Have we manifested a holy jealousy such as Divine love ought to produce in us? Must not some here confess that their love has by degrees grown cold, or at least lukewarm? Must not many of us acknowledge that we have been very carnal, so as to have been overjoyed with worldly prosperity, or overly dampened with worldly adversity?

Must we not acknowledge, many of us, that we have been slothful in the Master's service? Are there not some among in your Master's business, fervent in spirit, serving the Lord. But that has gone—your former zeal and fidelity have departed from you—unstable as water, you do not now excel. With this there has crept over some hearts a listlessness in prayer, a want of enjoyment in reading the Word, a deadness towards spiritual things, a carelessness of walk, a carnal security of spirit. Dr. Watts' verse might suit some of you sadly well—

"In vain we tune our formal songs,
In vain we strive to rise.

Hosannas languish on our tongues,
And our devotion dies."
Now, in such a case, my Brothers and Sisters, if you are conscious of an evil heart of unbelief in departing from the living God. If you are obliged to confess that the former days were better than now, and to admit that the consolations of the Lord are small with you—I do, in deep and anxious sympathy with your condition—exhort you to use from your heart the language of the Psalmist, "Cast me not away from Your Presence. And take not Your Holy Spirit from me."

You will perceive that a soul which can really pray thus has life—true spiritual life—still struggling within. An ungodly man does not ask that he may abide in nearness to God. Rather, he would say, "Where shall I flee from Your Presence?" He does not seek for God's Spirit. He is quite content that the evil spirit should rule him, and that the spirit of this world should be predominant in him.

But here is life, struggling, panting, crushed, painful life—but life for all that. The higher spiritual life which sighs after God. I have seen in the corner of the garden a little fire covered up with many damp autumn leaves. I have watched its feeble smoke, and known thereby that the fire still lived and was fighting with the damp which almost smothered it. So, here, these desires and sighs and cries are as so much smoke, indicating the Divine fire within. "Cast me not away from Your Presence," shows a soul that loves God's Presence. "Take not Your Holy Spirit from me," reveals a heart that desires to be under the dominion of that Spirit yet more completely.

Here are signs of life, though they may appear to be as indistinct and doleful as hollow groans far underground—such as have been heard from men buried alive—voices from the sepulcher, choked and ghostly, but telling of life in the charnel house, grappling with death, and crying out, "O wretched man that I am! Who shall deliver me?" Let us look at these words closely, since I have shown you how applicable they are to us, and how they indicate spiritual life. I think when David used them, he may have looked back in his mind to that portion of sacred history with which he was conversant.

He remembered when Adam and Eve, having rebelled against their Maker, were driven out from God's Presence, when the cherubim with flaming sword blocked the gate of Eden's blighted garden. "My God," he seems to say, "I, too, have offended. Your Presence is my Paradise, my Eden, all else is wilderness to me—barren, thorn-bearing wilderness. O drive me not out! Cast me not away from Your Presence! Let me but know You love me and I shall be in Eden. Let me but know that I am still Your child, Your favored one, and I will find in that sweet assurance my Paradise, my all. Let me be a courtier in Your palace, or even a doorkeeper in Your house, and I will be content. "But from Your Presence banish me not, else do You wither all my joys."

Did he think of Cain, too, and was his mind so distressed that he was half afraid lest he should become like that marked man who went out from the Presence of the Lord to be a wanderer and a vagabond, and find from then on no rest for the sole of his feet? Did he feel that if he were exiled from God's Presence he would be just as wretched as the accursed Cain, himself? Did the thought of that first manslayer put an emphasis into the prayer, "Cast me not away from Your Presence"?

Do you think he remembered Pharaoh, too, in that memorable night when the cloud that imaged the Presence of Jehovah came down between Israel and Egypt, and the dark side of it was towards Pharaoh? For God indignantly turned His back upon the haughty king, while His face shone lovingly upon His chosen, but afflicted people. Did he mean by our text to say, "Lord, turn not Your back on me. Cause not such trouble and confusion in my soul as ensued in Egypt's hosts when the night of Your wrath fell on it. O cast me not away from Your Presence"?

Is it possible that the penitent monarch, while penning this Psalm, thought of Samson, too, and therefore uttered the latter part of the verse, "Take not Your Holy Spirit from me"? Did he remember the strongman who could tear a lion as though it were a kid when the Spirit of the Lord came upon him, or smite the Philistines hip and thigh till he piled them up in heaps when God was with him—but who, when his locks had been shorn, and the Spirit was gone—was ignominiously bound, and with blinded eyes was made to do a mill horse's work?

Did he think of the hero of Gaza and say, "My God, take not Your Holy Spirit from me. Leave me not to be the sport of my enemies. Cast me not off as one whom You can no longer employ for high and honorable service. Take not Your Holy Spirit from me"? Or is it not very likely that if he thought of all these, yet his eyes were peculiarly fixed upon one between whom and himself there had been a very close relation? I mean Saul, his predecessor on the throne. That man had been chosen to rule God's people Israel, but he proved rebellious, and he was cast away from God's Presence, so that God would not hear him in the hour of distress.

No Urim and Thummim would give him a Divine response. No Prophet would regard him. No priest could present for him acceptable sacrifices. He was cast away from God's Presence, and the Spirit was finally gone from him. Even that ordinary measure of the Spirit which he had once enjoyed was gone. Saul was once among the Prophets, but we find him by-and-by among the witches. Saul had lost all prudence in the council chamber, all success in the battlefield. The voice of Him by whom kings reign had gone forth against him, and broken his scepter.

"Because you have rejected the Word of the Lord, He has also rejected you from being king." All this David remembered with a shudder, and his heart said to him, "What? Shall the son of Jesse be like the son of Kish? Shall the second anointed of Samuel be like the first, of whom the Lord said, 'It repents Me that I have set up Saul to be king' "? He became overwhelmed with dreadful apprehension and turned to the Lord with a bitter cry, "Oh, can it be, my God? Shall I also be cast away from Your Presence, and Your Spirit taken from me?" He bows himself in agonizing prayer with this as his petition, "Cast me not away from Your Presence. And take not Your Holy Spirit from me."

Give me your patient attention, you who love the Lord, while I try to give you many reasons why such a prayer as this should arise out of the depths of your hearts, and leap from your lips. As for the first petition of the text, "Cast me not away from Your Presence," my Brethren, we have need to present it, for God's Presence is to us our comfort amid affliction. He is "a very present help in trouble." It is our greatest delight–of all our true joys it is the source and sum. We call Him by that name, "God our exceeding joy."

The Lord's Presence is our strength. God with us is our banner of victory. When He is not with us we are weaker than water, but in His might we are Omnipotent. His Presence is our sanctification. By beholding the Glory of the Lord we become like He. Communion with God has a transforming power upon us. This, too, is our highest glory–angels have no brighter honor. And this shall be our Heaven hereafter–to dwell in the immediate and unveiled Presence of the Lord in His own Palace forever.

I cannot, however, dwell at length on this first part of the text, and therefore I have summarized the reasons for its use. But the second I shall ask your attention to in greater detail. "Take not Your Holy Spirit from me." Remember, my Brethren, it was the Holy Spirit who first of all regenerated us. If we have, indeed, been born again from above, our new birth was by the Holy Spirit. "Not of blood, nor of the will of the flesh, nor of the will of man, but of God," are we made this day spiritual men. If, therefore, we have not the Spirit, or it is possible that the Spirit is taken from us, the very essence of our spiritual life is gone. We are utterly dead, we are no longer numbered with the living people of the living God.

The Holy Spirit is not to us a luxury, but a necessity. We must have the Spirit of God or we live not at all in a spiritual sense. If any man has not the Spirit of Christ he is none of His. Without the supernatural work of this Divine Person upon our nature we are not numbered with the family of God at all. Remember, my dear Friends, that into the Holy Spirit you and I, when we professed our faith in Jesus, were baptized. We were immersed "into the name of the Father, and of the Son, and of the Holy Spirit." And this day, without the Holy Spirit, you and I are fraudulent professors, baptized deceivers, and arrant hypocrites.

If we were not, indeed, baptized into the Holy Spirit, how dare we be baptized into the outward symbol? As he who, if an unworthy communicant, eats and drinks condemnation to himself, even so does the unworthy participant in Baptism. This day we are bearing a false profession, we wear a fictitious name, we are as those who said they were Jews and were not, but did lie. We number ourselves with the people of God, but if we have not the Spirit we shall at last be numbered with the castaways. See to this, I pray you, and O may the preacher see to this himself!

Remember, too, that the Spirit of God is to each one of us the Spirit of adoption. "You have not received," says the Apostle, "the spirit of bondage again to fear, but you have received the Spirit of adoption, whereby we cry, Abba, Father." Without the Spirit of God, then, we have no Spirit of adoption. We have lost that best of all blessings, the sonship, which places us in possession of all the treasures of Heaven as joint-heirs with Christ.

In the wilderness it was the sonship of our Lord which Satan assaulted when he tempted the Savior. "If You are the Son of God," said he. Christ the Lord, however, stood fast upon this point and was not moved—and therefore He conquered. Let anything come between us and the distinct recognition of our sonship towards God and we are undone. Lord, if it so pleases You, suffer Satan to rob me of all my goods, as Job was deprived of all his treasures. And let the desire of my eyes be taken from me, and my eyes, themselves, no more behold the sweet light of day.

But "take not Your Holy Spirit from me," for then my very relation to You would vanish from my heart. While I can say, "My God, my Father," I have enough, though all else is gone. But if You are no Father to me, or I have no Spirit of adoption towards You, then I am undone, indeed. "Take not Your Holy Spirit from me," is a necessary prayer, for to do so would be to end our spiritual life, to cast us out as mere pretenders, to treat us as trees twice dead, plucked up by the roots.

Further, let us not forget that it is by the Holy Spirit that we have access to God. "We have access by one Spirit unto the Father," says the Apostle. Now, access to God is among the richest of our privileges. Let a man be able to take his burdens to God and it little matters how heavy they may be. Let him be able to tell his needs to his Father, and it little signifies how great those needs may be, for God will supply them all according to His riches in glory by Christ Jesus. But take away the Mercy Seat, or block up the road by which the Believer reaches it. Withdraw his power in prayer, and his faith in the promise—and all this you do if you take away the Holy Spirit from him—then is the Believer ruined, indeed.

Praying in the Holy Spirit is the only true praying. O may we never cease from it! "He helps our infirmities: for we know not what we should pray for as we ought." Without His teaching, then, what stammering prayers, what wandering prayers, what prayers that are not prayers at all we should offer! We must have the Spirit or else our great resource and remedy of prayer becomes unavailable. On your knees, then, you that have wandered and deserve to be forsaken and deserted of the Holy Spirit! I beseech you cry mightily, "Take not Your Holy Spirit from me," and let your plea be in the name and merit of Christ Jesus the Savior.

Moreover, Brethren, the Holy Spirit is our great Instructor. In these times, when errorists of all kinds are anxious to mislead us, some from the side of credulity, and others from the side of skepticism, we have need to pray every day, "Take not Your Holy Spirit from me." One says, "Lo, here!" Another, with equal vehemence, cries, "Lo, there!" We have not only, "another gospel," but we have fifty other gospels now preached. Though there is but one foundation and one salvation, yet there are those among us who proclaim with earnestness this, and that, and other doctrines as fundamental, though their teaching is of the flesh, and not of God.

The young and unwary must often have cause, in great bewilderment, to enquire, "How shall I know the Truth? By what means shall I discern the way?" Now, the Spirit of God is given to "lead us into all Truth," and reverently sought, He will be given to all who lack wisdom—to teach them the things of Christ, by taking those precious things and revealing them unto their hearts.

But oh, without the Holy Spirit our patient and Infallible Teacher, we should be like a child in the woods when the sun has gone down, wandering here and there, torn with briers and fearful of the wolf, crying in the dark for its father. Or like a traveler lost on one of our southern downs, surrounded by a clinging mist, not knowing which way he goes, and in constant danger of falling from some lofty cliff into the sea. "Take not Your Holy Spirit from me." You puzzled and bewildered children of God, here is a prayer for you—and God fulfill it to you according to His infinite mercy.

Again, I pray that I may be helped to magnify the Holy Spirit in your esteem, making you to love Him and worship Him more than ever. Dear Brethren, we want the Holy Spirit as our Comforter. This is one of His names, the Paraclete, the Comforter. He has come on purpose to appease the griefs of His children, and bring peace into their minds. Now, whatever our troubles may be, if we have such a Comforter, we can afford to welcome them.

Our adversities may be innumerable, but with the Holy Spirit's Presence, we rise above them all. But, O my God, if the Comforter is gone, then my brain reels, my spirit sinks, I give up the conflict, I cannot endure to the end—for only by His consolations shall I in patience possess my soul.

Though I might enlarge, I must not, for time reproves me. The Holy Spirit is our Sanctifier, and when we feel sin raging within, how can we hope to conquer without His aid? If He should leave us, if He who began the work does not keep His hand to it, how will it ever be complete? Holiness is too Divine a work to be worked in us by any inferior hand. He who made the first rough draft must put in the perfecting stroke, or all will remain incomplete.

And He, also, is our power for practical service—the "power from on high" for which Apostles tarried of old. If the Holy Spirit is not with the preacher, vain are his pleadings with men. If He is not with the teacher in his class, with any worker for God—what is their labor but beating the air, or reasoning with the waves? If no other person can pray this prayer from his inmost soul, at least the preacher can.

It rises up, as the Lord knows, from the very center of my heart. I dread beyond all things the Spirit's withdrawal. Death has not half the terror of that thought. I would sooner die a thousand times than lose the helpful Presence of the Holy Spirit. I will just one moment allude to a controversy which has raged around this text, and then pass on. Some have said, "Then a true saint may be cast away, lose the Spirit of God, and perish." The argument being that there is no need for a man to pray for that which God is sure to give, or pray against an evil which God will never inflict.

The answer is briefly this—I should not dare to pray, "Cast me not away from Your Presence. And take not Your Holy Spirit from me," if I had not the promise that He will not cast me away from His Presence, nor take His Holy Spirit from me. Instead of it not being right to pray for what God will give, I venture to say it is not right to pray for what God will not give. The promise is not a reason for not praying, but the very best reason in all the world for praying. Because I earnestly believe that no real child of God will ever be cast away from God's Presence, therefore I pray that I may not be.

And because I am well persuaded that from no really regenerated soul will God ever utterly take His Spirit, therefore, for that reason above all others do I pray that He may never take His Spirit from me. I say, again, it is absurd to argue that a thing which God promises to give is not to be asked for, for has He not Himself said, "I will yet for this be enquired of by the house of Israel, to do it for them"? The fact that the continuance of the Holy Spirit is the subject of an inspired prayer rather strengthens, than weakens the certainty of the promised blessing.

Moreover, be it remembered, that God may partially take away His Presence and His Spirit, and yet, after all, never remove His everlasting and eternal love from that person. For He may only withdraw for a season, for wise reasons, to return again afterwards with fullness of Grace. Against this partial desertion we are, however, allowed and encouraged to pray. Once again, remember that when a man has sinned, as David did, and is bowed down as David was, he cannot always pray in language which would be precisely suitable for a well-assured saint.

He has doubts as to whether he is saved, and therefore he does well to pray on the lowest ground as though he were not surely a saint, but might prove an apostate after all. It is most natural for a backslider to use expressions implying the very worst, expressions rather of fear than confidence, rather of distress than repose. David cries like Jonah out of the belly of Hell, "Cast me not away from Your Presence."

The lower down we get, the better. I frequently find that I cannot pray as a minister. I find that I cannot sometimes pray as an assured Christian, but I bless God I can pray as a sinner. I begin again with, "God be merciful to me, a sinner," and by degrees rise up again to faith, and onward to assurance. When assurance is gone, and faith is weak, it is a great comfort that we may pray a sinner's prayer–the words of which may be inaccurate as to our actual condition, but correctly describe our doubts and fears, and supposed condition.

II. But now I shall pass on to take these words and use them as THE VOICE OF AN ANXIOUS CHURCH. The true Church of God may well pray, "Cast me not away from Your Presence. And take not Your Holy Spirit from me." Brethren, I shall speak pointedly to this Church, over which the Holy Spirit has made me an overseer. Let us, my dear Brethren, remember that there have been Churches of old which God has cast away from His Presence.

Where are the Churches of Asia that were once like golden candlesticks? Where are Sardis, Thyatira and Laodicea? Can you find so much as a relic of them? Are not their places empty, void and waste? Look at the Church of Rome, once a martyr Church, valiant for the Truth of God, and strong in the Lord–now the very personification of Antichrist, and utterly gone aside to the worship of images and all manner of idolatries–an apostate and defiled thing, and no more a Church of Christ at all.

Now, what has happened to other Churches may happen to this Church and we ought to be very earnestly on our guard lest so it should be. In your own time you yourselves have seen Churches flourishing, multiplying, walking in peace and love. But for some reason not known to us but perceived by the Watcher who jealously surveys the Churches of God, a root of bitterness has sprung up, divisions have devoured them, heresy has poisoned them, and the place that once gloried in them scarcely knows them now.

Existing they may be, but little more–dwindling in numbers, barren of Divine Grace–they are rather an encumbrance than power for good. Remember, then, Beloved, that the power of any Church for good depends on the Presence of God, and that sin in the Church may grieve the Lord so that He may no more frequent her courts, or go forth with her armies. It is a dire calamity for a Church when the Lord refuses any longer to bless her work, or reveal Himself in her ordinances.

Then is she driven of the wind here and there like a boat derelict and castaway. The Lord may, because of sin, take away His Holy Spirit from a Church. The spirit of love may depart, the spirit of prayer may cease, the spirit of zeal and earnestness may be removed, and the Spirit which converts the souls of men may display His power elsewhere, but not in the once-favored congregation. Let me impress upon you that all this may readily happen if we grieve the Holy Spirit as some Churches have done.

My Beloved, let me refresh your memories with the recollection that the great power of the Church does not lie in the power of her organizations. You may have good schemes for work wisely arranged and managed, but they will be a failure without the Divine energy. Too often excellent methods are rigidly adhered to, and confidently relied upon, and yet, without the Holy Spirit they are sheer folly.

We are told that in unhappy Paris, when first the mails were stopped, the drivers of the mail carts took their seats upon their boxes and sat there, though no horses were forthcoming. Red tape commands as much reverence as the magic cord of the Brahmins. Formal routine satisfies many. Preachers, deacons, and teachers sit on the boxes of their mail coaches for the appointed time, but the power which moves the whole is too much forgotten, and in some cases ignored.

Souls are not saved by systems, but by the Spirit. Organizations without the Holy Spirit are windmills without wind. Methods and arrangements without Divine Grace are pipes from a dry conduit, lamps without oil. Even the most Scriptural forms of Church government and effort are null and void without the "power from on High."

Remember, too, that the power of the Church does not lie in her gifts. You might, every one of you, have all wisdom and be able to understand all mysteries. We might all speak with tongues and be numbered among the eloquent of the earth–but our Church might not flourish for all this. Gifts glitter, but are not always gold. Gifts may puff up, but they cannot build up if the Holy Spirit is not there.

Strife and divisions, emulations and jealousies are, through the evil of our nature, the very frequent consequences of the possession of great talents by a Church–and these things are unmingled evils. Nor does the power of the Church consist in her wealth. When the Spirit is with her, sufficient treasure is laid at her feet, and the "daughter of Tyre is there with a gift." But if the Spirit of God is gone, we might say of all the money that was ever poured into ecclesiastical coffers by those who sought to strengthen her, "Your money perish with you!"

Gold avails nothing to a Church devoid of Divine Grace, it does but increase the evil which is corrupting within. O you vainglorious Churches–you may gild your domes, you may make your pillars of alabaster, and cover your altars with precious stones–you may clothe your priests in scarlet and in fair white linen, you may make your ceremonies imposing, your processions gorgeous, and your music enchanting–but all this avails nothing if the Spirit of God is gone! All that remains for you is as sounding brass, and a tinkling cymbal.

Nor, and here let me press this upon you, does the strength of a Church lie merely in her doctrines. I know not that Laodicea held false doctrines, yet was she nauseous to the Lord. Orthodox Churches may become lifeless corpses. Truth may be held in unrighteousness. Creeds most accurate may be but the cerements in which a dead Church is wrapped to be carried to her burial. Men have had sound views of the Truth of God, and yet have been unsound in life, and sound in nothing else but in the sleep of carelessness.

Nor does the strength of a Church lie in her numbers. Congratulate yourselves that your membership is counted by thousands, but if you become a mob and not an army, or an army without a Divine Leader, and without the enthusiasm which only the present Spirit of God can give—what are your numbers but the source of difficulty, corruption, and failure? You are like so many grains of sand that cannot unite. You are altogether broken, and poured out like water if the Spirit is gone.

What availed the number of the Scribes and priests of old when God had left them to their own blindness? What can the largest flock of sheep do without a shepherd? What is a large Church without the Lord's Presence but a mass of chaff to be scattered with a whirlwind, or to rot on the threshing floor? So, too, is it with the past history and the prestige of a Church. It is vain to depend on these. There is far too great an attitude among us to fall back on what our fathers did, or what we ourselves achieved ten or twenty years ago. My word to you, my dearly Beloved Church, is, "Hold fast that which you have, that no man take your crown."

Our crown as a Church has been this—we have been a soul-winning Church. We have had nothing else whereof to boast, but this is our claim—we have sought the souls of men, and God has given them to us. To Him be all the glory. Shall we lose that crown through slackness and lukewarmness? It must be so unless we cry again and again, "Take not Your Holy Spirit from us." The Holy Spirit we want to abide with us in all the excellency of His glorious power. And if we have Him not, woe is the day. Our Shiloh shall become a desolation, and this beautiful house of our assembling shall become a hissing and a reproach.

Brethren, I will use an image which will come home to your minds at once. Any Church of God from which the Spirit has departed becomes very much like that great empire with whose military glory the world was dazzled, and whose strength made the nations tremble. France, mistress of arms, queen of beauty, arbiter of politics—how soon has she fallen! I have heard many reasons given for her sudden overthrow, but I scarcely believe any of them to be sufficient to account for such a fall.

In an hour, like a lily broken at the stalk, she has withered. On a sudden, as though the hand of God had gone out against her, her glory has departed. Why was it? I do not believe that it was any lack of courage in her soldiery, nor do I even think that there was more than usual deficiency of skill in her commanders. Her hour had come, she was weighed in the balances and found wanting, and her prowess failed her as in a moment. The nation once so great now lies bleeding at her victor's feet, pitied of us all, none the less, because her folly continues the useless fight.

Just so have we seen it in Churches. May we never so see it here. Everybody may be saying, "How wondrously that Church flourishes! What power! What influence! What numbers!" And on a sudden some radical evil which had been eating out the very soul of the Church may come to its issue–and then, as in a moment, all the apparent prosperity will subside–and the Philistines will rejoice. May it not be so! May our prayer be, "Take not Your Holy Spirit from us." Travelers in Egypt point to spots where once grew luxurious vegetation when the soil was constantly irrigated by the rich stream of the Nile. But now the irrigation, having ceased, the sand of the Libyan desert has conquered the fertile ground and annexed it to the wilderness. After this sort, Churches irrigated by the Spirit once produced rich harvests of souls–left of the Spirit the sand of the world has covered them–and where once all was green and beautiful there is nothing but the former howling wilderness.

It awakens melancholy reflections when we hear of the bodies of old Egyptian kings, proud lords of millions of men, dragged by our discoverers out of their secret chambers in the pyramids and exposed to every vulgar eye. The great sarcophagus has had its lid uplifted, and the monarch who once ruled the world has been taken out and his corpse unrolled for the sake of a little old linen, and an ounce or two of the embalming gum. Poor mummy! Once a Pharaoh whose voice could shake a nation and devastate continents–now used to heat an Arab's kettle or to furnish an object for a museum. So with a Church–alive by the Divine indwelling–God gives it royalty and makes it a king and priest unto Himself among the sons of men. Its influence is felt further than it dreams. The world trembles at it, for it is fair as the sun, clear as the moon, and terrible as an army with banners. But when the Spirit of God is departed, all that remains is its old records, ancient creeds, title-deeds, traditions, histories and memories!

It is in fact a mummy of a Church rather than a Church of God, and it is better fitted to be looked at by antiquarians than to be treated as an existent agency. May we never come to this! May the Tabernacle abide in prosperity till the Temple of God shall be among men. Let our whole Church lift up the prayer,

"Cast me not away from Your Presence. And take not Your Holy Spirit from me."

III. But time outruns me, and therefore I must close by regarding this as THE CRY OF AN AWAKENED SINNER. Not properly, nor accurately, but still instructively I may use it. O unconverted Man, if you are, indeed, anxious about your soul, pray this prayer, "Cast me not away from Your Presence. And take not Your Holy Spirit from me." Say you thus to the Lord, "O You most merciful God, pronounce not yet that word, 'Depart, you cursed.' My God, cast me not away as reprobate.

"Let Your long-suffering spare me a little longer, till Your Grace has saved me. Let me still stand on praying ground and pleading terms with You! 'Take not Your Holy Spirit from me.' It is true I have not Your Spirit as I gladly would have it, but still I hear Your Word. O let me not be denied the hearing of Your Gospel which by Your Grace may bless my soul. Still have I Your Holy Book, and Your Spirit's voice is heard there—may it lead me to Jesus. O take not away Your Book from me! Shut me not up in Hell, where I shall feel the threats, but never know the promises of Your Word.

"Sometimes Your Spirit touches my conscience—hard as my heart is—it sometimes trembles. Sometimes I feel myself inclined to love You if I could. I feel some sighing and yearning after You. Take not these beginnings of Grace from me. O God, I wait upon You in the hearing of Your Word, and sometimes I hope Your power, Your life, will come to me, and I, even I, the chief of sinners, shall yet be saved. O take not away that hope utterly and forever. Swear not in Your anger that I shall never enter into Your rest, but rather turn Your pitying eyes on me and break my heart this day, and bind it up with the dear Savior's love. Save me, O save me, with Your great salvation, for the sake of Jesus, Your Son." Have you prayed that prayer, dear Hearer? It shall be heard. But hear what God speaks to you—it is this—"Believe you now this day, and trust in Jesus and you shall be saved." Come now and put yourself before the Cross. Trust yourself for time and for eternity in His dear hands, who there poured out His soul unto death for sinners. Then shall you know without a doubt that He will never cast you away from His Presence!

"Him that comes to Me," says Jesus, "I will in no wise cast out." Then shall you know that the Spirit shall not be taken from you, for He is with them that believe, and He shall abide in them forever. God bless you, every one of you, for Christ's sake. Amen.

SERMONS IN CHRONOLOGICAL ORDER

SERMONS IN BIBLICAL ORDER

Printed in Great Britain
by Amazon